PIRATES

PIRATES

A History

TIM TRAVERS

Cover illustrations: (front) Captain Kent – the romantic image of a pirate captain, as imagined by Howard Pyle, the American illustrator, who did more than any other individual to imprint on the modern mind what a pirate looked like. *Author's collection*; (spine) skull and cross bones taken from a Howard Pyle illustration. *Author's collection;* (back) a version of the Jolly Roger flag, *c.* 1704. *Courtesy of Joel Baer*.

First published 2007
This edition published 2009

The History Press Ltd
The Mill, Brimscombe Port
Stroud, Gloucestershire, GL5 2QG
www.thehistorypress.co.uk

© Tim Travers, 2007, 2009

The right of Tim Travers to be identified as the Author
of this work has been asserted in accordance with the
Copyrights, Designs and Patents Act 1988.

British Library Cataloguing in Publication Data
A catalogue record for this book is available from the British Library

ISBN 978 0 7524 4852 7

Printed and bound in Great Britain

Contents

Acknowledgments   6

1   The Pirate World   7
2   From Classical Piracy to the Medieval Mediterranean   51
3   Piracy in the Northern World   67
4   The Elizabethan Sea Rovers and the Jacobean Pirates   83
5   Buccaneers of the Caribbean   97
6   The Madagascar Men   163
7   Death to the Pirates   181
8   The Barbary Corsairs of North Africa   205
9   Pirates of the Eastern Seas   235
10   The Road to Modern Piracy   263

     Epilogue   281
     Abbreviations   285
     Definitions   286
     List of Illustrations   287
     Maps   292
     Notes   297
     Bibliography   309
     Index   314

Acknowledgments

Any attempt to write a history of piracy must gratefully rely on numerous authors and selected archives. These are listed in the bibliography, but special thanks are due to the librarians and archivists of the British Library, London; the Public Record Office, Kew; and the National Maritime Museum, Greenwich. Valuable, too, was the inter library loan office at the University of Victoria, as were the students of my pirate history seminar at the University of Victoria. Many thanks are also due to those who generously supplied lodging and hospitality in England, especially Patricia Rogers, and Jo and Charles Cumberlege. Others who kindly helped along the way with information and encouragement include Chris Archer, Peter Fothergill-Payne, Richard Unger, and Patrick Wright. Thanks also to Jonathan Reeve, publisher, for his patience as the manuscript went over the time limit. Most of all, Heather gave up much of her time to solve all computer problems, and thanks to her, the manuscript and the author both survived. Of course, all errors are due to the author alone.

The Pirate World

The 'golden age' of piracy in the West lasted from the 1680s to the 1720s, and during this time some 5,000 pirates roamed the seas. Who were these pirates? A great many were sailors who became unemployed after major European wars ended. Others came from the hard grind and exploitation of the Newfoundland fishery. Still other pirate recruits came from ships that pirates captured, and whose crews either volunteered or were forced to join. This was especially the case with captured slave ships, where conditions for the crew, let alone the miserable slaves, were brutal. And many African slaves also joined as willing or unwilling pirates. Then there were indentured servants from the colonies who found their lives unendurable and were happy to try piracy. Many individuals went 'on account' as pirates simply to improve their lot in life, and others were attracted by the promise of wealth that could not be obtained in any other way. Some perhaps joined pirate crews for political or ideological reasons, and democracy did generally rule on pirate ships. Merchant and navy ships were notorious for poor conditions and bad treatment, and so sailors from these ships often decided to try their luck with pirate ships. In fact, mutinies on merchant ships in particular were often caused by lack of provisions and tardiness in paying their crews, so that most of the crew would turn pirate. Altogether there were many reasons to become a pirate at this time, and there was always the lure of treasure to attract men unhappy with low wages and poverty stricken lives.

How then to enter the world of the pirates of the late seventeenth and early eighteenth centuries? One way is to listen to what they said about themselves. A good start is an early eighteenth-century mock trial, in which a group of pirates pretended to put themselves in court in order to both criticize and make fun of the judicial system of the day:

Attorn. Gen: An't please your Lordship, and you Gentlemen of the Jury, here is a Fellow before you that is a sad Dog, a sad sad Dog; & I humbly hope your Lordship will order him to be hanged out of the Way immediately. He has committed Pyracy upon the High Seas, and we shall prove, an't please your Lordship, that this Fellow, this sad Dog before you, has escaped a thousand Storms, nay, has got safe ashore when the Ship has been cast away, which was a certain Sign he was not born to be drown'd; yet not having the Fear of hanging before his Eyes, he went on robbing & ravishing, Man, Woman and Child, plundering Ships Cargoes fore and aft, burning and sinking Ship, Bark and Boat, as if the Devil had been in him. But that is not all, my Lord, he has committed worse Villanies than all these, for we shall prove, that he has been guilty of drinking Small-Beer; and your Lordship knows, there never was a sober Fellow but what was a Rogue. My Lord, I should have spoken much finer than I do now, but that, as your Lordship knows our Rum is all out, and how should a Man speak good Law that has not drunk a Dram. However, I hope your Lordship will order the Fellow to be hang'd.

Judge: Heark'ee me sirrah, you lousy, pitiful, ill-look'd Dog; what have you to say why you should not be tuck'd up immediately, and set a Sundrying like a Scare-crow? Are you guilty or not guilty?

Pris[oner]: Not guilty, an't please your Worship.[1]

This mock trial gives an insight into the humour, as well as the fears, of the pirates. This skit was performed on an island off Cuba in 1722 by a pirate crew commanded by Captain Anstis, and recorded by Captain Charles Johnson, the eighteenth-century historian of piracy. The pirates well knew that they had committed or were about to commit crimes that would result in the hanging of many of them, or at the least produce an untimely death of some kind. So this mock trial was a way of getting over their fear of hanging by making fun of it, and at the same time showing a defiance of the law in pursuing their piratical ways regardless.

Captain Charles Johnson's book is one of the key sources for Western piracy in the Golden Age of piracy from the 1680s to the 1720s. Entitled *A General History of the Robberies and Murders of the Most Notorious Pyrates*, it was first published in 1724, and subsequently in several further editions. Unfortunately, no one knows who Captain Charles Johnson was, since this name was a pseudonym, although some older authorities consider Johnson might have been the author Daniel Defoe. Some wonder if Johnson was the playwright Charles Johnson (1679-1748), who did write a play called *The Successful Pirate*, while still others consider that Johnson must have been a sailor or even a pirate, judging from his inside knowledge of the sea and his connections to many pirates. Whoever he was, Johnson's book contains biographies of many of the most famous pirates of the day such as Avery (or Every), Blackbeard (or Teach), Rackam, Roberts, Kidd, and the two female pirates, Mary Read and Anne Bonny. By cross checking with documents from the English High Court of the Admiralty, Colonial Office records, trial reports, and other official sources, it seems that Johnson was generally quite accurate, although details were sometimes wrong, and speeches were probably mostly invented.[2]

The world of the pirates has been explored in a large number of books, but the present volume tries to extend the time and space of piracy by going back to classical and medieval piracy and forward to modern piracy, while also widening the search to include Asian and South Asian piracy. Yet the greatest volume of archival and other resources easily available relates to the period from about 1600 onward in regard to Caribbean, Atlantic and Pacific piracy, and so a number of chapters deal with this area. First hand accounts of this period are particularly useful, and some are to be found in the British Library, London. Yet our modern image of the pirate is very strongly formed not from archives or from modern books, but by one or two late nineteenth- and early twentieth-century children's books, by the lurid illustrations of the American Howard Pyle at the turn of the century, and by the cinema.

Undoubtedly the most influential children's book is by Robert Louis Stevenson, whose *Treasure Island*, published in 1883, introduced some memorable fictional pirate characters, such as Long John Silver, Blind Pew, Ben Gunn, and Israel Hands, the last being the name of a real pirate. Stevenson had read Charles Johnson and this accounts for the authentic pirate 'feel' to the book. *Treasure Island* continues to be read and republished, and introduces the strange concept that murderous pirates are especially suitable for children's literature. This must be explained partly because we are no longer frightened of piracy, which has retreated to the periphery of the world. Thus piracy belongs to an imaginary world rather than a real world, and so pirate stories can safely be read by children. The children's theme continued with the highly successful drama of *Peter Pan, or The Boy Who Wouldn't Grow Up*, by another Scotsman, J.M. Barrie, which was produced in 1902. This play introduced Captain Hook, whose image is based partly on the pirate Blackbeard. Hook is the unpleasant leader of a group of pirates, who pursue a number of children. Once more, the situation is potentially frightening, but is resolved through magical means, and children can feel safe watching the play.[3]

Pirate books for children continue to be published, such as the Pirate Hunter series for teenagers, and it is the combination of exotic locations, daring adventures, and pirates who are on the social boundaries of society like outlaws and highwaymen, who are a suitable distance from real pirates, which make these stories popular.[4] Some of these books are illustrated with the work of the American author and illustrator, Howard Pyle, who produced a very romantic image of the pirate, which has now become the standard of what a seventeenth- or eighteenth-century pirate really looked like. Pyle's pirates are shown doing both imagined and genuine pirate activities, such as forcing captives to walk the plank, pirates being marooned, pirate craft sneaking up on ships, pirates torturing prisoners to force them to reveal where their wealth is, pirates fighting pirates, pirates burying treasure, and evil looking pirates like William Kidd.[5] Meanwhile, there has been a surprising resurgence in scholarly pirate historiography in the last dozen years or so, some of which might have been stimulated by the emergence of modern piracy, and others perhaps by the creation of a new genre of pirate film.[6]

Pirate films generally fit into four overlapping categories. First, the 'Swashbuckler' style of film, starring actors such as Errol Flynn and Douglas Fairbanks, in films such as *Captain Blood* (1924, 1935), based on the novel by Rafael Sabatini, published in 1923; *The Black Pirate* (1926); and *The Black Swan* (1942), another film based on a Sabatini novel published in 1932. The theme in these films tends to be the misunderstood pirate who eventually turns out well, but the central image is the handsome, charismatic, bare-chested, cutlass swinging, dare devil of a pirate, carefree, and yet caring of his men and usually a woman. The second film category would be the 'patriotic' pirate film, in which the pirate hero wages war against an unpleasant enemy of his country. Examples include *The Sea Hawk* (1924, 1942), based on yet another early Sabatini novel published in 1915, with the enemy being nasty Spain, a frequent antagonist, as in *The Spanish Main* (1945). Then there is *The Buccaneer* (1938, 1958), about the American pirate Jean Laffite, who helps the Americans against the British at the Battle of New Orleans. The third film category relates to pirate parodies and comedies, which poke fun at the stock characters and themes of the swashbuckling and patriotic era. Needless to say, this genre requires an established set of pirate characters and films to parody, and also signals that the original pirate genre is now tired and seriously in need of new directions. The comedy genre started around the 1940s, with films such as *The Princess and the Pirate* (1944), starring Bob Hope, and continued with many more recent films such as *Abbott and Costello Meet Captain Kidd* (1952) and *The Crimson Pirate* (1952). These films often include an evil Spanish governor or similar unpleasant tyrant, and the required female interest. The newest example of this genre is *The Pirates of the Caribbean* series which is mainly a parody, but contains a certain amount of swashbuckling, and a love interest. Lastly, a fourth category is the children's film. Following the previously mentioned connection between piracy and children's literature, a number of children's films have been released, starting with many versions of *Treasure Island* (1920, 1934, 1950, 1972, 1990). The children's film *Long John Silver* appeared in 1954, and, as might be expected, *Peter Pan* was also turned into a film, in 1953, and again in 1991 under the title *Hook*. *Peter Pan* also became a musical in 1954 and a television adaptation in 1976. In some ways, *The Pirates of the Caribbean* films are also children's films, while the Gilbert and Sullivan musical/opera, *The Pirates of Penzance* (1983), really also belongs to the parody genre.

Overall, in regard to film, the swashbuckling and patriotic style pirate films held sway from the 1920s to the 1950s, then these genres ran out of steam, and were replaced to a considerable extent by parodies and comedies. These too seemed to have run their course until *The Pirates of the Caribbean* series, which managed to breathe new life into the pirate film with a mixture of swashbuckling, comedy, science fiction, and a dash of children's entertainment. One point is worth making before leaving the topic of the cinema, and this is that the handsome type of pirate portrayed by film stars such as Errol Flynn is rather far from reality. In contrast, for example, the real pirate John James is described in 1699 as 'a man of middle Stature, Square-Shouldered, Large jointed, Lean, much disfigured with the small pox, broad Speech, thick Lipped, a blemish or Cast in his left Eye…' A descriptive selection of a list of pirates, who ran away with the ship *Adventure* in September 1698, is described thus, so that they could be identified if captured:

> John Lloyde: of Ordinary Stature, raw boned, very pale Complexion, darke hair, remarkably deformed by an Attraction of the Lower Eyelid.
> John Peirce: Short, well sett, swarthy, much pockfretten.
> Andrew Martin: Short, thick great lipps, black bushey hair.
> Tho Simpson: Short and Small, black, much squint eyed. [7]

And so on. All of these pirates were quite young, in the fifteen to thirty-five age bracket. Many had eye problems, and some were marked by small pox or other diseases. However, as might be expected from their rough backgrounds and life styles, seventeenth- and eighteenth-century pirates were not quite like those portrayed in the modern cinema. What then was the real pirate world like?

Democracy

Among Western pirates in the seventeenth and eighteenth centuries, a very significant aspect of their lives was the concept of democracy onboard a pirate ship. The pirates did not call it democracy, but they were well aware that the rules, written and unwritten, which they lived under as pirates, were very different from the regimented and hierarchical lives of sailors onboard merchant and naval vessels. Some pirate captains introduced specific rules for living onboard, such as the rules of Captain Bart Roberts, Captain Phillips and Captain Lowther. These rules laid out four basic areas of pirate conduct: the system of division of treasure among the officers and crew; the regulation of life aboard the ship; the reward system for those injured in engagements; and the punishments for infringements of the rules. Every man that came aboard a pirate ship where these rules were followed had to sign articles, usually on a bible, to show that he agreed to obey these rules. It is of interest that Roberts produced twelve rules, Lowther eight, and Phillips nine.

Roberts tended to be stricter, tougher and more of a disciplinarian than other captains, which perhaps accounts for the larger number of his rules. Thus Roberts had rules to forbid dicing and gambling for money, which was a frequent cause of trouble onboard pirate ships, a rule that candles and lights were to be out at eight o'clock at night, though drinking could carry on after this on the open deck, and a rule to prevent boys or women being brought onboard. Roberts also had rules that demanded the crew keep their pistols and cutlasses in good order, that musicians onboard should be able to rest on the Sabbath, but for the other six days and nights be ready to play, and a rule that no crew member should talk of breaking up their way of living until each man was able to share £1,000. This last rule was designed to offset the perennial problem of pirate voyages, when some pirates wanted to end the voyage with what they had, and others wanted to continue. Other rules related to duels as a method of dealing with conflict onboard, and a rule outlining punishments both for pirates leaving their station in battle, and for deserting the ship, which last was a problem when a group might try to take over a ship and depart, or when an individual might desert and perhaps inform the authorities. Then there was the usual rule for distributing treasure, and for compensating those who were wounded in battle. Of significance is Roberts' first rule, which spelled out the democratic intent of the pirate life:

> Every Man has a Vote in Affairs of Moment; has equal Title to the fresh Provisions, or strong Liquors, at any Time seized, & use them at pleasure, unless a Scarcity make it necessary, for the good of all, to Vote a Retrenchment.[8]

In actual fact, not every one had a vote, since men who were forced to join a pirate crew were judged unreliable, and were narrowly watched by the old hands. Certain officers such as the surgeon were often compelled to join a pirate ship and were also thought to be less enthusiastic. Of course, rules were all very well, but enforcing them, and having pirates obey them, was not an easy matter in an equal democracy. In Roberts' case, he was able to hold his crew together for four years. This was no mean feat, although some crew did desert him, and there was too much drinking, which in the end left Roberts' ships vulnerable when the Royal Navy caught up with them. Captain Lowther's eight rules were very much the same, except that there were fewer rules regarding conduct onboard, and the last two rules spelled out particulars. Lowther's rule number seven stated, 'Good Quarters be given when called for', presumably to save the lives of those victims that wanted to surrender, and rule number eight stated that the first pirate to see a sail should have the best pistol or small arm onboard the victim. Lowther's rules did not prevent much dissension onboard his ships, and he was also accused of cruelty. Lowther's ship was eventually caught while the crew was careening it (cleaning the bottom of the hull of barnacles and weed), and Lowther either shot himself ashore, or was shot by a fellow pirate.[9]

Captain Phillips' articles were again much the same as those laid out by Roberts. Thus there was one for the safety of the ship, which forbade firing arms onboard, or smoking in the hold without a cap to the pipe, or carrying a lighted candle without a safety case. If this happened, the perpetrator should receive Moses' Law – 40 stripes, lacking one, on the bare back. Phillips' articles included the usual threat against those wanting to run away – and Phillips killed two men that attempted this, while keeping a secret from the company was also a crime. These last two crimes were to be punished by marooning, a favourite punishment of the pirates, though it seems not to have happened very often. Phillips' last rule forbade the pirates from molesting a 'prudent Woman' without her consent, which would be punished by death. It is not clear if this rule was obeyed, and one of Phillips' crew, when about to be hung, did bewail his lack of chastity. The end of Phillips' career was rather gruesome because seven captives onboard from several of his piracies combined to overthrow the pirate crew, and Phillips was hit with a mallet which broke his jaw, and he was then battered to death with a carpenter's adze. Subsequently, Phillips' head was cut off, pickled, and hung from the masthead.[10]

These rules show what the pirate captains intended rather than what actually happened, but there was a definite appeal to real equality and democracy. In this regard, Charles Johnson expanded on the customs of the pirate way of life. Firstly, Johnson pointed to the role of the quartermaster, who was a kind of civil magistrate onboard, carrying out punishment for minor problems by 'drubbing or whipping' the trouble maker. The quartermaster was a sort of trustee for the whole ship's company, and also was first onboard any prize, and organized the division of spoils. Next, Johnson wrote of the captain's powers onboard, which partly depended on the kind of man he was. Roberts was a strong captain, but even he found that he needed to use a small group of insiders to help him rule. By pirate tradition, the captain was only permitted to be captain by the will of the crew, and could be deposed at any time. But a pirate captain had certain rights, 'The captain's power is uncontrollable in chase, or in battle, drubbing, cutting, or even shooting any one who dares to deny his command.' This meant that it was during battle that the captain had total power. Similarly, the captain reserved the right to deal with prisoners in any way he saw fit. Otherwise, for example, when deciding where to sail, the crew would vote on this, and would also vote on whether to attack a particular ship or place onshore. Thus the captain had very few privileges, except perhaps a better cabin than others, and a higher percentage of the treasure captured. Needless to say, some captains ruled by fear, some were quickly deposed, and some were able to retain command for the short period they usually had before their piracy came to an end.[11]

The question of the origins of pirate democracy is much debated. Essentially, did this life of democracy come about for practical reasons, or was there an ideological element to it? Certainly, pirates had no wish to live under the kind of rough justice they experienced onboard merchant and navy ships, and certainly there was a rejection of the hierarchical social world the pirates came from. Beyond this, there is the often quoted speech by Samuel Bellamy, a pirate captain, who reportedly wanted to marry a certain Maria Hallett of Eastham, Massachusetts, but her parents wanted a wealthier man. So Bellamy went to sea looking for shipwrecks to recover valuables from, and turned to piracy when he could not find any wrecks. Ironically, Bellamy drowned in 1717 when he was captain of the captured slave ship *Whydah*, which struck a sand bar. Before this happened, Johnson either invented or paraphrased a speech in which Bellamy addressed the captain of a sloop he had just captured:

> …you are a sneaking puppy, and so are all those who will submit to be governed by laws which rich men have made for their own security, for the cowardly whelps have not the courage otherwise to defend what they get by their knavery; but ___ ye altogether; ___ them for a pack of crafty rascals, and you, who serve them, for a parcel of hen-hearted numskulls. They vilify us, the scoundrels do, when there is only this difference, they rob the poor under the cover of law, forsooth, and we plunder the rich under the protection of our own courage.

Bellamy asked the captured captain to join his crew, but the captain refused, so Bellamy started off again:

> You are a devilish conscience rascal … I am a free prince, and I have as much authority to make war on the whole world, as he who has a hundred sail of ships at sea, and an army of 100,000 men in the field; and this my conscience tells me: but there is no arguing with such snivelling puppies, who allow superiors to kick them around at pleasure.[12]

It is hard to say how accurate this speech is. It may reflect Johnson's attitude as much as Bellamy's, but it is very likely that many pirates harboured similar anti-establishment views. Hence, Bart Roberts compared the miserable life of underfed and mistreated merchant sailors to the wonderful possibilities that could happen with piracy, and frequently drank the following toast, 'D__n to him who ever lived to wear a halter.'[13]

These anti-establishment views can be seen in the clothes the pirates wore, for example, 'Calico Jack' Rackam, whose shirts opposed the sumptuary (anti-extravagance) laws of the time, or Bart Roberts' fine clothes, or the gold chain and gold toothpick that the pirate John James happily wore round his neck.[14] Then there was the free spending, normally the activity of a gentleman of means, by newly enriched pirates, who drank, caroused, gambled, and threw money away recklessly. Other anti-establishment attitudes came through in the brutal treatment of unpopular merchant captains and officers as revenge when they were captured, for example, the pirate Philip Lyne claimed to have killed thirty-seven masters. Conversely there was better treatment if the individual had been a kindly captain, as happened to William Snelgrave when his ship was taken at Sierra Leone. The pirates were about to dispatch Snelgrave when one of his crew pushed forward and said, 'For God's sake don't kill our captain, for we were never with a better man.' This was enough to spare Snelgrave.[15] On the other hand, pirates often wanted to make themselves gentlemen through the simple means of getting enough wealth to act as gentlemen. So in 1721, one pirate crew made a rich haul of some 9,000 pounds sterling from a valuable ship, enough to make them 'gentlemen of fortune', while the pirate Captain Howel Davis tried to entice the crew of the captured ship *Princess* to join him, saying 'he would make gentlemen of them all' if they would join his crew. And it is the case that the great majority of pirates, when they were not forced, and when they did not mutiny for lack of food or pay, set out to improve their lives by obtaining material goods and wealth if they possibly could. And some pirate treasure was remarkably large, as in the loot of the French pirate Jean Hamlin, who sent ashore in 1683 as much gold dust as could be carried by eight slaves, plus 150 pigs of silver and 120 bags of coins.[16]

Africans Onboard Pirate Ships

Yet there was one component of almost all pirate crews which normally did not share in the democracy onboard, and this was the African slaves. Many

Africans were captured when slave ships were taken by pirates off the coast of West Africa, or on the way to the Caribbean and the Americas. It is well known that when Roberts' ships were taken by the Royal Navy in 1722 somewhere between 70 and 75 Africans were also captured, having served on Roberts' fleet. The question to be asked in Roberts' case is whether these Africans were forced, or were volunteers, and in general, one can say that they were forced into working on his ships. Partly for this reason, no African slaves from Roberts' ships were executed, and instead they were sold into further slavery. On the other hand, when a member of Roberts' crew testified at his trial, he said that two Africans with loaded pistols forced the crew of a ship at St Christopher to sign ships' articles. In this situation, these two Africans were probably willing participants. On another occasion, a privateer turned pirate was blocked in the port of Soulière, near St Augustine, in 1700, by the Royal Navy ship *Lizard*, which found there were 400 blacks in arms onboard the privateer. These Africans were evidently active pirates.[17] It is also known that onboard Blackbeard's ship in his last fight there was an African named Black Caesar, 'a resolute fellow, a Negro who he [Blackbeard] had brought up, [entrusted] with a lighted match in the powder room with commands to blow up when he should give him orders.' Black Caesar duly attempted to blow up the ship but was prevented by others onboard. When the trial of Blackbeard's pirates was held, Black Caesar refused to bargain with the authorities, although four other African pirates did try to turn state's evidence. However, black slaves were not allowed to testify by law in South Carolina, and in the end Black Caesar, and the other four African pirates, were hung along with the rest of Blackbeard's crew.[18]

Another incident involving Africans occurred in 1721 when Richard Taylor and a large number of pirates at Madagascar decided to go and try and seek a pardon in the West Indies. An eye witness recorded that, '…thereupon the sd. Richard Taylor with a hundred & twelve white men & forty Blacks voted to go to the West Indies and came onboard the *Cassandra*…' This sounds as though the forty Africans had the choice of a vote, and could decide whether to continue piracy or seek a pardon. On the other hand, Africans were frequently forced onboard pirate ships, and had no choice. Their normal fate on a pirate ship was to do the hard labour. Yet some Africans were no doubt happy to have escaped transportation as slaves, and were willing to join the pirate crew as active participants.[19]

Marooned!

Democracy onboard pirate ships relied partly on adherence to the articles or rules drawn up by captain and crew. Marooning was one of the punishments decreed by Bart Roberts, yet the word itself had a different history from the commonly understood practice of abandoning individuals on desert islands. Initially, the word 'maroon' was derived from the word for escaped African slaves, who often fought against the Spanish, and were called 'cimarrones'. The French and English reduced this word to 'maroons'. By the 1660s, Caribbean pirates called themselves 'marooners', because of their occasional practice of marooning victims, while sometimes those marooned were the pirates themselves.

An example of pirates calling themselves marooners is that of Thomas Lawrence Jones and his associates. Jones gave a long story to the High Court of the Admiralty in 1723 that explained how he eventually came to be a marooner. Jones' account starts with him serving on a ship called the *Merrie* in 1720, when it was taken off the Guinea coast by the pirate Howel Davis. Soon after, Davis was killed, and Bartholomew Roberts became captain. Jones claimed that he and 14 others were forced to join Roberts' ship, the *Ranger*. Subsequently, some ships were captured by Roberts, and then a sloop was taken, which was named the *Good Fortune*. Jones claimed that he was forced to sign articles on the *Good Fortune* by two 'Negroes with loaded pistols'. Now occurred a violent episode that Jones did not relate in his testimony, in which he had a fight with Roberts over the death of a friend who had been killed by Roberts because this friend, in a drunken state, had insulted Roberts. According to Charles Johnson, Roberts ran Jones through with his sword, but Jones fought back and severely beat Roberts as he was pinned underneath a cannon. Jones recovered from his wound, but was given a severe whipping by the crew of the *Good Fortune*, who administered two lashes per crew member on the unfortunate Jones. Jones resented this treatment, and resolved to desert Roberts, which he achieved by sailing away at night with other malcontents on a captured brigantine under the command of Captain Anstis. Now, finally, according to Jones, these deserters from Roberts resolved 'to live a marooning life – till they would have an answer to a Petition to his Majestie for a Pardon…'[20] So Jones and his shipmates captured two more ships, in one of which they sailed to 'a marooning Key…' According to Johnson, this Key was an uninhabited island off the south-west coast of Cuba called Rattan. (This island, actually called Roatan, is close to what is now Honduras.) This petition from Anstis' crew was signed in 'round robin' fashion, to prevent the detection of ring leaders, and Johnson records the petition in full. It essentially condemns Roberts as wicked, while Anstis, Jones, and the rest of the crew sought a better life for themselves. Meanwhile, Anstis, Jones, and the rest of the pirates took a number of French, Spanish and English ships, lived a 'maroon' life on Rattan [Roatan] and other islands for eight months, and sent a second petition. No answer coming to their appeals, Jones and eighteen others eventually left off pirating and sailed to England and dispersed, living free for eight months before being captured. Johnson notes that Jones later died in London's Marshalsea prison.[21]

Turning from marooners to ships' articles, it is well known that some pirate captains in the early eighteenth century required their crews to sign these articles, which usually included marooning as a punishment for various crimes against the crew. Thus Captain Phillips' articles on the *Revenge*, in 1723, included three articles that mentioned marooning. Article 2 read, 'If any Man shall offer to run away, or keep any secret from the Company, he shall be marooned, with one Bottle of Powder, and Bottle of Water, one small Arm, and Shot.' Article 3 read, 'If any Man shall steal any Thing in the Company, or Game, to the value of a Piece of Eight, he shall be maroon'd or shot.' It does not seem that Captain Phillips or his crew put the first article into practice – in fact, according to Johnson, two members of the crew who attempted to leave the ship were simply killed by Phillips, thus contradicting Article 2. Of course, there may not have been a suitable island or land close by for marooning in these two cases. Meanwhile, Article 4 read, 'If at any time we should meet another Marrooner [that is Pyrate,] that Man that shall sign his articles without the consent of our Company, shall suffer such Punishment as the Captain and Company shall think fit.' It is worth noting that only a few of Phillips' crew were voluntary pirates, and so Phillips no doubt wanted to keep as strict a hold as he could over his crew.[22]

Another pirate who set out ship's articles was Captain George Lowther, on the *Delivery*, in 1721, but it is notable that none of his eight articles mentioned marooning. Instead, all crimes against the ship and crew were to be punished according to what the captain and majority of the company should see fit. This was obviously a more flexible system, and did not preclude marooning. Ironically, Lowther and some of his men marooned themselves on the island of Blanco (near Tortuga), in 1723, to avoid capture by a South Sea sloop from Barbados. Lowther was taken by surprise

while careening his ship, which made the ship and crew extremely vulnerable. Johnson reported that Lowther probably shot himself on Blanco, being
found dead with a burst pistol by his side.[23]

The next pirate whose articles Johnson lists was the famous Captain
Bart Roberts. Johnson treats the case of Bart Roberts in the greatest
detail, since he evidently had very good information on Roberts' career.
In regard to Roberts' articles, dated around 1720, two of them mention
marooning. The first article, no. 2, declares, 'Every Man to be called fairly
in turn, by list, on Board of Prizes, because, (over and above their proper
Share,) they there on these Occasions allow'd a Shift of Cloaths: But if
they defrauded the Company to the Value of a Dollar, in Plate, Jewels, or
Money, MAROONING was their Punishment.' Johnson added the comment that marooning was a barbarous custom, but noted that if the robbery
was between individuals, rather than against the whole crew, then the
guilty one would be put ashore, not in an uninhabited place, but where the
guilty party would suffer hardship. This would obviously be a lesser punishment than marooning on a deserted island. The second article mentioning
marooning was no. 7, 'To Desert the Ship, or their Quarters in Battle, was
punished with Death, or Marooning.' It is notable that in Roberts' mind,
as with Phillips' articles, marooning was clearly a particular punishment for
those who transgressed against the ship and crew as a whole.[24] It seems that
Roberts also used marooning as a punishment when the pirates' victims
fought back – thus in 1722 when a French ship resisted Roberts' two ships,
the remaining prisoners were marooned on the most desolate island that
Roberts could find.[25] On the other hand, Roberts rescued thirteen naked
sailors marooned on the island of Dominica in 1720 by a Spanish coast
guard ship, who understandably joined Roberts' crew rather than remain
marooned.[26]

These examples are from the early 1720s when pirates were under particular stress from renewed naval efforts to capture and eradicate them, and
so pirate captains tended to be stricter in dealing with their crews. But of
course, marooning was practiced earlier, from at least the sixteenth century.
It also occurred sometimes by accident of fate, when a sailor would be left
ashore somewhere, as happened to a Moskito coast native man called William
the Striker. On a raid in the South Seas, Captain Watling and his buccaneers
anchored at the Juan Fernandez Islands in 1681, and were forced to leave
suddenly as three Spanish ships hove into sight. Left ashore was William the
Striker, who had become hidden 'under a treed slope' – although Watling

and his crew did send a canoe to try to find him before leaving, but could not. William had to wait three years until 1684 when another South Seas voyage under Captains Cook and Eaton visited the Juan Fernandez Islands, and William was rescued from his marooned state. William Dampier, who was present, described the touching scene as William the Striker came to the beach as another Moskito native, called Robin, joined others as they went ashore in canoes. Robin waded through the surf and 'running to his brother Moskito man, threw himself flat on his face at his feet.' Then they embraced, and William was brought onto the ship.[27]

Sometimes, however, men actually wanted to leave their ships and be marooned. This was the case with four English sailors who apparently left a privateer of their own free will in 1687, and marooned themselves on the same Juan Fernandez Islands. They were rescued by a ship called the *Welfare* in October 1690.[28] Much more common, though, was marooning as a malicious act. This happened in November 1715 when the third mate of the *Anglesea*, John Rolf, decided to take over the *Anglesea* at Buena Vista. Rolf succeeded, and put the master of the ship on a desolate island, where he died.[29] A better known example occurred in 1698, when Joseph Bradish, the mate of the *Adventure*, together with others, took over the ship, complaining of lack of provisions, and sailed away, marooning the surgeon, the captain's mate, and three others on an island they called Polonoys, six miles from Sumatra. Some others were left in a long boat at the same place.[30]

Naturally, the most famous of the marooned was Alexander Selkirk, the alleged model or prototype of Defoe's *Robinson Crusoe*. Selkirk sailed with William Dampier in 1703, as part of a privateering cruise by a two ship fleet on the coast of South America, hoping to capture the Spanish treasure fleet. The expedition was not a happy one, and to make matters worse, the captain of one of the ships, the *Cinque Ports*, died, leaving command in the hands of a twenty-one year-old first lieutenant called Thomas Stradling. Selkirk was the quartermaster on the *Cinque Ports*, and he argued bitterly with Stradling over the seaworthiness of the ship. Selkirk was so angry with Stradling, whom he detested, that he asked to be left behind on the Juan Fernandez Islands. He was put ashore with bedding, sea chest, provisions, tobacco, navigation instruments, books, powder and shot. At the last minute Selkirk changed his mind, gesticulating frantically from the shore, but Stradling would not take him onboard again. This was in October 1704, but it turned out that Selkirk was fortunate in his decision, since the *Cinque Ports* was wrecked soon after, and the eight survivors imprisoned by

the Spanish. Meanwhile, Selkirk remained on his island for the next four
and a half years until February 1709 when Captain Woodes Rogers, again
with Dampier aboard, dropped anchor and was surprised to see smoke and
a wildly waving individual. This was Selkirk 'cloth'd in Goats-Skins who
looked wilder than the first Owners of them'. Selkirk had lost the art of
speech, but was healthy, and had trained young goats and the island cats to
keep him company, and when depressed would 'sing and dance with them.'
Selkirk was rescued, and appeared in the pages of Woodes Rogers' book, *A
Cruising Voyage Round the World*, published in 1712. Selkirk appropriately had
become 'a better Christian while in this solitude than ever he was before',
which was a kind of stamp of approval of his story.[31]

Defoe's *Robinson Crusoe* came out in 1719, and the coincidence of
Selkirk's and Robinson Crusoe's stories strongly suggested that Defoe
used Selkirk as his model for Crusoe. This was particularly the case because
Defoe was clearly very interested in privateers and piracy, writing briefly on
the pirates Gow and Avery, and fictionalising piracy in his books on Captain
Singleton and the further adventures of Robinson Crusoe. Nevertheless,
a recent book argues persuasively that the original model for Robinson
Crusoe's story of marooning was not Selkirk but Henry Pitman. It seems
that Pitman was convicted of being involved in the Duke of Monmouth's
rebellion in England, and was transported to Barbados as a ten year convict.
Despairing of his life, he and a few others escaped from Barbados in a small
boat in 1687 and eventually wound up on the island of Salt Tortuga, off the
coast of Venezuela. There they met with some pirates under the command
of one Dutch Yanche or Yanky. This pirate had himself marooned some
English buccaneers on Cow Island, close to Hispaniola, after arguments
over prizes. Pitman found Yanky devious, and in fact Yanky and his crew
sailed off to go raiding, leaving Pitman and his companions marooned on
Salt Tortuga. Notably, Pitman bought an Indian from the pirates before they
left, in order to use the Indian's skill as a survivor – an obvious reference to
Man Friday in *Robinson Crusoe*. Pitman was rescued from Salt Tortuga by a
pirate ship after three months on the island, being readily accepted because
he was a surgeon, although Pitman apparently left his seven companions
behind. Ultimately, Pitman reached London, and wrote a slim book entitled *A Relation of the great suffering and strange adventures of Henry Pitman,
Chirurgeon*, which was published in 1689. The connection between Pitman
and Defoe is strengthened by the fact that Pitman's book and Defoe's book
were published by the same publishing family in London, the Taylor family,

at St Paul's Churchyard, and round the corner in Paternoster Row, respectively. Finally, another connection is that Henry Pitman made his living after returning to London by mixing and selling medicines at Taylor's publishing shop in St Paul's Churchyard, where he very likely met Defoe.[32]

Women Pirates

In the Western world, piracy was normally the domain of men rather than women. There were a number of reasons for this, chief among them being that in the seventeenth and eighteenth centuries, women were thought to create considerable unrest on ships, leading to conflicts, fights, disorder, and murder. There was also a convention at the time that considered that women brought bad luck to a ship. Another reason for the absence of women pirates was that women were not considered to have the required physical strength to work a ship. It was also not easy for women to serve onboard a ship in disguise, since it was extremely difficult to hide their sex on a ship where privacy simply didn't exist, although there are a few examples of some women who did serve on a ship.

In fact it was possible in the eighteenth century for women to accompany their husbands to sea in the Royal Navy if their husbands were of the rank of warrant officer or less. A very few captains in the Royal Navy also brought women onboard in peace time, although this was strictly illegal. It was much more common for women to enlist as soldiers on land, and many women were to be found in Napoleon's army, either in official female units, or disguised as men, or as wives of senior officers. In the Royal Navy, it was rare for women to serve in disguise, but one example was William Prothero, a private marine onboard HMS *Amazon*, who was found to be a Welsh girl of 18 following her lover to sea. Another woman who started as a soldier, and became a sailor, was Mary Anne Talbot, born in 1778, one of the sixteen bastard children of Lord William Talbot. She became the mistress of Captain Bowen in 1792, who enlisted her as a foot boy called John Taylor in his regiment, and they sailed on HMS *Crown*, bound for Santo Domingo. There she became a drummer boy, and was present at the battle of Valenciennes, where Bowen was killed. Later she joined the French navy as a cabin boy, but was captured by HMS *Brunswick* where she served as a powder monkey. She was badly wounded in 1794, and wound up in London in 1796, where she was pressed by the Navy, but revealed her sex. She continued to wear sailor's clothes, and found that her inheritance had been wasted by her guardian. After a spell in debtor's prison, she became servant to a publisher, and died in 1808.[33]

Another woman who disguised herself was Hannah Snell. She served in the marines, and onboard Royal Navy ships. Born in 1723, she fell in love with a Dutch sailor, and married him, but he abandoned her when she was pregnant. The child died, and she enlisted in Fraser's Regiment of Marines in 1746. She deserted, and joined HMS *Swallow* as an assistant steward and cook to the officers' mess. She was wounded at the assault on Pondicherry in India, and allegedly used a native woman to dress her wounds, in order to maintain her disguise as a man. Snell enlisted on two ships, and continued to try to find her Dutch husband. Aboard these ships she was apparently nicknamed 'Molly' because of the smoothness of her face, and then 'Hearty Jemmy', on account of her popularity. Her disguise as a man still continued. Then she discovered that her Dutch husband had been executed in Genoa, and so she paid off from HMS *Eltham* and made a few appearances on stage in London, dressed in either her soldier or marine uniforms. Subsequently, she ran a pub in Wapping, London, called appropriately *The Female Warrior*. Snell married twice more, but then the strain of her life told on her, and she was judged to have become insane. She died at Bedlam Hospital for the insane in London in 1792, but was buried at Chelsea Hospital among the other soldiers, as she had wanted.[34]

Of course neither Talbot nor Snell were pirates, but they did demonstrate that it was possible for women to serve onboard ship in disguise. It is noteworthy that these two women served in roles that required courage but generally not physical strength. Celebrated as actual women pirates were Mary Read and Anne Bonny. Both women grew up in situations that required them to be dressed as men, and it was as men that they wound up on the pirate ship of 'Calico Jack' Rackam. Mary Read had served earlier in the infantry in Europe, and this stood her in good stead when she fought a duel in place of her lover on Rackam's ship, and killed the sailor who was to fight her lover at a later hour. As a pirate she was an active participant on Rackam's ship. Anne Bonny ran away from home with a poverty stricken sailor, and they sailed for Providence, hoping to pick up privateering work. Here she met Jack Rackam, abandoned her husband, and went onboard his ship. Read and Bonny wore men's clothes onboard Rackam's ship, but they also sometimes wore women's clothes. Read and Bonny were captured off Jamaica in 1720, along with the rest of Rackam's crew, and went to trial. As it happened, both were pregnant, and so escaped hanging for this reason (see Chapter 7).

Besides Read and Bonny, an earlier female pirate was the Irish smuggler and pirate, Grace O'Malley. She was born around 1530 in Connaught, on the west coast of Ireland. Her father was a local chieftain, who possessed castles and a fleet of ships that were used for trading, smuggling and piracy. It seems that Grace grew up sailing in her father's ships, and cut her hair short and dressed in boy's clothes to show that she was familiar with the sea. Her nickname, 'Granuaille' meant 'bald', since she had cut her hair short. Grace married twice, probably both times for economic as well as romantic reasons, and produced four children. Her first husband was killed, but her second husband lived at Rockfleet Castle in County Mayo, commanding Clew Bay. Grace operated from Rockfleet Castle and Clew Bay for the rest of her life, where the O'Malleys possessed some twenty ships, most of them being galleys. These galleys were propelled by thirty oars, and had onboard some 100 musket men. Another source relates that the O'Malleys owned three galleys with 200 fighting men, meaning that each galley had sixty odd musket men onboard. Presumably these galleys stayed close to shore, but they certainly raided locally and also took passing merchant ships. In the early 1570s, Grace created too much trouble with her raids, and a government force led by Captain William Martin launched a punitive raid on Clew Bay and Rockfleet Castle in 1574. Apparently, Grace compelled Martin to retreat, but in 1577 on a plundering raid against the lands of the Earl of Desmond (surely an over-ambitious plan), Grace was captured and spent time in Limerick jail. Lord Justice Drury described her as 'a woman that hath … been a great spoiler, and chief commander and director of thieves and murderers at sea to spoil this province.'[35]

In 1588, Grace O'Malley reportedly helped massacre Spanish sailors who came off the wreck of their ship, the *El Gran Grin*, in Clew Bay, after the Spanish Armada failed. It seems that Sir Richard Bingham, governor of Connaught in 1588, was responsible for ordering most of the slaughter of these Spanish sailors. It was also Bingham who held a low opinion of Grace, and impounded her fleet. Grace was now in poor financial condition, since her second husband had died in 1583, and she appealed to Queen Elizabeth. Bingham meanwhile arrested her brother and one of her sons, and so she went to England, meeting Queen Elizabeth at Greenwich Palace in September 1593. This must have been an interesting occasion, although nothing is recorded of the meeting except for a suspect ballad or two. Judging by later events, Grace probably bought safety from Bingham by promising to fight the Queen's enemies. The Queen instructed Bingham to provide for Grace, and he did release her son and brother, but continued to be hostile until he retired in 1597, when Grace's fortunes improved. She died in 1603, and it is relevant that Grace's son supported the English crown and was made Viscount Mayo in 1627.[36]

Grace O'Malley was very much a woman, chieftain, and pirate of her time, often embroiled in regional battles, and profiting from trading and raiding until she came up against the Queen's governor, Bingham. Similar to Grace's story were the female Chinese pirates of the nineteenth and twentieth centuries, who raided locally, and operated according to the cultural norms of the time (see Chapters 9 and 10). In general, female pirates in the Western world in the golden age of piracy (1680s to 1720s) were very scarce, as might be expected because of the social restrictions of the day, and it is interesting that some pirate captains even attempted to control the presence of women onboard. It is well known that one of Roberts' rules read, 'No Boy or Woman to be allow'd amongst them. If any Man were found seducing any of the latter Sex, and carried her to Sea, disguised, he was to suffer Death.' According to Johnson this rule was less to protect women (and boys) than to prevent discord onboard, and he cynically wrote that the sentry put to protect any woman captured, actually reserved her favours for himself. This apparently happened to the captive Elizabeth Trengrove onboard Roberts' ship in August 1721. Another pirate, Captain Phillips, stated more ambiguously that 'If at any time you meet with a prudent Woman (i.e. not a prostitute or a loose woman), that man who offers to meddle with her, without her Consent, shall suffer present Death.' Presumably, a less respectable woman could be handled as desired by the crew. On the other hand, the rules of Captain Lowther had nothing to say about women, and it is known that the Red Sea pirates badly mistreated their female captives.[37]

As a final note, the lack of women onboard pirate ships is sometimes cited as a reason for pirate homosexuality.[38] Yet there is a lack of evidence on this score, although one or two items tend to suggest that in Western piracy there was some homosexuality. In their buccaneer voyage in the Pacific in 1680–1681, Bartholomew Sharp recorded in his journal that in January 1681 William Cooke accused Edmund Cooke of buggering him,'…his Master had oft times Buggered him in England … in Jamaica … and once in these seas before Panama.' The captain put Edmund Cooke in irons, although this event may have been connected to a power struggle onboard for the captaincy of the ship. In any case, Sharp does not add any comment, which suggests he did not find the problem very unusual.[39] That homosexuality existed is evident, as in the case of the cabin boy Richard Mandervell, who in 1721 accused his master, Samuel Norman, of forcing him to wash the partly dressed Norman onboard ship at Oporto. Norman apparently called Mandervell 'Son of a Bitch' when he objected.[40] As mentioned elsewhere, the system of matelotage in Hispaniola, among the cattle hunters of the island, and in the logwood camps of Campeche, whereby two men shared all their possessions, hunted together, lived together, and left each other their goods upon death, suggests some may have been in homosexual relationships (see Chapter 5). Among the Barbary corsairs, European observers, often priests, certainly emphasised homosexual relationships in Algiers, although the horror they expressed stemmed partly from their desire to paint the situation in Algiers in the darkest colours in order to arouse publicity to help free the Christian slaves held there. One lurid story of the Barbary corsairs comes from a Christian priest who suggested in 1647 that young Christian captive boys were:

…purchased at great price by the Turks to serve them in their abominable sins, and no sooner do they have them in their power, [then] by dressing them up and caressing them, they persuade them to make themselves Turks. But if by chance someone does not consent to their uncontrolled desires, they treat him badly, using force to induce him into sin; they keep him locked up, so that he does not see nor frequent [other] Christians, and many others they circumcise by force.[41]

Finally, Chinese pirates in the early eighteenth century apparently used homosexuality to recruit young pirates to their junk fleets, while the question of homosexuality, although forbidden by the authorities, seems to have been a more open matter among Chinese pirates (see Chapter 9).

Overall, though, the question of homosexuality among western pirates remains an undecided issue due to lack of sufficient evidence. Many pirates sailed together on a long term basis, such as John Swann and Robert Culliford, but that does not prove a homosexual relationship.

Drink and Food

Whether pirates were men or women, what did they have to eat and drink? Pirates were notorious for heavy bouts of drinking alcohol, and usually drank anything they could get their hands on, whether it was plundered wine, brandy, cider or beer. When Captain Snelgrave, commander of a slave

ship, entered the mouth of the Sierra Leone River, his ship was captured by
the pirates Thomas Cocklyn, Howel Davis, and the Frenchman La Buze (or
La Bouche). Snelgrave watched as the pirates:

> …hoisted upon Deck a great many half hogsheads of Claret and French
> Brandy; knock'd their Heads out, and dipp'd Canns and Bowls into them to
> drink out of; And in their Wantoness threw full Buckets upon one another.
> And in the evening washed the Decks with what remained in the Casks. As
> to bottled Liquor, they would not give themselves the trouble of drawing the
> Cork out, but nick'd the Bottles, as they called it, that is, struck their necks off
> with a Cutlace; by which means one in three was generally broke.

Logwood cutters in Campeche (on the Yucatan peninsula of Mexico), were
renowned for their drinking bouts, punctuating each toast with a cannon
shot. Another scenario that provided for communal drinking was when
pirates would gather to take a vote onboard their ship, they would usually
first prepare a bowl of punch and then get down to decision making. For
example, when the pirate Howel Davis was elected as commander, the election system required that 'a counsel of war was called over a large bowl of
punch, at which it was proposed to choose a commander…' In the same
way, when a decision had to be made over shipmates who had broken the
rules of the pirate crew, as in the case of Roberts' crew 'a large bowl of
rum punch was made, and placed upon the table, the pipes and tobacco
being ready, the judicial proceedings began…' After capturing a ship, pirates
would often celebrate, for example Captain Spriggs' men spent the day 'in
boisterous mirth, roaring and drinking of healths…' Later on, Spriggs' crew
captured Captain Hawkins' ship for the second time, in the evening, when
the pirates were 'most of 'em drunk, as is usual at this time of night…'[42]

In fact, there was hardly any activity onboard a pirate ship that was not
associated with drinking at one time or another, and this was an age in
which heavy drinking was normal. But some pirates such as Roberts tried
to control alcohol, while others such as Blackbeard found that rum drinking kept his crew happy, which allowed him to remain as captain. Yet sailing
ships of the seventeenth and eighteenth centuries are complicated pieces of
machinery, and a drunken crew would find it hard to work such a ship, so
pirate crews simply could not have been drunk all the time. And in general,
the heaviest drinking took place when a pirate ship was in harbour or being
careened in some hidden bay. Port Royal, in Jamaica, long a well known

pirate haunt, provided as many as 100 taverns in 1680 for the pirates and other sailors. Occasionally, such drinking and debauchery let the pirates down, as when Captain Roberts' crew was taken by surprise by the Royal Navy in 1722 and 'the greatest part of his men were drunk, passively courageous, unfit for service'. In the same way, Blackbeard himself spent the night in drinking before being killed in battle, and possibly would have made a better plan if he had been clear headed.[43]

Pirates also obviously drank simply to quench their thirst. Since water could quickly go bad onboard ship, beer and other alcoholic drinks were a substitute for water. Pirates also drank for social reasons, in order to help maintain solidarity. Then there was drinking for comfort in cold weather; or as part of pirate rituals; or for medicinal purposes. But the drink that is most often associated with Western pirates was 'bumboo', a mixture of rum, water, and sugar, flavoured with nutmeg. The key ingredient was rum, and indeed rum tended to be part of most peoples' lives in the Caribbean in the seventeenth and eighteenth centuries.

As far as food was concerned, pirates ate anything that was available. Turning once again to Captain Snelgrave, he noted that the pirates who captured his ship ate 'Cheese, Butter, Sugar, and many other things, they were as soon gone.' Then Snelgrave was served slices of boiled ham laid on a ship's biscuit, but he also observed the live fowls on his ship – geese, turkeys, chickens and ducks, being dispatched and thrown into a large cauldron – along with Westphalian hams and a pregnant sow. The cook boiled them all together and the pirate crew feasted happily on the result.[44] Another common source of pirate food was the sea turtle. Turtles were kept alive by being turned on their backs, and they survived for long periods of time due to their low metabolism. This therefore provided fresh meat for pirate and other crews who killed the turtles as they needed them. A case in point was the experience of Captain Anstis' pirate crew, who waited on an island off the south-west coast of Cuba for news of a pardon. Not having any food except rice for these nine months, they subsisted almost entirely on turtle meat seasoned with rice.[45] In fact, food was always a problem for pirates, who either had to capture ships with provisions onboard, or raid local ports and villages, or buy whatever food they could. A case in point was the pirate Captain Gow, who sailed into Porto Santo, near Madeira, in 1725, and needed to buy water and provisions, since they were very short of both. The Governor was not speedy enough with the provisions, so he was kidnapped, and as a result Gow obtained a cow and calf, a good number of fowls, and seven butts of water.[46]

Food shortages were always a logistical nightmare for pirates on long or even short voyages.

Normally, in areas where ships were close to land, like the Caribbean or in the Mediterranean, food could be replaced without too much trouble. But long voyages off the Americas, and especially sailing across the Pacific, were logistical nightmares. The buccaneer, William Cowley, reported such difficulties in the 1680s. Cowley's ship stopped at the Juan Fernandez Islands for goats and fish and green vegetables for the crew, and then sailed along the Pacific coast of South America, where men had to be put ashore in May 1683 because they were suffering from scurvy, (due to lack of Vitamin C). Later, Cowley's ship set off across the Pacific toward the Philippines, a distance of 3,000 miles, where many men were sick from scurvy again. The ship sailed on further east and by February 1684, rats had to be caught and given to sick men since there was no other food. By March all onboard were starving, and now only the ship's cat was left, which was killed to make broth for the sick. The ship went on to the Ladrones Islands, where coconut milk and fruit revived the crew, who also bought 50 hogs from the local Governor. Eventually, Cowley arrived back in England in 1686 after a three year voyage, which had been marked by the ever present problem of scurvy, as well as actual starvation.[47]

Yet the food that was usually associated with Western pirates was called Salmagundi. This dish may have been of French origin, and spread from the buccaneers of the Caribbean to pirates and sailors in the Atlantic, West Africa, and Madagascar. Salmagundi was a highly spiced cold salad composed of chopped pieces of meat of any variety, roasted and marinated in spiced wine, then mixed with palm hearts, cabbage, anchovies, pickled herring, hard boiled eggs, onions, olives, and any other vegetables that could be found. Finally, the dish would be seasoned with garlic, salt, pepper, mustard, freshened up with oil and vinegar if available, and all mixed thoroughly together. The dish protected against scurvy to some extent, and provided a contrast to the heavily salted food generally available. It would normally be served with beer, and it is of interest that Captain Bart Roberts was sitting down, drinking beer, and eating Salmagundi for breakfast, when his ship was surprised by the Royal Navy in 1722.[48]

Swearing

Pirate behaviour included much swearing, yet the overall range of late seventeenth century and early eighteenth century swearing seems quite limited, even if intensely felt. As an example, in 1691 a shoemaker in Boston was overheard swearing at his wife, 'God damn you!', 'the Devil rot you!', and the 'Pox take you', for which crime he spent two hours in the stocks. Pirate swearing during the same period does not seem to be nearly as terrible as might be expected by modern readers.[49] But it certainly shocked contemporaries. When William Snelgrave was taken by pirates in 1719, in the mouth of the Sierra Leone river, he wrote later that the 'execrable oaths and blasphemies shocked me to such a degree that in Hell itself I thought there could not be worse.'[50]

The most common swear words of the day concerned the word 'dog', as in 'you sad dog', 'you long dog', or simply 'you dog'. Also common were 'Damn you' or 'Damn me', 'son of a bitch', 'damn your blood', 'God's Zounds' and words related to disease or death such as 'pox'.

In 1697, when William Kidd got into a heated argument with his gunner, William Moore, Kidd simply concluded the argument by saying, 'You are a dog to give me those words.' The seeming mildness of the swearing was belied by Kidd's next action, which was to pick up a bucket and hit Moore on the head, so that Moore died the following day.[51] The pirate Charles Vane used the 'dog' word in 1718 when trying to get information out of a prisoner, 'Damn you, you old Dog, then tell where your Money is … If we find you in one Lye, we'll Damn you, and your Vessel also…'[52] Similarly, when Captain Roberts, aboard a merchant ship called the *Margaret*, was accosted by pirates in 1722, and Roberts delayed in rowing over to them, the pirates called out to him, 'You Dog, You Son of a Bitch. Why have you not come aboard us?'[53]

Beyond the 'dog' word, there were the 'damn' and 'blood' words. In 1718, Robert Hudson, feeling unfairly treated 'cocked his Piece … and said, Damn your Blood, I'll kill you, for sending me on the Main Yard in the Storm…'[54] When Bart Roberts' pirate ship, the *Royal Rover*, captured Thomas Grant, master of the *Experiment* in July 1719, Grant was lucky to live. He reported that one pirate immediately said to him, 'Damn You where's your Money.' Grant was wise enough to tell them, but then he was noticed by the pirate Walter Kennedy, who knew him from before. Kennedy swore, 'Damn you I know you and will sacrifice you.' Kennedy then punched Grant in the mouth, and would have killed him, but other pirates kept Grant out of the way while Kennedy ran about with a cutlass looking for Grant.[55] Similar sentiments were expressed by the pirate Richard Taylor when he heard in 1721 that the Royal Navy was after him and his ship, 'Damne my Blood

God forgive me for swearing...' This seems to indicate that he mildly regretted his blasphemy. At around the same time, in 1722, a pirate recorded a crew mate swearing at another, 'God's Zounds Damn you, you long Dog.'[56] When the *George Galley* was taken by John Smith or John Gow in 1724, one of the mutineers, James Williams, who seems to have been an unstable personality, did not like the request of the master's clerk that he be allowed time to say his prayers before being killed, 'God Damn yr. Blood say your Prayers and be damned.' Williams also pressed a reluctant crew member to shoot the mate of the captured ship, saying if he did not, he, Williams, 'would make the Sun and Moon shine through him...'[57]

Captain Charles Johnson recounted some swearing episodes, but toned them down for the publication of his book. Johnson tells the story of Harry Glasby, originally taken off the *Samuel* in 1720 by Bart Roberts. Glasby was a sober individual, who did not wish to be a pirate, and tried to escape, but on recapture by Roberts' crew, was in imminent danger of being executed. However, one of Roberts crew stood by Glasby, saying, according to Johnson, 'G__ d__ n ye gentlemen, I am as good a man as the best of you; d__ n my S__ l if ever I turned my back to any man in my life, or ever will by G__ ; Glasby is an honest fellow ... and I love him, D __ l d__ n me if I don't ... but d __ n me if he must die, I will die along with him.' So Glasby was saved, but not his accomplices. Johnson certainly paraphrased this speech, but it must have been close to the original, since he knew a great deal about Roberts and his crew.[58]

In 1727, after being falsely accused by a fellow crew member of murder, John Ashley unleashed what he evidently thought was a severe bout of swearing against his accuser, John Prie, 'You son of a Bitch how can you tell such a damnd Lye when you know we sailed under a Dutch jack [flag] you Dog you are the cause of my ruin ... It was yourself Rot you that was the Master...'[59] It was in fact John Prie who decided to kill the master of the ship *Young Lawrence*, swearing upon his decision, 'Curse my Body, but I will...' The same John Prie, looking for a particular individual, shouted, 'Where's the son of a Bitch god Damn my blood Ile be through him...' On another ship, taken by the pirate Joseph Cooper, master of the *Night Rambler*, one John Upton tried to escape, but was given a box on the ear, and called 'son of a Bitch'. Upton was also fired at, but luckily the ball passed through his hat and not his head.[60]

The conclusion, therefore, is that of course the pirates did swear, but probably no more than the ruder elements of society at that time, and by modern standards pirate swearing was rather mild.

Buried Treasure

The question of buried pirate treasure is an exciting one, but unfortunately very few pirates buried any treasure for a number of reasons. First, and most important, very few pirates managed to keep any of their treasure, because it was all spent in gambling, drinking, womanising, and other pleasures, so that there was nothing left to bury. Secondly, many ships that were seized contained items that could not easily be buried, such as bales of cotton, calico, muslin, and silk, provisions, bulky goods, wine, brandy, spices, and of course, slaves. Thirdly, when pirates did capture treasure such as jewelry, gold dust, bars of silver, and so on, it was shared out very carefully among the pirate crew, so that no large amount was left to bury. Fourthly, when pirates returned to their ports or sought protection for their treasure in different safe locations, they had to pay off greedy and corrupt colonial Governors, such as Nicholas Trott of the Bahamas, and with what was left usually tried to turn their treasure into land or property or ships, so again there was nothing left to bury. Fifthly, even if there was some treasure buried, it would be recovered quite quickly by the pirates who buried it. Sixthly, although some pirates such as Henry Avery's men in the Red Sea, collected between £700 and £1,000 pounds each, others often made very little. So of course, there was nothing for them to bury. In one case, there was not enough treasure to go around a group of pirates on St Mary's Island, Madagascar. The loot was supposed to be distributed to 14 pirates by Captains Tew, Rayner, Mason and Coats, but there simply wasn't enough to distribute, so these 14 pirates formed themselves into two groups of seven men each, and fought it out. The result was that 'one of the said Sevens were all killed, and five of the others, so that the two which survived Enjoyed the whole Booty.'[61] Finally, the buried treasure that does exist is usually to be found in children's stories (*Treasure Island*), or in film versions of what pirates were supposed to do with their plunder (*Blackbeard the Pirate*, 1952).

Nevertheless, one or two pirate stories do suggest some treasure is buried. For example, a young sailor named Morgan Miles reported in 1721 that he was at St Mary's Island, Madagascar, in 1720, when Captain Stratton of the *Prince Eugene* traded with the pirate Edmund Conden, captain of the *Flying Dragon*. It seems that a large amount of silver dollars were transferred from the *Flying Dragon* to the *Prince Eugene* after Conden bought the cargo of the *Prince Eugene*, which consisted of useful pirate requirements such as muskets, powder, wine and brandy. Stratton then sailed to Chesapeake Bay on the eastern coast of North America, and at the entrance to the York River, rowed six bags of silver ashore at night, and according to Miles, buried the treasure 'in the sand'. Stratton was then captured and brought to England, where he refused to tell the High Court of the Admiralty anything because he claimed his case was a criminal matter and therefore he was not obliged by law to answer any questions. It is not clear what happened to the buried treasure, but probably it was recovered by the authorities.[62]

Another case of buried treasure was the effort made by William Kidd to preserve his wealth, obtained during his long voyage to Madagascar, the Red Sea, and the coast of India, from 1697 to 1699. On this voyage Kidd was supposed to hunt for pirates and French ships, but perhaps Kidd became a pirate himself. Kidd returned to New England in 1699 from this voyage, during which time he had taken two valuable ships, claiming them to be captured under French passes, but he now wondered if he would be seen as a pirate, and he therefore decided to split up his treasure. This was actually a common tactic of pirates who feared arrest. So Kidd gave some bags of gold and silver to friends, such as 'Whisking' Clark, Duncan Campbell, Major Selleck, and Thomas Way, for safe keeping, and he probably sent some more treasure to his wife in New York. Kidd had sailed to Gardiner's Island before confronting Lord Bellomont, Governor of Massachusetts, in Boston. Bellomont had been one of Kidd's original backers, but Kidd was unsure of Bellomont's intentions toward him, and so he decided to bury a large part of his treasure in order to use it as a bargaining chip if needed. Kidd therefore bribed John Gardiner to bury the treasure on his island and keep it safe. This treasure amounted to 50 pounds of gold and 50 pounds of silver and a chest with medical drugs. There were also items such as spices, muslin, silk and calico clothes, which were hidden rather than buried. Most of the gold and silver was buried by tradition in Cherry Tree field on Gardiner's Island. But Kidd was never able to reclaim this part of his wealth, since he was arrested and put in jail by Lord Bellomont who hoped to benefit himself from Kidd's treasure. So, after Kidd's arrest, Bellomont sent orders for John Gardiner to dig up Kidd's treasure and deliver it to Bellomont, which Gardiner did. Undoubtedly, everybody involved siphoned off parts of Kidd's treasure, including Gardiner, but Bellomont was able to ship to England what he claimed was the full extent of Kidd's treasure that he had been able to recover. This amounted to some 1,100 ounces of gold, 2,350 ounces of silver, and 41 boxes of various jewels, silver coins, and valuable cloths. Perhaps the whole treasure was then worth about £10,000. This was a small percentage of what Kidd was supposed to have plundered, but Kidd probably plundered less than was publicly imagined, while he had sold much of his treasure during his voyage, and some was placed with friends and family and never recovered. Eventually, Kidd was hung in London in 1701, and now only one thing is certain, there is no buried treasure left on Gardiner's Island.[63]

Treasure was also supposedly buried by various pirates, including William Kidd, on Oak Island off Nova Scotia. Kidd himself did not bury anything on Oak Island since he is not known to have visited there. In fact, treasure of any kind buried on Oak Island by any group of pirates or visiting ships is very improbable. This is because after many heroic attempts to locate treasure there over at least two centuries by treasure hunters, such treasure has not been found. No pirate or ship's crew would ever bury and conceal their wealth in such a difficult location that it couldn't be easily recovered. But there is another location where treasure is much more likely to be found, and this is St Mary's Island, off the ocean coast of Madagascar. Here, many pirates like Henry Avery, fresh from looting Muslim ships in the Red Sea and elsewhere (see Chapter 6), would either use the island to transship their enormous treasures home to the Caribbean, or the Americas, or Europe, or they might sell parts of it to traders like John Plantain on St Mary's Island, or they might actually stay on St Mary's Island for some years. In all those years, very large amounts of treasure passed through the island, from the 1680s to the 1720s. So, some of that treasure seems likely to have stayed on the island. Perhaps there are caches of treasure left behind, possibly at Ranter Bay, where the trader Plantain lived, since Plantain himself claimed to be very rich in gold and diamonds.[64]

One very specific location of treasure, allegedly buried by the pirate Blackbeard (Edward Teach), is recorded by the sailor and part time artilleryman in India, Clement Downing. According to Downing, when he was in India in the early eighteenth century, he met with a Portuguese man named Anthony de Silvestro. This man claimed to have been with Blackbeard when the pirate was killed. Silvestro reported that at York River, Chesapeake Bay, near Mulberry Island, Blackbeard's pirates buried 'considerable Sums of Money in great Chests, well clamp'd with Iron Plates.' Downing researched the story a little, and found that there was indeed an island called Mulberry Island, and stated:

> If any person who uses those Parts, should think it worth while to dig a little way at the upper End of a small sandy Cove, where it is convenient to land, he would soon find whether the Information I had was well grounded.

Fronting the Landing-Place are five Trees, amongst which, he [Silvestro] said, the Money was hid.

Downing added a rather plaintive request that if any one should benefit from his account, he hoped that they would remember him for his information. Downing obviously hoped for a finder's fee, but as of the present, no one has yet found any of Blackbeard's treasure at Mulberry Island, or anywhere else. Another explanation for the lack of success in finding this treasure is that Downing or Silvestro confused the Blackbeard story with the story of the burial of treasure from Captain Stratton's ship, previously mentioned, since that burial of treasure took place in exactly the same location, at the head of the York River in Chesapeake Bay, as recounted above. Moreover, Downing himself happened to give evidence to the High Court of the Admiralty only a year or two after the Stratton case was heard by the same High Court, so Downing probably confused the two stories in his memory.[65]

One last place where pirate treasure can actually be found is in the wrecks of pirate ships. The most famous of these so far is the *Whydah*, the ship captained by the pirate Samuel Bellamy. This ship was lost in a gale near Cape Cod in April 1717, with 144 onboard, of which only two survived. The *Whydah* was carrying four and a half tons of treasure, mainly gold and silver, but the ship was wrecked in only a quarter of an hour, and the remains of the wreck then spread out along the coast for some four miles. Scavengers quickly arrived on the scene, but the *Whydah* itself vanished under the sea until the wreck was rediscovered in 1984 by underwater searchers led by Barry Clifford. A large amount of treasure has been recovered from the *Whydah* wreck so far, including over 8,000 coins, 17 gold bars, 14 gold nuggets, and assorted amounts of gold dust and gold nuggets. This is certainly a very large treasure trove, yet the *Whydah* clearly held more when she sank. Another wreck that has been recovered is that of Blackbeard's *Queen Anne's Revenge*, which grounded at Beaufort Inlet, North Carolina. Many objects, including cannon, a ship's bell, and a urethral medical instrument for treating venereal disease, have been recovered, but so far no treasure.[66] Finally, it is of interest that the pirates themselves looked for ship wrecks in order to recover whatever treasure they could. One such wreck was found at Salt Key, near the Turks Islands, in 1686, where a ship with a great deal of bullion had gone down on a half moon reef. Divers went down soon after and recovered a large amount of bullion. The wreck was reported as lying at Latitude 20 degrees, 15 minutes north, not far from Porto Plato.[67]

Weapons

What weapons did the pirates fight with, and how were they used? The first and most obvious weapon was the Cutlass. In the cinema, pirates are often seen fighting with straight swords, such as a rapier. These straight swords took a considerable length of time to learn to use effectively, and so they were not used by pirates. Instead, pirates most often owned the cutlass, a shorter, heavier, curved sword. The cutlass seems to have come into use from about the 1590s onward, and proved valuable because it was effective in close quarter fighting, which was the normal situation when pirates boarded another ship, or were defending their own ship. Cutlasses were also strong enough to cut heavy tackle, ropes and wood. It was very important, too, that cutlasses were easy to learn to use.

Knives, daggers and machetes were also carried, and were obviously valuable for a variety of tasks onboard ship, as well as for fighting. The next most useful weapon was the Pistol. Pirates found pistols very handy for the quick, sharp moments when a ship was being boarded and rapid fire power was needed. However, not every one possessed pistols, which could normally only be obtained by capturing them from pirate victims, or from a captured ships' armory.

It is important to note that pistols changed from the very awkward match lock pistol to the more convenient flint lock pistol around 1700. Both types of pistol had to be loaded from the muzzle, with the ball and powder rammed home, plus a wad, and then the pan filled with powder and closed. But with the match lock a burning match had to be applied to the pan, while the flint lock only required a spark from the flint to set off the pan, and thus the pistol itself. When the powder was damp from rain or humidity, or there was a high wind, pistols could easily misfire (a 'flash in the pan' only), and this happened frequently. Nevertheless, with the flint lock pistol, the pirate system was to wrap two or three pistols in a sash hung over the shoulder. This meant that one pistol could be fired and then another in quick succession, without the time consuming problem of reloading – and generally only two or three shots were needed in the short, sharp fights that pirates found themselves in. Pistols could also be tucked into the waistband, although this was awkward, uncomfortable and unsafe. Fire-power could also be obtained through the musket. This weapon required the same reloading system as the pistol, and also changed from match lock to flint lock around 1700. Occasionally, pirates found muskets useful as ships approached each other, since a few musket shots might frighten the opponent and bring the fight to a quick conclusion. But muskets were not as common as pistols in the pirate armory.

Pirates spent a lot of time boarding ships, and here the grenade was critical. For example, Blackbeard's crew used grenades, which were thrown onto the deck of the target ship just before boarding, and which burst with clouds of smoke as well as throwing off pieces of metal. This obviously aided the attack through injury, intimidation, noise and confusion. Charles Johnson describes Blackbeard's 'several new fashioned sort of grenades, viz. case bottles filled with powder and small shot, slugs, and pieces of lead or iron, with a quick match in the mouth of it … and as it is instantly thrown onboard, generally does great execution, besides putting all the crew into confusion…'[68]

The heaviest weapon the pirates used was the cannon. Most pirate ships carried cannon, which could be used to disarm or frighten other ships into surrender, but, most importantly, to fight off naval ships or larger merchant ships that also carried cannon. By and large, the more cannon onboard the better, because this naturally created a more powerful pirate ship. Normally, however, pirates wanted to capture ships intact and not sink them, so pirate crews tended to find large numbers of men more valuable than cannon, since these large numbers of men could more easily overwhelm their victims. Thus cannon would only be used as a last resort. One instance, in which a pirate crew did not succeed in a cannon fight occurred in 1697 when the *Mocha* frigate, captained by the pirate Robert Culliford, came across the well armed merchant ship *Dorrill*, which had about 30 guns. The *Mocha* had 22 cannon, a relatively large number for a pirate ship, and came up with the *Dorrill*, at which point the *Mocha* fired two:

> …forechaser [bow] Guns into her, but before they had fired another they had received both his broadsides … they were as good as the Pirates Guns they had not past 3 or 4 broadsides … soe the Pirates disheartened, said they [would] get nothing here but broaken bones & if we loose a mast where shall we get others they had then rec'd a shott in their foremast a 6 pounder which had gone right through the hart of it…

The pirate crew voted against continuing the fight and the *Mocha* sailed away. This was the normal result when a pirate ship faced a well armed opponent, since gunnery required more skill and discipline than a pirate ship usually possessed.[69]

Cannon came in various sizes and shapes, ranging normally from the large and very heavy twenty-four pounder to the smaller six or eight pounder – measured according to the size and weight of the cannon ball. Cannon were muzzle loaded, and had to be run out to fire outside the gun port. This was heavy work and required a number of sailors. Then the recoil of the shot would send the cannon back inboard for re-loading. The kind of shot fired from a cannon could be varied according to the target – cannon could be loaded with missiles of different kinds for anti-personnel work, sometimes called small shot; there was chain and bar shot for damaging sails and masts; or round shot for smashing the opponent's ships' sides and opposition cannon. Pirates might also carry a carronade, a short heavy weapon for a quick, devastating fire, or swivel guns for anti-personnel work. Gunnery was a difficult art, and so gunners were much sought after by pirate crews and given higher rewards when prizes were captured – in Captain Roberts' articles, gunners received a share and a half, along with masters and boatswains, while Captain Phillips' articles gave gunners a share and a quarter, along with masters, boatswains and carpenters. Captain Lowther's articles also gave gunners a share and a quarter, together with doctors, mates, and boatswains.

Cruel Pirates?

Sometime during the night of 4 June 1629, the Dutch East India Company ship, the *Batavia*, struck a reef off the west coast of Australia. The reef was part of the Abrolhos Islands, 80km off the mainland, and the *Batavia* was on its way from Holland to Batavia (modern Djakarta), to trade in spices. Among the officers of the *Batavia* was the commander, Francisco Pelsaert, the skipper Ariaen Jacobsz, and Jeronimus Cornelisz, in charge of the ship's cargo. The *Batavia* was the flag ship of the Dutch East India Company, and was large enough so that it carried 341 people onboard, including thirty-eight passengers – men, women and children. During the voyage, trouble arose when Jacobsz assaulted two women onboard, while Jacobsz and Cornelisz also hatched a plot to mutiny and take over the ship, which was carrying a very great deal of coins, gold, and goods, to the value of half a million pounds sterling. Their strange plan was to attack a female passenger, as a result of which Pelsaert would discipline the crew, which would be viewed as too harsh, and which would then lead to mutiny. In fact Pelsaert did not make any arrests, and the plan failed. As part of the plan, Jacobsz deliberately steered the ship off course, which only led to the wreck of the ship. After surveying the islands on which the ship was wrecked, Pelsaert, Jacobsz and a few others set off for Batavia in an open boat, to bring rescue to the wrecked survivors. The boat voyage itself was epic, and took thirty-three days. The boat arrived safely at Batavia, and Pelsaert then set off back to the wreck site in a Dutch ship, the *Saardam*.

Meanwhile, back at the wreck site, Cornelisz had been busy. He was a bankrupt pharmacist from Haarlem in Holland, and also a member of a heretical Anabaptist sect, which probably forced him to leave Holland. The ship-wrecked Cornelisz decided that his mutiny could still work if he recruited a small group of followers. He was aware, too, that Jacobsz would blame him for the previous attempt at mutiny, and the wreck of the *Batavia*. So Cornelisz planned to capture the rescue ship when it arrived, and depart with his followers and the treasure of the *Batavia*. If Pelsaert did not return, then they would simply build a boat and still depart with the treasure. In the mix was the idea, undoubtedly derived from his religion, that he would create a new kingdom. In order to achieve all this, Cornelisz decided that he and his followers had to kill all the rest of the passengers and crew of the *Batavia* that had survived the wreck. There then ensued a bloody regime that rivals any other pirate murders in history. Cornelisz did not do the killings himself, but his personal charisma and religious fervor compelled his followers to do the dirty work. Thus:

> Jan Hendrycks confesses that one day he had been called by Jeronimus [Cornelisz] into his tent and that he gave him to know that at night time he must help with the murder of the Predikant's family. At night, Zeevonk [another mutineer] has called outside Wiebrecht Clausen, a young girl, whom Hendrycks stabbed with a dagger, and inside all people – the mother with her six children – had their heads battered in with axes…[70]

This scene was repeated until some 125 men, women and children were murdered. When Pelsaert returned with the rescue ship, a short battle took place, and Cornelisz and his mutinous followers were defeated. Retribution was predictably fierce – Cornelisz had his hands cut off and he was hung. Other mutineers were flogged, keel hauled and hung from the yard arm. Cornelisz's second in command was broken on the wheel. Altogether seven mutineers were executed, and two were marooned. Jacobsz survived, because, even under torture, he did not confess to planning mutiny, and since he was part of the boat that sailed with Pelsaert to Batavia, he was not implicated with Cornelisz. He probably wound up in prison in Batavia.[71]

The wreck of the *Batavia* unleashed terrible cruelty by the mutineers, who can be seen as pirates through their mutiny. Perhaps Cornelisz used radical religion as a motivation for his crimes, or perhaps he was simply an unbalanced individual with considerable powers of persuasion. Yet in regard to pirates generally, the application of torture and cruelty was varied, as might be expected. Some pirates were cruel, and some were not. However, it was a rough age, and in the East it seems that torture among captives taken by Chinese pirates was sometimes unusually brutal. According to an account by John Turner, chief mate of the *Tay*, captured by the Chinese pirate Ching Yih in 1806–1807, one prisoner 'was fixed upright, his bowels cut open and his heart taken out, which they afterwards soaked in spirits and ate…'[72]

Among Western pirates, by far the most common reason for cruelty was when captives were tortured to reveal where treasure could be found aboard the ship or port the pirates had just captured. Other reasons for cruelty were because the ship attacked by the pirates offered resistance, causing death and injury to the pirates, or because a harsh and disliked captain and officers happened to be captured by pirates who knew them from previous experience. Some pirates might also have revenge in mind from their unpleasant previous service in the merchant or naval marine, or if the captured ship had harmed friends or compatriots. Some pirates had ideological reasons, for example, hatred of Spain, because of previous cruel treatment by Spaniards of their captives. And in general, the first moments when pirates swarmed onto a ship and captured it, and then began furious looting, tended to be the most dangerous moments for the officers and crew of the captured ship. Finally, another reason for cruelty was that a pirate captain might simply be an unbalanced and sadistic individual.

Typical of a situation where torture was applied to find hidden wealth was the Red Sea capture by Henry Avery of the Muslim ship, the *Gunsway* or *Ganj-i-Sawai*, belonging to the Moghul emperor Aurangzeb. According to one eye witness, the treasure in the *Gunsway* was very great, but 'little in Comparison to what was onboard, for tho' they put severall to the torture they would not Confess where ye [the] rest of their treasure lay…' Probably there was no more treasure because it seems very unlikely that among all those tortured nobody would reveal the location of more treasure.[73] Equally unpleasant treatment was meted out by the pirate Captain Low (or Lowe) who took a Portuguese ship, which offered some resistance. According to Johnson, 'Low tortured several of the men, to make them declare where the money (which he supposed they had onboard) lay, and extorted by that means, a confession that the captain had, during the chase, flung out of the cabin window, a bag with 11,000 moidores (Portuguese gold coins), which as soon as he was taken, he cut the rope off; and let it drop into the sea.' This was enough to set Low off, who 'raved like a fury, swore a thousand oaths, and ordered the captain's lips to be cut off; which he broiled before his face, and afterwards murdered him and all the crew, being thirty two persons.'[74] Low and his crew continued their bloody ways when they next captured a Spanish sloop of six guns and seventy men in the Bay of Honduras in March 1722 or 1723, which had previously taken five English sloops. Possibly this was the reason that the crew voted to kill all the Spaniards. So the pirates 'fell pell-mell to execution with their swords, cutlasses, pole axes and pistols, cutting, slashing and shooting the poor Spaniards at a sad rate.' Some Spaniards jumped into the sea, but a canoe chased after them, and the majority were hit on the head and drowned. One unfortunate Spaniard, weak and suffering from wounds, came back to Low's ship, and begged for quarter (mercy). This was not forthcoming because, 'one of the villains took hold of him, and said G__d d__n him, he would give him good quarters presently, and made the poor Spaniard kneel down on his knees, then taking his fusil [musket], put the muzzle of it into his mouth, and fired down his throat.'[75]

This cruelty was not practiced in order to discover where treasure was located, but as a more general rage against opponents, especially those who resisted the pirates' attacks. And perhaps the pirate violence of the 1720s was a reaction against the ruthless war being waged against them by the authorities.[76] Nevertheless, Low was evidently an unbalanced individual, distinguished by his cruelty. Among Low's other cruel exploits was the burning alive of a cook on a captured French ship, since the cook 'was a greasy fellow [who] would burn well in the fire; so the poor man was bound to the main-mast, and burnt in the ship…' Then there were the Portuguese friars who were hung at the fore-yard, but let down before they were dead, and this was repeated several times 'out of sport', wrote Johnson. Another Portuguese passenger looked too sad for one pirate, who cut open the passenger's bowels with his cutlass, which immediately killed him. Low seemed also to specialize in cutting off the ears of his chief captives, thus Captain Willard from the New England ship *Amsterdam Merchant*, lost his ears, his nose was slit, and he suffered other cuts to the body. Nathan Skiff, captain of a whaler from Nantucket was bloodily whipped around the deck, then his ears were cut off, and he was shot dead. The masters of two more captured whale boats near Rhode Island suffered miserably, one was ripped up and his entrails taken out, the other had his ears cut off, and he was forced to eat them, seasoned with salt and pepper. Captain Thompson, commanding a ship of 14 guns, was forced to surrender to Low because his crew would not fight, and he too had his ears cut off. Possibly the ear cutting was symbolic – perhaps to silence authority?[77]

It is noteworthy that Low appeared to take his bloody revenge against specific individuals and groups: the masters and captains of ships, French and Portuguese captains and crew, and against New England ships' masters and captains. This last was because one Rhode Island Governor had made considerable efforts to capture Low. Eventually, Low's extreme behaviour alienated even his own crew, who mutinied and put him into a small boat, which was captured by the French. Low was then hanged in Martinique by the French in 1726. Low was one of those pirates, like the French pirate L'Olonnais (see Chapter 5), whose character was simply more brutal than the rest, possibly stemming from Low's rough upbringing in Westminster, London.[78] Another pirate captain, who sailed with Low for a while, Captain Spriggs, also practiced some cruelties, though to a lesser degree than Low. After capturing a certain Captain Hawkins' ship twice, Spriggs' pirates were so annoyed at having chased and taken a worthless ship the second time around, that they set upon Hawkins and laid him flat on the deck. Then Hawkins was forced to eat a dish of candles, and finally beaten for a while. Later, Hawkins and his crew were marooned on Roatan Island, though they were given a musket, powder and ball. Hawkins and his crew survived, partly because they were ferried to a nearby island by two men in a canoe, and were eventually rescued by a passing ship.[79]

Spriggs' crew applied other cruelties, one of which was a familiar procedure to pirates. Called 'sweating', the idea was to stick lighted candles around the mizzen mast, below decks, and then the pirates formed a circle around the mast. The prisoners were then forced to run around the mast, within the pirate circle, as the pirates prodded them with penknives, forks and compasses to keep them moving while music played. According to Johnson, prisoners could keep up their running for about 10 to 12 minutes before they collapsed. In this particular case, the captain of a captured ship was sweated because he did not answer questions truthfully. Other familiar tortures included 'woolding' – twisting a rope around a person's head with a stick as lever until the pressure caused the eyes to protrude and considerable pain. Henry Morgan was reputed to have used this treatment to persuade the inhabitants of Panama City to reveal where their treasures were to be found. And in general, Morgan's men during his several raids, ruthlessly broke captives on the rack, and used fire, to persuade them to disgorge their wealth. Spriggs also practiced 'blooding', as did Captain Shelvocke, in which a captive would be pricked with needles, and then put in a barrel with cockroaches. Continuing with Spriggs, an unusual event occurred later when his ship took a boat, coming out of Rhode Island, containing a cargo of provisions and horses. For fun the crew rode the horses up and down the deck at full gallop, shouting and hallooing. Not surprisingly, two or three pirates were thrown, at which the pirates fell upon the ships' crew and beat and cut them for bringing horses without proper boots and spurs. Less pleasant was the treatment of a ship from St Eustatia, captained by Nicholas Trot. Wanting some diversion, Spriggs' crew hoisted the men as high as the main and fore tops and then let them run down fast, so that they 'broke all the bones in their skins', which pretty well crippled the crew. After some whipping, Trot and his crew were then released on their sloop. Spriggs' eventual fate is unknown, although he is likely to have perished ashore on the island of Roatan in 1725.[80]

Spriggs and his crew were a milder version of Low, and seemed to epitomize the later more aggressive attitude of pirates in the 1720s. Similarly bloodthirsty was one of the crewmen sailing with the pirate captain Matthew Luke – perhaps really Matteo Luca – whose ship was caught off Hispaniola by the *Launceston* in 1722. Matthew Luke claimed to be a Spanish 'guarda costa' (coast guard), enforcing Spanish navigation laws under a commission from Puerto Rico. When taken, Luke's crew of fifty-eight was composed mainly of Spaniards and mulattos. However, one bloodthirsty member of the crew confessed to killing twenty-eight English men 'with his own hands'. Matthew Luke was put in irons, and forty-three of his crew hanged.[81] Another example of an individual who dispensed rough justice was the English pirate Walter Kennedy. He seems to have followed the pattern of Edward Low in coming from a tough background, in his case, pick pocketing and house breaking in London, which translated into a violent attitude to life and piracy. Kennedy sailed with both Howel Davis and Bart Roberts, and then went off on his own as a pirate captain. When Kennedy was on the *Royal Rover*, as part of Roberts' fleet, the *Royal Rover* captured the *Experiment* in 1719, whose captain was Thomas Grant. Kennedy tried to kill Grant but some crew members kept Grant out of the way while Kennedy

ran about with a cutlass looking for him. Another story comes from the
sailor Edward Green, who served onboard the *Loyal Merchant*, taken earlier
by Howel Davis. He claimed to have been wounded by Walter Kennedy
and others, who 'put a Rope about his neck & drew him up under the
main top & kept him hanging there about a minute & let him down again
and then put a Rope round his Head and tyed it across his Ears & twisted
it untill he was almost blind and insensible…' This obviously was woolding,
and was employed to persuade the captive (Grant) to show where the ship's
wealth was hidden. However, it is not clear how much of the torture was
carried out by Walter Kennedy himself.[82]

When Kennedy and his crew decided to retire from piracy, he aimed
his ship toward Ireland. But Kennedy was illiterate and his navigator was
ignorant, so their ship was wrecked in Scotland while on the way to Ireland.
Kennedy eventually wound up in London, running a bawdy house in
Deptford. There one of his prostitutes, obviously annoyed with Kennedy for
some reason, gave evidence against him, and he was imprisoned in Bridewell
prison and reformatory. The same prostitute, still angry, found a witness
whose ship was taken by Kennedy. She evidently hoped to send Kennedy to
the gallows. This witness was called Grant – probably the same Grant who
was tortured earlier. Perhaps to try and save himself, Kennedy turned state's
evidence and gave the names and locations, where he knew them, of 13 of
his former shipmates. This did not help him because Kennedy was hanged
at Execution Dock, Wapping, on 19 July 1721.[83]

Moving forward in time, the pirates of the 1820s in the Caribbean and
the Americas, and especially off Cuba, practiced some of the worst cruelties in pirate history. One who survived such an attack in 1823 reported on
it in the *American Monthly* for February 1824. Sailing on a ship called the
Mary from Philadelphia to New Orleans, the *Mary*, with a very small crew,
was easily captured by pirates speaking a mixture of French, Spanish and
English. The author of the story was slashed on the head with a cutlass and
then tied to the foremast, facing the stern. If the author is to be believed, the
unfortunate captain was brutally tortured to reveal where wealth was hidden. Refusing to speak, the pirates cut off his arms at the elbow. At this, the
captain understandably gave way and told the pirates where the specie was
hidden. Not satisfied, the pirates then burnt the captain to death on a bed of
oakum soaked with turpentine, while filling his mouth with combustibles.
Equally unhappy was the boatswain who was fixed to the deck with nails
through his feet and his body spiked to the tiller. Then the remaining sailor

was forced to kneel in front of a swivel gun which was fired, wounding him severely in the head. Finally, the pirates also shot the ship's dog and cut out the dog's tongue. With everyone else dead, the pirates turned to the author, and cut off his clothes with a knife, which revealed more money. At this critical point, things would have gone badly for the author except that a ship providentially arrived, compelling the pirates to leave. One last problem was that the pirates scuttled the *Mary*, which began to sink. Fortunately, the ship and the author were saved.[84]

Overall, pirates were often cruel, but this was a cruel age. And apart from unbalanced individuals, the conclusion is that most pirates, if they tortured prisoners, normally did so for specific reasons, usually to discover where treasure was hidden, or to exact revenge for past injuries. This latter situation occurred when a former master of a ship, by name Skinner, who had dismissed some of his crew and refused them wages, was captured by pirates that included one of those dismissed by Skinner. This pirate eyed Skinner and said, 'Ah, Captain Skinner! Is it you? The only man I wish to see; I am much in your debt, and now I shall pay you all in your own coin.' Skinner trembled in every joint, as he had good reason to do, for he was fastened to the windlass, pelted with glass bottles, and then whipped around the deck until the pirates were weary. At last Skinner was shot through the head.[85] So pirates did frequently inflict injury and death, even if for reasons that to them seemed necessary. This explains, but does not reduce the pain of the victims, and there were times, as in the 1820s, when pirate cruelty spiked, and victims did suffer very severely.

Death, Repentance and Hanging

The final end for many pirates was hanging. In the seventeenth and eighteenth century, hanging was not a pleasant end for an individual because the 'long drop', which broke one's neck, was not introduced until the 1870s in England and elsewhere. Instead the pirate (or any other person sentenced to hang), was left to slowly choke to death after being 'turned off' with the short drop. This short drop might take 15 minutes or more to choke the victim to death, so that sometimes the condemned person would hire the jailor to hang on to his legs and so hasten the conclusion. Equally, friends might run forward and also quicken the end in the same way. Nor was this all, because hanging was a very public spectacle, and the crowd would shout out curses and lewd comments to the victims, and throw dead cats and dogs and excrement into the crowd, as well as at the hangman. If the hanging was well organized, the pirate would be exhorted to penitence by the prison chaplain, called the 'ordinary', on the gallows platform. This individual made a nice income by selling to broadsheet sellers in London the last words of the condemned. As an example, the ordinary at London's Newgate prison, Paul Lorrain, was worth the enormous sum of £5,000 when he died in 1700. After exhortations by the ordinary, the pirate or any other condemned individual would be allowed to sing psalms and make a farewell address before being turned off. On the positive side, the execution-bound pirate would be given drams of rum or other spirits as he made his way by cart from Newgate or Marshalsea prisons to Wapping, on the River Thames, where Execution Dock stood and where pirates were specifically hung. Consequently, many were quite drunk by the time they reached the gallows. Some pirates also would wear ribbons and hold nose gays in their hands, as a final gesture to the unkind world. After hanging, the dead pirate would be chained to a stake at the low water mark of the Thames, and the water allowed to wash over the pirate three times, to signify the authority of the British Admiralty over pirates. If the pirate was sufficiently well known, the body would be taken down and resurrected at Tilbury, the entrance to the Thames, as a warning to other pirates and would-be pirates.[86]

Starting in 1700, pirates could be tried and hung anywhere in the colonial world, and the largest mass hanging did take place at Cape Coast Castle, West Africa, when some 50 of Roberts' crew were hung in 1722. This was in the middle of the period of the greatest number of pirate hangings, perhaps 400 to 500, which took place between 1716 and 1726 in the Anglo-American world. This was part of the ruthless campaign to exterminate piracy conducted by Britain and other countries in the early 1700s. If the numbers are correct, this meant that around one pirate in ten was hung at this time. To put this in perspective, 2,169 men and women were hung just at Tyburn in London between 1714 and 1783, for a rate of thirty-one to thirty-two per year. This means that pirates were being hung at a slightly higher rate, except for the obvious fact that overall pirate numbers were clearly very much smaller than the whole population of England. Thus, if caught, pirates stood a good chance of being hung. And if all other means of dying as a pirate are included, perhaps one pirate in four was executed, died of natural causes, or was killed, in this period. Also, while in the previous century only the captain and ring leaders tended to be hung, by the eighteenth century most

of the pirate crew would hang. In this context, Johnson provides considerable detail on the manner of the hanging of Bart Roberts' crew. Several of
Roberts' pirates were not inclined to show remorse for their lives, indeed
one pirate called Sympson exclaimed just before he was hung that he saw
a woman in the crowd whom he had lain with three times. Another pirate
called Hardy, finding his arms tied behind his back, merely observed that
he had seen many hangings, but in no case had he seen any brought to
the gallows with their hands tied in this manner. But others did express
remorse, for example a certain Scudamore, who requested an extra three
days to say his prayers and study the scriptures. At the gallows, he sang the
first part of the 31st Psalm through by himself. A deserter from the Royal
Navy, Armstrong, was hung onboard the *Weymouth*, and spent his last hour
lamenting his sins, and singing some verses of the 140th Psalm. Equally, one
young man, Bunce, made a pathetic speech at the gallows, blaming his youth
for having been tempted by a life of power, liberty and wealth. He begged
God's forgiveness, and asked the spectators to remember God in their early
years, so that they would not go astray. Some pirates did therefore turn to
religion at the end of their lives, and Johnson gives an example of this in the
case of two pirates from Captain Phillips' crew, John Archer and William
White, who were hung at Boston in 1724. Johnson records that these pirates
both blamed alcohol for the start of their problems, and Johnson printed
their joint and lengthy religious submission on the gallows:

> Oh! That in this Blood our Scarlet and Crimson Guilt might be all washed
> away! We are sensible of an hard Heart in us, full of Wickedness. And we
> look upon God for his renewing Grace upon us. We bless God for the Space
> of Repentance which he had given us; and that he has not cut us off in the
> Midst and Height of our Wickedness.[87]

One pirate who had an unfortunate hanging was William Kidd in 1701. He
was well supplied with drink by the time he got to the gallows at Wapping,
and shouted out his innocence while accurately enough blaming his prominent backers, such as Lord Bellomont, for his present condition. He was to
be hung with three others, one of whom, the sickly Darby Mullins, called
out pathetically just before hanging, 'Lord have mercy upon me! Father
have mercy upon me!' The other two pirates were French, who naturally
prayed in French before their deaths. Kidd shouted again that his backers
were greedy men, and then as he was turned off, the rope broke. Kidd fell to

the mud of the Thames below. Sometimes this accident was seen as an inter-
vention by God to spare an innocent man, but the sheriff's deputies brought
him up again to hang a second time. By now Kidd was sober, and reportedly
either committed his soul to God, or said farewell to his wife and daughter
in New York City, before his second hanging.[88] Yet for one unusual pirate, it
was not necessary to be faced with hanging to find repentance. According
to one account, the pirate Edward England was living in poor health and
poverty on St Mary's Island, Madagascar, in 1721. He 'seem'd very penitent
some time before his Death, and hoped that GOD would forgive him his
Sins, desiring his Companions to leave off that Course of Life.' This account
claimed that Edward England's death was caused by 'the severe Stings of his
Conscience for his Wicked Course of Life, and the Injuries he had done to
several, by robbing them of their Properties.'[89]

In fact, pirates about to meet death were understandably quite varied in
their attitudes toward their terrible situation, some penitent, some defiant. At
New Providence, in the Bahamas, under the new and reformed Governor,
Woodes Rogers, Captain Augur and a number of his crew were condemned
as pirates in October 1718, and sentenced to hang. It appears that Woodes
Rogers did not have authority for this action, having no commission for
the trial, and he only appealed rather vaguely to the Laws of all Nations. In
any case, the sentence was to be carried out, despite some concern that the
residents of New Providence, long a pirate haven, would come to the rescue
of the condemned pirates. However, this did not happen, and eight pirates
were hung in November 1718. Some of these pirates were penitent, others
were not, while the oldest, aged 45 (which was old for a pirate), William
Cunningham, had been a gunner with Blackbeard. He expressed contrition,
while Captain Augur, aged around 40, simply drank a glass of wine to the
health of the Governor and the Bahamas Islands before being turned off.
The most surprising behaviour was that of Dennis Macarty, aged 28, who
wore blue ribbons at his neck, wrist, knees and cap. Macarty appealed to
the crowd saying that he knew a time when the residents would not have
let him die like a dog, and appealed to the spectators to have compassion
on him. The crowd was too cowed by soldiers to help him. Macarty kicked
off his shoes, saying he had promised not to die with his shoes on, and so
he died shoeless. Thomas Morris, aged about 22, was dressed with red ribbons, and criticised the new Governor. Before dying he defiantly said that
he wished he had been a greater plague to the Bahamas Islands. Another of
the condemned, William Lewis, aged about thirty-four, only desired liquors

to drink with the other condemned and with the crowd of spectators. In contrast, William Ling, aged about thirty, was penitent and told Lewis that water was more suitable than liquors to drink at this critical time. The most reviled pirate, according to the account, was William Dowling, aged about twenty-four, who was said to have been a pirate for some time, and was rumoured to have murdered his mother in Ireland. Nevertheless, all these pirates apparently joined in reading prayers and psalms before being conducted to the place of execution.[90]

In regard to this group execution in the Bahamas, age did not seem to have an effect on the attitude of these pirates to their unpleasant end. The youngest was 18 and the oldest, as noted, was 45. One of the two pirate ring leaders was Macarty (the other had died), and it was Macarty who had dealt harshly with his captives, and this same bravado appeared as he faced death without his shoes. This pirate group also appeared surprised by the toughness of Woodes Rogers, and certainly hoped that New Providence's former pirates would assist them. But the tide had turned against piracy, and the correspondent who sent Johnson the details of this New Providence trial and execution observed that there were few who watched the hangings that did not deserve the same fate, being former pirates, but they had been pardoned by a recent Act of Grace. These spectators at the hanging now reluctantly recognized that the world was changing. The golden age of piracy in the West was over.

Now, before returning later to this golden age of piracy, the story of piracy really begins with the ancient world.

2

From Classical Piracy to the Medieval Mediterranean

Pirates are the eternal outsiders, riding the shifting boundary between honesty and crime at sea. The line between piracy and legal maritime activity was a very fine one – for example, in the ancient period the distinction between piracy and customary raiding did not really exist. As an example, what is the reader to make of the casual exploit in Homer's *Odyssey*, perhaps composed somewhere around the eigth century BC, when the hero sailed:

> …to the Cicones, to Ismaros [on the Thracian coast]; there I sacked a city and slew the men, and taking from the city their wives and many possessions we divided them, that no man for me might depart deprived of an equal share. Then, indeed I ordered that we should fly with nimble foot…[1]

Perhaps Homer was thinking back to the violent twelfth century BC when raiders like Homer's hero sacked cities, and went after treasure and women. The whole purpose was spoil, 'Silver, gold, bronze, horses, cattle and sheep, women, above all, treasure and women.'[2] At a lower level of raiding, there must also have been many freebooter groups, often composed of just three or four men in small boats, scrounging what they could get. Later on, much of the raiding that took place in coastal regions of the Mediterranean was a by product of the wars between the Greeks and the Persians, between Athens and Sparta, and other local wars. Thus one Polycrates became a tyrant and pirate in the sixth century BC. He was an ally of the Egyptian king, Amasis, and according to the historian Herodotus, captured the island of Samos between about 535 to 532BC. Polycrates raided rather successfully:

> …wherever he decided to strike in a campaign, everything went well for him. He got himself one hundred penteconters [a 50 oared ship] and a thousand archers, and he harried and plundered every state without distinction … He captured a great number of the islands and many of the towns on the main-land [of Greece. Among his conquests were the Lesbians … he beat them in a sea battle, and it was they who in chains dug the whole of the trench around the fortification in Samos.[3]

Even so, it is hard to determine if Polycrates can strictly be called a pirate because of his large scale operations and alliance with Egypt. Also it seems that the concept of piracy did not really begin to emerge until 478BC, during the creation of the Delian League, a group of city states and Greek islands led by Athens, which was formed to protect against the Persians, act against pirates, and restore order to the Aegean region after the Persian invasion of 480BC.

No doubt it was always difficult to differentiate between piracy and authorized raiding during the long periods of warfare in the ancient world. During the Peloponnesian War of 431–404BC much of what may seem to be piracy was really mercenary privateering on behalf of one side or another. It also appears that the Greek word 'peirates', meaning one who assaults, only stems from around the third century BC.[4] On the other hand, Athens tried to control piracy during the fourth century BC, and Athenians evidently understood who was a pirate and who was not. Similarly, during the short rule of Alexander the Great (336-323BC), he clearly differentiated between pirates and legitimate maritime activity, and attempted to rid his empire of pirates. Thus Alexander told his admirals Hegelochus and Amphoterus in 331BC to rid the seas of pirate fleets, which had flourished while Alexander was locked in his struggle with the Persian king Darius. Particular mention was made of Crete, which supported piracy and ran a large slave market.[5] Another reference to pirates during Alexander's reign occurs when five pirate galleys, which had allied themselves with Persian forces in the eastern Mediterranean, entered the harbour of Chios in 331BC under the mistaken impression that Chios was under the control of the Persians. However, Chios was actually in Macedonian hands, and the surprised pirate crews were 'killed then and there'. Clearly, Alexander himself saw a clear distinction between pirates and other groups.[6]

Following the death of Alexander in 323BC, the wars of his Successors spawned pirates, privateers and mercenaries in large numbers. Notable among this group were the pirates who assisted Antigonus the one-eyed, and his son Demetrius, in their siege of Rhodes in 305-304BC. The historian Diodorus records that pirates, merchants and traders all provided cargo and transport ships for Demetrius. Even though Diodorus remarks that these merchants and traders gathered around Demetrius in order to enrich themselves from the misfortunes of others, Diodorus still distinguishes between the pirates and these other potential plunderers of Rhodes. The same distinction between pirates and others is made by Diodorus when he relates that Demetrius sent out pirates and soldiers to attack Rhodes by sea and by land. Subsequently, the maritime defenders of Rhodes sailed out and defeated a fleet of Demetrius' ships, which included some pirate ships, commanded by the pirate Timocles. Diodorus notes that Timocles was the chief pirate, and his ships consisted of three 'deckless ships', presumably meaning fast galleys with just one bank of oars. Once again, Diodorus makes a clear distinction between pirates and Demetrius' other ships. In this case, despite the efforts of Demetrius and Antigonus, the siege of Rhodes failed. This father and son adopted the use of extremely large siege engines, requiring thousands of men to work them, because they mistakenly believed that bigger is better. One of these engines was a truly enormous siege tower, nine stories high, inside which were 3,400 soldiers. But one night, the Rhodians fired bolts that dislodged some of the iron cladding that protected the wood beneath, and then followed up with fire arrows that set the tower on fire. Consequently, the tower had to be withdrawn. The siege was eventually abandoned, and a treaty was signed. Following this, the island of Rhodes, on behalf of all the Greeks, took the lead in attacking the pirates of the Mediterranean, and, according to Diodorus, purged 'the seas of these evil doers...'[7]

Romans and Pirates

Despite this effort by Rhodes, by the time the Romans emerged as a Mediterranean power, pirate raids were still a constant problem. These pirates were difficult to deal with because Rome did not emphasise sea power, and pirates were able to operate quite easily from the Mediterranean coast of Cilicia (eastern Turkey). These Cilician pirates took slaves, ransomed prisoners, and attacked coastal ports and towns. It was alleged that the Cilician pirates had a thousand ships, which were adorned in gold, silver and purple, and that they sailed in squadrons commanded by admirals. Another pirate base was Crete, where pirates sailed out to take captives for slavery, since Crete continued to run a very large slave market.[8] In this context, in the year 74 or 75BC, a young Roman by the name of Julius Caesar was captured by Aegean pirates. He was on his way to Rhodes to study rhetoric, but was taken by pirates operating from the island of Pharmacusa, off the coast of Caria. Reportedly, Caesar was offended by the low ransom of 20 talents demanded for him by the pirates, and raised it to 50 talents. This was an error because back home in Rome the dictator Sulla, an enemy of Caesar's family, had confiscated Julius Caesar's property and that of his wife. Consequently, the ransom took some 40 days to collect, although during this time Caesar and the pirates became reasonably friendly, even if Caesar promised to return and crucify his captors. After the ransom was deposited, Caesar was released, and true to his word, borrowed four galleys and attendant soldiers, and returned to capture the pirates and bring them to Pergamon. Caesar wanted immediate execution, but the local Roman governor was not used to such decisive action, especially because pirates and local merchants had evolved a mutual system of living and benefiting together, and so he forbade execution. But Caesar, showing the decisiveness of his future career, ordered the execution of the pirates anyway. Then, in view of their friendly relations during his captivity, Caesar took aside the 30 principal pirates and promised that their throats would be cut before crucifixion – a more merciful conclusion to their lives than the drawn out death of crucifixion.[9]

Meanwhile, the Romans found that piracy from Crete was sufficiently damaging that several attempts to take Crete were launched, for example the failed assault by Marc Antony in 72BC. It is reported that the fetters that Marc Antony placed in his ships were then used to bind the Roman prisoners on Crete.[10] Romans were not used to failure, and in 69BC the Roman general Metellus launched three legions against Crete and conquered the island via a series of sieges and with considerable brutality. However, the situation for Rome became graver through the ravages of the Cilician pirates. Despite Metellus' success, in 69BC the pirate Athenodorus captured Delos and desecrated the statues of their gods. Plutarch notes that pirates went on to plunder a further thirteen sanctuaries and 400 cities. Ships were attacked as well, also the harbor of Ostia, and then pirates captured two Roman praetors, dressed in purple, as well as the daughter of Antony, carried off from the port of Misenum, and ransomed. The final straw – and the most dangerous for Rome – was the threat by pirates to capture the grain fleet from Egypt in 67BC, which would be disastrous for the food supply of Rome.

Consequently in 67BC, the Roman general Pompey, who had probably already been planning the campaign strategy, was appointed to command the fight against the pirates. Pompey was given 270 ships for the campaign, and started by guarding the grain supplies from Sicily, North Africa, and Sardinia. He then divided the Mediterranean and the Black Sea into thirteen commands, with the idea of isolating the pirates into small groups that could be dealt with separately. Pompey himself commanded a fleet of sixty ships. The campaign went well, though a recent analysis argues that the campaign only took four months, was a rushed job, and was really just aimed at securing the grain supply. In addition, Pompey's victory over the pirates was hyped up and over emphasized since the threat of the Cilician pirates remained. Subsequently, Pompey led 100 ships to the Cilician coast, with numerous siege engines onboard because it was thought that the only way to defeat the pirates was to capture their land bases. However, it seems that the pirates did not fight, recognizing their likely defeat, but simply surrendered in return for good behavior, and resettlement as farmers. So Pompey simply gave them pardons.[11]

The Cilician pirate threat had been removed for the time being, but full suppression of the pirates in the Mediterranean did not come until the rule of Octavian, who was named senator in 28BC, and then titled Augustus in 27BC. Augustus essentially got rid of the pirates by capturing the borders of the Mediterranean, thus denying pirates the use of ports and land bases. Following this, the Pax Romana generally kept the Mediterranean safe for traders until the gradual collapse of the Roman Empire in the fifth and sixth centuries. During this collapse, the Roman Empire was frequently assaulted by northern pirates, as well as by Franks and Saxons in the third and fourth centuries, and by Picts and Scots, and later, by Angles and Heruls.[12] The decline of Rome meant that the Mediterranean eventually became prey to a very large number of new threats, including Vandals, Arabs and Muslims, Vikings, and later, Normans, and once more, Cretans. These national and ethnic groups might be termed pirates, raiders, freebooters, or semi-authorised fleets. Once again, it is very difficult to distinguish between a pirate and a legal raider as part of warfare.

In the fourth and fifth centuries, one of the naval and land threats to Rome was the tribe known as the Vandals, who eventually migrated to North Africa. Their naval strength was not overwhelming, but the historian Procopius describes one maritime victory over a Roman fleet in 468, when the Vandal ships found the Romans unprepared and at anchor in a bay:

> And when they [the Vandal fleet] came near, they set fire to the boats which they were towing, when their sails were bellied by the wind, and let them go against the Roman fleet. And since there were a great number of ships there, these boats easily spread fire wherever they struck … And as the fire advanced in this way, the Roman fleet was filled with tumult, as was natural, and with a great din that rivaled the noise caused by the wind and the roaring of the flames, as the soldiers together with the sailors shouted orders to one another and pushed off with their poles the fire-boats and their own ships as well, which were being destroyed by one another in complete disorder. And already the Vandals too were at hand ramming and sinking the ships, and making booty of such of the soldiers as attempted to escape, and of their arms as well.[13]

The Medieval Mediterranean

The Vandals were followed by later Mediterranean raiders of all sorts as the Mediterranean became a battleground for maritime supremacy between three principal entities: the Muslims, the Byzantines, and the Christian West. Looking ahead, the Muslim eruption into the Mediterranean began in the seventh century, and achieved very considerable successes until the Byzantine resurgence around 750. Eventually, Byzantium dominated the Mediterranean by the tenth century. Despite this, Muslim attacks continued through the ninth and tenth centuries, although in the end these attacks did not succeed in dominating the Mediterranean. Then, from the eleventh to the fifteenth centuries, Western Christian shipping predominated in the Mediterranean, although during this time Muslim emirates and Ottomans continued their attacks on Western Christian and Byzantine shipping. Constantinople fell to the Ottomans in 1453, and through the sixteenth century the Ottoman attacks intensified. As might be imagined, these competing and constantly fluctuating rival powers in the Mediterranean made for a very complex situation, leading to a bewildering mixture of piracy, privateering, corsairs, and state sponsored raiding. As one historian wrote:

> Outright illegal piracy on the one hand and legitimized corsair activity under the licence of political authorities … on the other, were endemic throughout the Mediterranean from the twelfth to the sixteenth centuries. No region or time period was free from them, and there was no maritime city, state, or people whose seamen did not participate in them.[14]

In this context, and in the discussion of medieval Mediterranean piracy, it will obviously be difficult to distinguish between piracy and other more legitimate or semi-legitimate attacks. With this warning in mind, and turning back to the earlier Muslim offensives in the seventh century, the Muslims started raiding in 634 and attacked North Africa, Constantinople, Spain, southern France, and a variety of Mediterranean targets such as Cyprus, Sicily, Rhodes, Sardinia and Crete. Muslim pirates eventually operated from a number of bases such as Fraxinetum in southern France, Monte Garigliano near Naples, and strongholds such as Bari, Palermo, and Tarentum. According to one source, these bases operated as an outer pirate screen of raiders, behind which the main Muslim fleets protected Muslim trading routes, and were able to launch major attacks.[15] Defending against these operations was Byzantium, which fended off serious Muslim attacks against Constantinople itself in the seventh century and the early eighth century, and established maritime superiority by the tenth century before finally falling to the Ottomans. Among some of the tactics the Byzantine navy used against its opponents, including pirates, was to use one galley to engage an enemy galley and then use another galley to ram the opponent at the stern. Another idea was to ram and puncture the enemy galley and so fill it with water, causing it to sink. Of interest also is the Byzantine method of communicating at sea by using flags and purple cones as signals. Finally, the celebrated Byzantine Greek fire was used, which ignited on contact with water, and whose ingredients were a closely guarded secret.[16]

Crete: 827–963

In particular, the Byzantine naval revival by the tenth century enabled Byzantium to recapture Crete in 963 after more than a century of occupation by Muslim pirates. Crete had been captured in 827 by Spanish Muslims, following a number of their raids against the island. These Spanish Muslims were exiles from Cordoba in Spain as rebels against the local Emir. Under their chief Abu Hafs, these Spanish Muslims sailed to Crete from Alexandria. Abu Hafs ordered his followers to burn their boats, so they could not retreat, but in fact they met little resistance in Crete. They set up a fortress and surrounded it with a moat, 'khandaq' in Arabic, from which the place name of Candia emerged. For the next 135 years, Candia acted as a stronghold for these pirates, alleged to number 10,000, who raided the coasts and islands of Greece, and were apparently financed by the city elites of Crete. Eventually, after several abortive attempts by the Byzantines to take Crete, one Nicephorus Phocas led a powerful Byzantine fleet of some 3,000 ships against the Muslim defenders of Crete in 960. Only Candia held out, and was besieged for eight months. Among the incidents relating to this siege was the symbolic announcement to the defenders of Candia, that their relief fleet had been destroyed, through the method of loading the Byzantine siege artillery with the severed heads of Muslim soldiers and firing them into Candia. Similarly, knowing that the defenders of Candia were starving, Phocas had an unfortunate live donkey fired into the city by a stone throwing machine, so that the donkey landed on its back, and lay with its legs waving in the air, to the amusement of the Byzantines. Yet another incident had an Arab woman of terrible appearance standing on the battlements of Candia, uttering curses and threats, and even undressing with indecent gestures. The Byzantine besiegers thought she was a witch, and fell into confusion, but one soldier simply shot her off her position, and resolved the crisis. Eventually, Candia could not hold out against starvation and fell in March 961.[17]

Similar to Crete was the case of Majorca, which was a Muslim island from 902 to 1229, and was a favourite lair for pirates. It should be noted here that the operations of these Muslim corsairs from Crete and Majorca and other centres in the ninth, tenth and following centuries, were partly piracy, but more than piracy in the sense that most Muslim corsairs at this time considered their activities to be a form of jihad, intended to advance the frontiers of the Muslim world.[18] Then, in the tenth century Byzantium began to recover a number of areas from the Muslims such as Cilicia and Cyprus, while the pirate bases of Garigliano and Fraxinetum was closed down in 915 and 972 respectively. Part of the reason for Muslim decline in the Mediterranean at this time, and with it Muslim pirate attacks, was the rivalry between different Muslim powers such as the Fatimids and the Ummayads. Later, under the Ottomans, Muslim naval power was to grow again, but in the meantime, two further semi-piratical powers emerged in the Mediterranean – the Normans, and the sea going cities of Pisa and Genoa.

The Normans

The Normans were a Viking/Frankish entity. They evolved from being Viking raiders and settlers in the area of Normandy to being an aggressive outward-looking group, which conquered England, and created empires in southern Europe and Sicily. The Normans used land warfare to build their empires, but also became sea raiders. It is difficult to know whether they can be called pirates, or perhaps more accurately, one can visualise the Normans as starting out as pirates, like their forebears the Vikings, but winding up as established powers in parts of Europe and the Mediterranean.

At first, the Normans reacted to Muslim attacks. Before the destruction of the Muslim bases at Garigliano and Fraxinetum, these centres launched attacks on southern Europe, as did Muslim ships based in North Africa. The Bishop of Cremona reported that, 'no-one coming from the west or north to make his prayers at the thresholds of the blessed apostles was able to get into Rome without either being taken prisoner by these men or only released on payment of a large ransom.'[19] This situation gave some Norman knights and families the excuse to liberate southern Europe from the Muslims, although they also attacked Byzantine lands. Thus, among the Norman knights was a freebooter named Robert Guiscard, who from the 1050s and 1060s led the Normans in the lengthy conquest of southern Italy and Sicily from the Byzantines. It is reported of him that he 'shrank from no violence and nothing was sacred to him; he respected neither old age, nor women and children and on occasion he spared neither church nor monastery.'[20] Among his exploits was the successful siege of the city of Salerno in 1076, strangely enough with the aid of Muslims, Greeks, and Richard of Capua. He attempted to attack Constantinople itself in 1080, took Corfu in 1084 and aimed at the island of Cephalonia in 1085. Robert's methods were to build large castles on his ships, covered with hides to protect crossbowmen and prevent fire. He also used catapults on his ships, as well as Greek fire, and crowded the rigging with crossbowmen to keep down the fire of defenders. Then he sailed close to castles located in the ports he was besieging and overwhelmed the castles.[21] It is interesting that the start of a fight between ships at this time used tricks such as hurling bags of lime onto the enemy to blind the sailors, and the application of soft soap to make the decks slippery for boarders.[22]

Robert Guiscard's brother, Roger, also took a leading part in the successful but lengthy Norman effort to conquer Sicily, and carried on the struggle after Robert's death in 1085. Apart from the two Guiscards, the most noteworthy Norman admiral during the height of Norman expansion was a certain George of Antioch. In 1146 he captured Tripoli in North Africa, and in 1148 he led a fleet of 250 ships to capture the port of Mahdiyya in what is now Tunisia. In 1147, George of Antioch found time to mount a large scale campaign among the Greek Ionian islands and Corinth. It is reported that by the end of the campaign 'the Sicilian vessels were so low in the water with the weight of their plunder that they seemed more like merchantmen than the pirate ships they really were'.[23] Then in 1149, George of Antioch raided up the Bosphorus, picking off the rich seaside Byzantine villas along the way, although he failed to plunder Constantinople. Subsequently, Norman raiding slowed down for a few years, partially caused by the death of George of Antioch, and his master, Roger Guiscard. After this, another Sicilian fleet under Tancred of Leche sailed from Messina in 1185 and in a joint land and maritime assault took Thessalonica, the second most important port and city of Byzantium. The Byzantine historian Nicetas was not impressed by the Normans, and wrote of their sack of Thessalonica:

> These barbarians carried their violences to the very foot of the altars in the presence of the holy images … it was thought strange that they should wish to destroy our icons, using them as fuel for the fires on which they cooked. More criminal still, they would dance upon the altars, before which the angels themselves trembled, and sing profane songs, then they would piss all over the church, flooding the altars with urine.[24]

No doubt the Viking forebears of the Normans might have done the same in their earlier raids on monasteries and churches. Yet the Norman Empire in North Africa did not last long, and soon after George of Antioch's death in 1153, their Mediterranean empire began to slowly disintegrate.

Genoa and Pisa

Meanwhile, at much the same time as the Norman expansion, the fleets of Genoa and Pisa were demonstrating their piratical abilities too. Ships from Pisa and Genoa had assisted the Holy Roman Emperor, Henry VI, in taking Sicily back from the Normans in 1194, and already by the late eleventh century, Pisans and Genoese had driven the Muslims from Corsica and Sardinia, assisted the Normans in taking Palermo, and were raiding North African ports. The piratical activities of Pisa and Genoa increased very much after their fellow citizens were driven out of their trading quarters in Constantinople in 1182, due to anti-Western feeling, and for the next few years until the Crusade of 1204, a plague of piracy ensued. The net result was that by 1191 most Aegean islands were depopulated, or were simply used as ports by pirates. Efforts were made by Byzantium to control this piracy, either by buying off the pirates; or by the system of reprisal. Reprisal worked by taking over as compensation whatever property of the relevant city state in Constantinople could be found (i.e. if the pirate was Pisan, seize Pisan property of similar value in Constantinople, and alternatively, if the pirate happened to be Genoese, simply imprison a prominent Genoan in Constantinople until compensation was paid). Then there was naval action, as when the Byzantines employed a pirate fleet under one Stirione, a Calabrian, to capture the fleet of the Genoese pirate Gafforio. This was accomplished in 1195 and Gafforio was killed. A curious case of setting a pirate to catch a pirate, and not for the last time.[25]

Genoese and Other Pirates

Some well known pirates of the time included the Genoan, Guglielmo Grasso, who attacked Rhodes with a pirate fleet in 1192, killed all he found in the harbor, and plundered the town. He then managed to capture a ship carrying gifts for the Byzantine Emperor from the famous Saladin, which contained horses, mules, Libyan wild beasts, valuable metals and woods, plus Byzantine envoys. All aboard were killed except for some Pisan and Genoese merchants.[26] Then there was Leone Vetrano, another Genoese pirate, who captured a castle in Corfu and raided various other ports in 1199. A Venetian fleet in 1207 finally defeated Vetrano's pirate fleet. Vetrano was captured and subsequently put to death by impaling. Another pirate was Enrico Pescatore (the fisherman), who married Grasso's daughter, and attacked Crete with five round ships and twenty-four triremes in 1206. He landed an army on Crete and captured the capital, and then, following this, built some fourteen or fifteen castles to solidify his hold on the island. But Pescatore was brought to heel in 1211, when the Venetians forced him to surrender his castle of Paleocastro in Crete. Pescatore agreed to financial terms, and left Crete. But violent piracy resumed in the 1213–1214 period, when the pirate Alamanno Costa, yet another Genoan, operated freely before being captured in 1217 and put in a cage.[27] It must be admitted, however, that these Genoese pirates were perhaps more than simple pirates because of the number of ships and soldiers that they controlled, so for example, Pescatore styled himself Count of Malta.

There were attempts to control piracy in the thirteenth century with commercial treaties between most of the chief Mediterranean powers, which sought to regularize commerce and outlaw piracy. These measures included, by 1301, the establishment of the Office of Piracies in Genoa in 1301 to compensate foreigners for Genoese piracy. Genoa also established harsh penalties for piracy. For example, in 1230, pirate captains were hung in chains on the city walls until they presumably died, while the right hands of their crewmen were cut off, to prevent them from carrying on the pirate trade. Another unpleasant form of punishment involved some 50 Venetians in 1261 who were captured trying to escape from Constantinople, and their captors, assuming them to be pirates, blinded them and cut off their noses.[28]

Despite all this, piracy was common in the medieval Mediterranean, not just by Pisans and Genoese, but also, among others, by Venetians, Amalfians, Lombards, Provencals, Catalans, Spaniards, Greeks, Slavs and Muslims – for treasure, or for slaves, or for ransom. For example, a certain Muslim emir, Usamah, operated galleys from Beirut in the 1190s, which captured 14,000 Christians, and sold them into slavery. Usamah owed allegiance to the famous commander Saladin, but seems to have operated independently. Usamah's reign was brought to an end by the reconquest of Beirut in 1197 by the Crusaders.[29] Some of this piracy involved the fierce and ongoing rivalry between Venice and Genoa, in which freelance privateers, corsairs, or unlicensed pirates, simply attacked ships of the opposition if circumstances were favourable. Piracy became even more prevalent in the fourteenth century, with its general nature and casual normality revealed by one of the stories told in Boccaccio's *Decameron*, written between 1351 and 1353. The *Decameron* recounts a series of tales told by ten young refugees from the plague, who flee to the countryside, and tell stories over a period of ten days. In Boccaccio's Fourth Tale on the second day of storytelling, a wealthy merchant from the Amalfi coast, Landolfo Ruffolo, makes a bad business decision and is headed towards poverty. He concludes that either he must kill himself or become a robber. Not surprisingly, he decides to rob. He has enough money to buy a small, fast craft, and so becomes a pirate 'with the intention of stealing other men's goods, especially the Turks'. Within a year he has made even more money from pirating than from his original merchant venture, and so he decides to retire from the piracy business. Ironically, his pirate ship is driven into a bay by a storm, where events turn against Ruffolo, as two large Genoese merchantmen are in the bay and 'determined to seize it [Ruffolo's ship], like the rapacious, money loving men they were.'[30]

Boccaccio's tale shows that piracy in the fourteenth century Mediterranean was normal and something to be expected. In this context, Genoa's Office of Piracies ceased to operate in the early fourteenth century due to civil war, when the Genoese could no longer control their own ships.[31] There was also a pirate fleet of twenty-nine ships that operated off the island of Negroponte in 1346.[32] On the other hand, the convoy system, starting around the eleventh century, appears to have developed widely in the Mediterranean, and trade revived strongly in the twelfth and thirteenth centuries. Convoys continued to be used in the fourteenth century, particularly by Genoa and Venice, as maritime rivalries encouraged the growth of piracy. At the same time, the Ottoman capture of Constantinople in 1453 allowed Catalan, Sicilian and Italian pirates to flourish in the Aegean, which was now free from Byzantine control. Similarly, the island of Lesbos was infested with pirates until it too fell to the Ottomans in 1462.[33] By the late fifteenth century, the Ottoman navy began to dominate the eastern Mediterranean, and waged two wars against Venice, most successfully in 1499–1502. In general, the Ottomans tried to control piracy in the eastern Mediterranean, and although Ottoman forces were later soundly defeated in the famous galley battle of Lepanto in 1571, this battle did not have any lasting effect on the Ottomans.[34] Meanwhile, in the western Mediterranean, pirates operated through the fifteenth century, and could originate from North Africa, Genoa, Granada, Portugal, Castile, Catalonia or France. For example, in 1401, the king of Aragon wrote to the king of Castile, praising him for dealing with pirates and corsairs 'who go by sea robbing and stealing all they can not less from our vassals and friends than from strangers and yours and our enemies.'[35]

As always, it is hard to distinguish between privateers who were commerce raiders against their enemies in the ongoing rivalry of Mediterranean city states and powers, and straightforward pirates, who raided all and sundry. But a major change occurred around 1500 when the Barbary corsairs emerged in the Mediterranean as raiders. These corsairs had their own arrangements with North African regencies such as Algiers, Tripoli and Tunis, which were under the nominal sovereignty of the Ottomans. Meanwhile, Western pirates, especially English and Dutch pirates, were also now operating in the Mediterranean. Thus there was a Mediterranean pirate offensive by Western pirates between 1595 and 1605, and ultimately, by 1610, according to one author, the Mediterranean had again become a systematic hunting ground for pirates, who took ships without any religious or other justification. This situation, along with economic and political problems, and technical back-wardness, had much to do with the decline of Venice as a sea going power by around 1600.[36]

Venice did not go down without a fight, as shown by the capture in October 1584 of a large Muslim galley off Cephalonia by the Venetians. Gabriele Emo, commander of a Venetian squadron of convict galleys, cut to pieces 50 Muslims, 75 Turks, 174 Renegade Christians, and 45 women, while releasing 200 galley slaves.[37] But Venice suffered from the difficulty of man-ning their galleys – the larger galleys required 164 rowers on 27 benches. So, after 1545, convicts were sent from prison to the oars, eventually some 500 per year. And by 1595 all Venetian galleys were mainly rowed by convicts, with very few free men volunteering. Despite the effort to solve the man-power problem by using convicts in the galleys, it seems that 60 per cent of the convicts died of poor conditions, partly due to their meagre supply of food – five ounces of biscuits and one cup of wine per day being the allowance. As if these galley problems were not enough, Venice turned to building very large galleasses and galleons in the early 1600s, but these were very expensive and good crews were impossible to find. By 1611 there was only one great galley available, and that was leaking and unseaworthy.[38]

Unfortunately for Venice, at this time the city had to deal not only with Barbary corsairs and European pirates, but also with privateers sailing out of Naples and Sicily, and an enterprising group of pirates operating in the Adriatic. These Adriatic pirates, called Uskoks, lived in the port of Senj, near Fiume, and operated in the border area between the Hapsburg and Ottoman empires. They attacked Venetian ships, using rowed boats with a crew of about thirty to sixty, and had a reputation for being violent. Certainly,

Venice cut off the heads or otherwise executed those Uskoks they caught, and viewed Uskok society as evil:

> The most honored [Uskok] families, and those considered of the greatest merit, are those who for the longest time have traced their origins in a continuous descent from those hanged, cut to pieces, and foully massacred in other ways in their pursuits.

Venice believed that, 'All those things which are universally detested as contrary to every humanity, are always praised by them as proper to men of valor.'[39] The Uskoks attacked Venetian ships from the 1570s until they were brought under some kind of limits by the Hapsburgs after the Venice-Hapsburg war of 1615–1617.

The medieval Mediterranean was a very complex place, full of constantly changing powers, with a bewildering variety of pirates, privateers and corsairs who changed status according to desire and necessity. But these raiders were all really part of a fluctuating Mediterranean economic system, stimulated by the competition between Islam, Byzantium and the Christian West. Consequently, distinctions between piracy and legitimate maritime conflict cannot easily be drawn. As one historian of the medieval Mediterranean suggests 'Pirate and corsair crews were cosmopolitan. Captains of all races roved the seas in the service of anyone who would pay or license them.' So, emperors of Byzantium before the Fourth Crusade issued letters of marque to Western corsairs to fight against other Western corsairs. Genoese, Pisans, Franks, and perhaps even Muslims, served as corsairs for Byzantium in the thirteenth century. Greeks served the Muslim emirs of Aydin (in the area of Smyrna), in the fourteenth century. Hence, it can be concluded that in the medieval Mediterranean 'There was no sharp distinction between the peaceful merchantman and the pirate on the one hand and the man of war and the corsair on the other.'[40] This same difficulty will arise later with the Barbary Corsairs and the Knights of Malta, but at the same time as the medieval Mediterranean created a sea of pirates and corsairs, the northern world of Europe produced its own form of medieval piracy.

3

Piracy in the Northern World

Just as piracy in the Mediterranean world went through complex changes, so a similar evolution took place in the pagan north. Vikings were raiders from Scandinavia, and the name Viking may come from the word 'Vik', meaning creek or inlet from which the Vikings emerged. In general, however, Scandinavians were called the Norse, and pirates and raiders were differentiated from the Norse by being called the Vikings. The first Viking ships arrived off the shores of England and France in the 780s, although the traditional start of the Viking age of attacks on the British Isles and Western Europe is the Viking raid on the monastery of Lindisfarne, off the English coast of Northumbria, in 793. These raiders were probably Norwegians, and the Anglo-Saxon Chronicle recorded this attack with dismay:

> In this year dire portents appeared over Northumbria and sorely frightened the people. They consisted of immense whirlwinds and flashes of lightning, and fiery dragons were seen flying in the air. A great famine immediately followed those signs, and a little after that in the same year, on June 8, the ravages of heathen men miserably destroyed God's church on Lindisfarne, with plunder and slaughter.

The scholar and teacher, Alcuin of York, wrote to King Aethelred of Northumbria in similar style about the Lindisfarne attack:

> …never before has such terror appeared in Britain as we have now suffered from a pagan race, nor was it thought that such an inroad from the sea could be made. Behold, the church of St. Cuthbert spattered with the blood of the priests of God, despoiled of all its ornaments; a place more venerable than all in Britain is given as a prey to pagan peoples.[1]

What drove these Scandinavians to leave their normal trade routes and farms and become pirates? Many explanations have been offered, ranging from over-population in Scandinavia which lead to shortage of land for farming; to climate change of colder weather, resulting in less land for farming; to the desire for honor and treasure; to competition between chieftains to attract followers (fellows) and produce valuable results from raids; to social encouragement in Scandinavia for such expeditions and later for emigration; to the lack of strong European powers at the time to curb such piracy; to the pre-existence of Scandinavian trade routes, which showed the Vikings where the valuable targets were; to the realization that raiding was more productive than trading to obtain silver and treasure; to eighth-century economic growth in Europe providing attractive targets; and to the development of suitable ships (the well known Viking long ships), with the parallel improvement of sailing skills. As well, being pagan, the Vikings had no remorse about plundering vulnerable targets such as monasteries and churches, where valuable artifacts could be found, where there were no defenses, and where monks and servants could easily be taken as slaves. As important was the fact that wealthy monasteries were often located on isolated islands or coasts that could easily be raided from the sea.

These Viking raids brought howls of protest from monks and clergy who were the most affected, and this actually pleased the Vikings, because such tales produced the kind of propaganda that might make the next target more ready to surrender without a fight. A similar sense of outrage came from the Patriarch Photius, in regard to a Viking raid on Constantinople, and on monasteries along the Bosphorus, in 860:

> Woe is me that I see a fierce and savage tribe fearlessly poured round the city, ravaging the suburbs, destroying everything, ruining everything – fields, houses, herds, beasts of burden, women, old men, youths – thrusting their swords

through everything, taking pity on nothing, sparing nothing. The destruction is universal. Like a locust in a cornfield, like mildew in a vineyard, or rather like a whirlwind or a typhoon or a torrent or I know not what to say, it fell upon our land and has annihilated whole generations of inhabitants.[2]

Photius was determined to emphasise the indiscriminate destruction caused by the Vikings:

Nor did their savagery stop with human beings but was extended to dumb animals – oxen, horses, fowl, and others. There lay an ox and a man by its side, a child and a horse found a common grave, women and fowl stained each other with their blood. Everywhere dead bodies. The flow of rivers was turned into blood; some of the fountains and reservoirs could not be distinguished because they were level with corpses … Corn land was rotting with dead bodies, roads were obstructed, forests looked wild and desolate … because of bodies; caverns were filled up and mountains, hills, ravines, and gullies differed in no way from city cemeteries.[3]

The Vikings themselves wrote sagas and poems of their exploits, and one such stanza written around 925 by Egil Skallagrimsson extols the bloody deeds of the Vikings in a very evocative manner:

I've been with sword and spear
slippery with bright blood
where kites wheeled. And how well
we violent Vikings clashed!
Red flames ate up men's roofs,
raging we killed and killed,
and skewered bodies sprawled
sleepy in town gate-ways.[4]

The Vikings soon gained a reputation as blood thirsty raiders, who were supposed to employ such rituals as the blood eagle sacrifice, in which the victim's back is cut open, the ribs bent outward, and the lungs pulled out to resemble an eagle. This seems to have been an invention, and the Vikings were probably no more violent than the age they lived in. And despite the terror produced by these early attacks, Viking raids usually led eventually to settlement, then conversion to Christianity, and quite quickly, social integration. But what kind of people were these Viking pirates?

The Swedish Vikings, who travelled along the rivers of Russia, were known as the Rus, from which it is argued that the name Russia derives. These Swedish Vikings in Russia primarily wanted to capture slaves to trade, and were also involved in the fur trade. Amusing details of the lives of these particular Vikings come from two Arab travelers in the first half of the tenth century, Ibn Fadlan, a diplomat, and Ibn Rustah, an astronomer and geographer. Ibn Fadlan, sent on a mission from Baghdad to the town of Bulgar on the Volga in 921–922, paints a rather negative picture of these Swedish Vikings from the perspective of a cultured and sophisticated observer:

> They are the filthiest of God's creatures. They do not wash after discharging their natural functions, neither do they wash their hands after meals. They are as stray donkeys. They arrive from their distant lands and lay their ships alongside the banks of the Atul [the Volga], which is a great river, and there they build big wooden houses on its shores. Ten or twenty of them may live together in one house, and each of them has a couch of his own where he sits and diverts himself with the pretty slave-girls whom he has brought along to offer for sale. He will make love with one of them in the presence of his comrades, sometimes this develops into a communal orgy, and, if a customer should turn up to buy a girl, the Rus will not let her go till he has finished with her.

Ibn Fadlan was not impressed by their hygiene:

> Every day they wash their faces and heads, all using the same water which is as filthy as can be imagined. This is how it is done. Every morning a girl brings her master a large bowl of water in which he washes his face and hands and hair, combing it also over the bowl, then blows his nose and spits into the water. When he has finished the girl takes the same bowl to his neighbour – who repeats the performance – until the bowl has gone round to the entire household. All have blown their noses, spat, and washed their faces and hair in the water.[5]

Ibn Rustah, writing in the 940s to the 950s period, described their activities in a more positive manner, though his description of their island location may well be fanciful:

> They stay on an island (or peninsula) in a lake, an island covered with forest and brush, which it takes three days to walk round and which is marshy

and unhealthy ... They sail their ships to ravage as-Saqaliba [the surrounding Slavs] and bring back captives whom they sell at Hazaran and Bulgar [both towns on the Volga]. They have no cultivated fields but depend for their supplies on what they can obtain from as-Saqaliba's land ... They have no estates, villages, or fields; their only business is to trade in sable, squirrel, and other furs, and the money they take in these transactions they stow in their belts. Their clothes are clean and the men decorate themselves with gold armlets. They treat their slaves well, and they wear exquisite clothes since they pursue trade with great energy. They have many towns. They deal firmly with one another; they respect their guests and are hospitable and friendly to strangers who take refuge with them ... They do not allow anybody to molest their guests or do them any harm...

On the other hand, Ibn Rustah had a healthy respect for their prowess in battle, emphasising the Vikings' determination, 'If a group of them is challenged to battle, they stick together as one man until victory has been achieved.' Similarly, 'They are courageous in battle and when they attack another tribe's territory they persist until they have destroyed it completely. They take the women prisoners and make the men serfs. They are well built and daring, but their daring is not apparent on land; they always launch their raids and campaigns from ships.'[6]

These Swedish Vikings were warriors and traders, and over the period of their expansion into Russia they took over towns such as Kiev and Novgorod, attacked Constantinople in 860, and again in 941. In this last attack, the Vikings were defeated by the use of Greek fire, which forced them to jump overboard rather than burn alive. But by the end of the tenth century the Viking Rus had converted to Christianity, and by the 1040s they had assimilated and become Slavs.

What of the predominantly Danish Vikings in England? A similar pattern existed there where the Vikings started as raiders and pirates, then settled, converted to Christianity, and became traders, craftsmen and farmers. The town of York, the Viking Jorvik, has recently been excavated, and the results tend to emphasise the craft and trading aspect of the Vikings. York was taken in 866 by Danish Vikings, who ruled the town and surrounding area, with some interruptions, until about 954. The Vikings of York included leather workers, wood workers, metal craftsmen, jewelry makers, shoe makers, and traders of all kinds. This image of the Vikings as creative artisans and traders goes some way to offset the image of the Vikings as primarily savage pirates, interested only in booty and killing.

England suffered two main waves of Viking attacks, each followed by periods of settlement, one wave of attacks lasting from 835 to 934, and the second lasting from 980 to 1035. Similarly, in the case of Ireland, there were raids followed by periods of settlement. For example, there was settlement between the 830s and 870s, when the Vikings initially founded Dublin, among other small towns. The Vikings helped to foster commerce, and then there was another wave of settlement between 914 and the 940s. In between these more peaceful periods of immigration and land settlement in Ireland occurred the brutal early years of the tenth century, when the Irish Sea was infested with pirates, both Viking and Irish.[7] Thus, in 902 a Viking force was defeated in Dublin and the Viking pirates left for the Isle of Man and north-west England. Then in 914 further Viking fleets arrived on the Irish coast. Later, in 917, the Vikings Ragnall and Sitric led fleets to south-east Ireland. Sitric led his men up the river Liffey and re-established a base in Dublin, which was to be his main centre of operations. Meanwhile, Ragnall landed at Waterford, left the next year, and fought a battle in Scotland, on the Tyne – apparently a draw. In this fight Ragnall dividing his forces into four battles or groups, three in the front line, and one in reserve. The reserve battle was supposed to either force the victory or cover a defeat.[8] Back in Ireland, in 919, Viking forces defeated the O'Neill, King of Tara, and 12 minor kings. It also seems that in 919 Ragnall, and subsequently Sitric, gained control of the town of York, introducing a period of Irish-Scandinavian rule. Essentially, the Viking pirates, by virtue of their success in England and Ireland, were becoming kings in their own right, and so were really ceasing to be pirates by organizing armies and becoming involved as local and national rulers.

Thus from 865 to 954 the Danish Vikings arrived in England as invading armies, aiming at conquest and settlement rather than raids. The armies were small – perhaps 500 to 2,000 men, but large enough to leave piracy behind and become something else. These armies landed, established bases, and used the old Roman roads to move inland on horse, either capturing local horses to use, or bringing horses with them. Then they dismounted and fought in a shield wall style of battle. The object was either to loot and plunder, or to force the local inhabitants to buy them off with silver, coins, or other valuables. Ultimately the Vikings wanted land, to settle and farm, and to encourage others to follow as immigrants. Resistance was difficult, and Alfred of Wessex in the 870s, and again in the 890s, tried to deal with the Danish Vikings in a variety of ways. Alfred used local militias, constructed coastal defenses, built a fleet, fortified a series of strong places, retreated when defeated, and finally made treaties, which accepted Danish settlement in an area of eastern England known as the Danelaw. But these relatively large scale Viking operations really can no longer be called pirate raids – the Vikings had become Norse settlers in England.

Before this transition to settlement, what were the raiding methods of the Vikings? The original Viking tactic was to sail and row their famous long boats toward their target, and then find a suitable island or protected place at the mouth of a river or an inlet on the coast to act as a base. A suitable church or fort, or defended village, could also be used as a base. The Vikings would then leave their ships with a guarding force, and range inland. If the raid aimed at going far inland, the Vikings would use horses to reach their objective, and then dismount to fight. These horses might be brought by specially constructed ships (not easily done, but shown as possible in the Bayeux tapestry of Duke William's 1066 invasion of England), or as mentioned, could be captured locally.

Battle of Maldon: 991

A typical Viking raid has been preserved for us in poetry, and is known as the *Battle of Maldon*. This Danish raid was led by a well known Viking chief called Olaf Tryggvason, who lived in Dublin, and then later ruled in Norway as king. He was a pagan, and used the 'crack a bone' method of divination to plan his actions, although he later became a Christian. Olaf was an unusual individual, according to reports. He was an expert swimmer and mountain climber. He could run along the oars of his long boat while the crew was rowing. He could juggle three daggers in the air at the same time. He could strike equally well with both hands, and so could throw two spears at once. In the end, in the year 1000 he drowned himself rather than surrender to a strong Swedish-Danish fleet.[9] But this was in the future.

In the year 991 Olaf's aim was the small town of Maldon, near the coast in Essex, England, which could be reached by the Blackwater River. In August, Olaf's very large fleet of Viking ships raided on the east coast, and then came up the Blackwater River, on the flood, past the old Roman fort, and beached at Northey Island, where the Viking base was established. The Vikings then shouted across the causeway to the Saxon defenders that they would go away if paid gold. The Saxons were led by the local ealdorman, or king's deputy, Brihtnoth, whose colourful name meant 'battle bright'. Brihtnoth refused to pay ransom for the town of Maldon, and three of his Saxons stood firm on the narrow causeway, preventing the Vikings from crossing to the mainland. The poem then suggests some trickery used by the Vikings to cross the causeway, but also that Brihtnoth proudly invited the Vikings across the narrow causeway, which was partly under water, being high tide. Brihtnoth was perhaps over-confident, or much more likely understood that if the Vikings were paid to go away, they would simply raid somewhere else on the Essex coast.

The Saxons formed a small army composed of thanes, or warrior class men, supported by the local fyrd, or militia. For their part, the Vikings were all warriors, and some of the upper class were well protected with coats of mail and helmets. Both sides possessed shields – the Viking shields being very large to protect the whole body, with an iron boss in the middle to deflect arrows and spears, and painted in strong colors. These shields would be raised in the air if the Vikings wanted peace, but this obviously wasn't the case at Maldon. Both sides possessed spears, swords, axes, and some bowmen. However, the poem suggests that the principal weapons used first in this battle were bows. The battle started with a hail of arrows, then spears were thrown and also used as stabbing weapons, and finally, swords were drawn and used in the climactic part of the battle when all the spears had been thrown or damaged. Axes were another favourite weapon of the Vikings, but are not mentioned at Maldon.

Before the battle started both sides shouted insults, while each side formed the battle hedge or shield wall, with interlocking shields. Brihtnoth apparently first rode his horse up and down the Saxon line to make sure it was properly organized. Then he dismounted to fight. The leaders stood in the centre, accompanied by a standard bearer and a bodyguard of the chief warriors. After opening the battle with a hail of arrows and spears, the object of both sides was then to use spears and swords and brute strength to cut a hole in the opposing shield wall, and roll up the enemy from either side of the hole. The poem describing this battle, composed by an anonymous Saxon companion of Brihtnoth, has lost its beginning and end, but gives a strong flavor of the battle:

> Bow strings were busy, shield parried point,
> Bitter was the battle. Brave men fell
> On both sides, youths choking in the dust.

Brihtnoth was the focus of the Viking attack, and he was wounded by a spear. He knocked the spear out with the edge of his shield, and killed the Viking who had wounded him. A second spear hit Brihtnoth in the side, which was pulled out by a fellow Saxon and hurled back, killing the Viking who had wounded Brihtnoth. But Brihtnoth was again wounded, this time in his sword arm, and he dropped his sword on the ground. Now he was defenseless, and Brihtnoth was hacked down, together with two of his Saxon thanes. This death struck fear into some of Brihtnoth's followers, who fled from the battle:

> The sons of Odda were the first to take flight:
> Godric fled from the battle, forsaking Brihtnoth.
> Forgetting that his lord had given him often the gift of a horse.
> He leapt into the saddle
> Of his lord's own horse, most unlawfully,
> And both his brothers, Godwine and Godwig,
> Galloped beside him; forgetting their duty
> They fled from the fight
> And saved their lives in the silent wood.

This was actually the crucial moment of the battle, for the Saxon warriors thought that it was Brihtnoth himself who was riding away, since Godric had taken Brihtnoth's own horse. The Saxon line therefore scattered in alarm, and allowed the Vikings to break through the Saxon shield wall. But others continued to fight, and the poet names these Saxon heroes: Aelfwine, Offa, Aethelric, Byrhtwold, and Leofsunu. The veteran warrior Byrhtwold shook his ash spear, and encouraged the others:

> Mind must be the firmer, heart the more fierce,
> Courage the greater, as our strength diminishes.
> Here lies our leader, dead,
> A heroic man in the dust.
> He who longs to escape will lament for ever.

Still, despite this final show of bravery, the Saxons were defeated, and the victorious Vikings decapitated the corpse of Brihtnoth, and carried away the head. The monks of nearby Ely took away the body and buried it, less the head. Brihtnoth's widow, Aelfflled, apparently wove a tapestry to commemorate his life and death, but this has disappeared. Meanwhile, Olaf's Viking ships continued their raids on the east coast until a truce was arranged by Sigeric, the Archbishop of Canterbury, which involved the payment of 10,000 pounds of silver to Olaf and his followers. So Olaf gained what he had demanded at the beginning of his raid on Maldon, but he had had to fight for the ransom.

Such was a typical pirate raid by the Vikings in England, but the Vikings also ranged very far afield. They raided into the Mediterranean, to Spain, Italy, and North Africa, into Russia, and the Black and Caspian seas. As explorers and farmers, the Vikings also settled Iceland, Greenland, and reached North America in about the year 1000. Before this, in the early 800s the Vikings raided Western Europe extensively, and paid particular attention to the Franks. In 799, the Danish Vikings raided and plundered St Philibert's monastery on the island of Noirmoutier, then spent much time raiding the nearby Frisian islands. The Frankish empire was in discord in the early ninth century, and so it was relatively easy for the Vikings to raid at will – for example, the trading centre of Dorestad on the Rhine was attacked four times in the 830s, and a further four times between the 840s and the 860s. Meanwhile, on Easter Sunday 845, the Vikings under their leader Ragnar, attacked and plundered Paris. The West Frankish king, Charles the Bald, was forced to pay 7,000 pounds of silver for the Vikings to leave. However, this turned out not to be a clear Viking victory, since Ragnar, who brought back a bar of the city gate of Paris as a souvenir of his success, succumbed to an epidemic, together with most of his fellow Vikings. Nevertheless, Viking raids continued so frequently that a monk from St Philibert's monastery wrote in the 860s that:

> The number of ships grows: the endless stream of Vikings never ceases to increase. Everywhere the Christians are victims of massacre, burnings, plunderings: the Vikings conquer all in their path, and no one resists them … Angers, Tours and Orleans are annihilated and an innumerable fleet sails up the Seine and the evil grows in the whole region. Rouen is laid waste, plundered and burned: Paris, Beauvais and Meaux taken, Melun's strong fortress leveled to the ground, Chartres occupied, Evreux and Bayeux plundered, and every town besieged.[10]

The Vikings practiced their normal system of attacking where defenses were weakest, and either plundered, or accepted silver to go away. There was also the option of settling in easily accessible areas, or sometimes they were given land, for example as a result of Charles the Bald's internal Frankish struggles against his brothers. The best Frankish defense against the Vikings was to build fortified bridges on rivers that led to important towns and fertile areas, which could halt the water-borne Vikings, but these required cash, and often took a long time to build. Other defensive ideas were to fortify towns and monasteries, or simply to pay ransoms, which were in effect taxes on the population. Further possibilities were to make alliances or treaties with the Vikings, or simply to allow the Vikings to occupy areas around river mouths and coasts. Occasionally it was possible to fight back, and otherwise the last resort was to flee inland – so floods of monks were to be seen on the roads leading to Burgundy, the Auvergne and Flanders. These monks took with them their holy relics, so from the 850s to the 870s the monks of Tours took with them the body of their holy father, St Martin, from Tours to Cormery, then to Chablis, to Auxerre, and finally back to Tours when danger seemed over. Likewise, the monks of St Philibert's monastery took their holy relics further and further inland from the 830s to the 870s, until they landed up at Tournus on the Saone River in 875.[11]

Siege of Paris: 885

The Viking attacks on the Frankish kingdoms started changing in the 850s. They were no longer isolated raids, but calculated campaigns, just as in England, involving the taking of horses after landing, and raiding inland. Between 879 and 892, a large force of Vikings left England, ravaged the north and north-east land of the Franks, and then turned south toward Paris in 885. Paris was a small town at the time, yet offered considerable defiance against the Vikings. Paris was located on an island in the Seine, the Ile de la Cité, defended by two bridges, with towers at either end of each bridge. With these fortifications, Paris held out against the Viking siege for a year, from November 885 to November 886. The Vikings were led by Sigfrid, and were really aiming at the Marne country beyond Paris, and so were willing to bypass the town to achieve this aim. Consequently, Sigfrid addressed Joscelin, the bishop of Paris, in the following way:

> Oh, Joscelin, have pity on your self and on the flock entrusted to your care. For your own good listen to what I have to say. We ask only that you let us pass beyond your city: we shall not touch it. We shall strive to safeguard your rights and also those of [the Count of Paris] Odo...'

The bishop responded loyally with these words:'We have been charged with the protection of this city by our king Charles [the Fat], whose kingdom extends almost over the entire earth ... The kingdom must not allow itself to be destroyed;she must be saved by our city. If these walls had been committed to you as they indeed have been committed to us and if you had acted as you have asked us to act, what would you think of yourself?'

Sigfrid answered, 'My sword would be disgraced and unworthy of my command. Nevertheless, if you do not grant my request, I must tell you that our instruments of war will send you poisoned arrows at daybreak, and at day's end there will be hunger. And so it will be; we will not cease.'

Thus the siege began, with Viking catapults and poisoned arrows fired against the bridge tower on the right bank, while the Parisians poured burning pitch and oil onto the attackers. The tower held out, and the next day the Vikings produced a battering ram in conjunction with the catapults. The tower continued to resist, and the Vikings settled down into a long siege, with the obvious intention of starving the Parisians. By January 866, this was not working, so the Vikings decided on an all out blow – they divided their forces so as to attack both the tower and the bridge on the right bank. The tower attackers filled the ditch outside the tower with branches, straw, dead animals, and even dead prisoners, in order to cross over and reach the tower itself. Meanwhile, the bridge attackers launched three fire ships against the bridge to burn it down. But all attacks against both tower and bridge failed.

Then, winter floods in February 886 swept away one bridge and enabled the Vikings to bypass Paris. Some Vikings raided beyond Paris, but others maintained the siege on the right bank. This was a partial Viking victory, but the Vikings could not leave their rear unsafe with Paris still resisting. So Sigfrid offered to raise the siege with a ransom of just 60 pounds of silver. The Parisians refused, and appealed for help from their king, but little help came. Meanwhile Joscelin died in April, and secretly Count Odo left Paris to persuade Charles the Fat to help. Coming back to Paris, Count Odo was intercepted by the Vikings and his horse was killed beneath him. Swinging his sword to left and right, Odo made it back into Paris, while Charles the Fat's army reached Paris in October 886. But Charles did not attack the Vikings; he simply made a deal with them to spare Paris, and allowed the Vikings to proceed beyond Paris and raid in Burgundy. Outraged, Parisians refused to allow this to happen, forcing the Vikings to carry their boats overland around the city. Finally, Charles the Fat paid the Vikings 700 pounds of silver to leave the Seine. Ironically, justice prevailed later when Charles was deposed in 888, and Count Odo of Paris became king of the West Franks the next year.[12]

The siege of Paris came toward the end of the Viking raids on Western Europe – by the early tenth century, the raids had ceased due to increased fortress building and stronger resistance by the Franks. Only in Normandy were the Vikings successful when in the early tenth century Charles the Simple, now king of the West Franks, gave the Vikings under their leader Rollo, the town of Rouen and an area around the town. The reason for this was that Charles hoped to use Rollo to defend Rouen, the coast, and the Seine River, against other Vikings. Rollo and his fellow Vikings settled down, were baptized and soon assimilated into the native French culture. Hence, William the Conqueror, who invaded England from Normandy in 1066, was a Frank and not a Viking.

The Vikings started as pirates and then became settlers and farmers, and some became kings. Their raids were often very successful and they were frequently violent. Huge amounts of silver were transferred from Eastern and Western Europe to the Vikings. But their ultimate assimilation into the cultures they attacked is perhaps the most significant aspect of their raids. Finally, it is noteworthy that this political evolution did not stop outbursts of local piracy by Viking descendants – in the twelfth century there was a revival of piracy in the Irish Sea from the Orkneys to the Hebrides, aiming at kidnapping and ransom.

Medieval Pirates

The Vikings were not the only raiders of the northern seas in the medieval period. There were several pirates who hovered on the boundary between piracy and privateering, generally being used by one competing nation or another as commerce raiders. One such was the famous Eustace the Monk, born in Boulogne, who allegedly started as a Benedictine monk but turned into a troublemaker. Eustace sold his services to the highest bidder, whether King John of England, or Phillip II of France. His role as a pirate occurred when he was in the pay of King John but simultaneously attacked English shipping, causing him to flee to France in 1211. Matthew Paris, the medieval English historian and Benedictine monk, described him as a *viro flagitiosissimo* (a real pain), but Eustace was captured in a battle between French and

English ships in 1217 off Dover, and summarily executed, together with his crew.[13]

In the competition between medieval European merchants, operating when naval forces were few or non-existent, many ships crossed the line and became temporary pirates. In the 1380s and 1390s, conflict between the Hanse (a league of Baltic trading towns) and Denmark, led to commerce raiding and some independent piracy, with pirates operating out of towns such as Rostok and Wismar in the Baltic. The Hanse enlisted the pirates as privateers against Denmark, and after the end of the war, perhaps predictably, the pirates soon turned against the Hanse itself. This raiding developed into a bold group of pirates called *Vitalienbruder* (Brotherhood of Suppliers), who liked to think of themselves as 'Likedeelers', meaning equal sharers. These pirates set up a stronghold in the town of Visby, and among other actions, sacked Bergen in 1392, taking the leading merchants away for ransom. Two major efforts were made to destroy the *Vitalienbruder*, one by Queen Margaret of Sweden in alliance with Richard II of England, and the second by thirty-five ships of the Hanse in 1394. Neither was successful. Yet the *Vitalienbruder* were forced out of the Baltic by 1400, and transferred to Frisia and Gotland in the North Sea. Finally, in 1402, Simon of Utrecht, who flew the flag of the Spotted Cow at his masthead, led a Hamburg fleet which captured the last of their leaders, Godeke Michels (or Godekins), and Klaus Stortebeker (or Stertebeker). These two leaders were beheaded in Hamburg, together with all of their followers. Their heads were displayed to the people, putting an end to years of piracy on the seas.

Many legends surround these *Vitalienbruder*, and Stortebeker in particular. Stortebeker was allegedly a ruined nobleman from Frisia, whose name meant 'beaker at a gulp'. This was because he compelled his victims to gulp down at one swallow the contents of four wine bottles. His coat of arms naturally featured crossed drinking glasses. Stortebeker pictured himself as a kind of maritime Robin Hood, adopting the motto for the *Vitalienbruder*, 'Friends of God, Enemies of the World'. The legend goes that before he was beheaded, he requested that the mayor of Hamburg release as many of his companions as he could walk past after he had lost his head. The headless Stortebeker allegedly walked past twelve of his fellow pirates before he was tripped up by the executioner. However, his request was not honoured, and all seventy-three of his companions were executed. Another legend relates that after capture, the main mast of Stortebeker's ship was found to be filled with bars of gold, which was sufficient to pay for the Hamburg fleet action against the brotherhood, and also pay back the merchants who had lost their ships to the *Vitalienbruder*. In addition, there was enough gold for the citizens of Hamburg to create a crown of gold atop the spire of St Nicholas' sailor's church in Hamburg.[14]

Piracy continued in the northern seas, usually as a by product of commerce raiding and maritime conflict. For example, there was an epidemic of piracy by the merchant community in the 1450s when the weak monarch, Henry VI of England, was on the throne. And despite the growth of European navies in the sixteenth century, Klein Henszlein, the German pirate, operated in the North Sea until captured by a fleet from Hamburg. He was beheaded together with thirty-three of his crew in 1573, with the executioner 'flicking off' their heads in only forty-five minutes. The executioner claimed that he was 'standing in blood so deep that it well nigh in his shoes did creep.'[15] The execution of Henszlein and his crew emphasises the point that the age of the freelance raiders of the northern seas was slowly coming to an end, while the consolidation of European states meant that nation states by the sixteenth century were beginning to control violence at sea. Laws and law courts, legal privateers, the convoy system, and the creation of European navies – all helped to create the state monopoly of maritime violence, which now separated out a clear distinction between piracy and privateering.[16]

4
The Elizabethan Sea Rovers
and the Jacobean Pirates

In the sixteenth century, as trade expanded to the Mediterranean, West Africa, the Levant, the Caribbean, and eventually to the East Indies, pirates correspondingly preyed on these merchant ships. Also, as war engulfed sixteenth-century Europe, sea rovers in the shape of Dutch, French and English adventurers roamed abroad, either as real pirates, or as official or semi-official privateers. French pirates operated off the coast of West Africa, and created havoc there in the sixteenth century. Hence, while the Portuguese authorized the sinking of all foreign ships found off their colonial trading empire of West Africa, and the throwing overboard of their crews, French pirates were investigating the possibilities of this coast. For example, in 1542 French pirates attacked a Portuguese ship off Guinea:

> ...they robbed the crew and put them below the deck and nailed down the hatchways upon them, and by firing bombards at them they sent them to the bottom of the sea, where they perished, and only those of the crew escaped who happened to be on land and a shipmaster who escaped by swimming.[1]

English pirates raided Spanish ships in the Canaries, for example the pirate Edward Cooke captured a Spanish ship there in 1560, and for good measure took an English ship as well. Meanwhile, the pirate Thomas Wyndham sailed to West Africa in 1553 with three ships, backed by merchants from the city of London, which put him on the borderline between a privateer and a pirate. In this voyage, the crew suffered heavily from disease, but skirmishes with the Portuguese and African slave traders resulted in booty of 400 pounds of gold, 36 butts of pepper, 250 elephant tusks, and the complete head of one huge elephant.[2]

John Hawkins (1532–1595)

Hawkins was another sea rover who skirted the border line between privateer and pirate. Hawkins was born in Plymouth, England, and came from a sea faring and wealthy family. Hawkins' father traded overseas, and left a small fleet to his two sons when he died. John Hawkins evidently learned about the sea from his father, but his own interest was slave trading, capturing or buying slaves on the west coast of Africa, and then selling these slaves to the Spanish colonies in the Americas. Hawkins made several voyages in the 1560s with that purpose in mind. These voyages were financially successful, and Queen Elizabeth herself either invested in these slaving expeditions by including her ships in Hawkins' voyages, or at least tacitly encouraged or permitted Hawkins' slaving and piracy to take place. But problems arose with this slaving enterprise because the Spanish did not allow the trading or the sale of slaves in their colonies in the Caribbean and the Americas without a license. And Hawkins certainly did not have a Spanish license. However, Hawkins was normally able to overcome this by making deals with corrupt local Spanish officials, such as buying licenses, or by selling slaves to Spanish merchants who pretended to refuse the transactions but secretly accepted the slaves, or by simply forcing the locals to trade. Still, a particular difficulty arose with Hawkins' 1567-1569 voyage. After arriving off the coast of Guinea and Sierra Leone with his fleet of six ships (two of them being Queen Elizabeth's ships, the *Jesus of Lubeck* and the *Minion*, while another, the *Judith*, was perhaps commanded by Hawkins' cousin, Francis Drake), Hawkins apparently took and looted seven Portuguese ships. Following this, Hawkins managed to capture or buy some 400 to 500 slaves from Sierra Leone, and then sailed to the Caribbean and the northern coast of South America to trade or sell these slaves.

Hawkins' fleet managed to trade and sell most of their slaves at seven Spanish ports in the Americas with a mixture of bribery and force, but then fell afoul of a major storm in September 1568. Perhaps this was a hurricane, but in any case Hawkins and his fleet (now numbering ten ships, augmented from the original six by captured Portuguese and Spanish ships), needed to find a base to repair and refit. The place chosen was San Juan de Ulua in New Spain (now central America), and Hawkins' small fleet entered the harbour. For a while all went well, but on 17 September 1568, a Spanish fleet appeared, containing the newly appointed Viceroy of New Spain. The Spanish fleet also needed to enter San Juan, and this awkward matter was arranged by both sides exchanging hostages, although fifty of Hawkins' men took over the shore batteries on land. This was seen as a contravention of the fragile truce by the Spanish, and plans were laid to capture the English fleet. At night, 150 Spanish soldiers went onboard an empty hulk and towed it alongside Hawkins' ship, the *Jesus of Lubeck*, with the intention of boarding. Hawkins suddenly noticed the plot and responded to the Spanish battle cry of 'Santiago', with his English cry of 'God and St George, upon these false traitors, for my trust is only in God that the daie shall be ours.'[3]

Spanish reinforcements easily captured the English sailors manning the shore batteries. These sailors were either captured and made prisoners, or put to the sword. On board the *Jesus*, Hawkins cut the moorings of his ship, which drifted away under fire from the Spanish flag ship. One Spanish shot shattered the main mast of the *Jesus*, and the Spanish prepared to send fire ships against the *Jesus*. The first fire ship failed to ignite, but as the second bore down on the *Jesus*, Hawkins and a large number of men managed to transfer to the *Minion*, leaving behind the ten Spanish hostages, and the wounded from the *Jesus*. Hawkins called for help from Francis Drake aboard the *Judith*, but according to Hawkins, Drake abandoned Hawkins and sailed for home. Hawkins was able to sail out of the harbour in the *Minion*, but was forced to leave behind five or six ships, much artillery, and an unknown amount of treasure.

The voyage home was a disaster for Hawkins – men were so hungry that they ate every rat, parrot, dog, or monkey aboard, and then turned their attention to the leather fittings. Water also failed, and some drank sea water. Realising that starvation could not be prevented, Hawkins put around 100 men ashore at Campeche, the logwood centre on the Yucatan peninsula. Continuing hunger and disease forced Hawkins' ship and the remaining crew to put into Galicia, Spain, before they could reach England. It is alleged that off Spain, Hawkins came across three Portuguese ships, which he captured, and then cut off the legs of the Portuguese sailors and pitched them over-board, still alive. This cruelty, if true, is in contrast to the ten Spanish hostages whom Hawkins did not kill when the Spanish attacked the *Jesus* in the port of San Juan de Ulua. Perhaps Hawkins did not have time for this at San Juan de Ulua. Nevertheless, when the *Minion* finally arrived in Cornwall in January 1569, there were only some fifteen sailors left alive, though strangely some slaves still survived. The human cost of Hawkins' voyage was tremendous, 130 dead at San Juan de Ulua, and 52 taken prisoner, 100 left in Campeche, and 45 dead of disease on the way home. An unknown but small number came home with Drake in the *Judith*, and curiously enough, Hawkins seemingly forgave Drake for abandoning him at the crisis of the battle in San Juan de Ulua. Perhaps Hawkins took account of his family relationship to Drake, and he probably also needed Drake for his future trading activities.[4]

As a result of Hawkins' voyages, and especially the 1567-1569 expedition, the Spanish and the Portuguese certainly thought Hawkins was a pirate, and the Spanish saw the battle at San Juan de Ulua as their victory over a heretical English pirate. But since two of the ships on Hawkins' slaving and trading raid belonged to the Queen, the *Jesus* and the *Minion*, it seems that Hawkins was not quite a pirate, because he at least had the financial support of the Queen, if not a specific commission. Following this voyage, Hawkins' future career was as Treasurer of Elizabeth's navy, and as a trader. Surprisingly, he was even suspected of being a double agent for Spain, or of wanting to enter Spanish service, perhaps because of religious doubts about Elizabeth's Protestantism, but in the end this did not happen. In future years, Hawkins went to sea reluctantly, since he actually preferred to remain at home as a trader and send others overseas, such as his cousin, Francis Drake.

Francis Drake (1540-1596)

Francis Drake was born in Devon, England, where his father was a sheep shearer and a farmer, and then a priest. However, as a cousin of John Hawkins, Francis Drake was brought up with a number of other relatives in the Hawkins house-hold. He had gone on some of Hawkins' early voyages, including as mentioned above, the 1567-1569 slaving and trading expedition, which came to grief at San Juan de Ulua. Drake learned some lessons from Hawkins' voyages, one of which was to sail with a single small ship, or a very small fleet of similar ships, capable of hiding in bays in the Caribbean, and capable of going up rivers to make land-based attacks. It was also a good idea to find a refitting spot where such attacks could be planned, and to which it was safe to return. Another idea was to have some small cut up pinnaces aboard the larger ships which could be reassembled and launched to attack or discover places where larger ships could not go. A favourite spot for Drake was the secluded anchorage of Port Pheasant, some miles east of the small Spanish port of Nombre de Dios. Another safe location was the Isle of Pines, even closer to Nombre de Dios.

In 1572 Drake aimed to capture Nombre de Dios. This was a potentially valuable target, because the port annually stored silver and other treasures from Peru, which had been shipped to Panama, and then come overland from Panama to Nombre de Dios. With the treasure in store, the inhabitants of Nombre de Dios waited for the Spanish plate fleet to arrive and pick up the treasure. Having done this, the Spanish plate fleet would return to Spain via Havana in Cuba. So, in July 1572, having first stopped for provisions at Port Pheasant, Drake then left his three ships at a safe harbour in the Isle of Pines. Following this, Drake boarded three small pinnaces with some of his crew and headed toward Nombre de Dios. Drake landed near Nombre de Dios and then marched toward the port at night. It turned out to be fairly simple to capture the small port since there were only some thirty-five or forty inhabitants, although Drake himself and a number of his men were wounded by musket fire. However, the treasure house turned out to be empty, so the raid to capture silver and treasure was a disaster. To prevent total failure, Drake and his men then captured a Spanish merchant ship in the harbour of Nombre de Dios, which contained wine. Unfortunately, this was worth very little, and Drake spent the next several weeks sailing rather aimlessly around the Spanish possessions on the coasts of Central America and the north coast of South America, looking for Spanish ships to take. He had limited success with this, but as always, Drake had to worry as much about an adequate supply of food and water, which he obtained by capturing small ships or by raiding ashore.

Determined not to return until he had captured a valuable cargo of some kind, Drake decided to wait for the return of the plate fleet. He and his crew spent the autumn living ashore and then in January 1573, with the end of the wet season, he set out overland toward the town of Panama, hoping to raid the warehouses at Venta des Cruces, close to Panama, and also to intercept one of the mule trains bringing silver and treasure to Nombre de Dios. In the meantime, Drake lost his brother John to a gunshot wound, and another brother, Joseph, to disease. Others also died of disease, and when Drake set out toward Panama, he had only eighteen sailors with him, plus a valuable group of some thirty Cimarrons, escaped black slaves who were enemies of the Spanish. Learning that a mule train containing treasure was on its way, Drake and his men laid an ambush. But Drake's bad luck continued because one of his crew stood up just as the mule train approached, with his white shirt gleaming in the moon light, and this alerted the Spanish guards. The mule train turned back, and only some less valuable materials were captured. Yet Drake still refused to give up, and in April 1573, Drake teamed up with a French pirate who appeared on the coast, Le Testu, and once more laid an ambush close to Nombre de Dios.

This time, Drake succeeded. The mule train was ambushed and discovered to be carrying a full load of silver. A fight ensued in which Le Testu was mortally wounded, as were several other French pirates, but the Spanish guards were driven off. There was so much silver and gold that some had to be hidden in the ground in animal burrows, while Drake carried off as much as he could, and Le Testu was left lying beside the road. As Drake prepared to get onboard his ship, his crew discovered a small Spanish fleet waiting for them, but with typical determination, Drake constructed a raft and eluded the Spanish by sailing to a nearby island. Here he and his crew were rescued by his pinnaces. Drake then sent a party back to find Le Testu and recover the rest of the buried silver. The party discovered Le Testu dead, and much of the buried treasure recovered by the Spanish, but some was still found and taken back to the ships. Now Drake decided he had done enough and prepared to sail home. He divided up the treasure with the French pirates and sailed for Plymouth. He had been away for so long that he and his crew were given up for lost, but on Sunday 9 August 1573, his small fleet was sighted and, as the story goes, all those who were in church deserted the preacher, and ran to welcome Drake's arrival. Drake's share of the proceeds from his voyage was some £20,000 – a huge fortune at the time – and he further increased his take by apparently cheating the widow of his brother John of her share of the proceeds.[5]

Drake's success attracted the keen interest of Queen Elizabeth and other high placed investors, including Privy Council members, and in 1577 a major pirate raid was planned to the Pacific coast of South America. There was the usual attempt to keep the plans secret, especially from the Spanish, but the Spanish soon got wind of what was afoot, and tried to find out the exact targets of the enterprise. Meanwhile, investors, including the Queen, put in money and ships – the Queen's investment apparently being the ship the *Swallow*. Significantly, the Queen issued no formal commission, obviously in order to protect her neutral position with Spain. At this point one can ask: in this enterprise, which eventually became a voyage around the world – was Drake a pirate? Since Drake had no specific commission or license, then he was a pirate. Of course, this was also the position of the Spanish. But since the Queen committed a ship to the voyage, took a large part of the vast fortune with which Drake returned, knew what was happening, and did not forbid the voyage, or imprison or blame Drake after the voyage (in fact she knighted him), it is also fair to call Drake a privateer of a sort. As usual, Drake trod a fine line between piracy and privateer, but perhaps in this case closer to a privateer, unlike his earlier assault on Nombre de Dios, which was more purely piracy.[6]

Drake's new enterprise of some five ships left England in November 1577. A storm at the outset destroyed one ship, but Drake left again and sailed to the Cape Verde islands, where a Spanish merchant ship was captured and added to the fleet. The next landfall was Brazil, but along the way Drake and his friend, Thomas Doughty, who had been an original supporter of the expedition, became enemies. Drake seems to have suspected Doughty of trying to undermine his authority, and the situation became tense enough for Drake to call a trial at the southern location of Port St Julian, on the east coast of South America. Drake accused Doughty of incitement to mutiny, and treason for speaking ill of the Queen. Drake essentially forced and tricked the jury to find Doughty guilty, despite a claim of illegality by a friend of Doughty's, to which Drake replied, 'I have not quoth he [Drake] to deal with you crafty lawyers, neythar care I fore the lawe, but I know what I will do.' By now most of Drake's crew were really quite frightened of him, and thus Drake forced through the execution of Doughty. Doughty was actually beheaded, though not before Drake and Doughty had embraced in a final farewell. Just before he died, Doughty also asked Drake to forgive one of his supporters, Hugh Smith, and Drake agreed reluctantly, 'I forgive thee [Smith], but by the life of God … I was determined to have neiled thy ears to the pillary.' When Doughty's head was cut off, Drake held up the head and told the assembled crew, 'This is the end of traitors.'[7]

Why Drake felt the need to actually execute Doughty is not clear, though Doughty and his supporters may have been opposed to Drake's plan to turn the voyage into a pirate expedition. Drake may also have been afraid of mutiny among his small fleet, a perpetual problem in long voyages, and so wished to intimidate his sailors – which he certainly succeeded in doing. Whatever the reason, Drake and the fleet then continued down the coast of South America, through the Straits of Magellan, losing some pinnaces and two ships in the process – the *Marigold* perhaps ran aground, while the *Elizabeth* returned to England. Now reduced to one ship, the *Pelican* (possibly renamed the *Golden Hind*), Drake sailed up the Pacific coast of South America, raiding and capturing ships as he went. It is noteworthy that Drake made full use of his pinnaces in this voyage – they could more easily scout out targets or slip unseen into harbours – and were valuable for carrying raiding parties to shore. Thus Drake kept his ship about three or four miles off shore while the pinnaces scouted and raided.

Of significance was Drake's capture of a Spanish ship off the coast of Ecuador, which contained a large amount of gold, silver and jewels. Drake cut away the sails of this ship and let it drift away with its crew once the treasure had been transferred, although he did keep the black slaves he found onboard, presumably to do the hard work on the *Pelican*. The very next day, 1 March 1579, Drake came up with a Spanish treasure ship called the *Nuestra Senora de la Concepcion*. Trailing ropes and cables to slow down his ship and fool the *Concepcion* into complacency, Drake then brought his ship alongside the Spaniard. According to the Spanish captain of this ship, San Juan de Anton, someone from the *Pelican* shouted 'English! I order you to strike your sails!' Anton supposedly replied, 'What England demands that I strike sail? Come and do it yourself.' That is just what Drake did, the *Pelican* firing cannon which destroyed the mizzen mast of the *Concepcion*, and then Drake's crew boarded the Spaniard. Since the *Concepcion* did not have cannon, because the Spanish did not expect to use cannon in the Pacific seas, it was quite simple for the *Pelican* and its crew to take the *Concepcion*. This is borne out by the information that Anton was alone on the deck when the boarders from the *Pelican* arrived.[8]

The treasure found on the *Concepcion* was enormous, composed of gold, silver bars, and reales (silver Spanish currency). The gold weighed eighty pounds, there were thirteen chests of reales, and enough silver to use as ballast in the ship. Another source said there were 1,300 silver bars, and fourteen chests of reales and gold. It certainly took six days for the treasure to be transferred to the *Pelican*, and evidently this treasure, in conjunction with what was taken elsewhere, was sufficient to make Drake and his backers very rich indeed, to say nothing of the Queen. It was also the case that so much treasure would very likely make Drake welcome in England, and would undercut any notion of the Queen arresting Drake as a pirate. But Drake and his crew were not home free yet, and a difficult voyage ensued, including going aground near the Celebes in January 1580. The *Pelican* escaped this death trap when the crew threw overboard all they could, and a gale came up with the winds fortunately in the right direction, so the *Pelican* was able to sail off the rocks. After further adventures, the *Pelican* arrived at Plymouth in September 1580, with Drake and those who survived the voyage having been away almost three years.

As might be expected, Drake's first question was whether the Queen was still alive, and, if she was, how would he be received. Drake was reassured by a private message from the Queen, and he was soon in private conference with Elizabeth. Apparently, this private meeting took about six hours, and Drake gave the Queen a sample of some of the *Pelican's* treasures. Ultimately, Drake transferred some twenty tons of silver, gold and pearls to the Tower of London as the Queen's share. Other parts of the treasure went to investors and significant courtiers. Drake kept a very large amount of treasure for himself, and therefore became one of the richest men in England. Following his purchase of a landed estate, which was a prerequisite for knighthood, Drake was knighted by the Queen in 1581.

Despite this obvious public approval by the Queen, Drake was still regarded by many as a pirate, including apparently, Lord Burghley.[9] As before, Drake trod the delicate line between privateer and pirate, and this distinction was played out again in Drake's major raid on the West Indies from 1585-1586. The Queen invested £10,000 in this raid, which turned out to be a failure financially, and costly in lives. Next came the raid on Cadiz in 1587, which was clearly organized by the Queen and the Privy Council. The Queen invested four ships in the Cadiz venture, intending to stave off a Spanish invasion of England, but also hoping to make a considerable financial gain from the project. So Drake was no pirate in the Cadiz raid, which was a curious mixture of war and commerce. The next year, 1588, saw the huge Spanish Armada launched by Phillip II of Spain approach the shores of England. Lord Howard was the overall commander of the English fleet, and although Drake was given no specific command, he was given thirty-six ships, of which nine belonged to the Queen. Later, Drake was given a royal commission, so once more Drake was clearly not a pirate in the Spanish Armada fight. But somehow Drake managed to veer toward piracy again during the Armada, because in the early stages of the struggle Drake disobeyed orders, put out his stern lantern at night, which was supposed to guide the English fleet, and went after a Spanish ship that had lagged behind the other ships of the Armada. This ship was the *Rosario*, a Spanish pay ship, and the captain, one Valdes, surrendered without a fight. After the Armada was defeated, Drake was able to make money from this capture plus claim ransom money for Valdes and two other Spanish officers, while taking little part in the final Armada battle of Gravelines.[10]

Drake continued to be employed by the Queen, and set off on a final voyage in 1595 with some twenty-seven ships, aiming at Puerto Rico and the West Indies. The Queen invested both money and ships in this expedition. As it turned out, the voyage was a disaster, and Drake himself fell ill of dysentery. He died onboard his ship the *Defiance* in January 1596. He was buried at sea in a lead lined casket off Porto Bello, reportedly with trumpets sounding and cannon roaring. Drake's career revealed him to be a tough, money minded individual, who was fortunate to have the backing of Queen Elizabeth for most of his endeavours. At times, Drake was clearly a pirate, for example in his early raids in the Indies, and certainly the Spanish always saw him as a pirate. At other times, due to the Queen's need for income, Drake was free to pursue his own ends, even in the middle of the Armada battle. Perhaps the contradictory sub-title of the fine biography of Drake by the historian Harry Kelsey – calling Drake 'The Queen's Pirate' – sums up his ambiguous status well enough.

Jacobean Pirates

Of course, Drake was not the only Elizabethan privateer and pirate to operate at this time, since the High Court of the Admiralty happily issued some 100 'letters of reprisal' every year, allowing English ships to take Spanish merchants and foreign traders opposed to England.[11] Most of these ships sailed from the west country of England. But with the death of Elizabeth in 1603, the new monarch of England, James I, turned out to have very different ideas, since he saw pirates as the enemy of God and man alike. Great efforts were made in England to catch and hang pirates in the early seventeenth century, whether from England or Ireland or elsewhere, and as was often the case, the cheapest and most useful weapon against the pirates was the issuance of a General Pardon in 1612.[12]

A significant victory in this area was the reformation of the English pirate Henry Mainwaring (1587-1653), who raided in the West Indies, took 400 crewmen from the cod fishery of Newfoundland, and captured Spanish ships. But in 1616 James I offered Mainwaring a pardon, allowing him to keep his booty. Mainwaring accepted this offer and instead turned pirate hunter. Mainwaring also wrote several books, the first of which he dedicated to James I in 1618, explaining how pirates could be suppressed. Mainwaring described which ports the pirates used, how they operated, and how the King could prevent and eradicate the pirates. Strangely enough, given his own history, Mainwaring counseled the king never to grant a pardon, because pirates would readily accept such an offer and then go back to being pirates. Further, the courts should never believe pirates who claimed to have been forced to join a pirate crew, since Mainwaring claimed that almost all sailors joined willingly enough. Mainwaring also thought that Ireland was the chief source of piracy, and advised that Irish pirates could be eliminated by hunting them down in their land-based hiding places, where they hid like conies (rabbits). Of interest was Mainwaring's description of contemporary pirate methods – the pirate ship would lower its sails at dawn and wait for a merchant ship, and then clap on all sail and chase the merchant ship if it tried to flee. Or if the merchant ship foolishly sailed toward them, the pirates would use drags to pretend they could not sail any faster (as Drake did when capturing the *Concepcion*), and then suddenly turn on their victim. Mainwaring mentioned that pirates seldom used cannon, but preferred to board their targets. And, as expected, the pirates hoisted whatever flags enabled them to surprise their victims.[13]

Other pirates of the Jacobean era included Peter Easton, who ended by accepting a generous offer of employment from the Duke of Savoy in 1613. Easton lived in princely style in Villefranche after marrying a lady of wealth from Nice. Then there was John Ward, who turned Barbary corsair, as did Simon Danziker, or Danzer, or Simon Simonson, a Fleming. Ward survived to live a drunken but successful life in Algiers, although still pining for England. As for Danziker, after a spectacular career, he was tricked ashore in Tunis in 1616, and killed. Further pirates included the Nutt brothers, operating out of the south and west of England in the early seventeenth century. John Nutt captured a ship at the entrance to Dungarvan harbour in Ireland in 1623, which contained a dozen women, whom the pirates abused. Nutt was apparently especially taken by the wife of a Cork saddler, since he took her to his cabin and there 'had her a weke.'[14] Ultimately, John Nutt and his brother Robert were pardoned in 1633 and retired from the game. Then the Anglo-Dutch wars of the seventeenth century employed most sailors and so kept piracy in check, while a larger Royal Navy in the later seventeenth century, less corruption, and greater efforts by the courts, all reduced the pirate scourge, which had been particularly strong on the coasts of Ireland.[15]

Yet still piracy continued – often practiced by sailors who were not paid properly, or who were cheated of their provisions onboard their merchant ships. It is also the case that sailors who became pirate captains were often of the Royal Navy rank of master, normally a warrant officer rank below that of lieutenant and other officers, but in charge of the key matter of navigation. In the merchant navy, it was the similar rank of mate that provided a large number of pirate captains. Probably frustration over the lack of promotion led to much of their piracy, while their maritime skills were sufficient to get them elected as pirate captains. This was the case with Henry Avery or Every, who was originally first mate of his ship, while Edward England was mate in his sloop, Howel Davis was chief mate of his snow, Bartholomew Roberts was second mate of his ship, George Lowther was second mate of his ship, and John Smith or Gow was second mate and gunner of his ship.[16]

John Smith, Alias John Gow (Executed 1725)

As an example of a merchant ship mate who became a pirate captain, there is considerable information about John Smith, who often used the alias John Gow, and about whom a number of depositions of the High Court of the Admiralty exist. Smith and a number of fellow mutineers were aboard a merchant ship called the *George Galley* in 1725, which sailed from Amsterdam to Santa Cruz and then to the Straits. During a quiet time, a number of the crew decided to take over the ship, and devised a watchword to start the mutiny. The watchword for the attack was 'Who fires now', and the response was simply, 'The Dutch'. The plan was carefully worked out, in which three of the mutineers would kill the ship's chief mate, the surgeon, and the master's clerk respectively, using their knives, while the victims were asleep in their hammocks. A number of men were then to kill the master who was on deck. The watchword was duly given and the killing began, but it seems the throat cutting was not as efficient as it might have been. The chief mate was seen by one witness coming toward the main hatchway crying out, 'I'm a dead man. One of the Dutch men has killed me.' Another witness, Joseph Wheatley, later said that the chief mate, Mr. Jelfs, cried out in much the same words, 'For God's sake let me down into the Hold the Dutch man has struck me…' Meanwhile, the wounded surgeon made it as far as the deck, but he then fell down and was thrown overboard. The master had not been finished off either, and was wounded only. He was heard to call out, 'What's the matter. What's the matter.' John Smith/Gow went down below decks to fetch a pair of pistols and either Smith, or another mutineer called Williams, shot the master, who cried out in French, 'My

God I am killed.' He too was then thrown overboard. (The master was a Frenchman named Oliver Ferneau.) Then the unfortunate master's clerk was shot by Williams, but managed to crawl forward, and begged for time to say his prayers. But the clerk was apparently not given any time, since Williams cursed him 'God Damn yr Blood say your Prayers & be damned', and immediately forced a young seventeen-year-old sailor, Michael Moor, to shoot the clerk, saying that if Moor did not shoot the clerk, he, Williams, would make the sun and moon to shine through Moor. So Moor shot the master's clerk, and the unhappy clerk was in turn hoisted on the deck and thrown overboard.[17]

Now the mutiny was complete, and Williams, who seems to have been the ringleader, came out of the master's cabin carrying the master's sword in his hand, and also the master's watch. Williams gave the watch to Smith/Gow, and then slapped or struck the capstan with the sword, saying to John Smith, 'Captain Smith you are welcome to the ship.' Evidently Smith was the most experienced and most senior of the mutineers as a former mate, and was trusted to be a successful captain. However, after capturing a number of ships, Smith then headed to the Orkney Islands, where he is alleged to have had a sweetheart that he wanted to marry although the girl's father had previously refused marriage on the grounds that Smith had no money and no prospects. Now Smith demonstrated to his sweetheart's father that he was a ship's captain and had prospects, and the happy pair was just about to wed when Smith was betrayed to the authorities. Smith abandoned his sweetheart, and instead planned to rob a few houses on the Orkneys before leaving, but a gale coming up, his ship was driven on the rocks of Calf Island in the Orkneys. Smith tried to bargain his way out, but he and his crew were taken prisoner by various means, and transported to Marshalsea prison in London. At their trial in London, Smith/Gow refused to plead, and had to be persuaded by the use of cords tightened around his thumbs, and then by the traditional threat of pressing with heavy stones on his chest. Smith gave in and pleaded not guilty, saying his pistol went off accidentally when the ship's master, Ferneau, was shot. But the jury duly found Smith and eight others guilty of piracy, and they were all hung at Execution dock in Wapping, London.[18]

By the late 1720s the Atlantic seas around England and Europe were more or less free of pirates, but there were other areas of the world where pirates flourished in the seventeenth and early eighteenth centuries, namely the Caribbean.

Buccaneers of the Caribbean

Before the buccaneers commenced their activities in the West Indies in the early 1600s, pirates were already raiding in the Caribbean and elsewhere. One particularly brutal pirate was Jacques Sores, a fanatical Huguenot (Protestant) from Normandy. Sores attacked Havana in Cuba in July 1555 with a fleet of three ships and some 200 men. Expecting to find treasure, Sores was disappointed to seize only one emerald ring and a silver plate from the small fort in Havana. The Spanish governor offered to ransom the town of Havana, but changed his mind in the night, and attacked Sores with a few Spaniards, 220 slaves and a number of Indians. The attack did not succeed, and an enraged Sores killed his own Spanish prisoners, hung large numbers of slaves by their heels, burnt the town, and brutally ravaged the surrounding countryside. Entering the church in Havana, Sores and his soldiers desecrated the altar and gave the vestments to his soldiers as cloaks. Leaving the West Indies after this exploit, Sores became involved in the French religious wars, fighting against the French Catholics with much violence. Perhaps his most infamous deed was to capture a Portuguese ship off the Canaries in July 1570, carrying forty Jesuit missionaries among its passengers. Leading the assault to board the ship, in his Protestant zeal Sores threw the missionaries overboard, both alive and dead, together with their holy images, bibles and relics. He also massacred the 500 passengers and crew, allowing only six to live. Still, Sores did not have long to continue his career – he died in 1570. It is of interest that Sores' earlier commander, Francois Le Clerc, another Norman, had lost his leg in action some time in the 1540s, but was fitted with a wooden leg. He was therefore named Pie de Palo (Peg Leg), but despite this continued to attack Spanish possessions, and eventually died hunting Spanish treasure ships in the Azores in 1563.[1]

The French assault on the Spanish continued in the early seventeenth century with the emergence of the buccaneers in the West Indies. The word 'buccaneer' refers to those pirates and privateers who attacked Spanish ships and towns primarily in the West Indies, but later came to refer to other areas as well, such as the Pacific coast of South America. The word itself comes from the *boucan* or barbecue, a kind of grill on which the Arawak Indians roasted their meat, poultry and fish. *Boucan* can also refer to the place where the Indians dried and salted their meat. The 'boucaniers' were originally groups of mainly French hunters who lived on the island of Hispaniola (now Haiti and the Dominican Republic), hunting the wild cattle and pigs to be found on the island, which had been left by the early Spanish settlers. These 'boucaniers' or buccaneers, from around 1605 initially sold dried meat and hides to passing ships, before turning to piracy. They were also strong enemies of the Spanish, and were soon joined by an eclectic mix of all nations – runaway slaves, deserters, indentured servants fleeing from rough usage in English and French colonies, failed or dispossessed planters, social and political refugees, marooned sailors, and anyone else who sought to escape the law. The buccaneers were described as being:

> …dressed in shirts and pantaloons of coarse linen cloth, which they steeped in the blood of the animals they slaughtered. They wore round caps, boots of hogskin drawn over their feet, and belts of raw hide, in which they stuck their sabres and knives. They also armed themselves with firelocks [matchlocks], which threw a couple of balls, each weighing two ounces … They chased and slaughtered horned cattle and trafficked with the flesh, and their favourite food was raw marrow from the bones of the beasts which they shot.[2]

The buccaneers' life style was curious – they hunted in small groups of six to eight, but lived in two man 'marriages' called matelotages. These 'marriages' were arrangements of convenience, and the two men shared a hut, their dogs, their possessions, and protected each other. They drank brandy like water, lived rough, and when one died, the other inherited all that the deceased owned. There may have been homosexual relationships involved, but they also pursued women whenever possible, as Esquemeling (a French surgeon who accompanied the buccaneers and wrote of them) observed, 'the service of Venus is not forgotten'. Sometimes the buccaneers were able to afford a servant, and one episode has a young servant complaining that Sunday was a day of rest, at which his buccaneer master thrashed him and roared, 'Get on, you bugger; my commands are these – six days shalt thou collect hides, and the seventh shalt thou bring them to the beach.'[3]

The buccaneers were content enough with their life in the early seventeenth century, but the Spanish made the mistake of trying to rid Hispaniola of the buccaneers by conducting inland sweeps in the 1630s, with the idea of killing the cattle and hogs on which the buccaneers survived. However, this only drove the buccaneers to the coasts of Hispaniola and into piracy against passing Spanish ships. The buccaneers first used canoes for their attacks, and then one-masted sloops. Their technique was to surprise the Spanish ships if possible, but if not, to use their formidable hunting skills to pick off the crew on deck, and then sail or row around to the stern and jam the rudder. After this, the buccaneers would board and fight ferociously until their aim was achieved. Some buccaneers moved onto the nearby island of Tortuga (meaning turtle, since it resembled one), and by the mid seventeenth century, others had moved on again to Port Royal, Jamaica.

There were perhaps 500 or 600 buccaneers, and their rise to significance owed something to the decline of Spain, and the emergence of non-Spanish colonies in the West Indies such as St Kitts, St Thomas, Barbados, Nevis, Antigua, Curacao, Hispaniola, Tortuga, and Jamaica. Political rulers with an interest in the West Indies such as Cromwell, Charles II, and Louis XIV, also played a part by intervening in the area. The same situation arose with Dutch independence from Spain. All of these factors gave a window of opportunity to adventurers and interlopers, such as Pierre Le Grand, who, according to Esquemeling, managed to surprise and board a large Spanish galleon in 1665. Having killed the deck watch, Le Grand and crew burst into the captain's cabin, where the officers were playing cards. Le Grand held a pistol to the captain's chest, and demanded surrender, causing the captain understandably to cry out, 'Jesus bless us! Are these devils or what are they?' After this, according to Esquemeling, Pierre Le Grand did not stay in the West Indies, but simply sailed home to Dieppe in Normandy on the ship he had taken, using some captured Spaniards to supplement his crew. Pierre Le Grand then retired from piracy.[4]

Le Vasseur

Before this, the Frenchman Le Vasseur, yet another Norman and strong Protestant, and a military engineer, arrived on Tortuga in 1642. He was originally sent to Tortuga by the governor of the French colonies, so at that time he did not qualify as a pirate. Yet Le Vasseur had ambitions, and soon began to operate independently. Among other things, he built a fort on top of a steep hill on Tortuga with a good supply of cannon and ammunition, and a difficult approach path. This path changed half way up from a stairway to an iron ladder with rungs, which could be raised and lowered from the top. With wry humour, Le Vasseur called this formidable fort his 'Dove cot'. In 1643 Le Vasseur and his men turned back a large Spanish force, and impressed by this feat, lawless buccaneers were soon attracted to Tortuga. Le Vasseur refused French rule, took a percentage of all buccaneer booty, taxed the cow hides that came in from Hispaniola, and became very wealthy. Unfortunately, Le Vasseur's character began to change for the worse, and he built an iron cage at his fort, nicknamed the 'little hell', where he imprisoned his enemies and in which one could neither stand up nor lie down. One incident involving a silver Madonna emphasised his independence from France. When he obtained this valuable icon from one of the buccaneers, the French governor requested the piece, but Le Vasseur sent a wooden Madonna instead, remarking that Catholics were too spiritual to notice any difference. Finally, two of Le Vasseur's own followers murdered him in 1653, ostensibly over a mistress that Le Vasseur claimed for himself. The next year the Spanish captured Tortuga, only to abandon it later, allowing the French back in again in 1660. But Tortuga remained a pirate hang out, and became home to one of the most notorious pirates, the Frenchman L'Olonnais.[5]

L'Olonnais

L'Olonnais was so named because he came from Les Sables d'Olonne (the sands of Olonne), in Brittany, France. His real name was Jean Nau, but he became known as one of the cruelest pirates of the Caribbean.

Illustrations 1–37, 67, 70–72, 78, 81–91, 97–100 and 103 are the work of American illustrator, writer and teacher, Howard Pyle (1853–1911). It is Howard Pyle more than any other individual who established and imprinted on the modern mind what a pirate looks like and how he should behave. His illustrations are romantic and unrealistic, but they established what we now think of as the genuine pirate image during the golden age of piracy from the sixteenth century to the eighteenth century and beyond. For this reason many of his illustrations have been reproduced in this book.

Top left: 1 'A pirate as imagined by a Quaker gentlemen.'

Top right: 2 'A typical pirate.'

Above: 3 'Band of armed pirates.'

Left: 4 'A pirate takes aim.'

Middle: 5 'A pirate is shot.'

Below: 6 'Pirate Bold and ship.'

℟ Pirate Bold.

It is not because of his life of adventure and daring that I admire this one of my favorite heroes; nor is it because of blowing winds nor blue ocean nor balmy islands which he knew so well; nor is it because of gold he spent nor treasure he hid. He was a man who knew his own mind and what he wanted. *Howard Pyle*

7 'A Pirate at the wheel.'

Above left: 8 'A pirate stands over his victim.'

Above right: 9 'A typical pirate.'

10 'A pirate captain surveys the deck.'

11 'Captain Scarfield.'

12 'Flirting on deck.'

13 'Beach scene.'

14 'Marooned pirate.'

15 'Rescue on its way.'

16 'Stabbed in the back.'

17 'Buried treasure.'

18 'Pirates carrying treasure.'

19 'Discovered treasure.'

20 'Pirates make off with treasure.'

Above: 21 'Examining treasure.'

Right: 22 'Captain Mayloe shot Captain Brand through the head.'

23 'She would sit quite still, permitting Barnaby to gaze.'

24 'Burning the ship.' Pirates did often burn the ships they captured, partly in order to prevent their victims from sailing off and revealing where the pirates were, and what they had done. The crews of these captured ships were normally allowed to land or row away.

25 'Pirates used to do that to their Captains now and then.'

26 'So the pirate treasure was divided.' Dividing up treasure among a pirate crew was an important process, in which care was taken to make each share as equal as possible. Some skilled members of a pirate crew, including the captain, surgeon, gunner, and carpenter, would be given more than one share.

Left: 27 'Colonel Rhett and the pirate.'

Below: 28 'The pirate's Christmas.'

29 'He lay silent and still, with his face half buried in the sand.'

30 'There Cap'n Goldsack goes, creeping, creeping, creeping, looking for his treasure down below!'

31 'He had found the captain agreeable and companionable.' In the late seventeenth century many colonial governors were sympathetic to pirates, happy to share the spoils. This picture shows the pirate Thomas Tew being entertained by New York Governor Benjamin Fletcher in the 1690s.

32 'How the buccaneers kept Christmas.'

33 'A pirate fighting it out.'

34 'The burning ship.' Fire was always a grave threat, and precautions were taken on all ships to prevent this happening. Pirates usually operated at trade routes fairly close to land because that was where merchant ships were to be found, so crews could normally get ashore if there was a fire.

Left: 35 'Pirates fighting.'

Below: 36 'Dead men tell no tales.' Some pirate captains did murder their victims. This was especially the case in the nineteenth century, when one pirate captain in 1824 told his men 'dead cats don't mew', obviously instructing his crew to kill their captives.

37 'Daughter of Captain Keitt.'

38 Execution of Stede Bonnet. Stede
Bonnet was hung in Charles Town, South
Carolina in 1718. Bonnet was an unlikely
pirate, being a middle aged plantation
owner from Barbados. Bonnet holds a
posy of flowers, a common touch with
the condemned at hanging, and he is
executed using the short rope drop, which
took some time to produce death.

Above: 39 Cape Corso Castle. A depiction of Cape Coast Castle on the West African coast, where Roberts' large crew were tried, and some of them hung, in 1722. Cape Coast Castle was a Royal African Company factory where African slaves were held before being shipped to their destinations.

Left: 40 A wounded Spaniard shot by Capt Low's crew. This scene depicts an event after a Spanish ship was captured off Honduras by Captain Low. One of the Spanish sailors jumped into the water to escape but was recaptured. He begged for mercy but one of the pirates made him kneel down, and placing the muzzle of his gun in the Spaniard's mouth, pulled the trigger.

41 Captain Anstis' mock trial. This mock trial, which took place in 1722, on an island off Cuba, reflected the pirates' attitude toward the justice system of the day. Some pirate humour and some pirate fear both seem to be part of this trial, which was fully reported by Captain Charles Johnson.

42 A symbolic representation of a pirate captain. Note the fashionable clothes, wig and three cornered hat. Also the gentleman's rapier sword and flintlock musket.

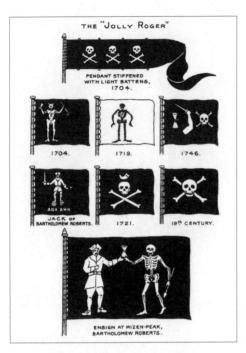

THE "JOLLY ROGER"

PENDANT STIFFENED
WITH LIGHT BATTENS,
1704.

1704.

1719.

1746.

ABH AMH
JACK OF
BARTHOLOMEW ROBERTS.

1721.

19TH CENTURY.

ENSIGN AT MIZEN-PEAK,
BARTHOLOMEW ROBERTS.

43 Different versions of pirate flags. Two of the flags were designed by the pirate captain Bartholomew Roberts – the lower left flag has Roberts standing on two of his opponent's skulls – A Bahamian's head and a Martinican's head.

44 Buccaneers attack a Spanish ship in a cannon duel. Normally, buccaneers preferred to take a ship by surprise or by boarding rather than in a fire fight, because Spanish fire discipline was often superior.

45 Title page of Esquemeling's *The Buccaneers of America*, first published in Amsterdam in 1678. Several other versions followed. Esquemeling is important for his first hand accounts of two of Henry Morgan's expeditions, and for his knowledge of the buccaneers.

46 Esquemeling's vision of a typical French buccaneer on Hispaniola. There were two kinds of buccaneer – those who hunted wild bulls and cattle in a two man operation, and those who hunted wild boars in teams of five or six men.

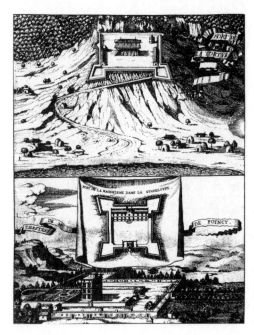

47 This is the buccaneer fort constructed on Tortuga by the French adventurer LeVasseur, in the 1640s. He ironically named it his 'Dove Cot'. Interestingly, the fort incorporates the latest 'bastion trace' outline, useful against cannon.

48 Henry Morgan's raid on El Puerto del Principe, Cuba. The buccaneers took the town, but found only 50,000 pieces of eight, since the Spanish were forewarned. Morgan also forced the inhabitants to produce and slaughter 500 cattle for the buccaneers, who were often short of food.

Right: 49 Portrait of the buccaneer Roche Brasiliano, a Dutchman, but named thus because of his long residence in Brazil. He raided along the coast of Central America, capturing several ships. He hated and tortured Spanish prisoners. But he spent all his plunder on alcohol and women.

Below: 50 Morgan's capture of Panama City in 1671. The buccaneers defeated the Spanish defenders of Panama City in a set battle outside the city, and then plundered Panama and surrounding area for several weeks. Panama was probably set on fire by some of the inhabitants.

ROCK. BRASILIANO

Above: 51 William Dampier, painted around 1697. Dampier was a buccaneer but also an acute observer of nature, and published his observations in a number of volumes. The books were readable, satisfied the public's desire for knowledge about the world, and made Dampier famous.

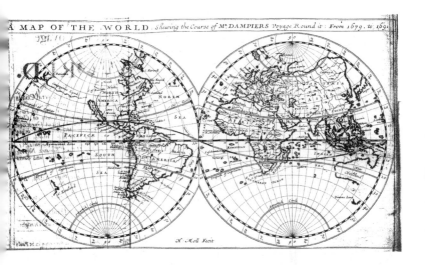

A MAP OF THE WORLD, *Shewing the Course of Mr DAMPIERS Voyage Round it : From 1679. to 1691*

H. Moll Fecit

Above: 53 Dampier's map of the world from his *A New Voyage Round the World* (1697). The map shows that Dampier was vague about North America, but that he knew South America and the Pacific, and in a later voyage he explored parts of Australia.

Right: 54 Hanging a pirate in the eighteenth century at Execution Dock, Wapping, London. At the time, hanging was a slow, unpleasant death due to the 'short drop' which did not break the neck of the condemned. Here, the chaplain, or 'ordinary', tries to elicit a last speech of repentance from the pirate.

Opposite below: 52 A map of the Americas from Dampier's book, *A New Voyage Round the World* (1697). It was in this area that the buccaneers operated and raided. Dampier himself joined some of these raids, but also circumnavigated the world.

Above: 55 A woodcut of the execution of one of Avery's crew in 1696. Bodies of the condemned were placed between the high and low water marks of the River Thames to signify the authority of the High Court of the Admiralty.

Left: 56 A copy of the first page of the 1700 piracy act of William III. This act allowed a seven man jury of officials or naval officers to be assembled anywhere in the world in order to try pirates and execute them if guilty.

57 A well known pirate, Charles Vane gained fame by refusing to accept Woodes Rogers' offer of a pardon in the Bahamas in 1718. Vane escaped by using a fire ship at night, and then pirated for two years, meeting up once with Blackbeard before being caught and hung in 1720.

58 Captain Charles Vane.

59 A report of the trial of the pirate Stede Bonnet and his crew at Charles Town in 1718. Bonnet was unusual in being a gentleman and man of means, who reportedly became a pirate in order to escape his wife. He was no mariner, and was hung along with most of his crew in 1718.

60 This pirate captain was known as 'Calico' Jack Rackam, due to his penchant for wearing white calico clothes. Rackam was not a very successful pirate, but gained posthumous fame for having two women pirates in his crew, Anne Bonny and Mary Read. He was easily captured, and tried and hung in Jamaica in 1720.

61 This picture shows the front page of the
very lengthy report of the trial of Captain
Jack Rackam and his crew, published in
Jamaica in 1721. The report also contains
the separate trial of the two women pirates
in his crew, Anne Bonny and Mary Read.

62 A portrait of Anne Bonny (or Bonn),
who served on Captain Jack Rackam's
ship. She abandoned a husband on New
Providence in order to run away with
Rackam, and became his lover. She was
captured and tried along with Rackam,
but was spared execution because she was
pregnant. She then disappears from history.

63 A portrait of Mary Read, who served on Captain Jack Rackam's ship. She had allegedly previously served in the army, which helped when she fought a duel with a sailor who threatened her lover. She was captured and tried along with Rackam, but was spared execution because she was pregnant. She died in prison.

Bartholomew Roberts doodgebleeven.

64 Captain Bartholomew Roberts, one of the most successful pirates. In his last battle in 1722, he dressed in a crimson waistcoat and trousers, a hat with a red plume, and wore a gold chain and diamond cross. He was killed in this battle against the Royal Navy, and thrown overboard as he had requested.

65 Captain Bartholomew Roberts again depicted in fine clothes. He carries a cutlass and a brace of pistols in a sash, as was normal. Roberts was unusual in not drinking alcohol, and in demanding strong discipline in his large crew.

66 Captain Bartholomew Robert's crew drinking at the slaving port of Old Calabar in 1721. The drink would have been rum or brandy. However, Roberts' pirates fought a battle with the local inhabitants here, and then set fire to the town.

67 'Extorting tribute from the citizens.' The prelude to torture, when pirates forced individuals to confess where their valuables could be found. This incident relates to the sack of Cartagena by buccaneers and the French in 1697.

JOHAN MORGAN
geboren in de Provincie van Wallis in Engeland
Generaal van de Roovers op Jamaica

68 Portrait of Henry Morgan. Technically not a pirate, Morgan launched several raids on Spanish towns, the most famous being the raid on Panama. Esquemeling writes that Morgan's buccaneers cruelly tortured many prisoners in these towns in order to find and seize their valuables.

The Spanish Armada destroyed by Captaine Morgan

Above: 69 Morgan fights his way out of Lake Maracaibo, which was blocked by a fort and three large Spanish ships. Morgan used fire ships and boarding to deal with the Spanish ships, and trickery to steal past the fort at night.

Right: 70 'Jack followed the Captain [Blackbeard] and the young lady up the crooked path to the house.'

71 'He led Jack up to a man [Blackbeard] who sat upon a barrel.'

72 'The combatants cut and slashed with savage fury.' When pirates boarded a ship, the fight was often violent, but also usually short. Blackbeard was killed in 1718 in a ship board struggle, and the fight was bitterly contested with cutlass and pistol.

73 The famous pirate Blackbeard (or Edward Teach) engaged in a fight for his life against Lieutenant Maynard of the Royal Navy. The fight took place in Ocracoke creek, North Carolina, in 1718. Blackbeard sustained many wounds before being cut down by a Royal Navy sailor.

74 After Blackbeard and his small crew were killed or captured, Lieutenant Maynard had Blackbeard's head cut off, and displayed it from his bowsprit. Allegedly, Maynard threw Blackbeard's body overboard, at which point the body swam around Maynard's ship.

75 A 1696 broadside or printed sheet of a ballad celebrating the piratical life of Henry Every (Avery). These sheets preserved the memory of Avery and this one presents him as a pirate who made his own future and fortune.

76 A government authorised version of the trial of six of Every's (Avery's) men. The first trial acquitted these crewmen. But in a second trial, one was spared and turned state's evidence, while the other five were hung as pirates.

77 Avery is presented here as the king of Madagascar. In fact, although he did put in to Madagascar on his way to the Red Sea, he was far from becoming the king of the island. A more likely king of Madagascar was the trader John or James Plantain.

78 'Kidd on the deck of the *Adventure Galley.'* William Kidd is here portrayed as an evil pirate, although there is some debate as to whether Kidd was actually a pirate or not.

Above: 79 William Kidd is here portrayed turning from good to evil. Historians are divided as to whether Kidd became a pirate, or tried to remain a privateer. The two major ships which Kidd took sailed under French passes, which permitted Kidd to take them legally. However, he was tried and hung in 1701.

Left: 80 Some of the most notorious pirates were hung and then placed in iron chains at a location where all ships' crews entering or leaving the River Thames would see them. Here, it is William Kidd hanging at Tilbury Point in 1701.

L'Olonnais established himself on Tortuga as the first of the large scale buccaneers in the early 1660s. What was different about L'Olonnais was that he successfully started raiding Spanish towns and ports ashore, although he also took Spanish ships when possible. Another thing that was different about L'Olonnais was that he tortured captives more brutally than most, to make them confess where their treasure and valuables were hidden. Stories abound concerning L'Olonnais' cruelty. According to Esquemeling, if his captives would not confess where their valuables were to be found, he would cut them to pieces with his cutlass, and pull out their tongues. Other tortures included burning with matches, or tying a cord about the prisoner's head and twisting it with a stick 'till his eyes shoot out', or putting the victim on a rack, and if the unfortunate prisoner did not immediately answer his questions, L'Olonnais would 'hack the man to pieces with his cutlass and lick the blood from the blade with his tongue, wishing it might have been the last Spaniard in the world he had thus killed.' Perhaps the most infamous of L'Olonnais' exploits took place on a raid on Nicaragua. Trying to discover ways to avoid a Spanish ambush, L'Olonnais cut open one of the prisoners with his cutlass, tore the living heart out of his body, bit and gnawed at it, saying to the rest, 'I will serve you all alike if you show me not another way.'[6]

It must be admitted that L'Olonnais was not alone in his cruelty, since a pattern developed in the Caribbean as other Europeans, often French, and generally deeply imbued with a hatred of the Spanish, did much the same. There was the infamous Montbars, from Languedoc in France, who is said to have read a book in his youth about the cruelty of the Spanish to the natives of the Americas. Montbars therefore practiced the same toward all Spaniards he caught. His nickname was the 'Exterminator', and he was known for cutting open the stomach of his victim, nailing one end of his intestines to the mast, and, by applying a burning torch to the backside of the unfortunate individual, making him run and dance to his death. Another unpleasant pirate was Roche Brasiliano, a Dutchman, who operated out of Jamaica, and who had sailed with L'Olonnais in the late 1660s. Brasiliano raided along the coast of Central America on his own behalf, and succeeded in capturing a number of ships, which he brought into Port Royal, Jamaica. One unpleasant trait of Brasiliano's was to roast alive those Spaniards who would not show him where their hog yards were located. Another aspect of Brasiliano's violent behaviour, according to Esquemeling, was that when drunk he:

…would roam the town like a madman. The first person he came across, he would chop off his arm or leg, without anyone daring to intervene, for he was like a maniac. He perpetrated the greatest atrocities possible against the Spaniards. Some of them he tied or spitted on wooden stakes and roasted them alive between two fires, like killing a pig…

Indeed, alcohol, together with gambling and brothels, soon took care of most pirate plunder, whether obtained by Brasiliano or any other pirate of the time. Esquemeling wrote that his own master would buy:

…a whole pipe of wine, and, placing it in the street, would force everyone that passed by to drink with him; threatening also to pistol them in case they would not do it. At other times, he would do the same with barrels of ale or beer. And, very often, with both his hands he would throw these liquors about the streets, and wet the clothes of such as walked by, without regarding whether he spoiled their apparel or not, were they men or women.[7]

Yet Brasiliano and Montbars were small operators compared to L'Olonnais, who took advantage of a brief war between France and Spain from 1667 to 1668 to launch a large scale raid against the towns of Maracaibo and Gibraltar on Lake Maracaibo in Venezuela. The inhabitants of Maracaibo, knowing an attack was coming, transferred their goods to Gibraltar, but L'Olonnais attacked Gibraltar, leading his men with the shout, 'Allons, mes freres, suivez-moi, et fait point les laches!' (Come on, brothers, and don't be cowards). L'Olonnais and his men took Gibraltar and spent a whole month plundering the town. The total haul from the area was 260,000 pieces of eight, plus jewels, silks, slaves, and a further 20,000 pieces of eight and 500 cattle as ransom, obtained by promising to burn the town unless the ransom was paid. Five hundred Spaniards died in the action, since they were put into boats, rowed out into the lake, and the boats then sunk. Following this, the pirates sailed to Cow Island, off Hispaniola, to divide up the treasure, and then on to Jamaica, where L'Olonnais sold an 80 ton, 12 gun ship to Brasiliano and another man, which started the piratical career of these two. Finally, it was back to Tortuga, where L'Olonnais planned another expedition. This was aimed at the Gulf of Honduras, where the pirates captured two towns. The expedition continued on to Nicaragua and the Isthmus of Darien, where the pirate ship ran aground. L'Olonnais and a landing party were ambushed by natives, who hacked L'Olonnais to pieces, roasted him limb by limb, and threw the ashes into the air. Such was the fitting end for L'Olonnais in 1668, but his death certainly did not end the reign of the buccaneers.[8]

This was because a large number of other buccaneers operated in the Caribbean, according to whether Spain and the relevant country were at peace or war. So, for example, the decade of the 1660s belonged to the English pirates and privateers, when the new king of England, Charles II, decided to try and force the Spanish to trade with English merchants, and to recognize English colonies in the Caribbean, such as Jamaica, captured in 1655. On the other hand, the period 1678 to 1683 belonged to French pirates and privateers such as Michel de Grammont, on behalf of French imperialism. De Grammont also raided Maracaibo in 1678, but found little there to plunder after the visit of L'Olonnais. De Grammont went on to capture La Guayra, the port of Caracas, in a clever night raid in 1680, and then with Laurens de Graff made an extremely profitable assault on Vera Cruz in 1683. This action earned some 1,200 men 800 pieces of eight each. The next year, France and Spain signed a peace treaty, although the Nine Years War (also called King William's War: 1689–1697) gave fresh impetus to the buccaneers again. Only in 1697, with the French attack on Cartagena, which included buccaneer ships, did the age of buccaneering come to an end.

Henry Morgan

Perhaps the most famous of the Jamaican buccaneers was Henry Morgan (1635–1688). Morgan came from a prominent military family in Wales, and he arrived in the West Indies in 1654, and perhaps served in the force that captured Jamaica in 1655. Morgan only operated for four years from Jamaica, yet he made a lasting impression in a series of large scale raids on Porto Bello in 1668, on the unfortunate towns of Maracaibo and Gibraltar in 1669, and on Panama in 1670–1671. Since Morgan always had a commission from the governor of Jamaica, Sir Thomas Modyford, for his various attacks on Spanish possessions, and since England was at war with Spain, Morgan was therefore a privateer and not a pirate, although Modyford's commissions usually referred to capturing ships at sea rather than land based operations. However, the 1670 expedition against Spanish possessions was viewed as a reprisal attack on the Spanish, since Spanish ships had earlier raided Jamaica. Even so, what turned out to be the Panama expedition might well be called piracy, since England and Spain signed the Treaty of Madrid in July 1670, and Morgan's commission, signed by Modyford, was issued several months after this peace treaty. In addition, Morgan captured the Spanish city of Panama in 1671, well after peace was supposed to exist between Spain and England. It is not clear if Morgan knew of the Treaty of Madrid when he attacked the city of Panama.

Morgan's reputation as an excellent commander, and his successful raids, attracted many buccaneers to his expeditions. In this context, the 1670 operation was no exception. To start with, in organizing what became the Panama attack, Morgan called on all willing buccaneers to attend a meeting on Tortuga on 24 October 1670. This meeting, according to Esquemeling, who accompanied the expedition as a surgeon, resulted in a fleet of thirty-seven ships and around 2,000 men. As usual, the first priority was to find provisions for such a large operation, and it was agreed that this would be achieved by raiding Spanish possessions. Then the buccaneers signed articles, with important articles relating to the future division of treasure, such as five or six portions for the captain, and the surgeons and carpenters receiving more than the ordinary sailor. There was also an article specifically setting out compensation for injuries received in action: loss of one leg – 600 pieces of eight, or six slaves; loss of one eye – 100 pieces of eight, or one slave; loss of both hands – 1,800 pieces of eight, or 18 slaves; loss of both legs – 1,500 pieces of eight, or 15 slaves. And in order to encourage bravery, the first man into a castle or fort or ship, and capturing the flag – 50 pieces of eight. Finally, the actual target of the operation was still to be decided – would it be Cartagena, Panama, or Vera Cruz? Panama was chosen because it promised to be the richest prize.[9]

With Panama decided, Morgan's force took the Spanish fort at the Isle of St Catherine (Old Providence Island), and collected some guides for the overland journey from the Caribbean side of the Isthmus of Panama to Panama City, which was on the Pacific side. The first obstacle was the fort of Chagres, at the mouth of the Chagres River, on the Caribbean side. Here Morgan employed Brasiliano, and his partner Erasmus Reyning, to lead the assault on the fort. According to Esquemeling, the first to enter the Chagres fort was a buccaneer who was shot by an arrow from the defenders. But the buccaneer pulled the arrow out and shot it back with lighted cotton attached, which set fire to the gunpowder in the fort and subsequently to the pales (palisade) defending the fort. However, the fort resisted for two days, and cost the buccaneers thirty-two casualties. Esquemeling states that Morgan then set forth to cross the isthmus in January 1671 with

1,200 men, while leaving large parties behind to safeguard his ships and Chagres fort in the rear. But the going was very rough indeed, mosquitoes and the heat sapped energy, Spanish sniping caused casualties, and the force ran so short of food that the men had to strip leather from their boots and cook it as a substitute food. This was partly because the Spanish were using a scorched earth policy to defeat the invaders. Nevertheless, Morgan showed great leadership skills, and eventually the discontented buccaneers emerged from the forest, found enough cattle to eat, and reached the outskirts of Panama City.[10]

At this point, the Spanish governor of Panama City, de Guzman, faced a problem. Although he had about 2,000 men, perhaps twice as many as the buccaneers, many of these, about 1,200, were Africans, mulattos, slaves and Indians, and there were few disciplined Spanish soldiers. De Guzman's force also had poor muskets, some being heavy harquebusses, or inadequate fowling pieces. But de Guzman did have 200 Spanish cavalry, and three leather covered light field pieces, seemingly copied from the leather cannon used by the Swedish king and innovator, Gustavus Adolphus. Esquemeling also reveals that de Guzman's force, or at least the trained soldiers, knew how to undertake the counter march – in which the first three ranks fired and then marched to the rear to reload the cumbersome match lock muskets, while the rear ranks moved forward to continue the fire. This was standard European practice from the 30 Years War (1618-1648), and shows how quickly military ideas spread from Europe to the Americas. De Guzman's defenders also formed up in accepted European style, with cannon in front, infantry in the centre, and cavalry on the wings. In the rear were two herds of wild cattle, brought along to bring disorder to the buccaneer ranks when unleashed. De Guzman wanted to maintain his tight formation, and allow Morgan's buccaneers to attack – which might have produced a Spanish victory if it had happened. But Morgan did not want to attack either, and set up his men in surprisingly up to date European fashion, with four roughly equal battalions, comprising an advance guard, a central main body, two wings, plus a reserve battalion in the rear. Then stalemate set in, for neither side wanted to advance – because the 30 Years War in Europe had already shown that it was safer to defend than attack. The ground was boggy also, which prevented the Spanish cavalry from maneuvering and outflanking, while Morgan's men were ready to form defensive musket 'squares' against the cavalry if attacked. For his part, Morgan sent out small parties to provoke the Spanish, but this did not produce a Spanish attack.[11]

Because Morgan and the buccaneers could not wait too long, for morale and logistical reasons, Morgan seized the initiative and wheeled part of his small army to the left onto a hill overlooking the battle ground. Probably this was just the advance guard, while Morgan's main body must have covered the move. De Guzman realised the danger and sent in his cavalry from his right flank, but these were stopped by the accurate musket fire of the buccaneers, who formed an oblong rather than a square, but they were effective nonetheless. The battle lasted for a limited time, with the Spanish cavalry doing their best to charge repeatedly against the main body of buccaneers, but they were forced back and destroyed by accurate musket fire. These repeated attacks by the Spanish cavalry probably occurred because the Spanish cavalry were the only force that de Guzman could really rely on. Then de Guzman recalls that he 'heard a loud clamour, crying, "Fall on! Fall on! For they fly"'. The buccaneers now saw that the left wing of de Guzman's army was running, which obviously spelled disaster for de Guzman's entire force. According to de Guzman, he then sent in the wild cattle, under the control of Africans and mulattos, against the buccaneers' rear. These too were easily dealt with by the buccaneers, who were certainly well used to dealing with wild cattle. Some of the cattle ran away, others were shot, and the only damage they did was to 'tear the Collours in pieces…' At the same time, de Guzman claims that he tried to lead his right wing cavalry in a final charge, but only one African and one servant followed him. De Guzman now very likely tried to portray himself as a hero, to avoid blame for the failure, since he then stated that he continued to advance, and was only persuaded to retire by a priest who beseeched him twice to do so and save himself. De Guzman rebuked him twice, but in familiar Christian symbolism, at the third request, when the priest said that 'it was mere desperation to Die in that manner and not like a Christian … I retired…'[12]

Now the way was clear to Panama City, where church bells were wildly ringing the alarm. Some 600 of de Guzman's army had died, and possibly around 200 buccaneers were casualties of one kind or another. Sporadic fighting continued in Panama City, and then fire broke out, most likely set by the Spanish themselves who had orders to set up 200 powder kegs around the city in the event of the city falling to Morgan. Or perhaps the fire was due to militiamen and slaves who ran from house to house with flaming torches, presumably to deny the buccaneers the wealth of the city. Morgan's men tried to stem the fire, which consumed the centre of the city and much of the suburbs, by blowing up or tearing down houses in the path of the fire.

But only some 300 houses remained out of about 7,000. The buccaneers also missed much of the treasure of the city, which was spirited away in the Spanish ship, *Santissima Trinidad*, which set sail for Lima. Meanwhile, according to Esquemeling, Morgan sent 150 men back to Chagres to announce his victory, and organised two groups of 150 men each to search for escaped citizens and seize their wealth.

Morgan and his men spent a month in Panama City, extorting valuables from the inhabitants and combing the surrounding countryside for fugitives and their wealth. Esquemeling claims that Morgan raped and badly mistreated numbers of women, and especially one woman of great beauty that Morgan desired for his own 'voluptuous pleasures'. When this was not forthcoming, Morgan threw her into a dark cellar and nearly starved her. Esquemeling claims to have witnessed this particular situation first hand. There was also torture of the inhabitants, to make them confess where their treasures lay, as Esquemeling luridly portrays. Esquemeling relates that prisoners were 'put to the most exquisite Tortures imaginable, to make them confess both other peoples Goods and their own'. In the confusion one unfortunate slave had probably stolen a pair of his master's taffeta breeches from which hung a golden key, and he was tortured on suspicion of possessing a hidden hoard. Morgan's men first put him on the rack, then put a rope about the slave's head, and twisted it, in the 'woolding' torture. They 'wrung [the rope] so hard, that his Eyes appeared as big as Eggs, and were ready to fall out of his Skull.' Following this, the buccaneers hung the slave up by his testicles, cut off his nose and ears, and singed his face with burning straw. Since the miserable slave had nothing to reveal and was close to death, they ordered 'a Negro to run him through with a Lance…' which ended his life. After similar kinds of persuasion, Morgan's men were able to collect about £30,000 from the inhabitants, and the buccaneers left the city on 24 February 1671, with a 175 mule train carrying the booty, plus about 600 prisoners.[13]

The triumphant buccaneers struggled back across the Isthmus of Panama, roughly herding their 600 prisoners along, who were short of food and water. The unhappy captives constantly beseeched Morgan to let them return to Panama, but Morgan refused, since he proposed to ransom them if possible, or if not, to sell them as slaves. However, he did allow the same beautiful woman he had thrown into the cellar in Panama to return to the city, since she had raised a ransom, even if this had been diverted by two religious persons. So Morgan simply took the two religious persons in her place. Finally, the long column of pirates and prisoners reached the fort at Chagres, which Morgan also hoped to ransom from the Spanish. However, the Spanish refused this offer, and Morgan was forced to simply demolish the fort. Then the time came to divide up the treasure from Panama City, but the sum total of about £30,000 was much less than expected by the buccaneers, and each man only received 200 pieces of eight. Morgan himself reportedly appropriated around £1,000, but the buccaneers were furious and strongly suspected that they had been cheated by Morgan. This may well have been the case, and Morgan probably did leave with more than he was entitled to, as Esquemeling argues.[14]

On the other hand, Esquemeling was a critic of Morgan, and Morgan's life in Jamaica would have been in danger if he had cheated his buccaneers too crudely and obviously, so perhaps the truth lies somewhere in the middle. In any case, perhaps because of fear of the buccaneers' anger, Morgan sailed off quickly, carrying with him the guns of the fort and all the powder. The buccaneers were mostly left behind, and many therefore stayed to raid along the coast of Central America, hoping to obtain more treasure. As for Morgan, he was welcomed back to Port Royal, Jamaica, yet his Panama raid was too much for the authorities in London, who came under Spanish pressure to punish him. At the same time, the Crown thought that Jamaican privateering and piracy in the Caribbean, while useful, was a danger to trade, and harmful to the English colonies in the Caribbean. Therefore, both Morgan and Modyford were sent to London for trial. Morgan apparently saved himself by offering professional advice on how to protect English colonies from the Dutch, with whom England went to war in 1672. This tactic worked so well that Morgan returned to Jamaica as deputy governor, and was later knighted. From then on Morgan turned to life as a plantation owner, but essentially ate and drank himself to death in 1688.[15]

William Dampier, Logwood Cutting, and Raiding the South Seas

The career of William Dampier, buccaneer and naturalist, nicely illustrates the changing fortunes of the buccaneers. He observed that the authorities in London and Jamaica had turned themselves against piracy, and so the buccaneers were, as he eloquently wrote 'put to their shifts, for they had prodigally spent whatever they got'.[16] Indeed, buccaneer spending was reckless in Jamaica, and Esquemeling tells the story of how one buccaneer paid a 'strumpet' five hundred pieces of eight 'only that he might see her naked'.[17] So the buccaneers were continually forced to either launch new expeditions, or seek new sources of income through logwood cutting in the Bay of Campeche (on the Yucatan peninsula). Logwood cutters numbered around 500 or 600, and cut the wood in order to produce the embedded valuable purple dye for the industries of Europe. (It is said that Henry Avery, the future Red Sea pirate, was a logwood cutter at this time.) Dampier described the process of logwood cutting as very heavy work amidst the mosquitoes, heat and water-logged mangrove swamps where the logwood trees grew. Dampier also noted that the cutters worked in small companies of three to ten men, living in pavilions, with beds raised above the water level. The cutters also signed a 'Short Compendium of Rules', which regulated their existence in a democratic way, and prohibited capital punishment. The cutters sold their logs to traders, who often paid them in rum and sugar. Not surprisingly, there were some prodigious drinking bouts, punctuated by the roar of cannon to signal the drinking of toasts. Dampier initially tried his luck as a logwood cutter, but failed to make any money from his efforts since a hurricane in 1676 destroyed his camp. Following this, Dampier took part in a raid on the port of Alvarado, near Vera Cruz, which was costly in casualties and yielded very little. Now somewhat desperate, he returned to logwood cutting, but left the business in 1678, shortly before the Spanish attacked the cutters where he had worked, and wiped them out. Dampier next sailed for England and got married, yet, restless as ever, thought to return to Campeche to trade goods, but only got as far as Jamaica. Here he sold his goods successfully in 1679, but then in 1680 became involved with one of the most well described of all buccaneering voyages, the large scale attack by the 'South Sea' men on Panama and the Pacific coast of South America.[18]

This raid, from 1680 to 1682, was widely described by several participants, including Esquemeling, Dampier, and the buccaneer Basil Ringrose, as well as in the private journals of other leading buccaneers, such as Bartholomew Sharp, John Cox, and an anonymous source. It is notable that both John Cox and Bartholomew Sharp dedicated their journals to the Duke of Albemarle, Governor of Jamaica, who was sympathetic to the buccaneers. Another journal by William Cowley discussed a later Pacific Ocean voyage. This first raid started off on the western tip of Jamaica as a dozen ships and about 500 buccaneers gathered. Captain Coxon, a former privateer from Jamaica, was elected admiral, and the fleet agreed to meet at the Isle of Pines, where

Drake had spent much time. The first target was Porto Bello, where Drake
had died and was buried at sea, which had been raided previously by various
buccaneers, including Morgan. Coxon's plan was to land some sixty miles
from Porto Bello and surprise the town by marching, rather than sailing, to
the town. However, according to Sharp's manuscript, an Indian saw the buccaneers as they closed in on Porto Bello, and called out 'Ladrones', meaning
robbers, and ran toward the town. Coxon thereupon cried out, 'good boys
you that are able to runn get into towne before we are descried, we had
then about three miles to Puerto Uello [Porto Bello].' But the Indian got
into town about half an hour before the buccaneers, and the alarm gun
was fired. Sharp recounted that 'ye foorlorne [the 'forlorn hope', the name
normally used for a lead attack group, who often died, hence lacking hope]
being led by Capt Robert Alliston ye rest of our party following up so fast
as they could before of ye clocke in the afternoon [mid-day] we had taken
ye towne ...' The Spanish soldiers retreated into the central castle called the
Glory, and about 200 of their soldiers tried to come out, but were forced
back. It does not seem that the Spaniards resisted very strongly. The buccaneers plundered the town for a day and then left, taking some prisoners
for ransom. On the way back to where their ships were anchored, the buccaneers took a Spanish ship, which led to the first of many problems relating
to leadership because it was found that Coxon had wrongly kept 500 pieces
of gold for himself. This was sorted out and everyone got 100 pieces of eight
per man.[19]

Subsequently, Coxon still proved a problem because when the buccaneer
group of some 300 men consulted over what to do next, he declared that he
wanted to go home. Coxon was apparently both hot tempered and thought
to be a coward, and at one point argued with the buccaneer Richard
Hendricks, firing his musket at him, but luckily missing. If Coxon's aim had
been better, he would have been severely punished by the buccaneers. Yet
Coxon must have had the necessary experience because he was still elected
overall commander, though, according to Bartholomew Sharp, 'wee were
forced to agree to make him our Generall by reason wee were very unwilling to brake our party soe he seeming then to be well satisfied it was agreed
and concluded on that wee should proceed toward the citty of Panama...'[20]
The buccaneers therefore set out for Panama City, with each group following their own captain under different coloured flags. Sharp's group followed
a red flag with green and white ribbons, Sawkins' flag was red striped with
yellow, Peter Harris had a green flag, Coxon had strong red colours, and

Edmund Cook flew a complicated flag of red striped with yellow, containing a hand and sword device. The buccaneers were helped very much by the local Kuna Indians, who supplied food, canoes and most importantly, guides. Nevertheless, the buccaneers were on their guard since the party had split up into different marching and canoe groups, 'We weare putt all to stand att this and thoughts rise amounge us yt these Indians only separated us to bring us all to distruction, so that wee had much grumblings amounge us, yt, they made signes we should nott be troubled att any thing.'[21]

The Indians proved loyal, and the first Spanish town the buccaneers came across was Santa Maria. This was taken by a charge led by Captain Sawkins, killing seventy of the defenders, with only two buccaneers being wounded, including Sawkins. However, there was little of value in the town, since the buccaneers had missed a gold shipment by just three days, while the Spanish governor, who could have been ransomed, made his escape by running fast for about a mile beside the river and could not be caught. Once more another vote was taken on whether to continue, and once more 'Our General Capt Coxon seemed unwilling, butt with much perswaifsion went…'[22] Meanwhile, the buccaneers took along as many Spanish prisoners from Santa Maria as they could, but had to leave many behind, and the Indians 'killed all ye poore soules yt were left…' The buccaneers pressed on, and arrived at the coast near Panama, but found the city had been warned of their approach. Consequently, three Spanish ships with some 300 men onboard sailed out to defend the city. Undaunted, the buccaneers boldly launched their canoes on each side of the Spanish ships, and then came under the stern to wedge the rudders, which prevented the Spanish cannon from being effective. Instead, the cross fire of the buccaneers' muskets proved decisive, so that one Spanish ship fled, one was taken by boarding, and one surrendered. Casualties to the buccaneers were eleven killed, and thirty-four wounded – one of the killed being 'Brave vallient Capt Peter Harriss [who] was shot through both his leggs bordeing of a greate ship.' Harris did not die straight away, but perished after the doctor cut off one leg which then developed gangrene.[23]

This sea battle was a considerable victory for the buccaneers, and they were then able to easily capture the Spanish ships inside the harbour of Panama because they were manned by very few men. One of these ships was the 400 ton *Santissima Trinidad*, which was renamed the *Trinity*, and turned into a hospital ship. Then, as often happened, an argument developed among the buccaneers over what was to happen next. Panama City itself was too strong to be attacked, so the choices were to either continue on into the South Seas, or return to the Caribbean. Coxon, true to form, wanted no more of fighting, and elected to return home, while Sawkins was made the new admiral. Coxon was anyway dismissed because of 'not behauving himself nobly in Line of Ingagement, [and] was something howled att by the Party…' Not only was Coxon relieved of his post, but he took the surgeon with him, and the best part of the medicines 'having no respect to the poor wounded men…' It seems that the desire to stay with the wounded was part of the decision by the buccaneers to remain in the South Seas, 'confidering ye condition of 34 poore wound/d. men were very unwilling to fee so many who had behaved themselves so bravely to perish, tooke up a resolution to stay in ye South Seas, till they were cured…'[24]

Coxon left to cross back over the Isthmus of Panama with some seventy men, while the remaining buccaneers, perhaps around 200, sailed south. Good luck produced a Spanish ship from Lima, which when captured contained 50,000 pieces of eight, plus wine and brandy, which certainly encouraged the buccaneers. Now the party had Sawkins as admiral in the *Trinity*, Sharp as commander of the recently taken Lima ship, Cooke as commander of a small ship, and two small barques containing seven men apiece. The decision was next made to attack the town of Pueblo Nuevo, in order to obtain fresh meat, which the buccaneers declared they had to have. Sawkins stormed ashore at the head of the attack party, but was killed, together with three others, and one man captured, who was tortured by the Spanish, making a 'dreadful noyse…' Following this, there arose the inevitable debate over who to elect as admiral, and where to go. John Cox wrote that 'here fell out a greater distraction amongst our men which was accationed by C/a Sawkins his men, for the lofs of their Commander, so 75 men left us…' It seems that Sawkins had been much liked, and Sharp much disliked, but Sharp made a speech promising to continue the South Seas voyage and make each man rich, and to stand by the wounded men, so he was elected admiral, while Sawkins' men departed, leaving 146 men to continue.[25]

The remaining buccaneers continued sailing south, but did not have much luck. The town of Arica proved too strong to capture, so the small port of Ilo (or Hilo) was taken and some provisions were found. By December 1680 they arrived at the Bay of Coquimbo. Here the buccaneers launched three canoes with thirty-five men against 150 Spanish cavalry, yet these odds did not daunt the buccaneers, whose captain told them that only five or six buccaneers should fire at a time, and only when sure of their mark. Coquimbo was captured because most of the defenders fled to the hills. There then took place a long debate with the governor of Coquimbo over a ransom – which the buccaneers always demanded if they could – but the governor declined to agree. The Spanish then opened the irrigation gates and tried to literally wash the buccaneers away. Realising there was nothing more to obtain from the town, the buccaneers left, carrying some silver plate and some jewelry. Then it was on to the Juan Fernandez Islands – a frequent stopping place for pirates because it was far enough off shore (some 400 miles off modern Chile) that the pirates were not bothered, and because the islands had plenty of goats, fish and water. The islands are steep sided and forbidding, and over the years several men were marooned here. This was also the case in January 1681 when the buccaneers departed the islands because they sighted some Spanish ships. This meant that they left behind a Moskito coast Indian, William the Striker (so called because of Moskito fishing skills), who was away hunting. William the Striker survived, and was later rescued in 1684.

There was also something of a mutiny among the buccaneers at the Juan Fernandez Islands because Sharp wanted to go home, having personally accumulated around 3,000 pieces of eight, some obtained by gambling. On the other hand, two thirds of the party had no money. It seems that a group of 'refactory' buccaneers went ashore and decided to turn out Sharp by signing a joint paper which named John Watling as admiral. Sharp was angry, but was made a prisoner. According to Sharp, the mutiny was led by John Cox and 70 men – but Cox's journal does not support this argument, calling Watling an usurper and nicknaming him 'Olliver' – a reference to Oliver Cromwell who usurped the crown of England. However the change came about, the new admiral was Watling, and the buccaneers decided to return to Arica and capture that town. An old Indian was captured and told Watling that Arica was well defended with thirteen copper cannon – but strangely, Watling refused to tell the crew what the Indian had said, and had the Indian shot. Consequently, when some ninety buccaneers attacked Arica in January 1681, there was a bitter fight, and they failed to capture the Spanish fortress in the town despite superhuman efforts. Watling was killed, along with twenty-seven others. Seventeen buccaneers were also wounded, leaving just forty-seven fit men to fight off 1,200 Spanish soldiers. The ships' surgeons were also left behind at Arica, either because they were drunk, or were occupied treating the wounded. Somehow the rest of the party reached their canoes and then got back onboard 'with heavy hearts to think we should leave so much Plate behind us…'[26]

Predictably, once more dissension reigned over who should become the new admiral of the buccaneers. John Cox complained that 'ye former disconters had not forgotten their old trade, but were every day for a new Broome…' There was also a severe water shortage, so the buccaneers agreed first to stand in to the shore for water, so 'that contented them for a while…' With a lack of seasoned leaders, the buccaneers voted Sharp in as their admiral once again, and the party returned to the Isle of Plate (off Peru, at the same latitude as the Galapagos Islands). The island was so called because Drake was thought to have divided up his treasure there. Here the buccaneers split up for the last time, with forty-five men refusing to serve under Sharp, including William Dampier, and Lionel Wafer, a surgeon. These forty-five men took one ship and two canoes and returned to cross the Isthmus of Panama. Meanwhile, the now much depleted group of buccaneers sailed south again in the *Trinity* under the command of Sharp, who redeemed himself somewhat, for they first captured a Spanish ship carrying 37,000 pieces of eight, and shared out the treasure, and then shortly after captured the Spanish ship *Santa Rosario*. Out of this ship the buccaneers took out much plate and linen and pieces of eight, but ignored 700 pigs of lead or tin 'not being able to pefswade our men to take in those pigs…' These pigs of lead or tin turned out to be silver, which the buccaneers missed, but they still managed to prevent the captain of the *Rosario* from throwing overboard a very valuable set of Spanish maps (called derroteros) of every Spanish port along the Pacific coast. Ringrose also reported in passing that the captain's wife was one of the most beautiful women he had ever seen in the South Seas.[27]

Now the *Trinity* headed south to the Straits of Magellan, where it seems that the African slaves onboard tried to revolt but were informed upon, and so failed. These slaves were simply kept onboard, as John Cox wrote, 'to do our worke…' The *Trinity* rounded the Cape and turned north toward the Caribbean. Along the way, on Christmas Day 1681, Sharp, still unpopular, apparently even feared for his life at this time, and therefore handed out three jars of wine to each mess, which did the trick. John Cox reported that the men killed a hog and a spaniel dog for their Christmas dinner and had much wine. Finally, the *Trinity* reached Barbados in January 1682. Unfortunately, the Royal Navy frigate *Richmond* was there, which frightened the buccaneers away, so they headed for Antigua. Here the governor of

Antigua refused permission for the crew to land. Consequently the buccaneers gave the *Trinity* to seven of their number who had lost all their money
gambling – a very common pirate problem – and everyone else then 'shifted
for himself'. Sharp and Cox returned to England, where they were tried for
piracy, but escaped the noose by presenting their carefully prepared journals
to the king, Charles II, and especially because of the value of the Spanish
maps they had captured onboard the *Rosario*. These maps or derroteros were
secret and very valuable, and it is surmised that Charles II arranged to fix
the trials in favour of Sharp and Cox because of the information they gave
the Crown. Sharp does not seem to have learned his lesson, since he partici-
pated in other piratical activities in the Caribbean and faced another piracy
trial on Nevis in 1687. With the probable connivance of the governor he
was freed, and perhaps even became governor of Anguilla. But in 1688 he
was sentenced to life in prison by the Danes on St Thomas, and there he
died sometime after 1699, crippled, and short of money.[28]

The 1680–1682 South Seas voyage was notable for friction among the
buccaneers, and for the several participants who wrote about their adventure,
including the well known authors William Dampier and Lionel Wafer. The
voyage did produce a sizeable number of pieces of eight for those who persisted to the end and did not lose it all gambling, while the buccaneers did
cause a considerable amount of bloodshed along the way. Drake and Morgan
had shown the way, but this new South Seas piracy revealed that while the
Spanish could not defend the whole Pacific coastline, they usually had good
intelligence about the buccaneers, and the larger towns were usually well
defended, although smaller towns, ports, and Spanish ships, were vulnerable.

Second Wave of South Seas Piracy

No sooner had the South Seas voyage finished than a second wave of South
Seas piracy descended on the Pacific coast when Dampier, Wafer, Edward
Davis and William Cowley, among many others, sailed from Virginia on the
Revenge in August 1683. This ship was under the command of John Cook,
who himself had served under Coxon in the previous voyage. Some of this
voyage is vividly described in the journal of William Cowley, who often
remarked on a wide range of topics. For example, while at the Cape Verde
Islands, Cowley, in one of several comments on race, wrote that the inhabitants of St Nicholas Island were Portuguese, but looked black – yet 'a man

being in danger of his life that calls them Negroes.' Turning to an account of this second wave of buccaneers, they first sailed to the Cape Verde Islands in order to get a better ship for their adventure. The buccaneers initially took a Dutch slaver, but this was too small, with only eight guns. So the buccaneers sailed on for the Guinea coast, and amusingly, cut the cable of a ship at St Jago, and tried to tow it away, but then discovered that the ship contained 300 men, so left it hurriedly alone. The next ship they tried to take turned out to be a Royal Navy ship, and that was also best avoided. It was along the African coast, past Sierra Leone, that Cowley went ashore with the ship's doctor, when the local king offered his 'black women' to them. The doctor stayed for this invitation, but Cowley casually remarked that he did not appreciate his woman because 'I did not like her hide.' However, it was near here that the buccaneers did manage to capture another slaver, this one Danish, and a bigger ship, with thirty-six guns. This became their flagship and was renamed the *Batchelor's Delight*. The reason for this name may have been because there were sixty female slaves onboard.[29]

Next, the buccaneers sailed around Cape Horn in a storm, which drove them far south, before meeting up with another pirate ship commanded by John Eaton. They agreed to co-operate and in March 1684 the small fleet sailed for the Juan Fernandez Islands, where Cowley noted that the captain sowed carrot, chive, and garden seeds, as well as boiled Brussels sprouts! Notably, the buccaneers came across the Moskito Indian William the Striker, who had been inadvertently marooned on the islands by Sharp nearly three years earlier. Cowley reported that the Spanish had left a plate on the island engraved with the message that they had courageously and violently chased away Captain Sharp. Yet William the Striker survived:

> This fellow had been hunted by the Spanish – he having nothing but Goates' skins to cover himself when we came there, he having been there alone neare three yeares, seeing no man in that time but those Spanish that had chased him with Doggs, he cutt his Gunn in pieces for Instruments to take ffifh [fish] and Goats.

Cowley and the others were obviously much impressed with William's survival skills, and were happy to rescue him. Now it was time for the serious business of pirating, yet here there came a hitch because the Spanish, as usual, had good intelligence on the buccaneers' arrival, together with other English pirates on the Pacific coast, and had sent 'expresses' to warn the entire coast line. The buccaneers learnt of this situation through the capture of small coastal ships, and quickly realised there was no point in attacking any major town or port.[30]

Keeping far off the coast to escape notice, the buccaneers sailed for the Galapagos Islands, although the Spanish prisoners onboard laughed and said that these islands were the Enchanted Isles and were not real. Despite this, Cowley as ship's navigator steered accurately to the islands, sailing down the latitude. On the Galapagos, Cowley observed the very large turtles and the friendly birds. The former paid dearly for their excellent meat by being easily captured and stored on the ships for future consumption. The buccaneers now sailed toward the mainland, but along the way Captain John Cook died at sea, so the buccaneers took him ashore for Christian burial, and elected Edward Davis as captain in his place. After several frustrated attempts at finding targets to raid, the two captains could not agree on future plans, and Captain Eaton decided to leave for the East Indies to make a voyage – meaning, to succeed in piracy. This created a crisis for Cowley, who wrote that he wanted to escape from the slavery on Davis' ship (as navigator he did not have the assistance of a mate), and therefore wanted to go onboard Eaton's ship, and asked Eaton to defend him. Cowley also believed that Eaton feared a mutiny on his ship because Davis' ship was bigger and offered better accommodation than Eaton's ship. There was therefore a competition for men, as Davis tried to lure Eaton's men onboard his ship, and especially the surgeon. Perhaps all this was simply justification for Cowley's desire to go pirating to the Indies, and abandoning Davis' ship. On the other hand, according to William Dampier, Davis and his men were the experienced buccaneers, while Eaton's men were just young beginners, and so the two captains could not agree on the future division of treasure, because Davis demanded the larger percentage of the take.[31] In the end, Eaton, with Cowley onboard, sailed for the Indies, while Davis and Dampier, and their crew onboard the *Batchelor's Delight*, headed for Peru.

Davis/Dampier, the Batchelor's Delight and Swan's the Cygnet

Looking first at the voyage of the *Batchelor's Delight*, this Davis/Dampier ship met up with another marauding ship, the *Cygnet*, commanded by Charles Swan. Together they raided the two towns of Paita and Guayaquil, getting little from the first, and some seventy slaves from the second. Then the small fleet sailed toward Panama again, hoping to intercept the valuable plate fleet that sailed from Lima to Panama with a fortune in pieces of eight and other treasure. This fleet only sailed once every three years, and, 1685 being the appropriate third year, ten pirate ships and about 1,000 men, both French and English, gathered in the Bay of Panama to try and intercept the Spanish plate fleet. Gaining intelligence from Spanish and Indian prisoners, the disparate group awaited the arrival of the Spanish fleet, although there were arguments over command, including an attempt to replace Davis with a tougher captain. This doubt about Davis' leadership skills turned out to be justified. When the Spanish fleet of fourteen ships hove into view, it was very well defended and carried some 3,000 men and 150 cannon. The French pirates refused to join the English buccaneers in a joint operation, while the English buccaneers, including Davis, did not feel strong enough to confront the Spanish fleet. The net result was a damp squib – the plate fleet sailed harmlessly into New Panama, and had in any case taken the precaution of unloading the treasure onshore before dealing with the buccaneers.[32]

Frustrated by this failure, the buccaneers split up, in one of the many break-ups that were always taking place amongst pirates. Dampier transferred to sail with Swan and the *Cygnet*, while Davis in the *Batchelor's Delight* decided to sail for home via the Straits of Magellan. Davis went on to a further successful career as a pirate, hauling in large sums of money on the coasts of Peru and Chile, perhaps as much as £100,000. Davis went home to New England, then was imprisoned in Virginia for his crimes, but was released, and finally settled in England in 1690. Davis still retained a fair amount of his booty intact in England, including three bags of Spanish coin, 142 pounds of broken silver, and some dirty linen. Davis continued his pirate career, and it was probably the same Edward Davis who met William Kidd at St Mary's Island in 1697, and sailed home with Kidd.[33]

Meanwhile, Swan and the crew of the *Cygnet* now attempted to track down another Spanish treasure fleet, this time the Manila galleons, which annually sailed between the Philippines and Acapulco, carrying trade goods and treasure to each destination. The *Cygnet* lay off Acapulco, but managed to miss the Manila galleon as the buccaneers happened to be onshore, hunting for food, as the galleon sailed past. Recriminations followed, and a subsequent raid onshore at Santa Pecaque only resulted in the death of fifty-four buccaneers, including the journal writer and pirate, Basil Ringrose. The death of Ringrose was doubly sad because he had not wanted to

continue the voyage, but felt compelled to do so due to poverty. The bodies of Ringrose and the others were 'stript, and so cut and mangl'd, that he
[Swan] scarce knew one man.' Following this further disaster, Swan and
Dampier opted to leave the South Seas and head for the East Indies, as
Cowley and Eaton had done earlier. Swan and Dampier managed to persuade their crew to pursue this journey, although Dampier first had to cure
himself of a tropical fever, which he achieved by being buried in hot sand
up to his neck for half an hour, in order to sweat out the fever. Happily the
cure worked, and the *Cygnet* set off for Guam, covering a tough 5,700 miles
in fifty-one days.[34]

By chance, another Manila galleon, sailing from Acapulco to Manila, with
a great deal of silver aboard, was now approaching Guam. The galleon was
warned off by the Spanish governor of Guam, yet as luck would have it, the
galleon got stuck on a sandbar nearby, and would have been a sitting duck
for the buccaneers had they pursued it. Here there arose a fatal rift between
the crew of the *Cygnet*, and Swan, who really wanted to be a trader and
not a pirate, and he refused to attack the Manila galleon. In fact, Swan said
of such an action, 'There is no prince on earth able to wipe off the Stain
of such Actions.' Consequently, the *Cygnet* sailed on to Mindanao, where
several months of feasting and drinking, plus Swan's autocratic behaviour,
brought about a final dissolution of the voyage. The result was that Swan
and some forty men chose to remain on Mindanao, while the majority of
some ninety buccaneers essentially took over the *Cygnet*, and elected to
sail onward. This continuing crew included Dampier, John Read, the new
captain of the *Cygnet*, who had been an old logwood cutter, and Josiah Teat,
the new master, who had accompanied the *Cygnet* from the Americas in
command of a small barque. This renewed voyage moved erratically in a
great sweep through the Philippines, to the South China Sea, then St John's
Island near Hong Kong, to the Pescadores, and back to Mindanao, where
they learned that Swan wanted to leave, although the *Cygnet*'s crew declined
to rescue him. Later, the crew found out that Swan was murdered before
he could leave Mindanao. Meanwhile, the *Cygnet* sailed on through the
Celebes, and finally reached New Holland, as Australia was then named.[35]

The *Cygnet* arrived on the north-west coast of New Holland, where
Dampier wrote down his impressions of the aboriginals. In his unpublished
manuscript, Dampier admired the aboriginals for their ability to survive
in an unpromising landscape. But in his published journal, Dampier saw
the aboriginals as 'the miserablest people in the world', differing 'little from

brutes'. They were 'long visaged and of a very unpleasing aspect, having no one graceful feature in their faces.' Their speech was a guttural noise like 'gurry, gurry', and they seemed to lack any curiosity about the buccaneers and their ship. The buccaneers spent two months in New Holland, then Read ordered the *Cygnet* careened, and when this was completed, the crew charted a course for the Cocos Islands, Sumatra and the Nicobar Islands. By this time Dampier was more than anxious to leave the *Cygnet*, since his naturalist interests were at odds with Read and most of the pirate crew. So Dampier confronted Read, and demanded to be set ashore, which was a buccaneer right. Read was angry, but consented because he thought that Dampier was far enough off the beaten track that he would not alert the authorities to the existence or course of the buccaneers. After arguments, Dampier and six others were set ashore on the Nicobar Islands, more or less marooned, with just an axe to trade. The *Cygnet* sailed on and left them to their fate in May 1688. Dampier and his companions then resolved to cross the rough 130 mile channel to Achin (Banda Aceh), on Sumatra's northern coast, where there was an East India Company factory. A nightmare voyage of five days and nights in an outrigger canoe caused Dampier to reflect on his life:

> I had a lingring View of approaching Death … and I must confess that my Courage, which I had hitherto kept up, failed me here; and I made very sad Reflections on my former Life, and look'd back with Horror and Detestation, on Actions which before I disliked, but now I trembled at the remembrance of. I had long before this repented me of that roving course of Life…

One can imagine that some of this repentance was for the benefit of his reading audience, but some of it seems genuine remorse for his buccaneering days.[36]

From this time on, for the next two years, Dampier served aboard trading vessels in the Indies and South Asia, and acted unhappily as a gunner for the East India Company fort in Sumatra. Dampier also acquired a half share in Jeoly, a tattooed Philippine prince, and eventually escaped from the fort to wind up back in England after an absence of twelve years. Along the way, in Achin, Dampier came across a member of the *Cygnet*'s crew who had deserted, and told Dampier that the ship had been pushed off course by monsoon winds which drove the *Cygnet* to the Coromandel Coast of India. Stories of what then happened to the buccaneers on the *Cygnet* vary. One version has half the crew deserting the *Cygnet* in India, some enlisting at an English fort, and others plundering the coastal villages. John Read took the *Cygnet* to the Bay of Bengal, where he took a rich prize in 1688, then left the *Cygnet*, and joined an American slave ship to sail back to New England. The crew of the *Cygnet* subsequently elected one James Smith as captain, and sailed on to Madagascar, where the *Cygnet* rotted at anchor, and the remaining crew joined the pirates on the island. A second version has Read losing half his crew on the Coromandel Coast of India, but then Read sailed away with the remaining crew to Madagascar. Here, Read joined a slave ship going to New York. At this point the *Cygnet* was turned over to Josiah Teat, formerly master of the *Cygnet*, who now became captain of the ship, and he also joined the Madagascar pirates. However, the *Cygnet* sank at her mooring at the port of St Augustine, Madagascar. A third version has the *Cygnet* arriving on the coast of Coromandel, India, where half the crew deserted to serve the Great Moghul of India. The rest, under Read, sailed to Madagascar, where Read and half a dozen of the crew went onboard a slaver bound for New York. Meanwhile, Josiah Teat took command of the *Cygnet*, but decided to abandon the ship and also serve the Great Moghul.[37]

William Cowley, John Eaton and the Nicholas

These complicated versions of the fate of the *Cygnet* do show some common themes of how the buccaneers tended to act according to their own particular interests. They often split up into smaller groups and into different ships according to inclination, like or dislike of captains and whether they had accumulated treasure, or gambled it away. Similarly, in a long voyage, few buccaneer crews had the discipline or leadership to stay together. In order to take another look at this phenomenon, it is worth while reverting to the story of William Cowley, who was last seen shifting from Davis' ship to join John Eaton's *Nicholas* as master, in the Gulf of St Michael.

Soon after joining the *Nicholas*, in October 1684, Cowley almost came to an untimely end. Going by small boat with seven others to get turtles and water on Lord Norris Island, in the Galapagos, the *Nicholas* was carried away by a current and thus basically marooned Cowley and his companions on Lord Norris Island. They caught fish, but there being no water on the island, Cowley and his shipmates moved on to Albemarle Island, which had turtles and birds but no water either. Trying to leave this island for King

James Island, the current forced them back. Here Cowley wrote that while he was cooking a large turtle the fire reminded him of Hell, and he had serious religious thoughts, just as Dampier did when faced with death. Cowley repented of his loose life, but unlike Dampier, Cowley had fearful visions of the fire and demons of Hell. At this moment, Cowley was suddenly faced with an aggressive sea lion, which he fought, and which he thought was a real devil. Recovering from this encounter, Dampier and his ship mates had just decided to sail to the Isle of Plata, some 500 miles away, when the buccaneers were delighted to see the *Nicholas* suddenly reappear. The marooned group got back onboard at 11p.m. at night, despite the heavy surf. Reunited, Eaton, Cowley and the crew of the *Nicholas* decided to commence sailing across the Pacific toward the Philippines in late December 1684, or early January 1685.[38]

Crossing the Pacific was always a voyage of extreme endurance, normally leading to a shortage of water and provisions. After some weeks, Cowley reported many cases of scurvy aboard, and how rats were caught on the ship, cooked, and given to the sick men to revive them. Soon all were sick and starving, but by mid March 1685, the ship reached Joanna Island, 8,600 miles from their starting point. Then it was on to the Ladrones Islands, the Marianas, known to Magellan as the island of thieves, where Cowley's crew fought with the Indians, whom he described as very large men. Apparently, four of the captured natives were brutally thrown into the water and shot. The *Nicholas* went on to Canton and Formosa, but captured few prizes except for a ship captained by a Greek, taken in April 1685, that yielded food and 2,000 pieces of eight. An Indian ship bound for Manila, captured in July 1885, produced only rice, and another ship heading for Japan, taken in September 1685, did have silks and velvet onboard, but no pieces of eight, because it would apparently be death for the crew if a single piece of eight was brought into Japan. It seems that the *Nicholas* also missed a Chinese junk carrying silver. A curious episode at the island of Sogo (Hong Kong Island) in the summer of 1685 had the crew assaulting the town, robbing the church of its plate, and taking away two Church Fathers, who they tried but failed to ransom. At this point, Cowley was relieved of his weapons, because he had become too friendly with the Church Fathers, and was suspected of running away with them. From now on Cowley watched for a place to leave the buccaneers, which he managed on 1 March 1686 at Timor. After this, he shipped onboard a Dutch ship, the *Sylida*, while Eaton and the *Nicholas* sailed past, bound for Batavia.[39]

Eaton and the *Nicholas* reached Indonesia in March 1686, and then they disappear from history, except that Eaton was alleged to have returned to England. Cowley meanwhile records his further adventures, calling in at the Cape of Good Hope (Bon Esperance), where four 'Hodmandods' (Hottentots) came aboard, which he described in another comment on race, as 'foul creatures'. At the end of June 1686, Cowley reported that he heard that Captain Davis was living in state at the court of the King of Siam with eighty Moors in attendance. In September 1688, Cowley was nearing Holland after some three and a half years voyaging, but nearly ended his life on the Lemon and Ore sands due to the captain's ignorance of the coast. At last, at the end of September 1686, Cowley came ashore in Holland, and reached London in October 1686. Later, in 1699, Cowley published the journal of his voyages, joining Dampier, Wafer and many others in publishing their journals for a public hungry to hear about the wider world and the exploits of the buccaneers.[40]

The Last Acts of the Buccaneers: Jamaican Laws; Port Royal Disappears, 1692; the Capture of Cartagena, 1697; and the War of the Spanish Succession 1701–1713

A number of events from the 1680s onward slowly turned the tide against the buccaneers of the Caribbean. In 1681 and 1683, anti-pirate legislation was passed in Jamaica, which at least for the moment turned would-be privateers into hunted pirates, and made the issuing of commissions more difficult. However, French and Dutch buccaneers, such as de Grammont and du Casse, continued to operate. Then in June 1692 a severe earthquake destroyed much of Port Royal, which was seen by some as a just retribution for the wild and ungodly life led by many of the inhabitants. First hand accounts of this earthquake are arresting – the Reverend Dr Emmanuel Heath was taking wine with the acting Governor of Jamaica, John White, when 'I found the ground rolling and moving under my feet, upon which I said, "Lord, sir, what is this?" White replied very composedly, being a very grave man: "It is an earthquake, be not afraid, it will soon be over."' However, it was not soon over, and there were later shocks, tidal waves, and a hurricane, as a result of which as many as 5,000 people perished. Other survivors saw 'whole streets sinking under water with men, women and children in them; and those houses which but just now appeared the fairest and loftiest in these parts were in a moment sunk down into the earth, and nothing to be seen of them.' More horrific was the vision of people whom 'the earth received up to their necks and then closed upon them and squeezed them to death with their heads above ground, many of which the dogs ate.'[41]

Another significant event was the sacking of the Spanish port of Cartagena (on the coast of modern Colombia) in 1697. Du Casse, French Governor of Santo Domingo (the western half of Hispaniola), and a former slaver, conceived of the idea of sacking Cartagena. He assembled some 700 buccaneers, plus Africans and locals, to a full number of some 1,000 men. But back in France, a certain Baron de Pointis, an experienced naval captain, got wind of the project, and decided to take it over. He appealed to Louis XIV, who placed him in charge, and so along with another 4,000 soldiers and sailors, and a small fleet, de Pointis sailed for Santo Domingo. Naturally, du Casse and de Pointis became bitter enemies, especially since du Casse and his independent minded buccaneers were ordered to submit to the orders of de Pointis. Somehow the two men and assorted buccaneers and French soldiers and sailors managed to co-operate sufficiently so that in the spring of 1697, the force combined landings and sea-based bombardments to capture a series of forts that guarded the narrow entrance to the Bay of Cartagena. These forts also guarded the city of Cartagena itself, yet each fort, isolated from its neighbouring forts, and low in morale, surrendered easily enough to the French attackers. Then the French assaulted the walls of Getsemani, the outer fort of the city of Cartagena. The French employed six very large mortars, hurling balls of twenty and thirty-six pounds, and a breach was quickly created. Du Casse, who had been wounded in a previous attack, personally led the buccaneers in a wild assault that captured the fort. De Pointis, who was himself wounded in the stomach, was very grudging in his comments on du Casse's leadership, saying unkindly that du Casse was not so 'nimble as the rest, despite all his good will, du Casse had so much trouble to climb it that he was out of breath by the time he got to the top, where he thought he should never recover his wind.'[42]

Now the French faced the city of Cartagena itself. Thinking rationally, the Spanish governor thought that little would be gained by defending the city, so he accepted an offer from de Pointis for the citizens to march out of the city with their personal possessions and not be harmed. Likewise, the churches of Cartagena were to be spared. So on 6 May 1697, the Spanish garrison and citizens left Cartagena in solemn procession, but the agreement did not extend to the treasure of Cartagena. In this regard, de Pointis

81 'An attack on a galleon.' Pirates did sometimes attack in small boats, and often from the stern of their target. Surprise was also always a useful weapon.

82 'Capture of the galleon.' This scene represents the occasion when Pierre Le Grand and his crew captured a Spanish galleon in 1665, and surprised the Spanish officers playing cards below decks.

83 'On the Tortugas.' Henry Pitman, perhaps the model for Robinson Crusoe, was stranded on Salt Tortuga Island with others in 1687. Salt Tortuga lies off the coast of Venezuela.

84 'Marooned.' Many pirates and their victims were marooned, the most famous being Alexander Selkirk, who was marooned on the Juan Fernandez Islands from 1704 to 1709.

85 'Walking the plank.' Very few pirates made their victims walk the plank. After all, wasn't it simpler to just throw the victims overboard? Possibly this myth came from the practice of pirates in the Roman era, who invited their captives to walk home.

86 'Buried treasure.' William Kidd did have John Gardiner bury most of Kidd's treasure on Gardiner's Island, Long Island Sound, in 1699. The treasure was shortly afterwards dug up and sent to Lord Bellomont in Boston after Kidd was arrested.

87 'Who shall be Captain?' Pirate captains were almost always elected by popular vote of the pirate crew, and did not fight to become captain. But pirates did sometimes fight each other.

88 'The bullets were humming and singing, clipping along the top of the water.'

89 'The Buccaneer was a picturesque fellow.' The Buccaneers of the seventeenth century were a very rough looking crew, unlike this individual. Buccaneers were usually based on Hispaniola and Tortuga, and lived by hunting wild cattle and hogs, before turning to piracy.

90 'Then the real fight began.' This picture depicts a mutiny, when some sailors decide to take over a ship. Usually there would be two or three ringleaders, then others would be signed up, and a signal would be agreed to start the mutiny – normally a password, or a cannon ball rolled over the deck.

91 'Captain Keitt.' A romantic and unrealistic image of a pirate captain. Many pirate captains started off as a mate or another senior position on a merchant ship before becoming a pirate. Only a few pirate captains, such as Bart Roberts, lasted more than a year or two.

92 Capt Edward England. A sketch of the pirate Edward England. He was reported to be kind hearted, and did not abuse his prisoners. He was removed as captain by his crew, and spent his final days in poverty and repentance at St Mary's Island, Madagascar.

Above: 93 Anne Bonny and Mary Read. These two women served as part of the crew on 'Calico' Jack Rackam's ship. There were extremely few female pirates in the West, so they gained considerable fame. They were captured along with the rest of Rackam's crew, and condemned to death. But both were pregnant, and so were spared the noose.

Below: 94 Capt Bart Roberts. Roberts was one of the most successful pirate captains, taking around 400 ships. He also managed to remain as captain for some four years, before being killed in 1722 on the coast of West Africa. Roberts was unusual in maintaining discipline on his ships, and was reportedly a non drinker.

Above left: 95 Captain George Lowther. Lowther is shown watching as his ship is careened. This was a difficult task in which the ship was heeled over, and the barnacles and weed scraped and burnt off the hull. Unfortunately for Lowther, his ship was taken in 1723 as it was being careened. Lowther escaped into the jungle where he was found dead with a pistol by his side.

Above right: 96 Captain Edward Low. An appropriate image of Edward Low, his twisting body reflecting his twisted personality. Low was an unusually cruel pirate captain, often torturing and killing his captives. He seems to have been an unbalanced individual, but he was caught and hung by the French in 1726.

97 'Henry Morgan recruiting for the attack.'

98 'Morgan at Porto Bello.'

99 'The sacking of Panama.' A romantic vision of the ruthless sacking of Panama in 1671 by Henry Morgan and his buccaneers.

Above: 100 'Blackbeard buries his treasure.' Blackbeard was rumoured to have buried his treasure on or near Mulberry Island, Chesapeake Bay. If he did, it has not yet been found.

Left: 101 Captain Teach. A portrait of Blackbeard. According to Captain Charles Johnson, Blackbeard did have a long, bushy beard, and he did set fire to lighted matches under his hat, and he did carry three brace of pistols in bandoliers.

Above left: 102 Captain Avery. A portrait of the pirate Henry Avery or Every. Avery was also called Long Ben, meaning that he was unusually tall. The picture relates to Avery's greatest feat in taking two very valuable ships from India. One of these ships did belong to the Moghul emperor of India, Aurangzeb.

Aboove right: 103 'Kidd at Gardiner's Island.'

104 The *Royal Ann*. A typical Royal Navy first rate. Rates were measured by the number of guns they carried – a first rate carried from 80 to 110 guns. The large crew of 780 men was required mainly to work the guns. These ships were not useful for chasing pirates because they were slow sailors, and could not enter rivers or go close to land.

105 The Captain's bridge protected by a grill against Chinese pirates in the 1920s and 30s.

106 Anti-pirate guard ready for action against Chinese pirates in the 1920s and 30s.

107 Lai Choi San. A well known female Chinese pirate in the 1920s, who commanded a fleet of 11 junks. She was to be obeyed, and obeyed she was.

108 Lai Choi San had singled out a large black junk with three yellow sails.

109 Lai Choi San's junk ready for action.

110 Two men bound hand and foot on Lai Choi San's junk after action.

111 Some distance to starboard lay the sinking junk – a victim of Lai Choi San.

112 Houses in the pirate lair of Bias Bay, near Hong Kong.

113 The house of torture in Bias Bay, the pirate lair near Hong Kong.

Avove left: 114 The powder magazine onboard Lai Choi San's junk.

Above right: 115 A typical pirate onboard Lai Choi San's junk.

cleverly decreed that the Spanish owners could keep 1/10th of their treasure if openly declared, and could keep 1/10th of any other treasure they knew about. A very large sum was raised by this means, eight million livres said de Pointis, twenty million livres said du Casse. This was all stowed away on the French naval ships, and then de Pointis offered the buccaneers some 40,000 livres instead of the 1.6 million to four million livres they were expecting. Complacently, de Pointis called the buccaneers mere banditti, 'the greatest part of them idle spectators of a great action.' De Pointis then sailed away for Santo Domingo and France, leaving du Casse and the buccaneers extremely angry. Du Casse and some buccaneers resolved to appeal to Louis XIV, but others decided to return to Cartagena and extort what they could from the unfortunate citizens, which turned out to be another five million livres or so.[43]

De Pointis' ships and the treasure made it back to France through several inept English fleets, while du Casse in France managed to win a settlement of 1.4 million francs to be distributed among the buccaneers. Predictably, little of this settlement got through to the buccaneers, while on their way back from Cartagena, the buccaneers had run into a number of English ships which separated the buccaneers from most of their hard won treasure. Finally, in September 1697, Spain, England and Holland signed the Treaty of Ryswick, which among other things, allowed these countries to pursue and suppress the buccaneers of the Caribbean. Those buccaneers who survived were then glad enough to be employed in legal ways during the widespread war of the Spanish Succession (1701–1713), at least until the Treaty of Utrecht in 1713 and the subsequent peace released yet another wave of pirates. But as far as the classic buccaneers were concerned, Cartagena was the last act of their unruly and adventurous careers.

Now the pirate story passes to the Madagascar men and their pirate lair on the island of St Mary's.

The Madagascar Men

In the 1690s, a number of pirates sailed to Madagascar and the Red Sea, hoping to capture the rich Muslim ships carrying pilgrims to and from Mecca, and to fleece the wealthy trading ships sailing to and from India. The Red Sea was also attractive because it provided easier pickings than the Caribbean. In June 1692 a ship from New York, the Jacob, captured four Red Sea ships and a great deal of treasure. The crew returned to New York via Madagascar in 1693, and news of the riches to be gained in the Red Sea spread. Soon, the Governor and Deputy Governor of Rhode Island were issuing suspect commissions to privateers, who evidently aimed to cash in on this treasure trove. Thus William Mayes, Thomas Wake and Thomas Tew all sailed for the Red Sea from Rhode Island, although Thomas Tew did not have a commission. These three joined Henry Avery at the Red Sea in 1695, with Avery as admiral of the small fleet, and subsequently these ships made a huge haul of treasure in the Red Sea. However, it was Thomas Tew who was particularly successful in his earlier voyage, taking a Muslim ship, so that the crew returned from the Red Sea and Madagascar to Rhode Island in April 1694, with £100,000 in gold, silver and elephant's teeth (ivory), which were sold to merchants in Boston.[1] In fact, John Banks of Rhode Island, who had a commission to sail in the Black Barke in 1694, declared that the Red Sea via Madagascar was known as a place 'where the money was as plenty as stones, and sand, saying the people there was Infidels, and it was no sin to kill them. Captain Thomas Tew about or near a year before coming hither with a mighty Mass of money…'[2]

Many of these pirates did come back from the Red Sea as rich men, for example a group of fifteen pirates from the Avery fleet arrived back in the Americas in 1696, and were now worth '£1,000 a man.'[3] Now it became apparent that Madagascar was an essential headquarters for those who raided in the Red Sea because it was a very convenient geographic location for them to refit and replenish with food and water, as well as enjoy rest and recreation. The main pirate stopping place was the island of St. Marie, off the north-east corner of Madagascar, known to the pirates as St Mary's. It was known that two agents of the wealthy New York merchant, Frederick Phillips, were operating to supply the pirates who stopped there, although pretending to actually trade in slaves. (In fact, there was also a lively slave trade going on at St Mary's.) The two agents were called Captain Adam Baldridge (he had previously killed a man in Jamaica, and then turned pirate around 1685, before landing up on Madagascar), and Lawrence Johnson. Baldridge and Johnson married local women on St Mary's, and exercised considerable power over the locals, while guarding themselves by building a fort with twenty-two guns. Other reports suggested the fort had forty or fifty guns and 1,500 men, with seventeen ships in harbour. Nevertheless, the happy time at St Mary's for the pirates nearly ended in the late 1690s when the local natives rebelled, destroyed the fort, and killed seven English men and four French men.[4]

Despite the troubles at St. Mary's, Madagascar continued to be a haunt of the pirates. A good example was the pirate Derick or Dirk Chivers, a Dutchman, who was elected captain of the ship *Resolution*. Chivers changed the name of his ship to *Soldado* (meaning 'soldier', perhaps a more militant name), and with his crew took four merchant ships in Calcutta harbour in 1696. Chivers demanded a ransom of £10,000 for their release, and when payment was not forthcoming, he hoisted 'bloody colours' and burnt two of the ships. Some of his pirates went ashore to expedite the ransom, and declared that they had no country – in fact had sold their country – and were sure to be hanged if taken. Thus they 'would take no quarter, but do all the mischief possible they could.' Chivers told the authorities in Calcutta that most of the pirates in the Red Sea area came from New York and had recently shared £700 each in New York after a recent voyage, and had sold their ship to the Governor of New York for £1,000. A short time later, some of the crew offered the Governor of New York £2,000 for the same ship, intending to go plundering again. As for Chivers' ransom demand at Calcutta, this was still not paid due to a fleet of Indian ships coming into harbour, so Chivers retreated to St Mary's in 1697 to refit the *Soldado*. The next year, Chivers and another pirate ship, the *Mocha Frigate*, under Robert Culliford, captured a huge prize, the *Great Mohammed*, worth at least £130,000. The plundering of the *Great Mohammed*, a pilgrim ship, was not pretty, with considerable torture and rape: the pirates 'ravished sixty women in ye most beastly barbarous manner…' according to one witness. Then both pirate ships returned to St Mary's in 1699. Later, when the Royal Navy arrived at St Mary's, the commander, Captain Littleton, offered Chivers, Culliford, and the other pirates a royal pardon, which they mostly accepted. Culliford was nevertheless tried in London, since his pardon was declared not valid, but he turned state's witness, and was happy to disappear into the back streets of London. Chivers himself died in a Bombay prison on his way to London.[5]

The Madagascar system was explained by an informant writing from Dublin in 1696. He reported that the pirate Thomas Tew pretended to load slaves at Madagascar, but his real intent was to go to the Red Sea to catch prizes. Tew and others would stop at Madagascar for victuals and water, and then it was on to Bab el Mandeb in the mouth of the Red Sea to wait for the traders who sailed from Surat and Madras in India at certain times because of the trade winds. Then they would take their ill gotten gains back to St Mary's, and on to New England 'where they have all been kindly received'. This last referred to New England governors and deputy governors who could be bribed, such as Walter Clarke, John Cranston and John Green of Rhode Island, Benjamin Fletcher of New York, and Cadwallader Jones and Nicholas Trott of the Bahamas.[6]

Bring the Pirates of Madagascar Home!

The reputation of St Mary's gained almost mythical status, suggesting the pirates and traders on the island had accumulated huge riches. Hence, an advice from the East India Company, dated November 1697, contained more information about St Mary's, exaggerating the number of pirates on the island and their wealth, but closed with the proposal that the pirates of Madagascar would accept a pardon if offered one. If the pardon was granted, 'they would leave that Villainous way of living, and return to their habitations.'[7] Some pirates did genuinely accept pardons, but this sense of large numbers of pirates on St Mary's, possessing very great wealth, stimulated very considerable interest in England in the early 1700s. Indeed, a popular ballad of the time went as follows:

> Where is the trader of London town?
> His gold's on the capstan
> His blood's on his gown
> And it's up and away for St. Mary's Bay
> Where the liquor is good and the lasses are gay.

Not surprisingly, therefore, petitions and proposals concerning St Mary's flooded in to Parliament and the Crown. These all pretended to be concerned with the threat posed by the Madagascar pirates, but the proposals were even more focused on the riches and treasure supposedly possessed by the pirates. In 1708, the Earl of Morton and the Honorable Charles Egerton, and others, petitioned the Queen for a chance to bring the pirates of Madagascar home, bringing their riches with them. Most of these riches would be paid to the Queen, but some treasure was preserved for the pirates themselves, and of course Morton and Egerton were to be trustees of this transaction. Then, in 1708, in conjunction with the Morton and Egerton petition, came a strange but compelling appeal from the wives and female relations of the wealthy pirates of Madagascar. These ladies wanted the Queen to allow the pirates to come home, and to permit the pirates to keep their wealth, but to share the wealth with the undersigned women. The petition was signed by some forty-five women and one or two men. (It is curious that the first name on the women's petition was that of Mary Read. She was illiterate and therefore signed her name with a mark. It is just possible that this was the same Mary Read who eventually sailed with 'Calico' Jack Rackam.) It seems that these women were signed up for this project by the supporters of one John Breholt, who in turn was supported by the previously mentioned Egerton and Morton. Breholt hoped to sign up the wives and relations of the chief pirates of Madagascar, and especially the wife of Captain Avery, whom Breholt thought 'might be very useful to them…' The incentive for these women was that they would be offered a share in the proceeds of the undertaking.

However, a deposition by one of these women, Penelope Aubin, stated that she had serious doubts about the undertaking, and advised Egerton to quit the affair. She therefore did not sign the petition. But certain other women who did sign the petition (Elizabeth Woodford, Barbara Ramsey and Ann Rupert) declared that Breholt offered them shares in the undertaking. All these women had taken part in a large meeting at the King's Head Inn in the Strand, London, which Morton, Egerton and other gentlemen attended. Breholt claimed to have ships ready for the expedition, and a pardon for the pirates of Madagascar, which would be produced by Morton. One of the women who signed the petition, Elizabeth Woodford, claimed in her deposition that her son-in-law was indeed one of the pirates on Madagascar.[8]

Central to these plans to capture a share of the wealth of the pirates of Madagascar was John Breholt. In June 1709, he was named in a letter to the Court of St James. Breholt was apparently trying to take advantage of delays in suppressing the pirates of Madagascar 'for want of shipping', and was therefore preparing the previously mentioned project in order to go where 'ye pyrates reside', namely Madagascar. John Breholt was possibly the same Breholt who earlier commanded a ship called the *Carlisle*, which was a privateer turned pirate. This Breholt was reportedly taken by Captain George Martin of the Royal Navy in 1700 at St Augustine, Madagascar, and claimed a pardon, although Martin stated that Breholt was since dead, and also called him George rather than John Breholt. Perhaps Martin was mistaken.[9] In any case, the promoter of the 1708-1709 undertaking, John Breholt, was unmasked by Lawrence Waldron, a barber surgeon, who in 1700 had sailed with John Breholt in the *Carlisle*. According to Waldron, he signed on with John Breholt, expecting to sail to England from the Carolinas. But once at sea, Breholt declared that the ship would go to Madagascar to pirate and make their fortune. However, Breholt and his crew were captured by the Spanish and incarcerated in Lisbon. No act of piracy being found against them, they were released after a year, and came to England, where Breholt and some comrades organized a fake scheme to find a ship wreck and take the treasure out of it. This scheme involved Lord Fairfax, and then Breholt organized a second fraudulent scheme to find a similar ship wreck, which involved Lord Rivers and other gentlemen. It is clear that John Breholt's scheme with Morton, Egerton and the supposed female relatives of the pirates was of the same fraudulent kind. Breholt's *modus operandi* was obviously to involve the naïve aristocracy, exploit their funds and respectability, and thus spring him to run away with the ships provided, and then go pirating again to Madagascar.[10]

Breholt's 1709 plan did not succeed, but it certainly worried the next promoter, the Marquis of Carmarthen. Carmarthen wrote a memorial to the Queen, complaining accurately enough of Breholt's 'pernicious design' to trade with the pirates of Madagascar, which plan had drawn in men of quality, but he asserted that Breholt's real plan was to run away with the ships and goods involved, and join with the pirates.[11] It did not take Carmarthen long to produce his own schemes for the Queen, which were either a plan to bring the pirates of Madagascar home with their wealth, giving a tenth part to the Queen, and allowing Carmarthen a share; or a far more ambitious plan to raid the French island of Reunion and the Arab kingdom of Muscat. This second plan would use the pardoned pirates of Madagascar to support the raid, which also required the Queen to provide five Royal Navy ships with Carmarthen as commander. Carmarthen also felt compelled to fend off the rival plans of the East India Company as well as Breholt's proposals.[12] It is relevant that Carmarthen's plans were no doubt influenced by his very considerable indebtedness, which, according to the diary of his father, the Duke of Leeds, amounted to the startling sum of £12,000.[13] Needless to say, Carmarthen's plan did not gain approval either, although he was soon involved in the war of the Spanish Succession as a naval commander, and managed to bring two Swedish ships as prizes into Portsmouth in 1710, which no doubt helped his financial condition.[14]

Henry Avery (Active 1693–1695)

Breholt's mention, above, of Captain Avery's wife, draws attention to the most successful Red Sea and Madagascar pirate of his time. Henry Avery or Every, had been chief mate aboard a navy ship, but, in 1693, was appointed chief mate of the *Charles II*, which, along with four other ships, was waiting at the port of Corunna to take part in an expedition to the Americas. The main idea of this expedition was to salvage valuable ship wrecks in Spanish American waters, but the Spanish authorities refused permission for the promoter of the expedition, Sir James Houblon, to carry on with the voyage. The net result was that, as the fleet waited at Corunna, wages were not paid, and food and necessities were very scarce. So Avery, who was an impressively tall and obviously capable leader, led a mutiny on 7 May 1694. The watchword for the mutiny was ironic, 'Is your drunken boatswain onboard?' The mutiny was easily undertaken and the *Charles II* sailed away from Corunna. As the ship sailed out to sea, the noise awoke the captain of the *Charles II*, Gibson, who was sick in his cabin. In a fright, Gibson asked Avery, 'Something's the matter with the ship, does she drive? What weather is it?' Avery coolly told him of the mutiny, 'I am bound to Madagascar with a design of making my own fortune and that of all the brave fellows joined with me.' Avery offered the captain a choice: join the mutiny, or be put ashore in a boat. Gibson chose to go ashore with some fourteen or fifteen others, and the *Charles II* sailed on, carrying 40 guns, a formidable amount of fire power, and some eighty men.[15]

Avery apparently did not tell the rest of the crew his real design for the voyage until the day after sailing, when the ship was 'abt. 20 or 30 Leagues' out to sea. It turned out that Avery's real intention, as he told the former captain, was to go via Madagascar to the Red Sea.[16] The crew accepted the plan, and the *Charles II*, now renamed the *Fancy*, quickly turned to piracy. Three English ships were taken at the Isle of May in the Cape Verde Islands, mainly for provisions, and nine sailors from their crews joined the *Fancy*, giving the pirate ship an establishment of ninety-four men. Then it was on to the Guinea coast of Africa, where the *Fancy* lured thirteen natives aboard, robbed them, and made them slaves. In addition two Danish ships were taken on the Guinea coast, producing elephants' teeth (ivory) and eight or nine ounces of gold per man. Here fourteen of the Danes joined Avery's crew. Then it was on to Madagascar, where the pirates watered, and sailed on to the island of Johanna (Anjouan). Here the *Fancy* plundered a Moorish ship, and later a French pirate, out of which forty men joined them. Now Avery's crew numbered some 170 men, about the right number for a pirate system that relied on boarding for success. Of these, 104 were English, 14 were Danes, and 52 were French. The slaves evidently did not count. Finally, the *Fancy* arrived at the Red Sea, but doubled back to Johanna when the winds were contrary, and then again set out for the Red Sea.[17]

On its way back to the Red Sea, the *Fancy* sailed along what the crew called the Ethiopian coast. When the inhabitants of a town called Mayd refused to trade with them, the crew 'burnt the town and blew up the Church…' Despite this, the *Fancy* lay there for about a month, and then headed again to the mouth of the Red Sea, and specifically to what was then called Babs Key or Rogues Island (Bab el Mandeb). There the *Fancy* was eventually joined by five other pirate ships, including one captained by Thomas Tew. Avery was elected commander of this fleet, possibly because the *Fancy* was the ship with the most cannon and men onboard (now 184 men). The ships waited for the Muslim merchant and pilgrim fleet to come down from Mocha (a port at the mouth of the Red Sea), on its way to India, which usually happened in late August and September due to the prevailing winds. However, after waiting for a month, a small captured grab (a galley) informed the pirates that the Mocha fleet had passed in the night. Avery and some of the pirate ships chased the Mocha fleet and caught up with one Muslim ship, the *Fateh Mohammed*, at the Cape of St John. This ship offered little or no resistance, and the pirates took out of her £50,000 to £60,000 of treasure. Then the pirates overhauled another huge Muslim ship, which they named the *Gunsway* (*Ganj-i-Sawai*). As it happened this ship belonged to the Moghul emperor, Aurangzeb, and was variously described as being of seventy guns and 600 or 700 men; or forty guns and 800 men, including passengers; or seventy guns and 1,000 men. This ship put up a stronger fight, and if it really did only have forty guns, would have been outgunned by the *Fancy* and another pirate ship, the *Pearl* (William Mayes captain). According to different witnesses the fight took either three hours, or two hours, or an hour and a half, and ended as Avery's crew boarded the *Gunsway*, assisted by the *Pearl*. The only man not to board the *Gunsway* was Avery himself. Huge amounts of gold and silver came out of the *Gunsway*, as well as many jewels, and a particular saddle and bridle designed as a gift for Aurangzeb, which was set with rubies. More treasure was unearthed as several members of the *Gunsway* were put to the torture to confess where their wealth was hidden. In addition, the pirates raped the women onboard, who were often of high caste status.[18]

As a result of this haul from the *Gunsway* and previous captures, the pirates netted between £800 and £1,000 per man. After disposing of some of the treasure locally, the *Fancy* headed back toward the West Indies, although Avery had to withstand a mutiny near Brazil over the destination of the ship. Some pirates were put ashore on the island of Reunion, and the *Fancy* eventually sailed into New Providence in the Bahamas in March or April 1695, where the Governor, Nicholas Trott, was known to be receptive to pirates. The crew of the *Fancy* gave Trott 20 pieces of eight and 2 sequins (a gold coin) per man, as well as the ship itself, so Trott permitted the *Fancy* and crew to come ashore and stay in two houses. One night a pirate broke a glass in one house and was made to pay 8 sequins for it by Trott! Following this, the remaining crew of the *Fancy* split up, with many remaining in the Americas, including Joseph Morris, who was 'left mad at Providence losing all his Jewels upon a wager', and Edward Short, who was killed by a shark. Avery himself and a few others arranged transport to Ireland, and thence to England. The authorities in England tracked down a number of the crew of the *Fancy*, and managed to hang five of them, besides persuading several to turn state's evidence. Yet Avery disappeared. To help his escape, he changed his name to John Bridgeman, and was believed by John Dann, a fellow crew member, to be headed for Devon, since Avery was a Plymouth man. John Dann also came across the wife of Avery's quartermaster boarding a coach at St. Albans, saying that she was going to meet up with Avery, but she naturally refused to say where she was heading. It seems equally possible that Avery was actually hiding in London, the easiest place to disappear because of its large population. Also, since St. Albans is north of London, presumably the coach was travelling from St. Albans to London. Either way, according to Captain Johnson, Avery tried to sell his jewels to some Bristol merchants, but was cheated, and died in poverty in Bideford, Devon. There is a moralistic quality to the supposed end of this Madagascar and Red Sea man, which seems a little unlikely for such a careful pirate.[19]

William Kidd (1654–1701)

Another famous visitor to Madagascar was William Kidd. He had been given commissions in London to capture pirates and French ships, the latter since England was at war with France when the commissions were issued in 1695. Kidd formed a financial agreement with several extremely prominent politicians in London to build a vessel, the *Adventure Galley*, to pursue these commissions. One of these politicians was Lord Bellomont, later governor of Massachusetts. However, a disappointing voyage frustrated Kidd's crew, and Kidd was faced with near mutiny at times. At one point Kidd quelled what he thought was mutinous behaviour by smashing a bucket on the head of his gunner, William Moore, calling him a 'Lousie Dog', and unintentionally killing him. At another point, Kidd sailed into a fleet of Muslim pilgrim ships at the entrance to the Red Sea, but was seen off by an East India Company ship, the *Sceptre*. Later, Kidd's *Adventure Galley* did capture two valuable merchant ships off India that both carried French passes, the *Rouparelle* and the *Quedagh Merchant*. When Kidd saw the French pass offered by the captain of the *Rouparelle*, he exclaimed joyfully, 'By God, I have got you! You are a free prize to England!' This indicates that Kidd felt he was not a pirate but a privateer. Kidd said much the same about the *Quedagh Merchant*, and he felt vindicated by these two French passes. With considerable treasure now onboard, Kidd headed for St. Mary's, Madagascar.

First into the harbour in 1698 came the *Adventure Galley*, with Kidd as captain. Some weeks later the *Rouparelle* and the *Quedagh Merchant* both arrived at St Mary's, with some of Kidd's prize crew in each. Also in St Mary's at the same time was the pirate Robert Culliford, who had many years earlier run away with a privateer in the West Indies captained by Kidd while Kidd was ashore. Therefore tension existed between Kidd and Culliford at St Mary's, and most of Kidd's crew deserted to Culliford. This was partly because Kidd was a severe captain, threatening to knock out the brains of those who opposed him, partly because Culliford offered a better chance of obtaining riches, and partly because Kidd wanted to delay dividing up their treasure until the crew reached New England. Kidd armed himself with muskets and pistols and barricaded himself in his cabin, with only a few supporters onboard. Kidd survived the cabin siege, and with a minimal crew transferred to the *Quedagh Merchant*, burnt the *Adventure Galley*, and left for New England. The *Rouparelle* was not seaworthy and sank in St Mary's harbour.[20]

Kidd's arrival in New England did not go well. Kidd was soon taken prisoner by Lord Bellomont in Boston, who felt the political winds of change. There was now a much more critical attitude towards pirates and pirate friendly governors, and Bellomont also well understood that he stood to make more money by capturing Kidd and receiving his share of the proceeds than by splitting the treasure with Kidd and many others. Kidd was brought to trial in London after spending more than a year in two very unpleasant London jails – the Marshalsea and Newgate. Kidd's trial in London showed that his political supporters wanted to get rid of him, and, as well, there was hostility from the East India Company, and the previously mentioned changing attitude toward pirates. Kidd found that the two French passes he had collected from the *Quedagh Merchant* and the *Rouparelle* had gone missing after he turned them over to Bellomont, and the trial seemed stacked against him. Thus the opening scenes of his trial make for sad reading:

> Captain Kidd: 'I cannot plead till I have these papers [the French passes]; and I have not my witnesses here.'

> Sir Salathiel Lovell [Recorder]: 'You do not know your own interest; if you will not plead you must have judgment against you.'

> Captain Kidd: 'If I plead I shall be accessory to my own death, till I have persons to plead for me.'

Sir Salathiel Lovell: 'You are accessory to your own death if you do not plead. We cannot enter into evidence unless you plead.'

Clerk of Arraigns: 'Are you guilty or not guilty?'[21]

Kidd was eventually forced to plead, but was found guilty of the murder of William Moore (it was judged to be premeditated), and also guilty of a number of counts of piracy against the *Quedagh Merchant*, the *Rouparelle*, and other ships. Kidd was therefore hung at Execution Dock, Wapping, London, in May 1701. Thus another Madagascar and Red Sea pirate earned the final sentence, although Kidd had naively failed to make use of his original political supporters to make a deal and thus save his life.

Kidd had left St Mary's in 1698, but according to Colonel Quarry, the aggressive customs collector for Pennsylvania, ships from New York were still following a trading round trip that threatened honest trade. Ships left from New York with a suitable cargo for Madras in India, then loaded up with brandy and wine for Madagascar, and sold the liquor to pirates who in exchange traded their treasure at cut rate prices to the ships. These traders then came back to New England and sold the pirate treasure at great profit. For example, Captain Giles Shelley sold his goods at Madagascar and took onboard seventy-five passengers, twenty-two Africans, and calico, ivory, 12,000 pieces of eight, and 3,000 Lyon dollars. He then returned to New England and made a good profit. And piracy still continued. For example, the pirate Ryder (or Rider) captured the ship *Beckford Galley* in 1698 while the captain was onshore trading at the port of Tullia in Madagascar. This Ryder was described as a middle sized man, of a swarthy complexion, churlish constitution, hair short and brown, and 'Apt when in Drink, to utter some Portegues, or Moorish words, he sometimes sayled with the Moores, and was left by a Pyrate att Fort Dolphin, on the East side of Madagascar…'[22] Rider disappeared with the *Beckford Galley* (possibly named for the wealthy West Indian planter and sugar merchant William Beckford), despite a message to all New England governors in 1700 to seize the ship.[23]

Edward England and Richard Taylor: Pirates

After a lull in piracy from Madagascar and in the Red Sea in the early 1700s, a revival took place after 1715, due to the end of the war of the

Spanish Succession, and the subsequent Treaty of Utrecht in 1713. Among the most significant Madagascar pirates were Edward England and Richard Taylor. England pursued a successful piratical career off the coast of Africa in 1719, capturing some twenty or more prizes in short order. One of the ships captured was renamed the *Victory*, and Richard Taylor appointed captain. According to Captain Johnson, Taylor was named captain because he was 'a fellow of most barbarous nature, who was become a great favourite amongst them [the pirates] for no other reason than he was a greater brute than the rest.'[24] After the African voyage, the crews of England and Taylor voted to go to the East Indies, and stopped at Madagascar on the way for water and provisions in 1720. Then the pirates raided along the coast of India, and returned again to Madagascar for provisions, where some of the pirates tried unsuccessfully to find whatever crew from Henry Avery's ship remained, but they searched in the wrong place, on the west side of the island instead of at St Mary's. Following this episode, the two pirate ships of England and Taylor went to the island of Johanna, where they took part in a violent fight with an East India Company ship, the *Cassandra*, with cannon fire killing and wounding many on each side. England's ship, the *Fancy*, forced the *Cassandra* ashore, but the *Fancy* also struck ground. The captain of the *Cassandra*, James Macrae, eventually surrendered to Taylor's *Victory*, and was close to being murdered when one of his old crewmen, with fearsome whiskers and a wooden leg, and stuck around with pistols, came 'swearing and vapouring upon the quarter-deck' and strongly defended the terrified Macrae. England was also sympathetic to Macrae, and advised Macrae to serve punch to Taylor in order to mellow him. This was done, and Macrae was even allowed to take the battered *Fancy* and get home if he could. Meanwhile, some of the pirates were much displeased with England for letting Macrae go free, thinking he would bring the East India Company against them. So, they deposed England, and marooned him with three others on Mauritius. There England and his companions put together a crude boat and sailed away to Madagascar, where he ended his career by subsisting on the charity of other pirates living there.[25]

However, Taylor was far from finished, and with the *Cassandra* and the *Victory* raided the coast of India, and then spent some time at the Dutch port of Cochin, enjoying a large amount of arrack (alcohol distilled from rice) and other necessities. This pleased the pirates so much that they gave the supplier three cheers, an eleven gun salute from each ship, £6,000 or £7000, and handfuls of ducats. In this good frame of mind, the pirates headed for Madagascar, but stopped on the way at the island of Reunion, now in company with the French pirate, Olivier La Buze or La Bouche. The pirates were fortunate because in the harbour was a large Portuguese ship, dismasted by a storm, that contained a very great treasure of diamonds, rubies, and other valuables, and also the Viceroy of Goa, who could be ransomed, all to the value of around £875,000. This was one of the greatest hauls of treasure ever taken by any pirate crew, and so each pirate received 42 diamonds as his part of the booty, plus other treasure. One jesting pirate complained that his large diamond, which had been judged equal to 42 smaller diamonds, was not as big as claimed, and so he broke his diamond into 43 smaller diamonds, boasting that 'he had a better share than any of them, for he had beat it, he said, into 43 sparks.'[26]

Now the question was what to do next, and hearing the guns of what was assumed to be a Royal Navy squadron come to hunt them, Taylor and the *Cassandra* sailed from St Mary's and called in at St Augustine on the west side of Madagascar. There the local natives brought onboard a letter left by Captain Matthews of the Royal Navy for another English man of war commanded by Captain Cockburn. According to a shipmate of Taylor's, the latter read out the letter to his crew, saying, 'Damne my Blood God forgive me for swearing heres a Squadron of Men of War sent to look after us but they don't much care for the seeing of us they are more upon the trading account but however lets stand one by another and take care of ourselves.'[27] Taylor was referring to the much deplored practice of Royal Navy captains trading on their own private account rather than chasing pirates, and ironically Captain Matthews was himself later court-martialled for private trading. Further evidence for this practice came when the Duke of Portland complained in a letter in 1723 that arrogant naval captains traded free of charge and so forced honest traders who could not compete, into piracy. A particular case was that of certain naval officers who stole a cargo of indigo off the trading ship *Nassau*, and then sold the indigo, but restored the ship back to its owners. On behalf of his officers, the naval captain unsuccessfully tried to justify the affair by saying that the indigo was condemned as French, and so a legitimate target.[28]

Returning to Taylor and the *Cassandra*, the crew decided to hide out on the east coast of Africa. Then the pirates split into two groups, one half sailing to Madagascar in a captured Portuguese prize with the idea of continuing their piratical life, and the other half (112 pirates and forty Africans) sailing in the *Cassandra* for the West Indies under Taylor with the idea of obtaining a pardon. The petition for a pardon was written from the *Cassandra*, anchored at the Isle of Pines, where Drake used to hide out, and addressed to the Governor of Jamaica. The petition, dated 10 April 1723, stated that the pirates now wanted to serve their King and Country, had only been led astray by evil associates from the island of Providence, and had not committed piracy for a year. It was signed by Richard Taylor, William Fox, and William Bates, and was agreed to by seventy English pirates and thirty-seven foreigners. The forty Africans apparently did not come into the matter. However, the Duke of Portland, on behalf of the Crown, refused a pardon for the pirates, causing Taylor's crew to send a second petition, saying that either they got the pardon or they were willing to stay and live amongst the Indians of Central America. The matter of the second petition was in the hands of Captain Laws of HMS *Mermaid*, who had sent a lieutenant with a letter to the pirates urging them to surrender. But as he told the Duke of Portland, the pirates were now in too strong a position to attack, their ship lying in a secure lagoon five leagues west of the Isle of Pines. According to Taylor, Laws asked the pirates whether this petition should go to Jamaica or not, which 'put us into a strange amusement…', either because the pirates had already made a deal with the Spanish, or because Laws was unable to decide where to send the petition. Nevertheless, Captain Laws sent his brother as a hostage to the pirates, while Taylor came onboard the *Mermaid*, to try to work out a pardon.[29]

The Duke of Portland was not impressed by Captain Laws' actions. He wrote that it was very strange that Captain Laws' ship stationed off Panama changed stations just as the *Cassandra* left Panama, implying that Laws had let the *Cassandra* escape. Another complaint was that the person negotiating with the pirates was actually Captain Laws' brother, who told the pirates that only Captain Laws could show mercy to them. Laws replied to Portland acknowledging that his letter to the pirates had been too kind, but argued that although his ship had left station just as a Royal Navy sloop arrived, still the combination of the sloop and Laws' ship could not have done anything against the pirates because onboard the *Cassandra* were ninety odd French pirates, seventy Indians, and a hundred English pirates. On the other hand, Taylor did tell Captain Laws that if the sloop had not arrived as Laws' ship left, his crew might have gone 'we know not whither…'[30] The end of the Taylor affair was that Taylor and his crew accepted a pardon from the Governor of Panama, either because Taylor threatened to kill everyone in the town of Porto Bello if a pardon was not forthcoming, or because Taylor and his crew had bribed the Governor of Panama, or because the Governor of Panama granted a free pardon to Taylor and his crew because he wanted the *Cassandra* to help defend against English ships. In fact, Captain Johnson claimed that Taylor later attacked English logwood cutters in the Bay of Honduras. Subsequently, the Duke of Portland complained to the Governor of Panama over the acceptance of Taylor and his ship into Spanish service, and received an amusing reply from the Governor of Panama, who declared that he had taken the *Cassandra* into his protection in order to make commerce safe. Still, the Spanish Governor suggested Portland might like to appeal to the Court in Spain, and ended with a flourish, 'Kiss your hands and am your most obliged Servant…' [31]

The Traders of St Mary's: Baldridge to Plantain

Finally, in this story of Madagascar and St Mary's, what happened to the traders who spent more time on the island of St Mary's than any pirate? Adam Baldridge, who left the ship *Fortune* in order to live on the island in 1691, was not only a trader but also a despot at St Mary's. He dispensed justice, kept a harem, and lived in very high style. However, his last exploit, when he invited a few dozen loyal Madagascar supporters onboard his ship for a party, and then sold them as slaves to the French on nearby Reunion, was one too many for the local tribes who rose against Baldridge in July 1697. They attacked his fort and warehouse, killing some thirty Europeans, including many pirates. Baldridge himself managed to escape and wound up living happily enough in New York, a far cry from St Mary's. Baldridge was followed by a certain Edward Welch, nicknamed 'Little King', because of his short stature. Welch ran the same compound, fort, and trading business as Baldridge, and included a whore house in his business activities. Welch was seriously wounded in a skirmish, and was eventually replaced by the most colourful of the Madagascar traders, John or James Plantain, who arrived in 1720. Plantain had been raised in Jamaica by parents who gave him the best education they could, which allegedly was 'to curse, swear, and blaspheme, from the time of his first learning to speak.' Plantain then learnt the sailor's trade aboard a small Jamaican sloop, and subsequently applied himself to the task of logwood cutting at Campeche. Later, he wandered to Rhode Island, and joined pirates who sailed to the coast of Africa. After this he served as a pirate on Edward England's ship, the *Fancy*, and then joined

Richard Taylor on the *Cassandra*, but was one of those who decided to stay on in Madagascar. Subsequently, Plantain served on the pirate ship *Dragon*, commanded by Edmund Conden. The *Dragon* seized a very rich Muslim ship from Jeddah at Bab el Mandeb in 1720, enabling Conden and his crew to rake in about £150,000. As a result each pirate received a share of some £2,000 each at St Mary's. It seems that Plantain and his two partners, James Adair and Hans Burgen, who had also very likely been on the *Dragon*, decided to settle down on Madagascar, and make use of their ill gotten gains to continue the trading business.[32]

Unlike previous traders, though, Plantain had political ambitions, and decided to become king of Madagascar. At the same time, Plantain was apparently homesick, saying in 1722 that he would give half of what he was worth in order to be in a Christian country.[33] But before Plantain tried to become king of Madagascar, he made himself a fort and compound in Ranter Bay, in the north of St Mary's, where he also established a harem containing a number of local girls bearing names such as Moll, Kate, Sue and Pegg. These ladies were outfitted in the best dresses, and some had diamond necklaces. Part of Plantain's wealth came from trading with the Royal Navy itself. It seems that Captains Thomas Matthews and Cockburn arrived at St Mary's in 1722 on the *Easter* and the *Lyon and Salisbury* respectively, and that Plantain came aboard with his private army of some thirty to forty armed natives. The captains agreed to trade spirits and goods (including spats, shoes, and stockings) for gold and diamonds. Plantain boasted to the sailors of the Royal Navy that if they would stay with him, he would build ships, and in a little while 'they should all be rich enough to buy Estates and that he had planted Sugar Canes and distilled as good Rum as any could be in the West Indies…' Meanwhile, in exchange for the spirits, Plantain bargained hard with his diamonds, taking them out of his pocket and saying to Matthews 'I'll give you all these for the Liquor if you'l take em but if you wont take them at the first word Ile put them into my pocket and they shall never come out again…' Matthews seized the chance to trade and accepted the diamonds in exchange for the spirits, which Plantain took from Matthews and hid under guard. It seems the transaction involved five bars of gold as well as the diamonds, but at this point there was a native attack on Ranter Bay, and Plantain had to leave in a hurry, without taking away the spirits. The navy was able to recover the spirits through the advice of a native, who knew where the spirits were hidden, although he had to be taken onboard to protect him from Plantain. So the spirits were taken back onto the Royal Navy ships, yet this was only a partial victory because the alcohol could not be touched by the crew for fear that the spirits had been poisoned.[34]

Captain Matthews would appear to have got the best of Plantain, but since Matthews was subsequently court martialled for using his ship for private trading, perhaps Plantain had the last laugh after all. Returning to Plantain's idea of becoming king of Madagascar, he launched a campaign, with his private army of natives and some pirates, against a local chief called Long Dick or King Dick. This fight started because Plantain was enamoured of the grand daughter of the king, by name Holy Eleonora Brown. She was called Holy because she knew the Lord's Prayer, the Creed, the Ten Commandments, and Christian precepts, and was named Brown because that was the name of her pirate father. King Dick refused to part with Eleonora, so Plantain's army attacked and defeated King Dick, and the latter was put to death in painful ways. Plantain took Eleonora back with him to Ranter Bay, where she advised him seriously on religious matters, and said her prayers morning and night. For his part, Plantain sent away most of his other wives, gave Eleonora twenty local girls as slaves, and dressed her in silks, diamonds and jewels. Plantain later launched an attack on another local king at Port Dauphin, where after an eighteen month siege, Plantain succeeded in taking the town. He then proclaimed himself King of Madagascar, but he and his compatriots were forced to leave Madagascar because of pending trouble with the local natives. Plantain sailed away in a small sloop taking Eleonora and his several children with him, and reportedly wound up on the Malabar Coast of India, serving with the Indian pirate Angrey. With this departure, the Red Sea pirates came close to ending their relationship with St Mary's and Madagascar – a pattern that had only lasted from the early 1690s to the late 1720s. Yet in this short time, St Mary's had seen significant piracy and the taking of vast amounts of Red Sea treasure. It is reported that some pirates still survived until 1730 on Madagascar, but these were the last of the breed.[35]

The end of the Madagascar pirates also paralleled the temporary end of the Western pirates, as the next chapter relates.

Death to the Pirates

In the western world of the Atlantic, the Caribbean, and along the coasts of the Americas, government forces were engaged in a concentrated campaign of suppression against the pirates in the period from roughly 1700 to the mid 1720s. Traders, merchants, slavers, and colonial governors combined to put pressure on governments to try to put an end to piracy in the West Indies and the Caribbean in this period, and an improved Royal Navy made this possible. It is too much to say that 'Piracy would come to an end by 1726', since there were occasional pirate attacks throughout the eighteenth century, and a very considerable resurgence of piracy in the early 1820s in the West Indies, to say nothing of what was happening in eastern seas. But certainly most of the well known western pirates of the early 1700s would come to an unfortunate end – with perhaps 500-600 Anglo-American pirates being executed between 1716 and 1726. Some 2,000 pirates were operating at any one time during the 'golden age' of piracy from the 1680s to the mid 1720s, and it is estimated that altogether around 5,000 pirates went 'on account' over this time frame. Rather than try to follow all their stories, it will be useful to focus on just three of the best known pirates of this time – Blackbeard, or Edward Teach, who was killed in 1718; 'Calico'

Jack Rackam, who was hanged in 1720; and Bartholomew Roberts, who was killed in 1722. [1]

Blackbeard (Active 1714/1715–1718)

Blackbeard gained more fame and notoriety from legends of his appearance and bravado than from his actual piracy. Charles Johnson's description of Blackbeard went a very long way to cementing the pirate's reputation with his extravagant description of the pirate's '…large quantity of hair, which like a frightful meteor covered his whole face and frightened America more than any comet that has appeared there a long time.' Johnson continued:

> This beard was black, which he suffered to grow of an extravagant length; as to breadth it came up to his eyes. He was accustomed to twist it with ribbons, in small tails, after the manner of our ramilies wigs [named for the battle of Ramillies in 1706, the type of wig being one in which there is a long plait or tail behind, which is tied with a bow at the top and bottom of the plait], and turn them about his ears. [Blackbeard actually seems to have produced several plaits instead of one.] In time of action, he wore a sling over his shoulders with three brace of pistols hanging in holsters like bandaliers [a common system to offset the slow and unreliable method of reloading the flintlock pistol], and stuck lighted matches under his hat, which appearing on each side of his face, his eyes looking naturally fierce and wild, made him altogether such a figure, that imagination cannot form an idea of a fury, from hell, to look more frightful. [2]

Johnson went on to describe three or four incidents, which also raised the profile and sinister image of Blackbeard, although it is noteworthy that these incidents do not involve piracy. In one incident, Blackbeard was supposed to have married a sixteen-year-old girl while at Bath Town in North Carolina, supposedly his fourteenth wife, and he allegedly invited five or six of his companions to his house, where he forced her to prostitute herself to them while Blackbeard watched. This seems just possible, but very unlikely. In another incident, Blackbeard was drinking one night in his cabin with Israel Hands, the captain of the sloop that sailed in consort with Blackbeard. Another pirate was also present, when Blackbeard blew out the candle, crossed his hands under the table, where he had two pistols, and shot Israel

Hands in the knee. The second pistol shot missed, or presumably the other man would have been badly injured also. The first shot disabled Israel Hands for life, and when questioned as to the reason for this, Blackbeard simply said that if he did not kill one of his crew, they would forget who he was. There may be some validity to this story, since Johnson reported that Israel Hands, after being pardoned, could be found later begging for bread in London, which might have been the only way Hands could survive, if he was crippled and unable to work.[3] In addition, if Johnson did come across Hands in London, he would have learnt many valuable details of Blackbeard's life.

Still another story related by Johnson has Blackbeard challenging his men to a contest, in which he and two or three others went down into the hold of their ship, and set fire to brimstone, to see how long they could stand the fumes. At length, some of the others cried out for air, so the hatches were opened, while Blackbeard was pleased that he had held out the longest. Again, this story is possible, although it relates to the image of fire and smoke that Johnson liked to emphasize with Blackbeard. Yet another fable, which stresses the diabolical image of Blackbeard, has the crew of his ship finding out that they had one more man onboard than was supposed to be there:

…such a one was seen several days amongst them, sometimes below, and sometimes upon deck, yet no man in the ship could give an account of who he was, or from whence he came, but that he disappeared a little before they were cast away in their great ship [the *Queen Anne's Revenge*]; but, it seems, they verily believed it was the Devil.

Pirates, like all sailors of the day, were very superstitious, so again this story is just possible. Yet the idea of the Devil onboard ship seems more likely to fit the 'devil' image of Blackbeard that Johnson is creating, rather than the reality of Blackbeard. This is borne out by the two immediately previous stories that Johnson relates: the brimstone story, mentioned above, where Johnson says Blackbeard used the brimstone contest to make his men believe he was the devil incarnate, and a second story in which Blackbeard is asked whether his wife knew where his treasure was buried, in case anything should happen to him. According to Johnson, Blackbeard answers, 'nobody but himself and the Devil knew where it was and the longest liver should take it all.' It is unlikely that Blackbeard buried any treasure [see Chapter 1], so this is almost certainly an apocryphal story, following Johnson's theme of emphasizing the 'hellish' image of Blackbeard.[4]

The reality behind Johnson's rather fantastical stories of Blackbeard is harder to pin down, including Blackbeard's actual name. There is no evidence besides Johnson for the pirate's real name, but it is possible that it was Edward Thatch or Teach, as related by Johnson, who is often reasonably accurate when discussing non-controversial topics. If so, Teach came from Bristol, and originally sailed as a privateer or slave trader out of Bristol, as many did at that time.[5] In regard to his piracy, Teach/Blackbeard (Blackbeard will henceforth be used as the more familiar name), originally sailed with the pirate Benjamin Hornigold out of New Providence in the Bahamas, in 1714 or 1715. By 1717 Hornigold had a thirty gun ship, probably the *Ranger*, while Blackbeard, as Hornigold's deputy, commanded a six gun sloop, with a crew of around seventy men. The two pirates sailed together and captured a number of small ships, and then in 1717, Blackbeard was appointed captain of the twelve gun *Revenge*, which belonged to Stede Bonnet – the strange, wealthy planter turned pirate, who knew little of the sea. Bonnet was happy to read his library of books onboard while Blackbeard went about the business of pirating. Meanwhile, Blackbeard and Hornigold parted company in 1717, when the latter was deposed by his crew for refusing to attack British ships. Hornigold would also shortly take the King's pardon, issued by George I in 1717, while Blackbeard continued as a pirate.[6]

Blackbeard's career started off well in November 1717 when he captured the French slaver, *La Concorde*, off Martinique, which he renamed *Queen Anne's Revenge*, possibly implying a preference for the Stuart cause, since Queen Anne, who died in 1714, was the last of the Stuart monarchs. Various reports give the number of the new crew of the *Queen Anne's Revenge* as around 150 men, with another fifty in an accompanying sloop, or a little later as 300 men, while the number of guns aboard the larger ship reportedly ranged from twenty-two to thirty-six guns. To command this number of men and keep them happy was a very difficult task, but Blackbeard seems to have accomplished this, partly through natural ability, and partly it seems by creating an image of himself as a tougher and larger than life pirate. This is all the more curious since Blackbeard apparently never actually killed anyone until his final battle. However, when a captured ship's captain described Blackbeard in late 1717, it was of a 'Captain Tach' – 'a tall spare man with a very black beard which he wore very long.' This image of Blackbeard is less riveting than Johnson's description, but shows that Johnson's lively description was not far from reality.[7]

In 1718 Blackbeard was in the Bay of Honduras, where he operated with the *Queen Anne's Revenge*, and the smaller sloop, the *Revenge*. Among the

ships they took was a bark of eighty tons called the *Adventure*, capable of carrying twelve guns, which appears later in the story of Blackbeard. A much
larger ship taken was the *Protestant Caesar*, out of Boston, which led them a
chase before she was finally cornered. The terrified crew rowed ashore and
hid in the jungle, no doubt watching as Blackbeard's crew plundered and
then burnt the prize to the waterline, so that the crew of the prize could
not 'brag when he went to New England that he had beat a Pirate.' This was
a reference to an earlier encounter between the *Caesar* and a sloop from
Blackbeard's small fleet, when the *Caesar* fought off the sloop. On the other
hand, Johnson maintains that the *Caesar* was burnt because she came from
Boston, where some men had recently been hung for piracy. Either way,
Blackbeard next headed to the Atlantic seaboard of British North America
in May 1718, following the pirate custom of raiding there in the summer,
and shifting to the Caribbean or the Guinea coast in the winter.[8]

In May 1718, Blackbeard and his fleet of one large ship, the *Queen Anne's
Revenge*, and three smaller sloops, arrived off the mouth of the river leading
to Charles Town, South Carolina. This was a clever move by Blackbeard, since
the pirates took eight or nine unsuspecting ships as they sailed toward Charles
Town, and a blockade could have done considerable damage to the economy
of Charles Town and its merchants and ship owners. Out of the ships that
Blackbeard took, some hostages were secured, from whom the pirates later
took cash and jewelry. Yet his only demand from Charles Town was for a medicine chest. This seems a small price for raising the blockade of Charles Town,
but Blackbeard's fleet was too small to take Charles Town with its population
of around 5,000, and the longer the pirate fleet waited outside the town, the
greater the danger of a Royal Navy ship arriving. Moreover, a medicine chest
was very valuable, and pirate ships usually compelled captured surgeons and
their medicine chests to join their crews, as sickness, wounds and death were
more than common onboard. Subsequently, after a week, Blackbeard sailed
north, toward North Carolina and Bath Town, where Governor Eden resided,
who seems to have been well disposed to the pirates.

In fact, Blackbeard was now apparently giving thought to the problem of
downsizing his large crew of pirates. He could not easily constantly satisfy
these pirates with prizes, and at the same time his fleet offered a tempting
target to the Royal Navy. Moreover, Blackbeard appears to have been contemplating asking for a pardon from Governor Eden. In order to achieve
these aims, Blackbeard first arranged to have the *Queen Anne's Revenge*
run aground on the complex shoals outside Bath Town, North Carolina.

After this, the *Adventure* also ran aground, while Stede Bonnet, still a part of Blackbeard's crew in the *Revenge*, was sent to Governor Eden, to ask for a pardon. While Bonnet was away, Blackbeard stripped the grounded ships of their contents, abandoned around seventeen of the crew on a barren island nearby, and left around 300 other crew ashore in the small village of Beaufort on the outer banks of North Carolina. Blackbeard himself hid out with around twenty-five trusted pirates in a captured Spanish sloop on the north side of Ocracoke Island. All of this seems to have been part of Blackbeard's plan to downsize and secure a pardon.[9]

On his return to the original *rendez vous* after some days, Stede Bonnet found Blackbeard gone. Furious at being abandoned, Bonnet sailed after Blackbeard in the *Revenge*, but missed him, and then resumed piracy himself, capturing a number of ships. It was not long before Bonnet was taken, and despite escaping once, he was hung at Charles Town in 1718, along with twenty-nine of his crew. Meanwhile, Blackbeard settled down to live at Bath Town for some six months, and he did receive a pardon from Governor Eden. Blackbeard renamed his Spanish sloop the *Adventure*, and with her took a Spanish prize whose profits he shared with Governor Eden and Deputy Governor Knight. A small crew lived aboard the *Adventure* at Ocracoke inlet, while Blackbeard himself either lived onboard, or at Bath Town, and the rest of the pirates lived normally at Bath Town. All seemed well, but to the south, Governor Spotswood of South Carolina, determined to revenge the blockade and losses caused by Blackbeard at Charles Town, disturbed by continuing piracy off his shores, and perhaps interested in taking over North Carolina as part of his empire, set out to kill or capture Blackbeard and his men. To do this, Spotswood chartered two sloops with shallow draughts, and manned them with about fifty-five men, under the command of two junior naval officers, Lt. Maynard and Mr. Hyde. Another force of 200 men was to march overland and roust out the nest of pirates in Bath Town – a bold and actually illegal move.

As it happened, Blackbeard was not in Bath Town at this moment, but onboard the *Adventure* at Ocracoke Island, entertaining guests. He had a crew of twenty-five men, since Israel Hands and the rest of the crew were ashore in Bath Town. Lt Maynard learnt where Blackbeard was located, and, as the senior officer of the two attacking sloops, he made sure that no ships entered or exited the area, to avoid alarming Blackbeard. In the early morning of 22 November 1718, Maynard's two sloops drifted toward Blackbeard's *Adventure*, and were quickly noticed. Blackbeard could have cut his cable and fled, but he obviously determined to fight, and probably considered his armament of a number of three and four pounder cannon superior. He may also have tried to lure the naval sloops onto a sandbar, but in fact both sides ran aground close to each other. At this point, Johnson has a lively tale of Maynard and Blackbeard exchanging threats. Blackbeard shouted:

> 'Damn you for villains, who are you? And from whence came you?' The lieu-tenant made him answer: 'You may see by our colours we are no pirates ... I will come aboard of you as soon as I can, with my sloop.' Upon this, Blackbeard took a glass of liquor and drank to him with these words: 'Damnation seize my soul if I give you Quarters, or take any from you.'[10]

Johnson was actually quite close in his reported dialogue, since Maynard later wrote that Blackbeard 'drank Damnation to me and my Men, whom he stil'd Cowardly Puppies, saying he would neither give nor take Quarter.' After this, the battle started with the *Adventure* opening fire, and nearly win-ning the fight with this single broadside. Around eleven Royal Navy sailors were killed, including Mr. Hyde, and twenty were wounded. However, Maynard arranged for the rest of his crew to be below decks, so these were spared. Then Blackbeard ordered his men to throw grenades onto the deck of Maynard's sloop, and under cover of the smoke boarded Maynard's sloop with between ten and fourteen pirates against Maynard and twelve Royal Navy sailors. The fight was very fierce, and at one point Maynard faced Blackbeard. Both fired pistols, and Blackbeard received a superficial wound. Blackbeard swung his cutlass against Maynard and cut the officer's fingers. As Blackbeard moved in for the kill, a navy sailor cut Blackbeard in the face or neck, saving Maynard. Several shots struck Blackbeard, but he kept swinging his cutlass. Another account has Blackbeard facing a Highlander, who gave Blackbeard the cut on his neck, at which Blackbeard said, 'well done, lad'. The Highlander was apparently quick witted, and retorted, 'If it be not well done, I'll do it better'. With that he gave Blackbeard a second stroke, which cut off his head ... On the other hand, Johnson states that Blackbeard received twenty-five wounds, five of them by shot, and as he was cocking his pistol to fire again, he suddenly fell dead on the deck.[11]

With Blackbeard's death, the fight went out of the remaining pirates, who either surrendered or jumped overboard to be killed or captured. On board the *Adventure*, an African pirate named Caesar tried to blow up the ship, but was stopped from doing so. Maynard hung Blackbeard's head from the bow sprit of his sloop, giving some credence to the story of the Highlander cutting Blackbeard's head off. Legend has it that Blackbeard's decapitated body then swam several times around the ship after being thrown overboard. No doubt the body was carried past the sloop by the current, but obviously did not swim. Later, ten of Blackbeard's crew were hung in South Carolina, through the efforts of Governor Spotswood, their bodies lining the road from Williamsburg to the James River. However, Israel Hands was pardoned, probably for giving evidence against the others. Maynard apparently gathered the treasure onboard Blackbeard's ship and split it with his surviving men, but got nothing from the Admiralty. He seems to have left the naval service shortly after the Blackbeard affair, and retreated into obscurity.[12]

It was the end of Blackbeard and his legend – although it leaves open the question as to whether Blackbeard really intended to honour Governor Eden's pardon, and whether he therefore really intended to give up piracy for ever. Blackbeard's life showed that although he was a reasonably successful pirate, his pirate career was actually quite short, from around 1714/1715 to 1718, so that it was really the creation of his image that has made him perhaps the most famous pirate of all time. The same might be said of 'Calico' Jack Rackam, who was more famous for having onboard two female pirates than from anything he actually achieved himself as a pirate.

'Calico' Jack Rackam (Hung 1720)

'Calico' Jack Rackam was so called because of his habit of wearing calico (white cotton cloth exported from Calicut in India, hence the name calico). His past is a mystery, and Johnson does not give any details of his earlier life, but he was originally probably a privateer, trader or slaver, as were so many others. Rackam actually emerges in history as the quartermaster of the pirate ship captained by the pirate Charles Vane. The rank of quartermaster was second only to the captain and required a responsible and capable leader. It was the quartermaster who spoke for the crew, managed discipline onboard, supervised the division of booty, called meetings when policy decisions had to be made, and acted as judge in ship board cases. Rackam must have been such a leader, and trusted by the crew.[13] Rackam's moment came when a French man of war hove into view in 1718, near Dominica. In the initial action, the French ship fired a broad side, which caused Vane to reconsider the wisdom of taking on such a large well armed ship. An argument broke out onboard Vane's ship, with Rackam leading the majority group that wanted to board the French ship, and Vane in the minority wanting to avoid battle. According to pirate rules, Vane, as captain in the middle of an action, had the authority to make critical decisions. Hence, Vane made the decision to flee, but this decision was later branded as cowardice by Rackam and the majority onboard. So a vote was called by Rackam, Vane was deposed by his crew, and Rackam was elected captain. Another source simply says that Vane's ship was beaten off by the French ship, so perhaps Vane was a little less cowardly than supposed, but he obviously did not satisfy his crew.[14]

Rackam allowed Vane and his sixteen supporters to sail off in a small sloop. Vane did not last much longer, because after a few piracies, his next ship was dismasted in a gale and driven ashore. Vane was captured in 1719, and hung in 1720. Meanwhile, Rackam plundered a few small prizes around the Leeward Islands, Hispaniola, Jamaica, and the Bahamas, before deciding to accept a pardon offered by Woodes Rogers in the Bahamas in 1719. Perhaps the reason behind Rackam's desire for a pardon was that he was hoping to become a privateer, because Britain was at war with Spain from 1718 to early 1720. After the war was over, Rackam probably lacked a source of income in the Bahamas, because in August 1720 he and a dozen supporters rowed out at night to the sloop *William*, and sailed from the Bahamas to continue piracy. Significantly, Rackam used his time in New Providence, Bahamas, to court a woman named Anne Bonny, or Anne Bonn, who was married to a penniless sailor. She abandoned her husband, and, disguised as a sailor, joined Rackam onboard as his lover. According to Johnson, she was soon discovered to be pregnant, and later went ashore in Cuba to deliver the child, before rejoining Rackam's ship. Strangely enough, among the other pirates who joined Rackam and Bonny in their escape from the Bahamas was another woman, also disguised as a man, Mary Read.[15]

The voyage of Rackam's sloop, accompanied by Bonny and Read, was short and not very rewarding. The *William* took fishing boats and a few small craft off Hispaniola and Jamaica, and then Rackam came across a group of nine turtle hunters from Jamaica in a small boat. These men allegedly came aboard Rackam's ship to exchange their catch for a bowl of punch, but were afterwards to bitterly regret this move because Rackam was shortly after surprised by a privateer, captained by a pirate hunter named Jonathan Barnet. Rackam apparently ordered the nine turtle hunters to immediately help weigh up the anchor, in order for the *William* to escape from Barnet. According to the turtle hunters, they refused, despite Rackam using violent means to persuade them. No doubt the turtle hunters coloured the story in their favour when on trial later, but it seems likely that Rackam wanted to escape from Barnet, and needed the man power to speedily weigh anchor, a heavy task that takes some time. On the other hand, a witness alleged that the turtle hunters had brought muskets and cutlasses onboard Rackam's ship, possibly with the idea of joining the pirate crew, and when the anchor was up, they helped in rowing the *William* away in the light breeze, in order to try and escape. Meanwhile, Rackam's crew refused to surrender – shouting 'they would strike no Strikes' – and, unable to flee, someone fired a swivel gun at Barnet's ship from Rackam's sloop. The privateer responded with cannon and musket fire, which brought down the *William*'s boom and cowed Rackam's crew. It appears that Rackam's crew surrendered very easily but that Read and Bonny and one other pirate continued the fight.[16]

At the various pirate trials in Jamaica in 1720, Rackam's male crew were found guilty and were hung, except for two Hispaniola-based French buccaneers who had been taken prisoner by Rackam, and were important witnesses. In a probable miscarriage of justice, the nine turtle hunters were also found guilty and hung, despite being onboard the *William* for a very short time before Barnet's privateer arrived. When it came time to try Read and Bonny, one or two interesting facts came up. One witness, Dorothy Thomas, who had been captured while paddling a canoe loaded with provisions, reported that the two women were onboard Rackam's sloop:

> ...and wore Mens Jackets, and long Trouzers, and Handkerchiefs tied about their Heads; and that each of them had a Machet [heavy knife or cutlass] and Pistol in their Hands, and cursed and swore at the Men, to murther the Deponent [Thomas]; and that they should kill her, to prevent her coming against them [as a witness]; and the Deponent further said, that the Reason of her knowing and believing them to be Women then was, by the largeness of their Breasts.

This has given rise to much speculation about Read and Bonny cross dressing, but the two French buccaneers testified that 'when they [Read and Bonny] saw any Vessel, gave Chase, or Attacked, they wore Men's Cloaths; and, at other Times, they wore Women's Cloaths...' Presumably therefore, there was no attempt to disguise themselves as men onboard Rackam's ship, which would have been very difficult or impossible on a small sloop, but in times of action, the two wore men's clothes, either because it was easier to be active and fight in that manner, or because it gave the illusion of there being more men onboard than there actually were.[17]

Another matter of interest is that Anne Bonny appears to have been the more prominent of the two women pirates in action, perhaps because of her relationship to John Rackam, or because that was her nature. According to witnesses, it was Anne Bonny particularly who handed gunpowder to the men – in other words, acting as what would in the Royal Navy be called a powder monkey – handing pre-packaged charges of gunpowder to the gunners onboard. And it was Anne Bonny in particular who on another occasion 'had a Gun in her Hand' when a sloop was taken, although the witness went on to say, 'That they were both very profligate, cursing and swearing much, and very ready and willing to do any Thing on Board.' It is curious also that the charges against Anne Bonny always include the alias 'Bonn', while she also used the alias 'Ann Fulford', but neither of these names appear in Johnson. And as discussed elsewhere (Chapter 6) the name Mary Read occurs in a 1708 proposal to bring the pirates back from Madagascar, although there is no means of proving this was the same Mary Read from Rackam's crew. In any case, the two women pirates were found guilty and condemned to hang, but both pleaded that they were quick with child, which would excuse them from immediate hanging since an unborn child was obviously innocent. Bonny's pregnancy was no doubt a result of her relationship with Jack Rackam, while Read's pregnancy probably stemmed from her relationship with a forced sailor on Rackam's ship, who was acquitted of piracy, and to whom she claimed to be married 'in conscience'. As a result, the women were inspected, and the pregnancies confirmed, although Johnson says that Read was very obviously pregnant at the time.[18]

As a result of their pregnancies, Bonny and Read were sent to jail rather than to the gibbet. It is known that Mary Read died in prison on 28 April 1721, perhaps of fever associated with child birth. Anne Bonny appears to have escaped the death sentence after giving birth, and was reprieved from time to time, according to Johnson. One tradition has it that Bonny's father purchased her release, and she moved to the Carolinas, presumably with her child, where she married a planter. Johnson also relates that the day that Rackam was due to be hung, Rackam was permitted to visit Bonny, yet she provided little comfort for him, saying that 'she was sorry to see him there, but if he had fought like a man, he need not have been hanged like a dog.' There was some justice in the remark, together with the idea that Rackam is now famous more for the presence of Bonny and Read onboard his ship than for anything he achieved himself. This is the more significant because there were extremely few western women pirates – and that both should serve together by chance on one ship is a remarkable coincidence.[19]

Bartholomew Roberts (Active 1718–1722)

The opposite may be said of the pirate Bartholomew Roberts, probably the most successful of all western pirates, who did not need any romantic attachments to build his reputation. Indeed, he was a rather austere and sober individual, who issued a series of strict regulations for his crews, including one which stated, 'No Boy or Woman to be allow'd amongst them. If any man were found seducing any of the latter Sex, and carried her to Sea, disguised, he was to suffer Death…' In contrast to Rackam, it was Roberts' discipline, audacity, and instinct for when to attack and when to leave an area that enabled him to succeed where others failed. But above all, it was Roberts' toughness in controlling his very large crew, including his clever management system of creating a privy council of 'half a dozen of the greatest bullies' onboard to support him, which enabled Roberts to successfully pirate for four long years before being killed by the Royal Navy in 1722.[20]

Roberts was Welsh, born in the village of Newydd Bach, near Fishguard Bay, around the years 1680–1682. His original name seems to have been John Robert, which he changed to Bartholomew Roberts, probably at the time his ship was taken by Howel Davis in 1719 and he decided to become a pirate. His shipmates nicknamed him 'Black Barty', because he was a dark featured individual, no doubt a typical Welshman in this respect. Roberts was second or third mate of the Royal African Company slave ship the *Princess* when the ship was captured by Davis. Roberts' rank is significant because it suggests that he, like many others who became pirate captains, believed they were unlikely to reach higher rank in merchant or slave ships. Indeed, according to Johnson, the reason that Roberts threw in his lot with Davis' crew was 'preferment', meaning that he aspired to higher rank and command. In other conversations reported by Johnson, which may have been invented by Johnson, but which probably did reflect Roberts' views, Roberts underlined his attitude when he frequently drank the toast, '"D –n to him who ever lived to wear a halter."' Similarly, Roberts explained why he became a pirate, as he:

'…frankly owned, 'twas to get rid of the disagreeable superiority of some masters he was acquainted with' … 'In an honest service', says he, 'there is thin commons, low wages, and hard labour; in this, plenty and satiety, pleasure and ease, liberty and power; and who could not balance creditor on this side, when all the hazard that is run for it, at worst is only a sour look or two at choking. No, a merry life and a short one, shall be my motto.'[21]

So it was that Roberts joined Davis' crew at Annabon on the Ivory Coast of Africa in June 1719. A few weeks later, Davis was killed at Principe Island in the Gulf of Guinea. The island was owned by the Portuguese, and Davis planned to deceive the governor in order to take the Portuguese fort without trouble and ransack the place, as well as enjoy the local ladies, including the wife of the Portuguese governor. Somehow the governor was warned, and set a trap of his own by inviting the unsuspecting Davis to the fort for dinner. As Davis and a troop of pirates happily walked up to the fort for dinner they were ambushed, and Davis was shot in the stomach. As he tried to get away, he realised he was being followed, and in a last gesture, fired shots from the two pistols he held, and then collapsed and died. Johnson wrote that Davis' end was 'like a game cock, giving a dying blow that he might not fall unrevenged.'[22]

The pirates wanted to revenge themselves on Principe for Davis' death and for the ambush which also killed more of their number. Because Roberts had visited Principe previously they accepted his advice on how to achieve the destruction of the fort. This was done by using broadsides from their ship, the *Royal Rover*, from a location that the guns of the fort could not cover. The fort was demolished, as well as the small town of Principe, plus some ships in the harbour. With honour satisfied, the crew of the *Royal Rover* turned to the election of a new captain. Somewhat surprisingly, Roberts was elected, despite having been with Davis' crew for only six weeks. Clearly the pirates onboard the *Royal Rover* recognized a sensible, courageous, and tough leader in Roberts, and they were not disappointed. Soon after Roberts took over command, the *Royal Rover* captured two ships, which supplied essential stores and a number of recruits. Then Roberts advised a cruise to Brazil, where he suggested there would be Portuguese trading ships that would be easy to capture. With the Brazil voyage, Roberts established himself as very much an Atlantic pirate, at ease in the West Indies, off Brazil, or on the west coast of Africa, all areas that he already knew from his slave trading days. The Brazil voyage also established Roberts as a cool and audacious captain, with good judgement.[23]

Although the first nine weeks off Brazil produced no prizes, Roberts' crew was rewarded by the sight of forty-two Portuguese ships lying in the harbour roads of Bahia De Los Santos – the Bay of All Saints. These ships were guarded by two seventy gun Portuguese men of war, so that the *Royal Rover*, with her twenty guns, would be opposed by 1,000 men and 500 cannon. But Roberts evidently had a low opinion of the Portuguese as defenders of their ships, and thought the fleet vulnerable. Silently, at night, the *Royal Rover* slipped in amongst the fleet and came up beside a merchant ship. A quick rush aboard her was sufficient to secure the ship. But Roberts really wanted to know from the captain of his prize which was the richest ship in the fleet, and promised to let the captain go if he would point out such a vessel, or he would suffer instant death if he refused. The captain quickly pointed to a Portuguese ship of forty guns and 150 men. The *Royal Rover* maneuvered beside the new target, called the *Sagrada Familia* (Holy Family), but they were observed, and the *Sagrada* prepared to defend herself. Roberts' crew quickly fired a broadside and boarded her with the usual intimidation of shouts and waving cutlasses. With the loss of only two pirates, Roberts became master of the new prize. According to Johnson, Roberts determined to keep the *Sagrada*, and prepared to defend her against the two Portuguese men of war. Yet these two Portuguese ships were not keen to fight, in fact one waited too long for the other to come up, and it was relatively easy for Roberts in the *Sagrada* to sail off, accompanied by the *Royal Rover*. The *Sagrada* proved to have a very valuable cargo – sugar, skins, tobacco and 90,000 moidores (Portuguese gold coins), together with jewelry, including a rich cross set with diamonds, ready to be presented to the King of Portugal.[24]

Roberts' crew sailed to the appropriately named Devil's Island, Guiana, with their prize, and enjoyed their newly acquired wealth in carousing and trading with the locals. But it was here that Roberts nearly came to grief. When a brigantine carrying supplies sailed past, Roberts embarked forty of his best men and sailed after her without any preparations. Not only did Roberts miss the brigantine, but adverse currents carried Roberts and his men away from the coast for several days, leaving them desperately short of water and food. Worse, when a boat was sent away to get help from the *Royal Rover*, the news came back that Roberts' lieutenant he had left behind in charge, Walter Kennedy, had simply sailed away with the *Royal Rover*, and had given away the Portuguese prize. Perhaps Kennedy did not expect Roberts to return, but neither did he send a boat to search for him. Kennedy was a tough and especially unpleasant character who did not live much longer. Meanwhile, Roberts and his men survived by tearing up the planks of the cabin to make a makeshift tub, held together with rope yarns, to fetch water for the desperate crew.[25]

Suitably refreshed, Roberts and his crew of 40 sailed for the Windward Islands, where they captured a few smaller ships at Guadeloupe to provide much needed supplies, and managed to avoid ships sent by the governors of Barbados and Martinique to capture them. As a result, Roberts designed a pirate flag with himself standing on top of two skulls, designated ABH and AMH, standing for A Barbadian Head, and A Martinican Head. In 1720, Roberts was able to carry out part of this threat, and hung the governor of Martinique from the yard arm. At about this time also, Roberts devised a set of rules for his crew, which aimed to produce a certain amount of discipline onboard, perhaps having Walter Kennedy in mind. Feeling some pressure in the West Indies, and with summer beginning, Roberts sailed for Newfoundland, and put into the cod fishery port of Trepassey (on the south coast of Newfoundland), in June 1720. Here Roberts essentially copied his feat of sailing among the Portuguese ships of Bahia, by sailing in amongst the fishing fleet, and cowed twenty-two ships into surrender, but this time in daylight 'with their black colours flying, drums beating, and trumpets sounding.' Roberts did not expect resistance, nor was there any. To confirm his reputation, and perhaps to punish those whom he saw as cowards, Roberts had the admiral of Trepassey brought onboard and flogged. Leaving Trepassey, Roberts burned all of the ships in harbour, with the exception of one galley into which he transferred several cannon and made her his new flagship, optimistically renaming her the *Fortune*. With this larger ship Roberts captured several French ships and others off Newfoundland, once more transferring to an even larger ship, which was named the *Good Fortune*.[26]

Finally, Roberts sailed for the West Indies, where more ships were taken, usually by a mixture of audacity and brutality. Next they headed to the African coast of Guinea, and on the way took a French ship which they named the *Royal Fortune*. Somehow they missed their navigation aim of stopping at the Cape Verde islands to refit, and were forced back to the West Indies, suffering terribly from want of water and food, so that men dropped away daily. The staggering crew actually made land at Surinam before recovering and heading for the West Indies again, where another ship was easily taken, which they renamed the *Ranger*, and so created a reasonably large fleet. Roberts then took time out to cheat the merchants of Martinique, pretending to want to trade like the Dutch interlopers, whose sign to the merchants that the Dutch wanted to trade was to fly a jack. Then it was on to Guadeloupe and Hispaniola, taking ships along the way by fighting or scaring them into surrender. At the latter place, as they were cleaning their ships and carousing, a certain Harry Glasby, a sober and reluctant recruit to Roberts, was nevertheless made captain of the *Royal Fortune*, but tried to desert, along with two others.[27]

Glasby and the two others were chased and caught, and brought to pirate justice. According to Roberts' rule number 7, 'To desert the Ship, or their Quarters in Battle, was punished with Death, or Marooning.' Part of the reason for the strictness of this rule concerning desertion was that the pirates feared the deserter would alert the authorities and bring them all to ruin. So Glasby was tried, along with the other two, but just before judgement was announced, one of the judges, Valentine Ashplant, who was afterwards hung at Cape Coast Castle, stood up to defend Glasby, 'By G—, Glasby shall not die; d—n me if he shall.' Ashplant may have known Glasby before, but in any case, he concluded his defense of Glasby by saying, '…I hope he'll live and repent of what he has done; but d—n me if he must die, I will die along with him.' To back up his defense, Ashplant produced a pair of pistols which easily convinced the pirate judges to acquit Glasby. Not so lucky were the other two deserters, who were quickly tied to the mainmast and shot dead.[28]

With this makeshift court out of the way, Roberts sailed for the island of Desirade (or Deseada), off Guadeloupe, a favourite haunt, where they might trade for provisions. Roberts' fleet now included another *Good Fortune*, a Rhode Island brigantine captured previously off Dominica after a bloody fight, which left some of the Rhode Island crew dead. A further excursion in the West Indies produced more ships captured, almost always for provisions. In fact, one of the most neglected aspects of the history of piracy is logistics, and Roberts, with a crew of around 300, always had to be thinking of restocking with food, water and clothes, to say nothing of sails, gear and cables. Having secured these provisions, Roberts headed for the African coast of Guinea in 1721, which he knew very well as a former slaver, intending to buy cheap gold dust. Along the way, the *Good Fortune*, with seventy men aboard, conspired to leave Roberts' fleet, some of the men hoping to give up piracy. The immediate reason for the departure was that a fight had taken place onboard, in which Roberts killed a man who had insulted him, as Roberts was now finding that he had to be tough to keep the frequently drunk pirates in line.[29]

The pirates arrived at Sierra Leone in June 1721, and learnt that two Royal Navy pirate hunters, the *Swallow* and the *Weymouth*, with fifty guns apiece, had left the month before and would not be back until December. With this threat thought to be removed, Roberts' men took two more ships, which were renamed the *Ranger* and yet another *Royal Fortune*. The latter ship originally contained a clergyman, whom Roberts' crew wanted to keep, saying that all he had to do for a share of prize money was to make punch and say prayers. But the clergyman refused, and the pirates allowed him to depart with his belongings, which apparently included several valuable items not actually belonging to him, while he left behind three prayer books and a bottle screw. This contact with a clergyman did not result in a change in behaviour, since at Old Calabar, a centre of the slave trade, the pirates fought a battle with the local inhabitants, and set fire to the town. Then along the coast a slaver named the *King Solomon* was sighted, and Roberts decided to take her by sending a long boat with around twenty men to board the ship. As was normal pirate practice, Roberts called out, 'who will go?', and the required number of brisk pirates volunteered. These brisk men volunteered partly because it gave them a reputation for courage, and partly because it provided them with a complete set of new clothes, which they were allowed to take for themselves out of a prize. The *King Solomon* was easily taken because her crew refused to fight – as must have happened most of the time – because there was no reason for sailors to defend with their lives what did not belong to them, and for which danger they would get little reward.[30]

The next port of call was Whydah, another slave trading port. Here a particularly unpleasant incident took place. Roberts' idea of forcing each ship in harbour to pay a ransom of eight pounds of gold dust worked well, except for one ship, the *Porcupine*, whose captain would not pay. Thereupon, Roberts sent a boat to the *Porcupine* in order to transport the slaves before burning the ship. Roberts' boat was under the command of a rather vicious pirate called John Walden, whose ironic nickname was 'Miss Nanny' on account of his toughness. Walden found that it would take too much time to unshackle the miserable slaves, so he set fire to the *Porcupine*. Some of the eighty slaves managed to break loose from the slaver and jump overboard, only to be eaten by sharks, while the rest were burnt to death or drowned. Following this nasty affair, Roberts intended to sail for the island of Annabon to refit, but contrary winds blew them south towards Cape Lopez. And it was here at Cape Lopez Bay that Captain Ogle, in the British man of war, *Swallow*, finally caught up with Roberts' fleet of three ships. Believing that the *Swallow* was a Portuguese sugar trader trying to escape from them as she tacked to avoid a sand bar, the *Ranger* set out after her, and too late discovered the truth. The *Swallow* opened fire at close quarters, and over a period of one and a quarter hours killed ten pirates and wounded twenty, as well as bringing down the

Ranger's top mast. The crew of the *Ranger* held a vote about boarding the *Swallow*, but this was not seconded, even though there was plenty of man-power aboard the *Ranger* – 113 men, including twenty Africans. So, lack of discipline, damage and confusion aboard the *Ranger*, and lack of leadership, all led to the only alternative – surrender. Some pirates crowded around the *Ranger's* powder store and fired a pistol into it, rather than be captured, yet the amount of powder was too small and only produced a minor explosion and severe burns for these half dozen pirates. The pirate captain of the *Ranger* was one Skyrme, who fought on although he lost a leg in the engagement. Another captured pirate was William Main, boatswain of the *Royal Fortune*, who happened to be onboard the *Ranger*.[31]

An officer from the *Swallow* addressed William Main, asking about the rest of Roberts' crew. Main said there were 120 of them "'…as clever fellows as ever trod shoe leather: would I were with them!'" "No doubt on it," says the officer. "By G— it is naked truth," answered he [Main], looking down and seeing himself, by this time quite stripped [of his clothes].' The pirates were secured, and the *Ranger* sailed into Princess Island with a skeleton crew from the *Swallow*. Then Ogle and the *Swallow* entered Cape Lopez Bay again while Roberts was at breakfast on the *Royal Fortune*, having just taken another trading ship, the *Neptune*. Roberts' ship the *Little Ranger* was also anchored in the bay. Roberts decided to try and sail past the *Swallow* in the *Royal Fortune*, but anticipated a fight. A deserter from the *Swallow* told Roberts that the *Swallow* sailed best into the wind, so Roberts decided the *Royal Fortune* would try to sail with the wind astern and escape in that fashion. Roberts dressed himself in a rich damask waistcoat and breeches, a gold chain and diamond cross around his neck, a sword in his hand, and two pistols hanging on a silk sling slung over his shoulder. Whether because the wind died, or because gunfire from the *Swallow* shot away the *Royal Fortune's* mizzen top mast, or because the steersman in the *Royal Fortune* panicked, the *Royal Fortune* lost way, and in two hours the *Swallow's* cannon battered the *Royal Fortune* into surrender. As for Roberts himself, an early charge of grape shot took him in the throat, and he settled onto the tackles of a gun, bleeding profusely, and died almost immediately.[32]

The Royal Navy surgeon on the *Swallow*, John Atkins, explained that the reason the pirates were so easily taken was that they lacked discipline. Certainly, as soon as Roberts was known to be dead, the pirates on the *Royal Fortune* seemed to lose heart, even though she had forty guns and the crew numbered 175 men, including forty-five Africans. It is also possible that many were drunk or hung over from the night before. Another factor was that the pirates of the *Royal Fortune* were unable to get close enough to board the *Swallow*, where greater pirate numbers might have told. Instead the battle turned into an off ship gunnery duel, in which the *Swallow* with more guns and better gunnery discipline would always have an advantage. And this was the case. Despite their victory, though, the Royal Navy had its own serious problems, due to very high losses of men to disease. In fact, the *Weymouth*, companion to the *Swallow*, started out with 240 men, but counting replacements, a total of 280 died. Both the *Weymouth* and the *Swallow* had to enlist large numbers of Africans to supplement their crews, as well as force sailors from trading ships. It turned out that the latter were useless because of their previous bad treatment and poor diet, while the African slaves often died. A letter from the *Weymouth*'s captain, Mungo Herdman, complained to the Admiralty that he had to buy fifty slaves to replace his dead crew, and had to feed them at his own expense. It seems that fourteen of the *Weymouth*'s fifty slaves died, and Herdman had to dispose of others cheaply, again at his own expense. Herdman requested compensation from the Admiralty.[33]

Another problem for the *Swallow* was that once the pirates were captured, they had to be transported to Cape Coast Castle, a Royal African Company port, in order to be tried. But their captors could only guard them with skeleton crews, and the pirates hatched two plans to overpower their captors and escape. These plans did not work because some of the pirates informed the Royal Navy officers of the potential take over, hoping for better treatment and to be spared the noose. Another problem for the Royal Navy, always avid for prize money, was the fact that Roberts' *Little Ranger*, which was supposed to be full of gold dust, lay deserted and empty in Cape Lopez Bay. The pirates had fled ashore, and it appears that the ship recently captured by Roberts, the *Neptune*, had the good sense to loot the *Little Ranger*, because the captain of the *Neptune* later sold fifty ounces of gold dust in Barbados. As it was, Ogle only found 10 ounces of gold in the *Little Ranger*, though he admitted to finding 3,000 ounces altogether from the other two of Roberts' ships. A final blow to the Royal Navy was the loss of both the *Royal Fortune* and the *Ranger*, taken as prizes, which were driven ashore onto the rocks under Saltpan Hill, Jamaica, by a hurricane, and broken all to pieces in less than an hour. Although this considerably reduced the Royal Navy prize money, all aboard were saved except for one sailor and two African slaves.[34]

Continuing the story of prize money, an ironic conclusion to the capture of Roberts' ships and crew was the unedifying argument over the distribution of such money in the years following 1722. Prize money from gold dust, other treasure, and the *Little Ranger*, brought into Rhode Island, might have been about £8,000 to £10,000. The Privy Seal took over, and eventually awarded £5,364.90 to Ogle, of which £1,940 was supposed to be head money for pirates captured and killed, for the benefit of the officers and crew of the *Swallow*. Ogle did not reveal that he had received this sum of money, despite petitions from sailors, wives and widows, until a publication in London forced his hand. Ogle, now knighted and on his way up the naval ladder, refused to pay any prize money to his crew, citing the large expenses of his new rank. Reluctantly he eventually agreed to pay the head money of £1,940 to his crew, which transaction finally took place four years later in 1726.[35]

While Ogle was cleverly managing his finances, the pirates of Roberts' crew who had been captured and transported to Cape Coast Castle, now faced trial. Johnson has very full details of this trial, the numbers involved, the details of a number of cases, and the last words of the accused before they were 'turned off' to swing in the air. This was a very large-scale trial, resulting in the following results:

Acquitted:	74
Executed:	52
Respited:	2
Into servitude:	20
To Marshalsea prison in London:	17
Killed in the Ranger:	10
Killed in the Royal Fortune:	3
Died on the way to Cape Coast Castle:	15
Died afterwards in the Cape Coast Castle:	4
Africans to be sold:	70
Total:	267

Ogle has almost the same figures except that he has seventy-seven acquitted, and seventy-five Africans to be sold. The relatively small number killed onboard the two ships points to the ease of the Royal Navy victory, while the fairly large number acquitted relates mainly to those who were judged to have been forced to join Roberts' crew. Of the two respited until a final decision was made, one died abroad and one was pardoned. Of the twenty sent into servitude to the Royal African Company, none were living by 1724, killed by disease and hard work. Of the Africans, nothing is known, except that they were sold and continued their slavery. Johnson was very conscious of the popularity of pirate confessions just before hanging, and reported several, including the only pirate hung onboard the *Weymouth*, who apparently asked the ships' crew to join him in the singing of two or three verses of Psalm 140 before he was triced up at the fore yard arm. On the other hand, many pirates called for drink before execution, and desired caps so they would look better at hanging. According to Johnson, the most pathetic speech was made by one Bunce, about twenty-six years-old, who claimed he had been lured into piracy by the possibilities of power, liberty, and wealth. He declared that his youth and inexperience, and his briskness in carrying out piratical acts, were only due to his lively nature. He begged forgiveness, exhorted the spectators to avoid sin, and ended with the rather too obvious simile, 'That he stood there as a Beacon upon a Rock (the gallows standing on one) to warn erring Mariners of Danger.'[36]

In general, the trial was quite lenient by the standards of the time, in that only around 30 per cent of those actually tried were executed. One wonders what Roberts would have made of the trial and of the behaviour of his crew during their fight against the *Swallow*. Nevertheless, the Royal Navy achieved what it set out to do. Consequently, Captains Archibald Hamilton and Barrow Harris wrote in letters to the Admiralty in 1723 that there were no pirates off West Africa by 1723 after Ogle left, and very few in the West Indies, although Spanish ships pretending to be coast guards were taking merchantmen in the latter location. In fact, there were very few Western pirates left by the late 1720s, despite the odd occasion, as in 1748, when a privateer from Cork turned pirate, taking Venetian and Swedish ships. Basically, the pirates had either been pardoned or done to death.[37]

Lord Muskerry Versus Captain Robert Harris (1722)

Yet sometimes the Royal Navy was actually too keen to catch pirates in this period, as one unusual case shows.

In the 1720s when the war against the pirates was in full swing, captains in the Royal Navy looked to capture pirates, make a name for themselves, and hopefully profit from their capture. The profit came from sharing out whatever the pirate ship might contain when captured, and also the head money that the Admiralty paid: £100 for a commander of a pirate ship, and £20 for every private man. This led to a certain zeal, sometimes misplaced.

One example of a mistaken identity occurs with the attempt of the Irish peer and naval commander, Lord Muskerry, to prove that the innocent merchant Captain, Robert Harris, was really a pirate.

The scene opens with an affidavit and deposition by Robert Harris in Boston on 13 August 1722. Harris claimed that on 4 July 1722, he was master of the sloop *Sarah*, lying in Trinity harbour in Newfoundland, close to the port of Trepassy. Trepassy was the centre of the cod fishery at the time, and a favourite haunt of pirates, who came to replenish their food supplies, and recruit or compel the fishery workers to join their crews. Harris saw a large ship enter Trinity harbour, which only flew a jack and no other colours, and he feared this was a pirate ship that had been reported taking ships off the Newfoundland banks. Harris therefore caused small arms to be prepared on deck, and he then hailed a boat that had put off from the other ship, asking who they were. The reply from the boat was shocking to Harris, 'Damn ye' or 'Pray God Damn ye'. The two men from the boat came onboard, one of them a naval Lieutenant, who cursed him, telling Harris they came from an English man of war. Harris then showed them his lawful Register and Clearance and invited them to a glass of wine. After this the Lieutenant left and Harris, obviously fearful, hove up the anchor of his sloop, and attempted to leave harbour.

At this point, the man of war fired several shots at the *Sarah*. So Harris let down his sails, the man of war's pinnace came to the *Sarah*, and its sailors forced Harris into the pinnace and onto the man of war. Harris was then thrust into the man of war's main cabin, and the Lieutenant locked the door. Sitting in the main cabin was the naval captain of the man of war, who said nothing but immediately gave Harris several blows with his 'woolded' cane – meaning a cane bound around with a cord. Harris caught hold of the cane and asked what he had done to deserve such punishment. The naval captain, who turned out to be Lord Muskerry, damned Harris and said that Harris had threatened to fire on his Lieutenant. At that, Muskerry laid on Harris again with blows to his face and head. When Muskerry ran out of breath, Harris told him that he, Harris, recalled that he had been with Muskerry when they were both in Lisbon, when Muskerry commanded a ship called the *Dover*. At this, Muskerry got angry again while Harris offered to pay money if he had offended. Once more Muskerry started battering Harris with his woolded cane, and so the unfortunate Harris attempted to escape through the cabin door.

Muskerry then fell to battering Harris again, giving him several dangerous blows, which almost deprived Harris of his senses. Then Muskerry ordered Harris into irons, calling him a Dog, but Harris could only crawl or creep onto the deck of the man of war. This again annoyed Muskerry, who gave him several more blows, at which point Muskerry changed his mind about the irons, and ordered Harris into the pinnace to return to his sloop. The sailors on the pinnace also removed the mainsail of the *Sarah*, preventing Harris' ship from sailing, so Harris later went ashore and desired to speak to Muskerry on land. Instead, one of Muskerry's officers told Harris he must pay £3 for the naval shots fired before he could get his mainsail back. He also told Harris that Muskerry was rather arbitrary, but that he, Harris, was lucky not to have been whipped from stage to stage through the harbour. Finally, Harris was told to go back onboard the man of war, and pay the £3, which he did, and got his mainsail back, while suffering further insults from Muskerry. Harris asked if he could leave harbour, but Muskerry refused permission.

Harris therefore spent the next night ashore in a miserable condition, and later pathetically described his wounds:

> …enduring abundance of pain in my head right side Shoulder and back having many Stripes severall of them Six Inches Long and three wide bruised to a Jelly, with many blows on my left hand and arm & Elbow my arm lying benummed and dead all the night and I received many blows on my fingers hands Left Arm and Elbow and in such a miserable and painfull Condition my Grief was the greater because there was no Surgeon in the Harbour nor any relief to be had but only from my Doctor's Box I had onboard…

Harris claimed to have been hit fifty times. Muskerry finally gave Harris permission to leave port, and it seems Harris learned at this point that his tormentor was Lord 'Muscarry' of the ship *Solebay*. After stopping to get medical treatment at the port of St Johns, Harris arrived at Boston on 31 July, and registered his affidavit and deposition against Muskerry shortly after. This material was then sent to the Admiralty.[38]

The Lords of the Admiralty somewhat naturally desired Muskerry to reply to Harris' charges. Muskerry replied on 7 December 1722, saying that he was pursuing a pirate ship, which he learned had gone into Trinity harbour. So Muskerry headed to Trinity harbour, and flew only his jack, hoping to surprise the pirate in the harbour. Muskerry claimed that as soon as he entered the harbour, he also hoisted King's colours. He found the sloop *Sarah* also carrying the same colours, and took her for the pirate he had been chasing. He sent his Lieutenant aboard the sloop, to bring the master (Harris) onboard the *Solebay*, which Harris refused. Then Harris made sail to leave the harbour, which increased Muskerry's suspicions. Muskerry fired two shots, but Harris kept going, so Muskerry fired a broadside. Harris was brought aboard the *Solebay*, and Muskerry asked Harris what he meant by abusing his Lieutenant by taking him by the throat and threatening to shoot him. (Harris did not include this detail in his deposition, and it may have taken place.) According to Muskerry, Harris said he would do the same again, that he cared not for any officer, and that the owners of his ship would protect him.

Muskerry wrote that because of this answer, 'I could not help reprimanding him [Harris] with half a dozen strokes with my Cane, but very far from what he is pleas'd to say in his Complaint to their Lordships, as to my detaining him it is most true being as I thought for the good of the Service believing he would give an account to the Pirates…' Muskerry also claimed that Harris was not in a hurry to leave Trinity harbour, and he ended his letter by writing that what he did was for the good and honour of the Service. Perhaps fearing that his account was not quite believable, Muskerry added a postscript suggesting that his officers would support his account.[39]

Predictably, Muskerry easily survived this complaint. In fact, Muskerry actually became governor of Newfoundland from 1733 to 1735, and finished his career in the Royal Navy in 1741 as captain of a first rate, the *Adventure*. Something of Muskerry's impetuous nature comes through in his next career, however, when he supported the Stuarts. This meant that he had to leave England and live in France, where he was given a very generous yearly income of £1,000 by Louis XV. Muskerry resided happily enough in Boulogne until his death in 1769. For his part, Harris seems to have been reasonably justified in his accusations against Muskerry, but simply continued his career as a merchant captain.

Nevertheless, the real significance of the Harris-Muskerry episode is that it is an example of the zeal with which the Royal Navy pursued pirates at this stage of the war of extermination against the pirates. And in this situation mistakes would be made because it was not always easy to tell who was a pirate and who was not.

Yet, if Atlantic pirates had by and large disappeared by the late 1720s, the Mediterranean was another story.

The Barbary Corsairs of North Africa

The name 'Barbary corsair' derives from the Arabic word 'barbar', referring to the Berbers of North Africa, and the word 'corso' referring to the practice of the galleys from North Africa going out 'al corso', hunting for Christian ships and captives. Technically, the galleys that rowed forth from the three regencies of Algiers, Tunis and Tripoli were privateers because they followed the instructions of the rulers of these North African towns, who were under the nominal control of the Ottoman Empire. In addition, there was always an element of jihad for these Muslim corsairs, who wished to expand the boundaries of Islam. Nevertheless, for Europeans, and especially for the inhabitants of Spain, Italy, Greece, and the Mediterranean islands, the Barbary corsairs appeared as pirates, raiding coasts and ships in search of captives to sell as slaves, or benefiting from the ransom payments of their captives. On the Atlantic coast, the Sallee Rovers, based in Salé, were more clearly pirates, many of them expelled from Spain in 1609, and by the late 1620s operating independently of the sultan of Morocco. On the other hand, the Sallee Rovers to some extent also saw their activities as a continuation of their holy war against the infidel. The Sallee Rovers aimed at wider horizons than the Barbary corsairs, raiding as far away as Iceland,

Wales, Ireland, and Newfoundland. The more spectacular of these raids were carried out by a Dutch renegade, Jan Janssen, renamed Murat Rais, who sailed to Reykjavik in 1627 and captured some 400 Icelanders. Four years later he surprised the inhabitants of Baltimore in southern Ireland, capturing some 120 slaves. Renegades were Christians who had converted to Islam, and were often used by the Barbary corsairs as ship captains and maritime experts.

The Barbarossa Brothers

The Barbary corsairs of North Africa moved into high gear with the arrival of the Barbarossa brothers. There were four brothers, Aroudj, Elias, Isaak, and Kheir ed-Din, who were all named Barbarossa because of the red beard of Aroudj, the eldest. Their father was one Jacob, an Albanian who had converted to Islam, their mother the daughter of a Greek priest, and the family resided on the Greek island of Lesbos. All four of the brothers became corsairs, though only two rose to fame, Aroudj and Kheir ed-din. Aroudj was captured by the Knights of Rhodes, and became a galley slave, but was ransomed. Starting with a small band, Aroudj then captured the island of Djerba around 1502 or 1503. Operating from there on behalf of the Ottoman Empire he captured two papal galleys and a Spanish ship carrying 300 soldiers and sixty passengers, and also took service with the sultan of Tunis. Carrying the fight to the infidel, Aroudj, sometimes with the aid of Ottoman forces, and sometimes leading a loose coalition of Moors, local tribesmen and dispossessed Muslims from Spain, attacked Spanish possessions on the coast of North Africa. For example, in 1512, he attacked the port of Bougie, whose ruler had been defeated by the Spanish two years before. However, at this siege, Aroudj lost his left arm to a cannon ball, and the siege failed. After a few more land-based operations, Aroudj was welcomed into Algiers by its ruler in 1516. Here, Aroudj showed his true colours by seizing the palace and town of Algiers with the support of Janissaries (the Ottoman army of Christian youths taken as a tax from the Balkans and converted to Islam; the Janissaries also recruited Christian renegades and Turks). Aroudj killed the ruler of Algiers in his sauna, while the ruler's widow committed suicide, and her companions were tortured to death. Aroudj executed all he suspected of opposing him. Next Aroudj turned west and attacked local rulers, but his cruelty and heavy taxation turned the population against him, and he was finally cornered by the Spanish in 1518, and killed. His head was displayed at the gate of Oran, and his body was nailed to the wall of the city of Tlemcen, lighted by the flares of four torches.[1]

If Aroudj was a part time pirate, but more of a land based adventurer, attempting to conquer Spanish possessions and the Arab and Berber tribes of North Africa, it was his youngest brother, Kheir ed-Din who dominated the maritime area. In honour of his brother, Kheir ed-Din dyed his hair and beard with henna, to produce a reddish hue, and was more capable than his brother, being a clever engineer and speaking six or more languages. He continued his brother's land-based campaigns in Tunisia and also made Algiers his base, finally capturing the strong Spanish fort in the approaches to Algiers, called the Penon, in May 1529. Even before this, Kheir ed-Din had successfully attacked Sicily and the Italian coasts, and operated profitably off the French coast. Consequently the Ottoman sultan, Suleiman the Magnificent, made him admiral in chief of his fleet in 1533, and Kheir ed-Din set about building a powerful Ottoman fleet of three decked galleys, reinforced with lead, and heavily armed. In 1534 Kheir ed-Din sailed with some forty of these galleys and sacked Fondi in Italy, perhaps seeking out the well known beauty, Giulia da Gonzaga, widow of the lord of Fondi. As it happened, Giulia was elsewhere, but 20,000 Janissaries landed near Fondi and carried off women and children. Next, Kheir ed-Din became involved in the struggle for Tunis, where he failed to retain control of the city against the local king, who was supported in bloody fights by Italians, Spaniards and the Knights of Malta. In revenge, Kheir ed-Din sailed for Majorca and allegedly carried away some 6,000 captives and considerable booty, selling his captives in the slave market of Algiers. In 1537, with a large fleet of 250 galleys, Kheir ed-Din devastated the area around Otranto in Italy, and then in the following year, 1538, he defeated a superior Christian fleet consisting of thirty-six papal galleys, sixty-one Genoese galleys, fifty Portuguese galleys, and ten galleys from the Knights of Malta. Kheir ed-Din's masterful command produced a victory, and gave the Ottomans control over the eastern Mediterranean for some thirty years.

There followed an unusual Ottoman alliance with France, since the French king, Francis I, used the Ottomans as allies in his struggle against the Holy Roman Emperor, Charles V. As part of this deal, Kheir ed-Din and his fleet of galleys spent the year 1543-1544 in the port of Toulon, planning future attacks against either Tunis, held by the Spaniards, or Italy, part of the domain of Charles V. Ultimately, Francis I was forced to bribe Kheir ed-

Din to leave France, handing over 800,000 ecus and much else, 'At Toulon there were thirty-two treasury officials filling sacks with 1,000, 2,000 or 3,000 ecus continually for three whole days and for the best part of the nights.'[2] So, in May 1544, Kheir ed-Din and his galleys plus a French fleet left the coast of France and sailed for Italy where towns and villages on the coast were plundered and burnt. At Reggio, in Calabria, men, women and children were chained and forced onto the ships. It is also alleged that Kheir ed-Din fell in love with the governor's daughter and made her his second wife. At Porto Ercole, thirty men were given up as tribute if the town would be spared, but the town was burnt anyway. The island of Giglio lost 632 individuals, while the heads of the leading inhabitants were cut off. The island of Lipari offered a bribe, but this was refused and Kheir ed-Din's artillery bombarded the main town until it surrendered. The population was brought in front of Kheir ed-Din who had the old men and women beaten, while the Janissaries found a group in the cathedral who 'were taken out, robbed of their clothes and cut open whilst still alive ...When we [the French] asked them why they treated these people with such cruelty they replied that among them such cruelty was deemed a virtue.'[3]

After this, Kheir ed-Din did not have long to live, but before he died in Istanbul of fever or the plague in 1546, he had time to raid Minorca and Mahon, carrying off another 6,000 people. Following this last attack, he began building a large palace and mosque in Istanbul, but he did not have much time to enjoy this final flourish. At his death, the Barbary corsairs lost their most famous captain, though others such as Dragut and Ochiali were to follow.[4]

The North African Corsair System: Raids and Attacks

The Barbarossas and subsequent corsairs certainly sought ships, money, and booty, but the main aim was to capture prisoners on land or at sea, who were then turned into slaves. These slaves might be ransomed or redeemed for cash, or more rarely exchanged for Muslim captives, or were purchased and put to work in different ways in North Africa. It has been estimated that between 1530 and 1780 some one million, or one and a quarter million Europeans were captured and made slaves in North Africa, principally in Algiers, Tunis and Tripoli, with further captives in Istanbul and Sallee. The high point of this activity was between 1605 and 1634, when corsairs from Algiers took some 600 European ships. Together with land raids, the result was some 35,000 captive slaves at any one time in the three Barbary regencies of Algiers, Tunis and Tripoli during the period 1580–1680. And because of the high attrition rate of the slaves – around 25 per cent per year due to plague, mortality from poor conditions, ransom, and some becoming Muslim – there was a need for another 8,500 new slaves per year.[5]

How did this whole system work? In the sixteenth century, before the galleon was introduced to the Barbary corsairs in the very early 1600s, their attacks were launched by the galley, usually operating in small fleets of two or three or more. Galleys were rowed by slaves, perhaps 150 to 300 per galley, which also contained around 140 soldiers. The aim was either to attack Christian ships at sea, or more easily, to raid the coastal areas of Italy, Spain and the Mediterranean islands. These raids usually took place at dawn, or involved some deceit, and the idea was to grab as many local inhabitants as possible. Villagers on these coasts had little recourse but to flee inland as fast as possible:

> Blessed was he who could flee his bed,
> That there was no other safety or shelter
> Than to run away leaving all his goods...
> The mother abandoned her own child,
> The husband his wife, the son his father,
> Never asking advice from anyone,
> But, by back roads, indirect and little-known,
> Everyone tried to flee the danger.[6]

The local authorities responded by building watch towers, and providing local militias, mobile cavalry patrols and naval forces to protect the coasts. There was also a special tune played by the local bugler when such raids came ashore, 'Moors on the Coast'. But a long cove-studded coast was hard to defend, and in the sixteenth century and early seventeenth centuries before protective measures became more effective, flight was still the best remedy. If the local inhabitants could not escape and were caught and taken onboard the corsair galley, the unfortunate victims still had a chance at freedom. This was because the corsair would frequently return after a day or two to the same location from where the captives had been taken, hoist a white flag or some other sign of treaty, and bargain for ransom payments for the captives. Families of the captives usually had little enough cash for this situation, being simple villagers, but ruthless financiers would arrive, and offer to advance the necessary ransom cash in exchange for the villagers' houses and farm land. There would also be a deadline for the payment of the ransom. As far as the corsairs were concerned, the ransom obtained in this manner would only be a small percentage of what their captives would fetch in the slave markets of North Africa, but it did provide instant cash for the corsairs, and also avoided the bother of keeping the captives secure and alive until the corsairs returned to port. If all went well, and the ransom was paid, the captives would return home to their now impoverished families, and often decided to move inland. In fact, one result of these corsair raids was a considerable depopulation of the coastal areas of Italy and Spain. As important, the corsair raids also had a considerable psychological impact.[7]

The other alternative to raiding on land was, of course, for the corsairs to attack at sea. Here the issue for the corsairs was complicated by the fact that the regencies of North Africa often had treaties with various European nations, so some ships were off limits. This particularly referred to French, Dutch and English ships at various times, but the corsairs were adept at attacking Hapsburg ships from Spain, Italy, the islands of Sardinia, Sicily, and the Balearics, plus ships from states sometimes allied with the Hapsburgs, such as Venice and Genoa. As well, ships of the Knights of Malta were in perpetual conflict with the corsairs, and could be captured if possible. Even if the Barbary corsairs took a ship that was supposedly protected by treaty, the corsairs cleverly provoked neutral ships, or used deceit when boarding such ships by claiming to find contraband onboard from prohibited states. If all this failed, the corsairs could still board, and pretend to find someone from an enemy nation. An example of this occurred when the French cleric Jean-Baptiste Gramaye was accused by corsairs of being a Spaniard onboard a neutral ship, though he protested he did not know a word of Spanish. Gramaye reported that the corsairs then 'whipped me with blows of a rope to the head, swearing that they would teach it to me well. Then, hearing me speak French and seeming to willingly believe that I had nothing in common with Spain, they insisted that I was a Jew.' This last suggestion was because Jews were thought to be worth large ransoms. Then Gramaye watched terrified as one passenger was thrashed almost unconscious, at the end of which the passenger was compelled to swear in writing that Gramaye was really a bishop in disguise, and his servant was actually a Knight of Malta.[8]

The corsair ships carried a large contingent of soldiers, perhaps 140 on a galley and 100–200 on a sailing ship. Because of this large number, plus the fact that the corsair galleys were usually faster than merchant ships, due to constant careening and the cut down character of their vessels, the corsairs had a high success rate once a ship was spotted. Then, the actual moment of capture was a terrifying one for those onboard the victim. The corsairs made as much noise as possible as they closed in on the unhappy ship, to psychologically disarm the crew. Shouting, cursing, banging the side of their ship, and clapping hands, the soldiers on the corsair ships wanted to have as easy a time in the actual capture as possible. Swarming aboard, rather than reducing their victim by cannon, the corsairs waved curved scimitars, wore turbans and flowing clothes, and altogether presented a terrifying picture. Also, because it was a tradition that if a ship offered any resistance, the first corsair aboard had the choice of one of the captured passengers as his slave, there was an understandable rush to get aboard the targeted ship. Then the rest of the corsairs wandered about the ship 'searching here and there on the bridge, in the waist, and at the bottom of the hold: with blows of axes they broke open the trunks … gorging themselves with booty, smashing into the stores, breaking the seals, and making an inventory all at the same time.'[9] The first rush onboard could also be dangerous for the crew and passengers due to the fury of the corsairs, following which came the search of the captured crew and passengers for their wealth and status. One account comes from Richard Hasleton, captured in 1582, as his ship sank after gunfire from two Turkish galleys. He was shot, but swam to one of the galleys, where he was stripped of his clothes, and the captain questioned him about his status, 'Which because I would not confess, he gave me fifteen strokes with a cudgel and then put me in the galley's hold, where I was six days, taking very little sustenance, lying in extreme pains by reason of my hurts…'[10]

The wealthy among the passengers would make every effort to conceal their status from the corsairs, since the wealthy would expect to have to pay a large ransom for their freedom. Hence, just before capture, there would be the hurried efforts of wealthy merchants to change their clothes to those of a peasant, and to conceal any coins and jewels, perhaps going as far as swallowing a gold coin or two. The ultimate option was to throw some or all of their wealth overboard. Thus one account showed how passengers, 'Threw the better part of their silver money, flashy dress suits, gilded swords, embroidered belts, boots, letters, and other indicators of wealth and quality helter-skelter into the sea … out of a desire to disguise themselves, to avoid the demands of a huge ransom.'[11] Of course the corsairs were well aware of such tricks, and spent some time examining the hands and teeth of their captives, which tended to give the game away. And, as in the story of Gramaye, the corsairs would sometimes choose one unfortunate captive to beat in order to get him to reveal which of the prisoners were worth large ransoms, and where everyone had hidden their wealth. But opinion seems to differ on the corsair treatment of their captives, one author praising the good behavior of the corsairs, especially in their treatment of female passengers, while another stressed the abuse of the corsairs. Certainly, the captives would be chained, hustled below deck, and kept in very confined quarters because the galley or ship would already have too many soldiers and rowers onboard. And sometimes the captive would be put to the oars immediately, as one wrote how within a very short time 'they put me in a Galley, stript off my Robes, shaved my head, and set me to an Oar, which was work enough for six of us to tug at.'[12]

Slave Captivity in North Africa

After this, the captives faced an unpleasant journey. This could be long, depending on the corsair voyage, and might result in death due to disease or lack of food and water, or the galley could head straight back to Algiers or another port. If the voyage had been a success, the corsair would fire guns as the galley or ship approached port, and if a galley, the rowers would be forced to row 'proudly', with a long stroke and exaggerated fall of the oar. Then, psychologically, must have come the hardest part for the captives, when they were paraded through town on their way to captivity before the slave auction, with the cheers and jeers of the town's inhabitants ringing in their ears. Joseph Pitts, captured in 1678, recounts his arrival in Algiers, where the first night was spent in the house of the ship's captain. Next day, the Dey (ruler) of Algiers took his one eighth pick of the slaves (and his one eighth of the cargo if it survived), after which Pitts was driven to the slave marketplace in Algiers, called the *badestan*, where he was obliged to stand from 8a.m. until 2p.m. while prospective buyers sampled the wares. Then came the auction, and Pitts recalled how the auctioneer tried to improve the value of the slave, 'Behold what a strong man this is! What limbs he has! He is fit for any work. And see what a pretty boy this is! No doubt his parents are very rich and able to redeem him with a great ransom.' Next, the slaves, whether male or female, were paraded a second time in front of the Dey, the governor of Algiers, who could repurchase any at the price that they were sold for in the auction.[13] It appears that the real auction then took place at the Dey's palace, since after the Dey had made his purchases, the traders made their final bids for the slaves, which were often twice what the original sale price had been. For these auctions, both at the *badestan* and in the Dey's palace, the slaves would be prodded, made to run and jump to show fitness, while the usual inspection of hands and teeth took place – the hands to establish rank, but the teeth to see if the slave could gnaw the hard biscuit and beef jerky of the galleys. Other more careful inspections would look at the hair cut, again to establish rank, and the earlobes to see if they had been pierced, which meant the slave was likely to be of higher status. More difficult was evaluation of age – obviously useful for judging the length of a slave's working life and ability to do hard work.

After purchase, slaves were divided into two categories: slaves for ransom, and slaves for work. Slaves for ransom were put to work, but the work needed to be of such a character that it did not damage the slave physically while awaiting the payment of their ransom. Slaves for work might find themselves doing the worst work – rowing in the galleys, or at construction onshore, especially the backbreaking work of building the mole in Algiers. The more fortunate slaves, and almost all the female slaves, would find themselves doing household work, carrying water, fetching bread, tending the gardens, nursing infants, sewing, or if capable, acting as clerks and shop assistants. Probably the hardest work was continually rebuilding the Algiers mole, as it was poorly constructed and frequently washed away by the sea. Huge stone blocks, weighing twenty to forty tons were cut from quarries about two miles away from the town, and then dragged on carts or sleds, hauled by 600 or 700 slaves, to the mole and dumped into the sea. The Dey set the quota for the slaves to fulfill, so many loads a day, which was required of the overseers who naturally made sure this was done, 'continually beating the slaves with their sticks, and goading them with its end, in which is a small spear, not unlike an ox-goad…'[14] To make matters worse, the slaves were chained together, or had heavy iron rings attached to their feet. Other tasks included building houses, road construction, working as farm labourers, and indeed any work that required manual labour.

At night the slaves were kept in 'bagnos', slave prisons, where conditions were unpleasant due to overcrowding, lack of sanitation, and heat. Some bagnos were very large – the Grand Bagno in Algiers was able to hold some 2,000 slaves, while others were much smaller, but regardless of the size, they tended to be miserable places. Describing a bagno at Porto Farina, near

Tunis, the Christian missionary Father Costa wrote that 100 or more slaves were crammed into a space:

> …about thirty paces square … and for the misery of the place, they have to stay on top of one the other and only with difficulty can one breathe … for there not being a window nor any breeze, and with the door closed, such is the fetor that it sometimes causes [men] to faint, and I do not speak of the quantity of every sort of animal waste … [and] at the break of dawn the Christians are let out and carried by the Moors off to work, and every night it is the same story.[15]

On the other hand, by the early eighteenth century, conditions inside the bagnos seem to have improved, with chapels, medical facilities and hospitals, shops run by the slaves, and bars to serve those who were allowed to drink alcohol, mainly renegades, and the slaves themselves. The overseer of the bagno was paid a sum of money, and he kept order so that the slaves who ran the bars and shops were fairly treated and could make a profit. In fact, some slaves were able to become minor entrepreneurs, working on a shared profit basis for their masters, taking advantage of the free time after daily work, and before being locked up in the bagno, to sell toys they had made, or to sell water around the streets, or to go into business as shopkeepers, or even to take the high risk of stealing goods and money.

Galley Slaves

Living in bagnos, being fed very little and being aroused at dawn to work at hard labour all day until an hour before sunset all took its toll on the slaves, so that mortality rates were quite high, perhaps around seventeen per cent per year. But it was life in the galleys that stands out as being the most traumatic experience of all for a slave. Galleys went out from the Barbary ports for cruises of around forty to fifty days twice a year, so the slaves would not be permanently confined to the galleys, but when not rowing would labour on land as previously described. However, galley slaves of the Ottoman Sultan in Istanbul would be permanently confined to their galleys, and often served extremely long terms, averaging around nineteen years in the late seventeenth century and early eighteenth century period. And these slaves simply never got off the galley but lived there for years. But whether rowing out of Istanbul, Algiers, Tunis or Tripoli – all faced a difficult time. A poem, originally printed in 1624, suggests the problems:

> He that's condemned to th'oar hath first his face,
> Eyebrows and head close shaven (for more disgrace
> Cannot betide a Christian). Then, being stripped
> To th'girdle (as when rogues are to be whipped),
> Chained are they to the seats where they sit rowing
> Five in a row together, a Turk going
> On a large plank between them; and though their eyes
> Are ready to start out with pulling, he cries
> 'Work, work, you Christian curs', and though none needs
> One blow for loitering, yet his bare back bleeds
> And riseth up in bunches, which the Turk
> With a bull's pizzle gives him, crying still, 'Work
> Work, dog', whilst some so faint, at th'oar th[e]y die,
> Being cast (like dogs) overboard presently.
> Their slavery done at sea, then they are laid
> In dungeons worse than jails, poorly arrayed,
> Fed with coarse horse-bread, water for their drink,
> And such sometimes puddles cannot worser stink.[16]

There needs to be some caution about descriptions of galley life, as in this poem, for there was an effort by Christian clergy to stress the cruelty in order to raise funds to redeem the captives. Nevertheless, being a galley slave was obviously a severe test of endurance. Rowers were shackled to the oar by their wrists and ankles to a chain that ran the length of the bench. There might be five or six rowers to each oar, who rowed by the method of rising and then pulling on the oar by falling back to the bench. Rowers could relieve themselves by going along their particular bench to a hole in the side of the galley, but often relieved themselves where they sat – it was said that one could smell a galley a mile away. Sleep was a luxury, since the rowers had to try to sleep where they sat, and sometimes had to row day and night. Clothing was simply a pair of breeches with no shirt to cover the chest. Food was meager in the extreme – two or three pieces of bread or biscuit, and some vinegar-laced water. With all this, the rowers were encouraged by the overseers who walked back and forth down the centre aisle, and lashed the bare backs of the slaves with a whip made of a bull's penis known as a bull's pizzle. Not surprisingly, many slaves died at sea and were thrown overboard or became too exhausted and sick to row in a future voyage. Fortunately, galley cruises were usually limited to around two a year, and during these two cruises, the time at sea was limited by the food and water and capacity of the galley so that the galley only spent a limited number of days at sea. And there was one positive aspect – galley slaves could actually benefit from the prize money obtained during a voyage. The crew was entitled to seven-sixteenth of the profit, and this included the galley slaves, though their master might take a percentage of that also. Yet, many slaves survived lengthy galley service, and there was the prospect of being appointed to a position onboard as a *scrivani* – a slave secretary who kept track of the lives of the slaves, and kept the financial books of the voyage. There were also *vagovans* – slaves who were the pace setters and organizers of the rowers, since achieving a good rhythm was vital, but as one might expect, difficult to attain. Overall, however, it is the image of the slave rowers being beaten to achieve maximum speed that remains:

> Under the least pretext, they [the overseers] would employ the Escurribanda, which consists of their rushing down the walkway and beating ten or twelve times the naked back of each [rower] with a tarred, knotted cord, and they deal with the two hundred and fifty Christians on a galley one after the other, without anyone escaping.[17]

The Redemption Orders and the Redemption System

Barbary slaves, whether on land, or at sea, always had hopes of redemption, that is being freed by the payment of ransom money. This was a system that became highly developed, with middlemen and charities raising money to provide ransoms. Of course, ransom was a well known European practice in medieval times, and as early as the twelfth and thirteenth centuries religious orders were created to redeem Christian captives taken during the Crusades. Thus, the redemption order known as the Trinitarians was founded in 1193, and the Mercedarians in 1203. These two orders later turned to ransoming slaves from the Barbary Coast, and other orders and charities joined the effort, such as the Congregation of Santo Cristo de Burgos, founded in 1569. Italian cities, such as Naples, Bologna, Lucca, Venice, Palermo, Genoa, and the Vatican itself, followed suit in the sixteenth and seventeenth centuries.

Soon, in Italy, preachers, churches, licensed alms collectors, local charities, towns and villages, and private families, all sought to raise funds for slave redemption. In Spain, from the time of Philip II, the state took over the supervision of ransoming slaves, with the Council of Castile being put in charge. The Council of the Indies gave money, as did private trusts and the Crown itself. These funds were divided into two kinds – *limosnas* for general redemptive use, and *adjutorios* for specific people.

And of course, as happened everywhere, private families gathered funds any way they could to liberate family members. The case of the author Miguel de Cervantes illustrates some of the problems of obtaining a ransom. Miguel de Cervantes was a rather obscure officer when captured in 1575, together with his brother Rodrigo, on his way from Naples to Spain. The family was not wealthy, so Cervantes' first effort was to send a letter to the Christian governor of Oran asking for help. But the Moor carrying the letter was intercepted, and strung up on the spot, while Cervantes suffered 200 blows for this appeal. The Trinitarians were able to secure the release of Rodrigo, being the younger brother and less important and thus cheaper. Meanwhile, Miguel had to stay in Algiers until the ransom of 750 ducats had been paid in full. Miguel's mother and sister were only able to raise 250 ducats, and charity provided another 300 ducats. 200 was still owing, which was eventually collected in Spain, and Miguel was released in 1580. It is recorded that when Miguel and eight fellow slaves landed in Spain they 'jumped ashore and kissed the soil'. It is also recorded that Miguel spent many years trying to repay the debts he owed, and he only started to become more secure financially after the publication of the first part of *Don Quixote* in 1605.[18]

Ironically, as charity funds for the redemption of slaves increased, so did the price that the Barbary states demanded for each slave, leading to inflation in the system. Another result of rising prices was the practice of the Barbary corsairs from the early 1700s of specifically capturing individuals for ransom, rather than using them for various kinds of labour. Before the 1700s the system was far from perfect since the slave had first to notify his family that he was a captive, and this could take months and years, partly because it cost money to send a letter, and slaves had little or no money. And some slaves, especially those on the sultan's galleys in Istanbul simply did not have the means of informing anyone of their situation. Then, even if a letter did arrive, there was obviously the question of raising the ransom, as mentioned, and in Italy authorities often requested the *fede* of slavery – a piece

of paper that identified the slave by name and description – and also certi-
fication that the slave's family was too poor to raise the ransom themselves.
It seems that some slaves in the Barbary ports were not above trying to take
the identity of a slave that had died, or even claiming to be that particular
slave when the ransom money was handed over. Thus it was necessary to
offer specific physical details of the particular slave to be ransomed, as in the
case of one Simone of Cavi, captured in 1582:

> Son of Romano and Catterina di Antonio of Cavi, around 24 years of age, [he
> is] with little beard, of fair skin, skinny of body, more tall than short in stature.
> With three marks on the body, that is: a cut on the thigh that was [from] birth,
> another cut on the temple from being hit by a rock, and another cut under
> the right eye that was [from] the point of a Moor's sword, from which eye he
> does not see, unless he holds it open like the other, but it is more white and
> bigger than the other, and [to keep it open] he had a string around his neck,
> where one can still see the mark.[19]

Simone should have been easy to identify with this description, and states
and charities began to compile lists of those held as slaves, with similar
types of description. Inevitably, though, there was a priority list of those to
be redeemed. First would be the slaves for whom specific funds had been
raised, then those who were thought to be at particular risk of becoming
Muslim such as women, children and young men. After this, clergy would
have a high listing, also those with good connections, and those with useful trades such as soldiers and sailors. Understandably, at the bottom of the
list were renegades who had changed their minds, but also the elderly, and
those nationalities without charities or representation. In this respect, certain nationalities did better than others, for example, Spanish slaves seemed
to be ransomed more quickly than other nationalities, probably because of
the efforts of the Trinitarians and Mercedarians, while the English, Dutch
and Germans fared less well.

This brings up the question of the method by which the redemption
transaction took place. The money raised for ransom might be entrusted to
the Trinitarians and Mercedarians, whose knowledge of the Barbary ports
and frequent visits there, plus experience in the ransom business, made them
efficient and reliable, and they did not charge a commission. Missionaries
from these orders would obtain passports and simply arrive in Algiers, Tunis
or Tripoli and negotiate with the local Dey the price for the release of as

many slaves as possible with the money at hand. Ransoms might also be entrusted to merchants and sea captains, who actually carried the money, or bills of exchange could be used. There was also a wide network of Jews who specialised in redemptions, but who tended to charge about a fourteen per cent commission. Prominent here as a professional ransom agent was Joseph Cohen of Algiers. Greeks and Armenians were also engaged in the ransom trade, as were renegades, who knew both sides of the ransom business, as did Moors from Spain who had settled in the Barbary ports. Others involved were the foreign consuls on the Barbary Coast who did much to organise the process, including drawing up contracts to allow slaves to go to Europe and try to arrange their own ransom. This system generally required hostages to be left behind, sometimes even the wife and children of the slave, who were sent to Barbary as surety, or there was the threat of retaliation against fellow slaves to make the European-bound slave adhere to his contract. One large problem in the redemption process tended to be the local Dey, who tried to unload the elderly, blind and infirm in place of those slaves requested by the negotiators, and often unloaded nationalities other than those from which the redeemers came. It was also possible for slave exchanges to take place, with Christian and Muslim slaves being exchanged through middlemen, usually with one Christian being equal to three or four Muslims.[20]

If all went well, the slaves on the list would be redeemed – but returning home was not so straightforward. Often redeemed slaves went through the Christian port of Leghorn, where they would wait for the ransom to be finalised. Then, by the seventeenth century in Italy and the eighteenth century in Spain, redeemed slaves would be quarantined, because of fear of the plague contracted on the Barbary Coast, for example the 1664 plague epidemic in Algiers. Quarantine took place in a lazaret – a house, a hospital, or sometimes a ship or an island – set aside for quarantine purposes. After approximately a month, the released slave, if healthy, would then join a procession to celebrate his deliverance. Whether in local towns or in the capital, the slaves would start their procession from a church of the Redemptionist order that had freed them, and would be accompanied by clergy, soldiers, members of the Redemptionist order, a band, and local townspeople. Banners were carried, and fireworks exploded. The ex-slaves were given meals, and in the case of Venice, a cash donation and the help of a gentleman for each slave to help them get started in life again. The processions were a method of raising donations for further redemptions, a way of fostering publicity for the Redemption orders involved, and an attempt to reintegrate the slave back into 'normal' society again. This was more than necessary because after several years of being absent a slave's home life and family might have altered considerably, and the frequently bleak financial picture and lack of jobs for returned slaves were serious problems. (This situation is somewhat similar to the problems faced today by prisoners recently released from jail, who often need help to reintegrate back into society.) In fact, as could be expected, redeemed slaves did find it difficult to reintegrate, judging by various written comments from them in Italy:

'In the meantime I have remained in a rented bed at [San] Tome, living miserably [and] not having anything of my own … Here I don't have anything: I'm living off charity…'

'Meanwhile, I am in the house of my wife, living in complete misery…'

'I live badly, in the house of my aforementioned sister in Castello, making a living when the chance comes to me to earn something…'

'I stay at Santa Margarita, in the house of my mother, who takes care of me since I have been stripped of everything, and if the opportunity presented itself, I would do the same work [as a sailor]…'[21]

Escape from the Barbary Coast

Finally, if redemption, as described above, seemed an impossible dream for those slaves without family money, charity, or connections, then escape was another possibility. Few captives actually achieved successful escapes, but because only those who escaped were able to publish their memoirs, so escaping appeared to the public as a viable option. The case of Miguel Cervantes, as mentioned above, is fairly typical. He probably decided to escape because he realised there would be little money from his family for ransom, since they were poor. In fact, Cervantes tried to escape from Algiers three times. The first time, with a few companions, Cervantes overpowered a guard, but they were soon recaptured, and as punishment Cervantes was sent to work in a quarry, crushing stones and hauling them to the port's fortifications. The second time, Cervantes tried to contact a ship via an intermediary, who was almost certainly a renegade. But the message was intercepted and Cervantes and his companions were found hiding in a cave. This time, the punishment was five months' incarceration in a dungeon, while his companions were either hung or impaled – Cervantes was lucky here – and he probably survived because he was bought by the Dey of Algiers, Hassan Pasha, in 1577. The third escape attempt was equally futile, Cervantes tried for another ship, but now he was betrayed by a renegade, and his subsequent punishment was another five months in a dungeon. Again, Cervantes was very lucky not to be more severely punished, but Hassan Pasha was probably safeguarding his investment. Eventually, Cervantes was ransomed, as described previously.[22]

One of the best known escapees was Thomas Pellow, who published his memoirs in 1740. Pellow was unusual in being a renegade, trusted by the ruler of Morocco, Moulay Ismail, and given command of a large military company of renegades. After spending several years in Morocco, Pellow married a local woman, who bore him a child. But Pellow decided on escape, and it was near the town of Meknes where he made his first escape attempt. He was similar to Cervantes in that he made three attempts to escape, and, in his first attempt, relied on an outsider to help the escape as did Cervantes. In Morocco, these intermediaries were called *metadores*, and for a particular sum, would guide the escapee to the nearest Spanish enclave. Pellow aimed at reaching the Portuguese garrison of Mazagan, and actually reached the walls of the city, when he unfortunately stumbled upon four Moors who captured him and delivered him to the nearest jail. Here he was befriended by the officer in charge, one Mohammed, who was involved in a local power struggle, and wanted to use Pellow for his own ends. Pellow was slated for execution and taken in hand by the executioner on the morning of the supposed execution, '[He] now had his knife ready in his right hand, and with his left hand had taken fast hold of my beard, the better to hold back to cut my throat', wrote Pellow later. But Mohammed was true to his word and spared Pellow, and even released him to return to the barracks where Pellow was supposed to have been living. It is not clear why Pellow was spared by Mohammed, nor why he did not receive any punishment subsequently for his escape attempt. Perhaps it was Pellow's rank as an officer in Moulay's army that saved him.

Some years later, in 1728 or 1729, Pellow made his second attempt, this time aiming at stealing a sloop in the port of Salé, and sailing to Gibraltar. Pellow's fellow escapees were two other renegades, but the third renegade, William Johnston, changed his mind just as Pellow and his friend William

Hussey were about to set forth to capture the sloop. Johnston apparently realised that his prospects as a soldier were much better in Salé than they would be as a penniless renegade in England, and so he threatened to betray the other two if they persisted. Angered by this, Pellow drew his sword and slashed Johnston in the face, at which point Johnston did report them to the governor of Salé. The governor brought the three renegades to a hearing, at which Pellow and Hussey turned the tables on Johnston by claiming that it was Johnston who was trying to escape, which was why they had slashed him in the face. Since it was two against one, the governor believed Pellow and Hussey and clapped Johnston in jail. However, Pellow was frightened by his narrow brush with the law, and did not try to escape again until 1737. By now he had spent 20 years in Morocco, having been captured very young, although his wife and daughter, both of whom he was fond of, had died earlier, perhaps of the plague. Perhaps because of their deaths, Pellow felt able to try to escape again, and he was also concerned that he would be killed in one of the various military expeditions in which he was forced to participate on behalf of the sultan.

Therefore, in 1737 Pellow set forth again from Meknes. He traveled by day, since, after twenty years in Morocco, he looked like an Arab, had a long beard, and spoke the language perfectly. The next few months were desperate times as Pellow walked south, trying to find a port where a European ship would take him onboard. At the outset Pellow joined a holy man and his group, but they were attacked by brigands almost immediately, and Pellow was robbed of all his possessions. Wearily he struggled on through the foothills of the Atlas Mountains, still heading south for the Atlantic Ocean. Then he met two Spanish renegades, who were earning a living as itinerant physicians. They gave Pellow some rusty instruments so that he could disguise himself as a similar physician. He was soon called upon to practice his craft, when a woman asked him to save her husband, who was in dire straits. Pellow decided to bleed him, the most common treatment for almost anything, but the lancet was too blunt to produce any blood. The patient cried out in pain, and so Pellow shifted to his red hot brand, a more radical treatment, and burned the man's head, at which the patient understandably cried out in pain. Pellow criticised the man for being 'a very faint hearted soldier', but was happy to stay for supper with the man's family. Leaving quickly the next morning before his mistreatment of the man could result in trouble, Pellow traveled for some six months more in the Atlas mountains before finally seeing the Atlantic Ocean. Unfortunately, the coastal path

Pellow took was infested with brigands, and he was soon set upon by a group of robbers, who shot Pellow in the leg, beat him unconscious, and left him for dead. Roused by the cold of night, his clothes bathed in blood, and in very poor shape, Pellow noticed a building close to him and he struggled toward it. Luckily the inhabitant took pity on Pellow, gave him food, and dressed his wound. Next day, Pellow set forth, limping, but anxious to keep going. He met next a kindly community of Jews, who again dressed his wound, and gave him food and lodging. Finally, he reached the port of Willadia, and was able to arouse the sympathy of one Captain Toobin, from Dublin, and captain of a ship. Usually, Christian captains were reluctant to help escapees such as Pellow, for fear that, if the slave was discovered, the captain and his crew would be severely punished. Nevertheless, Toobin took Pellow onboard and hid him below decks, and sailed for Gibraltar. The date was July 1738.

Pellow had finally escaped. Arriving in Gibraltar, he soon became the object of much interest, but a ship was leaving for London shortly, and Pellow went aboard. In London, interest in Pellow was equally high, but he managed to avoid the possibility of a procession, and sailed for Penryn in Cornwall in October 1738. There he did not at first recognise his parents, nor they him, but he was delighted to be home. Within two years a writer helped Pellow publish his story, and so he joined a small but useful group of escaped slaves whose memoirs gave some understanding of the Barbary corsairs and their slave taking and slave keeping societies.[23]

Another escape story has been preserved in the archives, and tells of how fifteen Christian slaves escaped from Algiers in July 1640. The story is told by two of the men, George Penticost and John Butler. Their plan of escape was to raid a house where muskets and ammunition were stored, and with these fight their way to a row boat in the harbour. The house was duly seized, although three men were lost in the fight, and so only twelve men got into the boat. Then two forts fired at them as they cleared Algiers harbour, but they were not hit. They were pursued by two boats and three frigates, which they fought off for five hours, resulting in three men wounded in their boat, but at five in the afternoon the pursuers left them and returned to Algiers. Then the remaining crew:

> ...rowed for Mayorka [Majorca] having no food meat nor drink. 3 days we rowed and found no land, and so dismayed us that we gave over for dead men. We prayed the Lord to deliver us, and in this our great distress the Lord sent

us a Turtle, who put his head to the boat, and we took him in to our great joy, which saved our lives. We ate the turtle raw and rowed hard that night and next day to port, the fifth morning from Algiers – greetings of great comfort and God's great Glory for our deliverance…[24]

There must have been many such escape attempts, a few successful, but most would be failures. Yet the nature of their slavery made the slaves willing to try.

The Knights of Malta

Surprisingly enough, the Barbary corsairs faced an enemy that was a mirror image of their own activity, namely the Knights of Malta. From the 1530s to the 1740s these knights and their licensed privateers also captured ships, slaves and cargo under a religious duty, but these were Muslim ships, slaves and cargo that the knights took. The Knights of St John were officially titled the Knights of the Order of St John of Jerusalem, better known as the Knights Hospitaller, which had been originally founded in the 1120s to look after the medical needs of crusaders and pilgrims to the Holy Land. The Hospitallers maintained their medical role but grew into a strong military order, and with the Knights of the Temple (the Templars), became the main Christian military religious orders in the Middle East. After the final failure of the crusades to the Holy Land by the early 1300s, the Hospitallers retired to the island of Rhodes. However, a prolonged siege by the Ottoman Turks in 1522 forced the Order to leave Rhodes, and they finally settled on Malta, given to them by the Emperor Charles V. The Knights of Malta were an order that attracted the junior sons of the nobility of Europe, especially France, where their families were happy to know that the Order asked for celibacy. On the other hand, another requirement, that the noble candidates were supposed to be able to swim, allowed some junior nobility to escape their parents' plans by claiming inability in the water. The Knights of Malta also possessed a considerable hierarchy of lesser knights and servants at arms, and an order of Sisters, which required the same noble origins as the men.[25]

Malta was well located geographically to intercept Barbary corsair ships, and the Knights of Malta did so with considerable success, especially because the Hospitallers also licensed independent corsairs to search for Muslim ships. Among these licensed corsairs in the sixteenth century was the famous captain Leone Strozzi, who had once belonged to the Order but later operated his own small fleet as 'the friend of God alone'. Another well known sailor was Mathurin Romegas, who often attacked several Muslim ships at the same time, and was undefeated and almost indestructible. One story has it that Romegas was submerged in his galley after a storm in the harbor of Malta in 1555, yet the next day knocking was heard and Romegas was rescued from under his galley, together with his pet monkey. However, it was Romegas' capture of a large Muslim ship in 1564, on its way from Venice to Istanbul with a valuable cargo worth 80,000 Spanish ducats, that precipitated the very destructive but ultimately unsuccessful Ottoman siege of Malta in 1565. The defense of Malta was led by de la Valette, aged seventy-one, the Grand Master of the Order, who had served on many voyages. De la Valette was previously captured by the Barbary corsairs in 1541 and survived a year at the oars in a corsair galley. Suffice to say that in the siege 600 Knights plus another 5,000 soldiers and local Maltese men faced 30,000 Ottoman warriors, including the renegade corsair Uluc Ali. After heroics on both sides, the problems of logistics, plague, and the strength of the Order's castles, defensive musketry and artillery, plus very tough defenders, carried the day against the Ottomans in a long lasting siege.[26]

Turning to the question of the ships of the Knights of Malta, the Order possessed galleys – eight in number in 1685 – plus one very large carrack, and this fleet increased into the middle of the eighteenth century. Each galley of the Hospitallers required thirty knights for a voyage, and each Knight Hospitaller had to serve four Caravans – a Caravan being a tour of six months. Later, sailing ships were deemed to be both more comfortable and effective, and so Caravans in a sailing ship lasted one year. However, if the Knight had completed his Caravans, and had also served three years on Malta, then he could retire to a sister house in Europe and recuperate. Also serving on the Knight Hospitaller galley were some 180 Christian soldiers, plus the rowers, who were a mixture of Muslim slaves, debtors from European prisons, and free Christians who were financially desperate enough to sign up for a voyage. The Knights of Malta continued to be very successful and still used the galley even after the sailing ship was introduced to Malta in the seventeenth century. The activity of the ships of the Knights of Malta declined in the late eighteenth century, because of changing political and economic circumstances, while the Barbary corsairs similarly declined in number and also became more reluctant to face the Knights at sea.

In the matter of administration, the Knights Hospitaller set up a tribunal in 1605 to regulate the independent corsairs they licensed, and this tribunal sought to keep a strict eye on these corsairs, especially which ships the corsairs were allowed to attack. This was not easy, since these licensed corsairs tended to attack not only Muslim ships, but also any ships that might be carrying Muslim goods, or indeed any ship that by some stretch of the imagination might be construed as a contraband ship – and these often turned out to be Greek ships. In the 1660s there were some thirty licensed ships operating out of Malta – quite apart from the Hospitaller's ships. These licensed ships were bound to pay out ten per cent of their gains to the Grand Master of the Knights Hospitaller. Then five shares went to the five Lances – essentially a spiritual and management bureaucracy in Malta. Then the captain was awarded eleven per cent, which also paid for the pilot and officers, and the remainder was divided between the investors in the voyage, and the crew itself. Meanwhile, the risky nature of these voyages is illustrated by marine insurance rates of around twenty-four per cent to thirty per cent interest, while the cost of borrowing to finance a voyage could be as high as forty to fifty per cent. It is also worth noting that most voyages took place in the summer months, while the winter months were spent refitting and relaxing among the Greek islands, where the licensed but idle captain and crew played cards and drank.[27]

The corsairs of Malta tended to rely more on their ship borne artillery than the Barbary corsairs, but like the Barbary corsairs, wanted to capture their victims with as little fighting and damage as possible. Obviously, the Maltese corsairs wanted to preserve the ship, cargo, crew and passengers of their victims in order to maximize their profits. This normally did happen without fighting since the Maltese corsair usually had the heavier armament and the larger numbers of crew and soldiers. Most valuable of all to the Maltese corsairs were the crew and passengers of the captured ship, who could be ransomed or sold locally in the Mediterranean, or back in Malta. Of course, captured Christian crew and passengers were theoretically useless to the Maltese corsairs, because they could not be sold or ransomed. As might be expected, the Maltese corsairs approached the captured crew and passengers in much the same way as the Barbary corsairs, stripping their captives, and choosing one of the officers or passengers to threaten with torture to reveal any cash hoards onboard. One example comes from a certain Jean Thevenot, a French passenger on a ship approaching Acre in the eastern Mediterranean in 1657. The ship was taken by a Maltese corsair who came aboard 'calling on God and devils alike to make themselves more frightening…', wrote Thevenot, who then found himself surrounded by these corsairs:

> …who, for most of the time, kept a pistol at my throat and a sword on my stomach, and desired me at first to undress myself, but, one pulling from in front, one from behind, one on top and one below, stripped me stark naked in a flash. I thought I was finished with them, when they began to jab their swords at me. And seeing that it was for a cheap ring that I had on my finger, I took it off quickly and threw it to them…

Later, onshore at Acre, Thevenot was rescued by the French consul, yet the actions of these licensed Maltese corsairs closely resembled those of the Barbary corsairs. And the system of slavery on Malta in terms of work, rowing on galleys, leg irons, slave prisons at night, the ability to run a business and make money in leisure hours, clothes and hair cuts to differentiate slaves from the local population, slave ransoms and slave exchanges – all these were not much different from slave life on the Barbary Coast.[28]

Ultimately, by the 1740s fewer licenses were being issued to the Maltese corsairs due to economic and political changes and the growth of European navies. As well, by the 1730s there were fewer Muslim ships to raid, since the Muslims of North Africa were largely shipping their goods with Christian merchants. Legal issues also undermined the freedom of operation of the Maltese corsairs, though in the early 1750s the corsairs thought up a new twist, and sailed under the flag of Monaco, and then under a series of other flags, including Russia. Nevertheless, the final decline of the Knights of Malta and their still active licensed corsairs occurred with the occupation of Malta by Napoleon in 1798. Napoleon did not like the religious orders, criticised the Knights of Malta as an 'institution to support in idleness the younger sons of privileged families', and also foresaw that Malta would prove a useful British base unless taken by the French. So in June 1798 Napoleon attacked Malta, and while some of the knights defended Malta, others deserted or refused to fight. Malta was taken, and Napoleon freed some 2,000 Muslim and North African slaves, thus putting an end to the Maltese corsairs.[29]

In North Africa, the end of the Barbary corsairs was a more complicated affair. The first blow was struck by American ships under Commodore Decatur, who in 1815 compelled the Algerian Dey to free all Americans held as captives, plus other concessions. The next year, in August 1816, a large Anglo-Dutch fleet of some twenty-six ships under Lord Exmouth made its way to Algiers and opened a massive bombardment of 50,000 cannon balls, and assorted fire bombs and shells, which reduced Algiers and its shipping to ruins. The defensive cannonade from Algiers was also severe, as one British lieutenant observed, 'Legs, arms, blood, brains and mangled bodies were strewn about in all directions. You could scarcely keep your feet from the slipperiness of the decks, wet with blood.'[30] Still, the Dey of Algiers recognised the futility of continuing, and agreed to release all slaves who had not already released themselves. Tunis, Tripoli and Morocco followed suit. But the Barbary corsairs would not give up their traditions so easily, and failed to openly renounce slavery. Only the occupation of Algiers by French forces in 1830 finally ended the Algerian slave trade, and persuaded Tunis and Tripoli to agree to terms as well.

Thus ended the 300 year rule of the Barbary corsairs. It was a time of piracy and commerce, based on the capture and sale of slaves, ships and cargo. More accurately, one could call the system used by both North Africa and Malta as commercial raiding, half way between privateering and piracy. One other story connected to the Barbary corsairs is of unusual interest, and that is the tale of captured Christian sailors and slaves who decided to 'take the turban' and become Muslim. These renegades were caught between two worlds and lived dangerous lives, suspected by both Muslim and Christian.

The Renegades

Over the course of some three centuries, from 1530 to 1780, a large number of European Christians were captured by the North African corsairs and became slaves. Their outlook was generally bleak, as has been described, but besides redemption or escape, there was one other option that could improve their lives, and this was to 'take the turban' and 'turn Turk', in other words, to become a Muslim and a renegade. Many renegades did well in business in North Africa, social mobility was very possible, and maritime expertise was particularly useful. Indeed, one Christian sailor, Edward Coxere declared that he found life better in a Tunis prison than back home in Yarmouth, England! As a result, conversion was quite a common procedure, and while the percentage of Christian converts to Islam varied according to location and time period, there seemed to be a fairly consistent rate of around twenty to thirty per cent, although one French source claimed that Provencals would put on a turban as easily as they would put on a night cap. According to the historian Linda Colley in her book on captives, of ninety-six crew saved from an English wreck in 1746, and sent to the sultan of Morocco as slaves, twenty-one had turned Muslim by 1751, for a conversion rate of 21.875 per cent. The historian Christopher Lloyd, in his book on English corsairs, stated that of 459 French captives in seventeenth-century North Africa, 149 'turned Turk' for a conversion percentage of 32.5 per cent. The redemptive orders also estimated that in Algiers between 1621 and 1627 there were the following renegades by country of origin: 857 Germans (138 from Hamburg), 300 English, 130 Dutch, 160 Danes, and 250 Poles, Hungarians and Muscovites.[31]

Renegades were a varied group – William Lithgow in his seventeenth century memoirs reported that Sir Francis Verney turned Turk in Tunis after running out of money. He spent two years as a galley slave but was redeemed by an English Jesuit. He became a common soldier, but still died in poverty in Messina. Others took the turban with the idea of improving their prospects – this was especially the case with unemployed European sailors after major wars ended. One unusual English renegade was John Ward (1553–1623), a pirate who turned Turk in 1615 and lived in Tunis. According to Lithgow, Ward had been a fisherman and a petty officer in the Royal Navy, but now Ward lived in Tunis in a palace of alabaster and marble with fifteen domestics, who were all renegades, all circumcised, but 'desperate and disdainful' wrote Lithgow. Ward was valuable to Tunis as a naval captain, ready with his squadron of ships to capture prizes, especially Venetian ships. Ward is alleged to have uttered these inflammatory words to the captain of King James' ship, the *Rainbow*, in the very early 1600s:

Go home, go home, says Captain Ward
And tell your king from me,
If he reigns king on all the land
Ward will reign king on the sea.[32]

Ward was a simple sailor, who struck it lucky with a number of rich prizes in 1605 and 1606, so that in 1606 he was able to make a deal to serve the Dey of Tunis. A visiting English sailor met Ward in 1608 and described him in less than flattering terms:

Very short with little hair, and that quite white, bald in front; swarthy face and beard. Speaks little, and almost always swearing. Drunk from morn till night.

Most prodigal and plucky. Sleeps a great deal, and often onboard when in
port. The habits of a thorough 'Salt.' A fool and an idiot out of his trade.[33]

This is actually a useful portrait of a fairly typical renegade. Like Ward, and
increasingly from the 1500s, Christian sailors and sea captains, who were
well versed in the arts of navigation and knew the Christian coasts, were
persuaded to become renegades. So, for example, on a Mediterranean raid
organised by an Albanian renegade in 1578, seven of his eight galliot captains were renegades, including one from France, one from Venice, one from
Naples, and three from Greece. Similarly, Father Dan, a priest dedicated to
redeeming Christian slaves in North Africa, wrote in the mid seventeenth
century that of thirty-five Algerian galley captains, twelve were Turks, one
a Jew and one a Hungarian, and the remainder were all renegades, from
Venice, Greece and Spain.

One celebrated naval renegade was Ochiali, or Uluc Ali, or Euldj'Ali. His
original name was Giovanni Galena, and he came from Licastelli in Calabria.
He was the son of a simple fisherman, but was captured in 1536 by another
famous renegade, Kheir ed-Din, admiral of the Ottoman navy and ruler of
Algiers. Giovanni was sold in the market of Istanbul and became a galley
slave, reportedly rowing the lead starboard bow oar. He suffered from ring
worm, which led to his nickname as 'the bald'. Insulted by another rower,
he converted to Islam in order to revenge himself on the man, although
another story has him converting in order to marry the daughter of the
owner. Giovanni took the turban and was renamed either Ochiali or Uluc
Ali, or Euldj'Ali, and soon rose in the ranks and displayed his ability as a
naval captain. He raided Sardinia in 1554, took part in the defeat of a Spanish
fleet at Djerba in 1560, fought at the siege of Malta in 1565, became pasha of
Algiers in 1568, and commanded the Ottoman left wing at the celebrated
battle of Lepanto in 1571. His squadron of ninety-five ships performed
better than any other Ottoman command in the battle, and he was subsequently made commander of the Ottoman navy. Earlier, Charles V offered
him the title of Marquis of Calabria in 1569, his birth place, but he refused,
though later, in 1572, he asked to be made a prince of Calabria. One story
has him anchored off Licastelli in 1562, intent on seeing his mother again,
but she reportedly rejected the chance of meeting up with her turncoat son.
More reliably, he is said to have raided Licastelli with the idea of punish-
ing those provincial nobles who had made his life a misery as a youngster,
and rewarding those inhabitants who would renounce Christianity and join

him in Algiers. As it was, Ochiali was supposed to have had 500 'renegades' in his household – these being young children kidnapped from the Balkan countries and enslaved.[34]

Ochiali's life was unusual in that he rose to very high rank among the Barbary corsairs, but was typical of many who chose to become renegades primarily in order to improve their lives. Others were not so lucky – a Corsican renegade called Hassan Corso (the name signifies he was a corsair), attempted to become the ruler of Algiers in 1556, at the urging of the local Janissary force. However, Corso was seized by the nominee of the Sultan, one Mohamed Tekelerli, and the renegade was put to death in a very unpleasant manner:

> After having stabbed sharp reeds into his fingers and toes they placed a red-hot iron crown upon his head. Then they impaled him alive on a sharpened stake by the Bab Azoun gate where he remained in public view, suffering the most dire agonies for more than half the day. He gave out the most terrible screams before dying of this torment.

Soon after, another renegade from Calabria, and a supporter of Corso, rallied some supporters, killed Tekelerli, and assumed control over Algiers before dying of the plague after just seven days.[35]

For the most part renegades did better themselves, especially in the naval area where maritime skills were much in demand. Renegades also often did very well in business, and there were few forced conversions from Christian to Muslim, although those renegades who made it back to their home countries somewhat naturally tried to emphasise the tortures that compelled them to take the turban. One such account came from the previously mentioned Thomas Pellow who in the early eighteenth century was taken by corsairs and made a slave in the house of one of the sons of the sultan of Morocco. Pellow described unpleasant tortures to make him convert, though it should be stressed that this account is very likely exaggerated, and may not have actually taken place. According to Pellow, his owner, Moulay es-Safa, beat him severely and burned the flesh off his bones 'which the tyrant did, by frequent repetitions, after a most cruel manner'. After much similar treatment, Pellow wrote that he was at last constrained to submit, 'calling upon God to forgive me, who knows that I never gave up the consent of my heart'. The method by which a Christian would signal that he was ready to turn Turk was a very simple one, merely raising the forefinger to the sky and uttering a few words of conversion. And this Pellow did.[36]

Other renegades told similar stories, for example, the narrative of Joseph Pitts, published in 1704. Pitts was the slave of two brothers in Algiers, who, according to Pitts, forced him into taking the turban. Pitts' account stresses the tortures he went through before agreeing to turn Turk. After lengthy verbal entreaties did not work with Pitts, his patron, the elder brother, went into a frenzy, had Pitts hung upside down and began to beat him on his feet, 'He being a very strong man and full of passion, his blows fell heavy indeed ... I roared out to feel the pain of his cruel strokes, but the more I cried, the more furiously he laid on upon me, and to stop the noise of my crying he would stamp with his feet on my mouth ...'. Two or three times Pitts asked him to stop and considered turning Muslim, but he held out, and finally 'seeing his cruelty towards me insatiable unless I did turn Mohammetan, through terror I did it and spake the words as usual, holding up the forefinger of my right hand ...'. The words that Pitts spoke to accompany the raised forefinger were the usual formula for turning Muslim and were, 'la illahi ill allah Mahommet resullallah'. Then the next step was circumcision, normally carried out at a surgeon's house, and then the red cap of slavery was replaced by the turban and the woolen djellaba.[37]

Pitts went on to give an elaborate account of what happened when a Christian voluntarily turned Turk. The apostate goes to the local dey (ruler) and his divan (council), and declares his willingness to become Muslim. He is immediately accepted, with no explanation necessary, placed on a horse with fine trappings, and paraded around the town. He is well dressed and carries an arrow, holding it straight up with his forefinger as he rides, with some twenty or thirty stewards riding beside him with drawn swords, signifying that if he changes his mind and repents he will be cut to pieces. There is music and drumming, and some of the crowd will give coins to encourage the convert. As soon as the ceremony is over, wrote Pitts, the renegade is enrolled in the pay of the local garrison and lives with the fellow soldiers. Finally, the circumciser comes and performs the ceremony of circumcision. The convert is now a fully fledged Muslim.[38]

A somewhat different perspective on the business of turning Turk comes from Thomas Baker, the English consul in Tripoli from 1677 to 1685. Baker's journal reveals his efforts to stop Christians turning Turk in Tripoli, for example a sailor in January 1680 wanted to turn Turk, but Baker was able to prevent this and put the sailor back on his ship, the *Francis*. At another point in November 1680, two sailors had turned Turk but now regretted this move, and Baker was able to write two letters of safe passage for them. In May 1681 Baker reported the story of three Christians – a French naval captain, his purser, and a Venetian gardener – who were surprised at an assignation outside Tripoli with women of the town. The Venetian gardener immediately turned Turk to escape punishment, while the women were set to ride through town on asses, facing backwards. The two Frenchmen paid $850 and were well beaten for their crime. Nevertheless, the renegade situation that seemed to preoccupy Baker the most, along with most Christian commentators, was the risk of young Christian boys turning Turk, with the presumption that they would be sodomised. In September 1680 Baker complained that three English boys had turned Turk, and that there were 300 such boys in Algiers. Baker continued to report stories of sodomy, for example in October 1680 when a Turk received 300 blows, not for sodomy with a boy, but for throwing the boy over the town wall and breaking both his legs. Then in June 1682 Baker was astonished that the son of a Dutch renegade was buggered by two Turks and this example was followed by thirty-four soldiers, with allegedly no shame or punishment for the transgressors![39]

It is difficult to tell how widespread the practice of encouraging youth to take the turban for the purpose of sodomy was, but certainly a homosexual culture was well established and accepted in North Africa. A typical Christian cleric, assuming the worst, wrote in 1647 that young slaves were purchased 'at great price by the Turks to serve them in their abominable sins, and no sooner do they have them in their power, by dressing them up and caressing them, [then] they persuade them to make themselves Turks'. If this did not work, force was then used. And according to one report, the famous Albanian renegade and eventual naval captain of the sea, Murat Rais (1534–1638), was captured as a youth at the age of twelve and given command of his first ship when he was still only twelve or thirteen by an infatuated corsair captain.[40]

The position of the renegade was a difficult one, caught between two cultures and two faiths, usually a willing convert, sometimes an unwilling convert. In the maritime area, renegades were essential to the Barbary corsairs as captains, navigators, shipwrights, artillery specialists, and possessing a good knowledge of Christian coasts and ports. It is especially in the naval area that many reached very high rank. Renegades would sometimes regret their choice, and try to buy a pardon back home, as John Ward attempted unsuccessfully in 1608. And others, like Thomas Pellow, did eventually escape and make it back to England, where he tried to justify his conversion and actions. But some renegades must have tried unsuccessfully to escape, as Thomas Baker noted in May 1681 when he reported that four renegades and two Christians ran away in a fishing boat from Tripoli, having looted the treasury for good measure. On recapture the two Christians were pardoned, being slaves, but two of the renegades were hung by their feet and then by the neck, while one drowned. Baker does not report the fate of the fourth renegade.[41]

Ultimately, the stories of the renegades are too diverse to summarise. They include simple opportunism, as in the case of Peter Lyle or Lisle, the Scots mate of the *Hampden*, who was caught stealing on his ship, and elected to escape punishment by turning Turk. Lisle was renamed Murat Rais, one of several of that name, and later became admiral of the Tripoli fleet from 1796 to 1815. Other renegades such as Ochiali seemed to have a deeper commitment. But at the least one must sympathise with their conflicted lives, belonging to neither world, and often subject to deep remorse for their decisions.[42]

Pirates of the Eastern Seas

Pirates of the Eastern Seas differed in one important respect from Western pirates – the former tended to see piracy as a way of life, while Western pirates usually saw piracy as a temporary job. Another difference was that Asian pirates had been operational for a very long time, while Atlantic and Caribbean pirates were a more recent innovation, though Ancient and Classical pirates had flourished in earlier times.

Chinese Piracy from Ming to Manchu

In more modern times, the threat of piracy on the coasts of China came to a head in the sixteenth century, during the period of the imperial Chinese Ming dynasty (1368–1644). At this time, foreign trade was prohibited, which led to smuggling, and only encouraged piracy. These smugglers turned pirates on the coasts of China were initially not actually Chinese but were often Japanese, and were known as the 'wo-k'uo', meaning simply Japanese bandits or pirates. It is reported that these Japanese pirates operated in large junk fleets, wore uniforms of red coats and yellow hats, and wielded a sword in each hand, which outmatched the Ming defenders. On the other hand, when the Japanese pirates were captured by the Ming they were steamed to death in large jars. However, some Chinese families, such as the Hsieh family, became involved in organising this Japanese smuggling and piracy, and eventually most of the pirates in the sixteenth century were Chinese rather than Japanese, in the ratio of about seventy per cent Chinese to thirty per cent Japanese.

Many of these Chinese pirates started out as legitimate traders, but were forced to become smugglers and pirates as a result of the foreign trading ban. The Ming bureaucracy believed that trade with foreigners only led to piracy, and therefore persecuted such traders. When these illegal traders were captured they suffered 100 lashes and confiscation of goods, while if humans or weapons were being carried, the punishment was death by strangulation. Despite all this, smuggling continued to increase through the 1520s and 1530s, with collusion from local families and lax military officers on the coasts of China. In 1547, the Ming general Zhu Wan was appointed to suppress piracy along the Fujian and Chekiang/Zhejiang coasts. He was quite successful in suppressing the merchant fleets that traded with the pirates, but he earned the dislike of powerful families that benefited from piracy, and so committed suicide in 1550 to avoid impeachment and disgrace. Zhu Wan had failed, and partly as a result, pirate fleets under the leadership of the merchant Wang Zhi now emerged to raid the south-east coast in 1552. These raids were very effective, and by 1554 the pirates were able to establish bases on land in order to raid even further inland. Ming armies were defeated in 1553 and 1554 by the pirates, and Ming soldiers were forced to retreat inside walled cities for protection. It seems that the merchant Wang Zhi actually wanted to return to legitimate trading, but the emperor and his bureaucrats refused to accept this option, and when Wang Zhi surrendered with the hope of a pardon, this was denied, and he was executed.[1]

The Ming tried to deal with piracy, ransom, and smuggling on the coast by training local militias, building city walls, arming defenders with gunpowder weapons, building new ships, and appointing more efficient military leaders. Equally influential was the opening of foreign trade to Chinese traders in 1567 (except with Japan), which undercut smuggling, plus the introduction of a fairer tax system (the 'one whip' system of one defined tax). Notable among the generals appointed to deal with the pirates was Ch'i Chi-Kuang, who was sent to the coastal region of Chekiang in the 1550s and 1560s to deal with the pirates. Chi-Kuang recruited tough peasants from inland areas, kept discipline by cutting off the ears of disobedient soldiers, and instituted the death penalty for units that retreated or failed. Chi-Kuang developed special tactical teams to deal with the pirates, which were called the 'mandarin duck formation', since they resembled a duck in outline. This well thought out formation was necessary to overcome the formidable fighting skills of the pirates. The centre of this 'duck' formation consisted of four pikemen, carrying pikes twelve feet in length. In front of the pikemen moved four soldiers, two with shields and swords to protect the pikemen, and two carrying bamboo trees with thick foliage to disguise the formation and confuse the enemy. Behind the pikemen marched two soldiers with weapons that discharged fire arrows, although normally Chi-Kuang did not believe in such weapons because he thought them unreliable, and perhaps because he could defeat the pirates without them. Chi-Kuang's idea was to attack with these formations and keep attacking, despite initial losses, at which point the pirates usually lost cohesion and retreated. Eventually Chi-Kuang enrolled an army of ten thousand men, which, together with the other advantages mentioned above, defeated the pirates by the mid 1560s. Chi-Kuang personally led his armies, and in one battle against the pirates, he shot to death the enemy commander.[2]

This period of Chinese piracy reached its height from 1547 to 1567. Then there was a renewal of piracy during the ill-fated Japanese invasion of Korea in 1592. Following this, in the early 1600s, there emerged the pirate Ching-Chi-Ling (also transliterated as Zheng Zhilong). Ching was a Roman Catholic convert who worked in the Portuguese factory in Macao, and acted as an interpreter for the East India Company in the 1620s. During the early 1620s Ching visited Japan where an uncle lived. In Japan, Ching married a Japanese lady, and this marriage produced a son, Koxinga, born in either 1623 or 1624, who later became a well known pirate. But before this, it was in Japan that Ching's uncle introduced Ching to piracy via his uncle's fleet of pirate junks. By 1627 Ching had built up a large pirate fleet of 400 junks, with a personal bodyguard of seventy-six Dutchmen, plus 300 Christian Africans, who were ex-slaves from Macao, dressed in colourful silks. Ching was active during the declining years of the Ming dynasty, at which time he gave up piracy and accepted a naval commission from the Ming, with the hope of promoting himself and his son to high positions in the Ming dynasty. Ching was in fact a key naval figure in the defense of southern China against the emerging Chinese imperial dynasty of the Manchus (1644–1912), but apparently was content to defend and did not go onto the offensive. In 1646 Ching either surrendered to the Manchus, or attempted to go over to their side. Either way, Ching was imprisoned by the Manchus, and was executed in 1661, some said through the death of a thousand cuts, but he was in fact beheaded.[3]

Ching was succeeded by his son Zheng Chenggong, commonly known as Koxinga. The Manchus had a great deal of trouble in dealing with Koxinga, who remained loyal to the Ming, because he operated a powerful fleet, taken over from his father, and he possessed bases in areas that were inaccessible by land. For some twenty years Koxinga sailed up and down the coast of China, burning and plundering – half pirate – half Ming defender. Koxinga was so successful that the Manchus were forced to order eighty sea coast townships to level their towns and move inland to escape his attacks. Koxinga next moved north in his offensive, as far as the Yangzi River, and in 1659 he even attacked the Manchus at Nanking. This however led to a crushing defeat for Koxinga outside the walls of Nanking, and Koxinga retreated south. He recognised that he did not have the forces or the ability to defeat the Manchus on land, and he was also less familiar with the northern sea coast, so he moved south to find a secure base. This turned out to be the Dutch controlled island of Formosa (Taiwan). In May 1661, with a fleet of 900 junks and 25,000 troops, Koxinga besieged the Formosan fortress of Zeelandia for nine months. The Dutch defender eventually surrendered, worried that if the fort was taken by Koxinga, the women and children might suffer a nasty fate, since Koxinga had a reputation for torture. With the surrender of this fort the rest of Formosa fell into Koxinga's hands, and the Dutch left. Koxinga then set his sights on Manila, but before he could attack the Philippines, he died in 1662. Koxinga's son took over, and held out in Formosa for twenty years, although he was defeated eventually by Admiral Shi Lang in 1683. There was a limit to what a purely naval force could do against a logistically superior Manchu dynasty.[4]

From the Tay-Son Rebellion to Chinese Piracy, 1770s –1810

Piracy emerged again in the 1760s, mainly in the islands around the mouth of the Canton River, including the future Hong Kong. These islands were called the Ladrones, meaning robbers or highwaymen, accurately so named by the Portuguese. Then in the 1770s, a rebellion in neighbouring VietNam, the Tay-son rebellion, pitted the Tay-son rebels against the rulers of VietNam. The Tay-son needed naval help, and Chinese pirates became involved on behalf of the Tay-son in the 1780s – chief among them being Ch'en Tien-pao. He was named 'General Pao, Virtuous Marquis', by the Tay-son leaders, and he recruited many Chinese pirates and a fleet of 1,000 junks. To maintain their resources, the Tay-son pirates raided into China on a regular basis, and the Manchu emperors found it difficult to defeat these pirates. Squadrons of gun boats did little against the pirates, because the gun boats crews feared the fierce Chinese pirates, and usually just fired their cannon to warn the pirates to escape. But if any pirates were captured by the Chinese authorities, they were executed if they were Vietnamese, and if they were Chinese dressed as Vietnamese, they were put to death by the painful method of 'slicing'. However, there was limited success in capturing these pirates, and so, just like their Western counterparts, the Manchus resorted to pardons. The idea was that the pirate followers might accept a pardon even if their leaders did not, and this should lead to dissension in the ranks, and so the pirates would turn on each other. Those pirates who surrendered were given cash, or attractive ranks in the army, or land. At the same time, pirates who surrendered were asked to produce the heads or ears of other pirates that they had captured. This general policy had limited success, because pirates realised they could turn themselves in more than once to gain extra money, and although some 1,700 did turn themselves in, causing bureaucratic headaches in resettling so many, piracy was still actually increasing in 1800. Nevertheless, in 1801 the Tay-son fleet was decimated in battle in VietNam, losing 50,000 men, most of their junks, and 6,000 cannon. The next year, Ch'en Tien-pao surrendered, and the last Chinese pirate Tay-son leader, Cheng Ch'i, was captured and beheaded.[5]

The Tay-son rebellion was over, but many Chinese pirates escaped back to China, and rather than compete with each other, seven pirate chiefs in July 1805 signed an agreement to co-operate. Ironically, therefore, the Tay-son failure actually provided the means for a revitalised Chinese piracy, and this occurred through the seven chiefs' agreement which really signaled the professionalisation of piracy in Chinese waters. Now there were strict rules of pirate co-operation in the agreement, much like the articles of Western pirates. For example, there were rules for the distribution of booty, rules for the care of wounded, and rules for the punishment of offenders. But there were differences from the West too, for example, the Chinese pirates were divided into six fleets (reduced from seven to six after one fleet commander surrendered to the authorities), and each fleet had its own coloured flags – Red, Black, White, Green, Blue and Yellow. In addition, because the pirates expected to make most of their income from protection money, one rule stated that boats that sailed without permission would be burned, weapons confiscated, and bosses executed. Another aspect that was different from Western pirates was the presence of women onboard the pirate junks. Married women were allowed onboard, and ship captains sometimes had as many as five or six wives aboard. The women worked the ship equally with the men, and sometimes commanded junks. According to the reports of one Westerner onboard a junk, there were also eight to ten concubines for the unmarried crew. Women who were captured were either kept for ransom, or assigned to crewmen as wives, or kept as concubines. And there also emerged a famous female commander of the entire pirate fleet – Ching Shi – who inherited the fleet from her husband, and ultimately commanded 800 large junks, 1,000 smaller boats, and a pirate structure of some 70,000 men and women. Yet another difference with the West was the prevalence of homosexuality. Many recruits for the pirate fleets were obtained through homosexual relations, and homosexuality was apparently common onboard. According to one Western witness, pirates 'committed almost publicly crimes against nature'. Discipline among the Chinese pirates also seems to have been more severe than in the West. Failure to surrender booty would lead to death or a severe whipping. Desertion led to the loss of one's ears. Raping a female captive led to death, but if the sexual relationship between the female captive and a crew man was by mutual consent, the crew man was decapitated, and the woman thrown overboard with weights attached to her legs.[6]

Other differences between West and East included the very large size of the confederation of Chinese pirates and their fleets compared to the small numbers and fleets of Western pirates. A further difference was the political ambitions of the Chinese pirates who aimed with the Tay-son rebellion to help seize power, and then, in China, to maintain control over large areas of the south China coast. There was also a strong measure of cruelty among Chinese pirates, which sometimes occurred among Western pirates too. For example, when the pirate chief Chang Pao captured nine rice boats, he tried to persuade the crew to become pirates. When three or four men resisted his offer, Chang Pao tied their hands behind them and hoisted them three feet from the deck where they were flogged until they were unconscious. Then they were raised to the masthead for an hour or more. The process was repeated until they either agreed to become pirates or died. The

Western captive, John Turner, captured and held by Ching Yih, a pirate chief in the Canton area in the period 1806–7, reported inhuman tortures for captured Chinese officers from the Imperial Navy:

> I saw one man ... nailed to the deck through his feet with large nails, then beaten with four rattans twisted together, till he vomited blood; and after remaining some time in this state, he was taken ashore and cut to pieces. [Another prisoner] was fixed upright, his bowels cut open and his heart taken out, which they afterwards soaked in spirits and ate ... The dead body I saw myself.[7]

Other bloody acts occurred in 1808 and 1809, when Chang Pao and his fleets attacked several villages in the Pearl River, Canton (now Guangzhou) area. Usually the pirates sought a ransom for sparing a village, but when the village resisted, the pirates could be ruthless. Thus, when the villagers of San Shan refused to pay, the pirates captured the village after hard fighting and plundered it for three days. As they left, the heads of eighty villagers were hung on the limbs of a banyan tree, and the women and children carried off to the ships. At another town and fort, Huang-pu, a violent struggle saw the pirates lose 200 men – so, stimulated by revenge, Chang Pao promised ten dollars for every Huang-pu head cut off. A witness saw one pirate with two heads hanging by their queues around his neck, with the pirate eagerly looking for a third head. As usual in these cases of resistance, the town was burnt.[8]

The pirates of the south China coast were commanded by a succession of capable pirate leaders, the first being the leader of the confederation, Cheng I. He was directly descended from pirates of the seventeenth century, one of whom had served with Koxinga, illustrating the importance of family connections among Chinese pirates. He consolidated his position in the confederation by placing his relatives, both men and women, among other fleets, with the latter becoming wives of influential pirates. Cheng I led the Red flag fleet of 200 junks, and 20,000 to 40,000 men, which swelled to 600 junks by 1807. Cheng I established shore bases for the pirates and helped unify the pirate confederation, but he died in 1807, either drowned or struck by a cannon ball. Cheng I's widow was a former prostitute, Cheng I Sao, also known as Ching Shi. To consolidate her hold on power, Ching Shi needed a partner, and she chose her husband's adopted son, Chang Pao. This individual, a fisherman's son, was initiated into the pirate world through a homosexual liaison at the age of 15 by Cheng I, and rapidly rose through the pirate ranks as a capable leader. Having selected Chang Pao as partner, Ching Shi and Chang Pao quickly became lovers, and then man and wife. Ching Shi ran the pirate confederation with an iron hand, and more important, was an excellent administrator. Chang Pao, a charismatic man, always elegantly dressed in purple silk robe and black turban, was the actual commander of the pirate fleets. He provided an ideology of rebellion to stimulate the pirates, and also posed as a defender of religion, with a temple onboard his command junk, which he consulted for direction over strategy and tactics. Chang Pao was a flexible and restrained commander, and the story is told that one day a pirate named Liu, whose father had died after being captured by Chang Pao's forces, aimed to stab Chang Pao with a poisoned knife. But Chang Pao, noticing a strange expression on Liu's face, had him searched and disarmed, and instead of having Liu killed, explained he was not responsible for Liu's father's abduction, and rewarded Liu with four silver dollars for his bravery.[9]

Ching Shi's ambition, and the growth of the pirate fleet to very large proportions (the previously mentioned 1,800 boats and some 70,000 men) eventually led to dissension among the pirates. Kuo P'o Tai, the commander of the Black Fleet, who had been a colleague of Cheng I, was jealous of Chang Pao's rise to power, and the fact that the Red fleet was bigger than his. It seems that Kuo P'o Tai was also extremely jealous of Chang Pao's relationship with Ching Shi, since he was in love with Ching Shi himself. In addition, Kuo P'o Tai had been brooding for some time over the fickleness of fate in regard to piracy, and was contemplating surrender, if he could be pardoned. Meanwhile, during one action, he refused to come to the help of Chang Pao, which led to an all out battle between the fleets of Chang Pao and Kuo P'o Tai. As it turned out, Kuo's fleet won, causing 1,000 casualties to Chang Pao, the capture of 321 of his men, and the loss of 16 of Chang Pao's large junks. Because of this action, Kuo P'o Tai was able to surrender his Black fleet to the Chinese authorities in early 1810, together with key members of the Yellow fleet, while Kuo himself was given a rank in the Imperial Navy. Before long others were surrendering too, and Chang Pao and Ching Shi were forced to recognize that the world was changing. So, to demonstrate their shift to a new allegiance to the Emperor, they set out to capture or destroy the remaining Yellow, Blue and Green fleets. Ironically, Chang Pao was accompanied in this venture by his former adversary, Kuo P'o Tai. When these fleets were largely dealt with, Chang Pao was well received by the Imperial authorities, and continued his successful career, rising eventually to command an Imperial military regiment as a Lieutenant Colonel. Chang Pao achieved all this, despite having started out as an illiterate fisherman's son. Ching Shi also surrendered and was allowed to retire gracefully, reportedly running a gambling house in Canton in her old age.[10]

Before the collapse of the pirate confederation, the pirates had been unusually successful in the period 1805 to 1810, due partly to appropriate tactics and weaponry. The pirate confederation was well organised in that its attacks were usually planned beforehand using information from shore based gambling dens, secret societies, and paid informers. The pirate attacks would aim either at junks close to shore, which generally provided necessary every day commodities and food, or at the valuable large ocean-going junks, which could provide considerable amounts of rice and other rich cargo. The pirates would also attack villages and government warehouses and forts ashore, which usually provided opportunity for ransom, captives for sale, and weapons from the government warehouses and forts. Normally, the pirates liked to attack through surprise or deception. One such attack took place in September 1808 when a heavily laden but well defended ocean junk was sailing from Vietnam to China. Unable to take the junk directly, the pirates took two ferries, concealed their men onboard the ferries, and then pretended to call for help from the junk. When the junk came alongside the ferries to assist, the pirates swarmed aboard while other pirate boats surrounded the junk. At other times the pirates would hide behind points of land, disguise their boats, or even swim with cutlasses over their shoulders and clamber aboard their targets.[11]

In general, the Chinese pirates liked to take junks by boarding, and, like most Western pirates, tried to establish a psychological edge through an image of terror, so that their victims would surrender more easily. The pirates stimulated themselves with drinks of wine and gunpowder, which produced red faces and glowing eyes, or ate the hearts of earlier victims to gain courage, and sprinkled themselves with garlic water as a charm against becoming casualties. Personal weapons used were the cutlass and the knife, and long and short bamboo pikes. A great variety of gunpowder weapons were available, including seven feet long gingalls, or blunderbusses, various unreliable match locks, and on the larger ships, cannon. These cannon fired shot ranging from six to twenty-four pounds, but the cannon tended to be fixed and could not adjust for range or direction, so the junk had to line up the enemy before firing. Other weapons included stink pots, containing gunpowder and Chinese gin for inflammation, thrown onto the decks of the target, where they broke and ignited. As in the West, fire ships were a useful weapon when the enemy fleets were too strong to be taken in other ways. However, the aim of the pirates was to board and capture the victim junk intact, in order to take captives alive, either for ransom or simply for sale. The pirates were not above cutting off fingers and ears of their victims to speed up the ransom process. One such raid took place in October 1809 on a village in the Pearl River delta. With their bound feet, the women of the village could not escape, so the pirates easily hauled 250 women aboard 'by their hair, and treated [them] in a most savage manner'. Protracted negotiations only led to the ransom of 100 of the women, presumably those with wealthier families. The other 150 women were sold to the pirate crew for forty dollars each. After the ransom process, profit could also come from sale of the ship's cargo, and then the ships themselves. Then there was the salt trade, which the pirates managed to take over by about 1805 in the salt producing area of Tien-pai. Finally, there was the well organised protection racket, in which the pirates forced almost all ships to pay for passes for their safe passage.[12]

Unhappy with such large scale pirate activities, the Manchu emperor decided it was necessary to eliminate this very significant threat to the coasts of south China. The generals the emperor appointed employed two or three different strategies. First was the 'militia and local boats' strategy of General Na-yen-ch'eng, which worked to some extent, but not enough force was applied, and this essentially failed by 1805. Consequently, as in the West, General Na turned to a 'Pardon and Pacification' campaign, which also worked to some extent, but not enough pirates surrendered. General Na was dismissed, and General Wu was appointed in his place. Wu also hired local boats, but these were defeated by 1809, so General Wu was replaced by General Pai Ling in 1809. Pai Ling's concept was to cut off the supplies of the pirates, and among other measures, to protect the salt trade by sending the salt inland instead of by sea. He also hired local ships to attack the pirates, with some success, but this too failed with a big pirate sea victory in 1809. Finally, it was not so much the tactics of the generals as internal dissension among the pirates that saw their reign come to an end in 1810, as mentioned above. In the short period of 1805 to 1810 these Chinese pirates succeeded through charismatic leaders, good organisation, strong discipline, and a keen desire for cash. Initially produced by the Tay-son rebellion, it is also notable that these very large pirate fleets only survived for five years before succumbing to internal rivalry – partly a victim of their own success.[13]

The end of the pirate confederation in 1810 did not mean the end of Chinese piracy, which continued well into the twentieth century. Yet there was one significant pirate explosion in the 1840s when the pirate chief Shap-'ng-tsai, with his lieutenant Chui Apoo, terrorised the area from the island of Hainan in the Gulf of Tonkin to Fukien province. As with previous Chinese pirates, these left the same trail of protection money paid, towns raided, goods stolen, men killed or ransomed, and women taken away for sale or concubinage. Shap's Chinese pirate fleet numbered some sixty-four junks and 3,000 crew. To counter this threat, a fleet of eight junks from the Chinese navy, three East India Company ships, including the steam paddler the *Phlegethon*, and the Royal Navy ship *Hastings*, pursued Shap's fleet into the Tonkin River in October 1849. The *Phlegethon* drew little water, and managed to cross a shallow sand bar, and trapped Shap's fleet in the river. In the late afternoon of 24 October 1849, the pursuing force hotly engaged the pirates, and Shap's junk blew up with a tremendous explosion. By 8p.m., twenty-seven of Shap's junks were in flames, and another twenty-four were destroyed. The low, flat islands at the mouth of the river were covered in Chinese pirates attempting to escape but the local Cochin Chinese either captured them, or used sampans to chase down and spear the pirates in the water. Shap himself escaped in a small junk, but later surrendered, and in the previous Chinese tradition of dealing with Chang Pao and Ching Shi, the authorities pardoned Shap and gave him a military commission. Chui Apoo held out for some further time, apparently in 1849 murdering two British officers in Hong Kong who had insulted him. Then his fleet was destroyed in two encounters near Bias Bay, close to Hong Kong. Like Shap, he surrendered to the Chinese authorities, but was kidnapped by the British and landed in a Hong Kong jail. He was sentenced to transportation for life, which he considered so insulting a sentence that he committed suicide in jail in 1851. This ended the Chinese burst of piracy of the 1840s, although much more was to come later.[14]

India and the Piracy of Kanhoji Angrey (1690s–1729)

In contrast to China, a somewhat different kind of piracy was developing along the coasts of India. Pirates had operated off India for centuries, including the Sanganians operating out of Kutch, and the Colee Rovers operating out of Gujerat. Indeed, Marco Polo wrote in the late 1260s that more than a hundred pirate ships came out from Gujerat every summer, bringing their wives and children with them. They stayed out all summer, and formed fleets of twenty to thirty ships, which acted as a sea cordon or blockade, so that no merchant vessel could escape them. There was a special emphasis on the west coast of India, due to strong trading links with the Indian Ocean, the Persian Gulf, the Arabian Sea, and the Red Sea. The west coast of India, sometimes known as the Malabar Coast, meaning the land between Bombay and Cochin, attracted pirates, especially after the coming of the Europeans in the early 1500s, following Vasco da Gama's arrival on the Malabar Coast in 1498.

It was along the west coast of India that there developed a remarkable struggle for power between several countries, groups and alliances. This situation was helped by the lack of a single strong power which might have controlled maritime security in the area. Among the contestants were the Europeans, who fought for trade dominance, pitting Portuguese, Dutch and English ships, trading bases, and companies, against each other. Of significance here were the enclaves established along the Indian coast by the Portuguese, especially Goa, as well as the creation of the British East India Company at the beginning of the seventeenth century, based at Surat and Bombay. Other significant competitors in the area included of course the Moghul Indian Empire. However, this empire was starting to break down, partly under the strain of internal feuds, rebellions, and costly military expeditions against the emerging Hindu power of the Marathas. Leading some of these very large Moghul military efforts was the emperor Aurangzeb (1658–1707), who was unable to defeat the Maratha hero, Shivaji (1627–1680). The Marathas thus also came to be a power in the region. Other contestants in the area included the Siddy, a naval force of Muslim descendants of Africans, who inhabited the port and fort of Janjira, and nominally owed allegiance to the sultan of Bijapur. Western pirates were another dangerous part of this coast in the late seventeenth century, including some of the Madagascar pirates such as Avery and Kidd (discussed in Chapter 6). The English sailor Edward Barlow, who unusually kept a diary, noted that he came across Danish pirates near Surat in 1687, who took Muslim ships and the Moghul's ships, because the Danes theoretically held a reprisal commission from the king of Denmark. Ten years later, in 1697, Barlow was in the same location again, and stated that locals feared what he called black pirates from Diu Point, near Surat. Other pirates included Muscat Arabs, who in 1696 swooped down on Salsette, a Portuguese town twenty miles from Bombay, killing the Portuguese priests and carrying off 1,400 captives. At this time these Muscat pirates possessed a very large and well armed fleet. Into this complicated, warring, and constantly changing mix on the coast of India, arrived Kanhoji Angrey (1669–1729), the founder of a dynasty, which the East India Company and the Portuguese called pirates. Angrey however, was normally allied with the Marathas, and so he can therefore also be seen as a Maratha privateer.[15]

Angrey originally served in the Maratha naval fleet – he was named deputy fleet commander in 1690, and perhaps admiral soon after. He continued to serve the Marathas, though endless civil wars within the Maratha ruling family and their supporters made it difficult to decide who exactly to serve. Nevertheless, Angrey insisted that foreign ships should carry his pass, the 'dastak', easily purchased for twenty rupees (the same rate as the Portuguese), which offered freedom from pirates and shore based attacks. Those who did not purchase the dastak, Angrey felt free to capture. Angrey strengthened his position by establishing a string of impregnable forts on the coast from Bombay to Goa, and by building up his navy. Around 1703, this navy consisted of ten ghurabs (frigates with sails, but with a bow like a galley) mounting sixteen to thirty cannon each, and fifty gallivats (fast rowing boats with sails) with four to ten cannon each. Singly, these ships were no match for the Europeans, but Angrey devised special tactics which proved very successful. When the larger European ships came close to shore, they slowed down in the shallow waters, which gave Angrey his chance as a large number of gallivats sped out from hiding, followed by the slower but larger ghurabs. The gallivats took care to stay astern of the European ships to avoid their cannon, and tried to cripple their victims and slow them down. Then came the ghurabs, which fired and wheeled away to give others their turn. As much as possible the shore-based guns of Angrey also came into play. The idea was to eventually board the European ship, relying on the man power superiority of Angrey's men – who anyway were better in man to man fighting than the Europeans.[16]

From around 1710, Angrey happily pursued East India Company ships, and indeed, any European and coastal ships that came into view of his ports. One unusual incident relates to Angrey's use of ransom as another source of pirate income. The story begins in 1709, when Captain Gerard Cooke and his family, passengers on the *Loyall Bliss*, were on their way to

Calcutta, where Cooke was to become the East India Company engineer. After a rough voyage the ship arrived, and anchored off Karwar. Here the nearly sixty-year-old chief factor of the East India Company, John Harvey, described as deformed, quickly became enamoured of Cooke's attractive thirteen or fourteen year-old daughter. By offering large sums to the Cooke family as a dowry, which Harvey obtained by private trading, as was usually the case, he secured her hand in marriage. However, Harvey died only two years later, and the fifteen year-old Mrs Harvey rapidly married the new East India Company chief factor at Karwar, Thomas Chown. The Chowns and two other ships set out for Bombay in 1713 and were ambushed by four of Angrey's ships. A very hot fight ensued, in which Angrey's ships prevailed, but during the contest Thomas Chown's arm was torn away by a shot. He died in his recent bride's bloodstained arms. Angrey brought Mrs Chown and the captains and mates of the East India Company ships to Colaba, Angrey's capital, where Angrey sought a ransom of 30,000 rupees for his captives. The Bombay Council of the East India Company readily paid the ransom, and Mrs Chown arrived in Bombay, where she very soon married another East India Company man, Thomas Gifford. Subsequently, Thomas Gifford obtained the pepper monopoly at Anjengo on the Malabar Coast, where he became wealthy by cheating both the East India Company and the local merchants. Retribution followed when the locals killed Gifford for cheating them, in 1721. This was not a pleasant demise, since the locals cut out Gifford's tongue and nailed it to his chest, and then fastened Gifford to a plank, on which he floated down the river. Mrs Gifford, still youthful, but now a widow three times over, escaped to Madras, where she appealed for help. What she wanted was to obtain her triple inheritances, and so she applied to the recently arrived Commodore Matthews, of the Royal Navy. This was the same Matthews who had called in at St Mary's Madagascar, attempting to capture pirates, but failed to achieve much except for private trading, for which he was court martialled (see Chapter 6). It seems that Matthews was brave, but otherwise 'void of common sense, good manners, or knowledge of the world'. Matthews quarreled with anybody and everybody, and especially with the Governor of Bombay, over the important question of who should fire the first salute. But in regard to Mrs Gifford, Matthews was very gallant, so that the attractive Mrs Gifford, still only twenty-six, lived in Matthew's house and then onboard his ship – to the scandal of Bombay. Subsequently, Mrs. Gifford returned to England, and became involved in long court cases against the East India Company over money. Earlier, of course, Angrey had obtained his ransom for Mrs Gifford when she was Mrs Chown, and was satisfied with this means of increasing his revenue, but now found he had to defend his interests when Matthews commanded a fleet in an ill fated attack on Angrey's fort at Colaba in 1721.[17]

Before turning to the question of Matthews and his attack on Colaba, it is worth noting the reason for the long 38 year fight which developed between Angrey and the East India Company. Commencing in 1718 the East India Company allowed Indian ships to fly the English flag, which robbed Angrey of his right to charge customs fees and the dastak from these Indian ships. Angrey strongly objected, and the struggle began. During this long period of warfare, the East India Company indulged in a series of incredibly incompetent attacks on Angrey's forts, usually resulting in casualties and miserable failure for the East India Company. For example, one such attack took place in November 1718, when one brave military captain marched up to the gates of Angrey's Khanderi fort, presented his pistol, and tried to shoot the lock off the gate. Instead the ball rebounded, hitting the captain on the nose, which caused him and most of the attackers to retreat. Most of these attacks failed due to lack of proper organization and planning, quite apart from the strength of Angrey's forts. But in a concerted attempt to deal with Angrey, the English and the Portuguese formed an alliance, and the Royal Navy headed by Commodore Matthews replaced the ineffective East India Company ships and sailors.

Focussing therefore on Matthews' attack on Colaba in 1721, some 6,500 Portuguese and English troops trained and secretly prepared to assault Angrey's fort from the land side, while a fleet of ten ships under Matthews was to bombard the fort in preparation for the assault. However, Angrey found out through his spies that Colaba was to be the target of this allied force, and speedily sought help from the Marathas, who provided 25,000 troops to help defend Colaba. The assault took place on 24 December 1721, and although a few English soldiers and sailors got into the fort, led by a certain Lieutenant Bellamy, who ascended the walls with colours flying, the rest were thrown back. Meanwhile, the Angrians counter attacked with a large force, including elephants, and the besieging army fell into disorder. The Portuguese army started to retreat, and were then routed by the Maratha cavalry. At the same time the English departed for their ships. Commodore Matthews was convinced of Portuguese treachery, and arrived at Portuguese headquarters in such a fury that he struck the Portuguese commander in the mouth with his cane. The Portuguese Viceroy was also badly treated and departed for his ship, claiming sickness, though an English doctor could find nothing wrong with him. Naturally, this violence from Matthews plus mutual recriminations disrupted the allied force. Indeed the Portuguese, who were disgusted at the constant drunkenness and quarreling among the English forces, and their treatment from Matthews, shortly after signed a peace treaty with Angrey.[18]

Things went from bad to worse for the East India Company – fighting broke out against the Portuguese, and Commodore Matthews departed on a private trading venture. Angrey began to attack Company ships as well as merchant ships, while Matthews, when he returned to Bombay, seems to have taken the side of Angrey in the latter's dispute with the East India Company. Astonishingly, as Matthews left Bombay in 1723 with his Royal Navy fleet, he sent word to the Viceroy of Goa that he would present him with an old woman's petticoat if he, the Viceroy, did not capture every single one of the East India Company's ships. Bombay was clearly glad to see the last of Matthews, who returned to England, where the Court of the Exchequer obtained judgement against him for private trading and misconduct in the sum of £13,676. Subsequently Matthews was cashiered from the Royal Navy in 1744 for failure and misconduct in a battle against a French and Spanish fleet in the Mediterranean. Bombay and the East India Company were no doubt very pleased that Matthews was now gone, although Angrey remained. Angrey's acts of piracy, or warfare, depending on one's point of view, continued until his death in 1729. Angrey is described as a strong man, at home on sea or land, fond of good living, yet deeply religious, a careful and astute leader, employing diplomacy as much as warfare. He collected swords, and encouraged learning. He had three wives, and many concubines, and was the father of seven legitimate children, which led to fighting between his sons for Angrey's kingdom on his death. Overcoming this, Angrey's sons continued attacking East India Company ships through the 1730s and 1740s. Especially striking was the capture of the *Derby* in 1735, a rich Company ship with enough gold onboard for the East India Company to operate for a whole year. It seems that nine Angrian pirate ships attacked the *Derby*, mostly from the stern as was their custom, a tactic made easier by the lack of wind that day. After losing the main and mizzen masts, the *Derby* and 115 passengers and crew surrendered. The inside story of this capture is that it was the custom of ships' captains to bring up two treasure chests to the top deck, containing around £2,000 as prize money to the crew if they fought stoutly and beat off attackers. The captain of the *Derby* neglected to do this, and the crew allegedly remained listless in the ship's defense. When seven men were killed and more were wounded, the captain of the *Derby* insisted on surrendering.[19]

Ultimately, Angrian piracy came to an end with the capture of the two main Angrian forts. First was the taking of Severndroog by Commodore James in 1755. Then James, Rear Admiral Watson, and Robert Clive, captured the fort of Gheria in 1756. British success in India had persuaded the majority of the Maratha forces to combine with the British in their assaults, thus depriving Tolaji, the current Angrian chief and an illegitimate son of Kanhoji Angrey, of much needed land support. In 1755, Commodore James in command of a small fleet of the Bombay Marine, plus a Maratha fleet, chased the Angrian fleet back into the protection of the Severndroog fort, known as the golden fort, with walls fifty feet high. James realised that a land based siege would take too long, and also realised that only very close bombardment from his flag ship, the forty gun *Protector*, would have an impact. So, after taking soundings, James sailed the *Protector* in close, in four fathoms of water, with the support of two smaller ships. On the second day of the cannonade, James organised the operation so that the *Protector* fired only two or three upper deck guns in continuous rotation at the main Severndroog fort, in order to keep the fort's return fire suppressed, assisted by the men in the tops with musket fire. Meanwhile, the *Protector*'s other side fired broadsides at two lesser forts across from the main fort. At midday, a magazine exploded in Severndroog fort, the defenders tried to leave by small boats, and soon resistance ended both at the main fort, and at the lesser forts. On his death, and in recognition of his success, James's widow erected a tower at Shooters Hill on Woolwich Common in England, known as Severndroog Tower, or perhaps more accurately as 'Lady James's Folly'.[20]

The next year, 1756, the Bombay Council of the East India Company decided to put an end to the Angrian pirates. A large fleet was assembled, consisting of eighteen Company ships under James, six Royal Navy ships under Rear Admiral Watson, and an army force of 1,800 European soldiers and 600 native troops under Robert Clive, including Maratha soldiers. The East India Company anticipated that Tolaji would attempt to bribe his way out of trouble, so part of their instructions read:

> It is probable that Torlajee may offer to capitulate, and possibly offer a sum of money, but you are to consider that this fellow is not on a footing with any prince in the known world, he being a pirate in whom no confidence can

be put, not only taking, burning, and destroying ships of all nations, but even the vessels belonging to the natives, which have his own passes [dastaks], and for which he has annually collected large sums of money. Should he offer any sum of money it must be a very great one that will pay us for the many rich ships he has taken…

The Company also wanted Tolaji dead or alive, to put an end to his piracy. And the Company was very keen to take Gheria by force of arms, because if the fort and Tolaji simply surrendered, the Marathas stood to gain a large part of Tolaji's wealth, whereas if the British and the Company forces compelled the surrender, then the Company stood to gain the maximum possible. This was the way it turned out, since a tremendous cannonade by 150 heavy guns over two days first of all burnt the entire Angrian fleet of some sixty-five ships, and secondly produced a huge explosion in the fort which caused a white flag to be raised on the second day. Tolaji himself surrendered to the Marathas, and was imprisoned for the rest of his life, while the Company hauled away a vast fortune including £130,000 in gold, silver and jewels.[21]

This action signaled the end of Angrian piracy after fifty years. However, since the Angrians, and especially Kanhoji Angrey, operated in alliance with the Marathas, it can be argued that some or most of this represented privateering rather than piracy. On the other hand, from the point of view of the East India Company, the Angrians were pirates.

Malaysia and the Philippines

The same ambivalence over the question of who was a pirate relates to South East Asia, where pirates or robbers had operated for centuries as a normal and even accepted way of life. After the Europeans arrived, and particularly in the eighteenth and nineteenth centuries, the old native state system was destroyed by the Europeans, who then used the suppression of piracy and local rivalries as an argument to justify the expansion of European, and especially British, influence in the region.[22] Generally speaking, during the period from the 1830s to the 1860s, British, Dutch, Spanish, and other European powers managed to suppress what was called piracy by the Europeans, but which would be given other interpretations locally. A bewildering variety of pirates/rebels/robbers/local rivals operated in the Indonesian, Malay and Philippine areas – the Ilanuns in

Mindanao (Philippines) and north-east Borneo; the Balanini in the Sulu chain of islands; the Dyaks in Sarawak and the Borneo area; the Bugis from Sulawsesi and Singapore; the Achin from north Sumatra; and the Malays of Johore (Singapore and north), from the Riau-Lingga islands, and Borneo and Brunei. Imperial and economic reasons motivated the European presence in this whole area, as well as lurid tales of piracy and mayhem against European ships, which required action. In regard to the last point, for example, a series of stories angered the European powers. One of these stories, if true, has Captain Gregory of the Dutch ship *Maria Frederika* being captured by Ilanun pirates in the early nineteenth century. The Ilanun took the ship to their stronghold at Tungku on the north east coast of Borneo, where Gregory and his first mate were buried in sand to their chests. Then an elderly chief with a white beard, carrying a heavy two handed sword, advanced on Gregory, swung the sword and cut Gregory's head from his body. The first mate died more slowly. Another story relates to Captain Ross of the ship *Regina* who was captured and tied to the mast of his ship, where he watched his son being drowned by the captors. Ross himself lost his fingers as they were cut off piece by piece, then there were further cuts, and he was finally burnt to death as the ship was put to the torch.[23]

Malays

In regard to the Malays, William Dampier is often cited as declaring the Malays to be a peaceable people in 1689. He thought that they were provoked into piracy by the Dutch, who prevented their trading. However, in 1687, in the Gulf of Thailand, William Dampier's ship encountered a Malay boat. Dampier remarked that the Malays had a reputation as 'desperate fellows, and their vessels [were] commonly full of men who all [wore] cressets or little daggers by their sides'. And when some men from Dampier's ship went onboard the Malay bark, the Malays killed half a dozen of them, although the Malays might have been apprehensive of the armed European sailors.[24] Regardless, after Raffles founded Singapore in 1819, the local chief Temenggong of Johore, from whom Singapore had been acquired, was strongly suspected of piracy. Up until that time, a local writer noted that:

...no mortal dared to pass through the Straits of Singapore. Jinns and satans even were afraid, for that was the place the pirates made use of to sleep and to

divide their booty. There also they put to death their captives and ... themselves fought and killed each other in their quarrels on the spoil ... All along
the beach there were hundreds of human skulls, some of them old, some fresh
with the hair still remaining, some with the teeth still sharp, and some without teeth. In fine, they were in various stages of decay.[25]

It seems that the Malays settled in various parts of South-East Asia, including Borneo. According to the account of a nineteenth-century European
resident of Sarawak, the Malays went out in fleets of ten to thirty war boats
or prahus. These prahus were ninety feet long, and carried a large gun in the
bow, with three or four swivel guns on the sides, plus some twenty to thirty
muskets onboard. Each prahu was rowed by sixty to eighty oars on two
decks, and carried around eighty to a hundred men. On top of the rowers
was a flat bamboo roof, which protected the ammunition and provisions,
and provided a platform from which to fight. Their method was to send
out small scout boats during the south-west monsoon season when trading
ships were plentiful. After a trading ship was sighted, the main prahus would
dart out from creeks and rivers and board the victim with blood curdling
yells. After taking captives and transferring the cargo, the prahus would burn
the captive ship to avoid detection, and return to their river lairs. By the
time of the north-east monsoon, the Malays would retire to their settle-
ments and await the next season.[26]

In regard to Singapore, it is argued that Raffles used the Malay piracy
threat to justify the elimination of Thai influence in the region, and to
expand British power on the peninsula. Thus the 1824 Treaty of London,
produced mainly to divide spheres of influence between the Dutch and
the British in the area, also contained a clause for the suppression of piracy,
and by the 1840s the Malay chief, Temenggong Ibrahim, was persuaded to
abandon what was partly a political fight between locals, and turn to trade
instead.[27]

Balanini and Ilanuns

Turning next to the Balanini, based on the island of Jolo in Sulu Sea, these
sea going peoples resented European intrusion, tried to stay independent,
and had spent many years in the islands of the Philippines capturing slaves
for their huge Sulu slave markets. According to the Royal Navy Captain

Keppel (later Admiral), in the 1840s, the Balanini operated large boats, to which were attached smaller sampans, carrying ten to fifteen men armed with muskets and small three pounder brass cannon. Their tactic was to take small boats by surprise, with the idea of selling the captives as slaves. A favourite device was for two or three Balanini to show themselves in full view, while the rest of the crew crouched hidden in the bottom of the boat. An unusual weapon was a long pole with barbed iron points by which the Balanini hooked their unhappy victims. However, by the 1850s they were under attack by the Spanish, although some years later, the Spanish were still assaulting Sulu, in 1871 and 1876. In the end, the Balanini pirate base of Tungku in north-east Borneo was only erased in 1879 by HMS *Kestrel*.

Then there were the Ilanuns, in Mindanao and north Borneo, who were much feared for their raids using their large prahus of several tons. These prahus had short masts, sported bow pieces and swivel guns, and were rowed by many slaves with a crew of fifty to a hundred. Together with the Balanini, these boats embarked on very wide ranging sea raids, so that the months of August to September were known as the 'Lanun Season'. However, a considerable number of the Ilanun raiders were eliminated in 1862 by the Sarawak screw steamer *Rainbow,* with the assistance of the government gun boat, *Jolly Bachelor*, which had earlier served with Admiral Keppel.[28]

This 1862 sea fight between these two British ships and six large Ilanun prahus and several smaller sampans, is reported in some detail by Harriette McDougall, a Sarawak resident. This missionary lady had a very low opinion of the Ilanuns, calling them 'pests of the human race', and thought of them as 'unmixed evil, because they are taught to be cruel from their childhood'. The sea fight began when three large Ilanun prahus were spotted off the port of Muka, on the west coast of Borneo. The *Rainbow* prepared for action by hanging planks and mattresses on the railings to absorb the rifle and musket shots of the Ilanuns, as well as providing some protection against spears and larger brass guns. This done, the tactic was to use grape and round shot against the Ilanun prahus at a distance, and then use the quicker and more agile steamer *Rainbow* to literally drive over the prahus one by one. However, the first prahu, seeing the danger, got into shallow water, where the *Rainbow* could not follow, so the *Jolly Bachelor* was sent to deal with this vessel. The second and third prahus were run over, and the pirates taken, killed, or escaped, while as many captives and slaves were rescued as possible. Subsequently, the rescued captives from these prahus told the captain of the *Rainbow* of the existence of three more prahus further out to sea. These were located, trying to use their long sweeps and sails to escape, but the *Rainbow* caught up with them, so that two of these were run over as before, and one was boarded. Overall, 165 captives and slaves were rescued, while only thirty-two Ilanuns were taken alive, the rest having been killed, or having escaped by swimming to the shore.[29]

Harrowing stories emerged from this sea fight. Some of the rescued captives were earlier attacked by the Ilanun pirates as the sea fight went against the pirates – one man 'came onboard with the top of his skull as cleanly lifted up by a Sooloo [Sulu] knife, as if a surgeon had desired to take a peep at the brains inside! It took considerable force to close it in the right place.' This man recovered, as did another who had a three barbed spear sticking in his back. From the prahus taken out at sea, a Chinese captive was seen swimming, holding his tail of hair in the air so that he would not be taken for a pirate. The rescued captives related how on the Ilanun prahus they were compelled to drink a mixture of salt water and fresh water, no doubt due to scarcity of drinking water. Food was a handful of rice and sago twice a day. The rescued Chinese captive said that when the Ilanuns took a ship that resisted, most onboard were killed. Those that were allowed to live were beaten with:

> …a flat piece of bamboo over the elbows and knees, and the muscles of arms
> and legs, until they were unable to move; then a halter is put round their
> necks, and, when they are sufficiently tamed, they are put to the oars and
> made to row in gangs, with one of their own fellow-captives as overseer to
> keep them at work.

This resembles the galley practice of the Barbary corsairs, as does the next comment, 'If he [the overseer] does not do it effectually, he is krissed [knifed] and thrown overboard. They row in relays, night and day; and to keep them awake, cayenne pepper is rubbed into their eyes or into cuts dealt them on their arms.'[30]

Harriette McDougall concluded her account by accurately pointing out two factors that enabled the *Rainbow* and *Jolly Bachelor* to succeed in their attack on the Ilanun prahus. The first was that the two ships met the Ilanuns in separate engagements – if the whole armada of six prahus and attendant sampans had been together, they might have overwhelmed the *Rainbow* and *Jolly Bachelor*. And secondly, the ammunition of the British ships only just lasted out the two engagements – at the conclusion of the second fight there was merely a little loose powder left in one barrel, and a few broken cartridges elsewhere. It seems unlikely that this one engagement, although dealing a severe blow to the Ilanuns, actually ended Ilanun activities, but no doubt it reduced their raids considerably.[31]

Dyaks

Borneo was also home to the sea going Dyaks from the Sarebas and Sekrang tribes. According to one source, these Dyaks, although head hunters, were really more involved in local rivalries and local piracy. But from the nineteenth-century missionary perspective of Harriette McDougall, the Sea Dyaks were definitely pirates, and this attitude was shared by Captain Henry Keppel, who hunted them down in the 1840s. According to Harriette McDougall, the Dyaks learnt piracy from the Malays, but developed their own style. The Dyaks built fast boats called bangkongs, ninety feet long and nine or ten feet broad, which drew little water. These boats could easily be disassembled, and either hidden, or carried to where they could be used, since they were only held together with rattan strips, and sealed with bark. The Dyaks would silently approach a ship at dusk or night and then overwhelm the crew with showers of spears, and either kill or capture their victims. The Dyaks were head hunters, and Harriette McDougall reported that she remembered one boat that had been recovered with only three fingers of the victims left in it, and blood on the sides of the boat where the heads of the victims had been cut off. The Dyaks raided on land as well as at sea, and often by river.

Sometimes, having destroyed a village and its inhabitants, they would dress themselves in the clothes of the slain, and, proceeding to another place, would call out to the women, 'The Sarebas are coming, but, if you bring down your valuables to us, we will defend you and your property.' And many fell into the snare, and were carried off. If they attacked a house when the men were at home, it was by night. They pulled stealthily up the river in their boats, and landing under cover of their shields, crept under the long house ... The pirates then set fire to dry wood and a quantity of chillies which they carried with them ... This made a suffocating smoke, which hindered the inhabitants from coming out to defend themselves. Then they cut down the posts of the house, which fell, with all that it contained, into their ruthless hands.[32]

The actions of the Dyaks and other pirates caught the attention of James Brooke – Rajah Brooke (1803–868) – who had become *de facto* ruler of Sarawak and agent for the Sultan of Brunei. Brooke mounted an anti-pirate campaign, because he believed the pirates disrupted trade, and he persuaded Captain Keppel to come to the rescue. Keppel arrived with HMS *Dido* and mounted a campaign in 1843 and 1844 to eliminate the Dyaks. Keppel was horrified by the head hunting activities of the Dyaks, having examined a Dyak house, which contained 'numerous human skulls suspended from the ceiling in regular festoons, with the thigh and arm bones occupying the intervening spaces…'[33] Keppel pursued the Dyaks relentlessly up the rivers of Sarawak and north Borneo where the Dyaks had their forts and houses. Keppel's tactics were fairly simple: pursue the Dyaks up river, although there were usually booms or felled trees laid across the rivers to halt Keppel's boats. These boats might be steamers, paddle wheelers, pinnaces and ship's cutters, depending on the situation. The Dyaks defended with musket and cannon fire, but they were almost always defeated by Keppel and his local allies. Keppel's men broke up the booms with axes, and then boldly attacked in frontal fashion, using muskets, cannon, and Congreve rockets. The Dyaks either then surrendered or were killed, but also melted away into the jungle to fight another day.

Looking at just one Keppel attack, there is his typical assault on the Dyak capital of Paddi in 1843. Moving up river with the tide, Keppel was in the lead in a ship's gig when they were swept around a bend in the river and as they hove in sight 'several hundred savages rose up, and gave one of their war-yells. It was the first I had heard. No report from musketry or ordnance could ever make a man's heart feel so *small* as mine did at that horrid yell: but I had no leisure to think.' Next, Keppel and the pinnaces and cutters that followed came across a barrier across the river – two rows of trees planted in the mud and held together by rattan strips. Keppel's small gig got through the barrier, and was in danger of being cut off, but managed to row back upstream, while the bigger boats behind cut through the rattan strips and opened a passage through the barrier. While the pinnace kept up a strong fire on the Dyak fort at Paddi on the river bank, other cutters from Keppel's crew landed the men, who straightaway ran for the fort, 'This mode of warfare – this dashing at once in the very face of the fort – was so novel and incomprehensible to our enemies, that they fled, panic-struck, into the jungle…' Soon the fort at Paddi was in flames, and Keppel's native allies were busy plundering and setting fire to neighbouring villages. After this, Keppel's force headed further up river, now aided by an 800 or 900 strong army of rival Dyaks. These 'friendly' Dyaks were provided with white strips of calico on their head dresses to distinguish them from the Dyaks that were being attacked, and also given a pass word, 'Datu'.[34]

Keppel's next move was to continue even further up the left hand fork of the river, which was defended with a barrier by the Dyaks. Keppel therefore decided it was the correct branch of the river to follow. A small well armed force of about ninety men in the pinnace headed up the river, although there were supposed to be around 6,000 Dyaks and 500 Malays to oppose them. There was a sharp fight, and an uncomfortable night for Keppel's force in the heavy rain, as Dyak spear throwing attacks continued through the darkness. It seems that signal rockets and Congreve rockets were discomforting to the Dyaks, as well as the accurate fire of the cannon and the rapid musket fire of Keppel's party. Moreover, the Dyaks' main weapon in this encounter was the spear, so there was an obvious technical imbalance in the conflict. When Keppel's force showed every intention of carrying on even further up the river, where the Dyaks had hidden their families and possessions, the Dyaks decided to bargain. Rajah Brooke conducted negotiations, and the Dyaks agreed to renounce their attacks. The campaign was not over, however, for Keppel's force then attacked other Dyak forts at a place called Pakoo, where the Dyaks were well fortified but had not had time to set up their cannon. A salvo from Keppel's force was enough to send these Dyaks into retreat, and Keppel's allies – a Dyak tribe called Singe – were active in taking the heads of Pakoo's defenders, 'I saw one body afterwards without its head, in which each passing [Singe] Dyak had thought proper to stick a spear, so that it had all the appearance of a huge porcupine.' As was customary, Pakoo was put to the torch, and so was the next Dyak fort at Rembas. In this fashion, the campaign of pacification continued, with one Dyak group after another being subdued.[35]

Yet the Dyaks were not to be so easily defeated, and in 1849 a major effort against them was launched by a number of Royal Navy vessels, by Rajah Brooke's ships, and by allied Dyaks. On 31 July 1849, this combined fleet cut off a major group of 150 Sarebas and Sakarran Dyak bangkongs returning from a raid. When the Dyaks saw they were cut off from their river retreat, they called a hasty council of war by the sounding of three strokes of a gong. According to Harriette McDougall, a subsequent yell of defiance showed that the Dyaks had decided to fight:

> The pirates fought bravely, but could not withstand the forces of their enemies. Their boats were upset by the paddles of the steamer; they were

hemmed in on every side, and five hundred men were killed, sword in hand; while two thousand five hundred escaped into the jungle ... The English officers on that night offered prizes to all who should bring in captives alive: but the pirates would take no quarter, in the water they still fought without surrender.[36]

The going rate offered by the British Admiralty for Dyak pirates captured or killed was £20, and Captain Farquhar of HMS *Albatross* successfully claimed £20,700 for his part in this action – an extraordinary fortune. The Dyaks who escaped into the jungle must have annoyed those who hoped for more prize money. (Similarly, Captain Sir Edward Belcher, on HMS *Samarang*, claimed 350 pirates killed in the Moluccas in 1844, at £20 each, which amounted to £7,000, but he also claimed for 980 pirates who escaped, at £5 each, for the sum of £4,900, the total being £11,900. Strangely enough, the total claim was accepted.) Returning to Farquhar, his action did much to put an end to Dyak raids, although the perspective of history shows that many of these Dyak raids were the result of local rivalries, and the piracy that did take place was usually local.[37]

The same can be said for almost all of the piracy of South-East Asia and the Pacific – what was piracy to Western imperial governments was traditional practice and local rivalry to the groups and tribes of the area.

Arab Piracy: The Qasimi

By the seventh century, the Muscat Arab raiders had already gained a reputation for piracy, and in the twefth century, they raided the coasts of India and Africa. In the sixteenth and seventeenth centuries the Arabs were formidable rivals to the Portuguese. Then, in the late eighteenth century and into the early nineteenth century, a confederation of tribes called the Qasimi attacked vessels of foreigners and other Arab ships from Muscat and Oman. The Qasimi (plural Qawasim) largely converted to Wahhabism, a stricter form of Islam, and in the period from the 1790s to the 1820s, raided a large number of ships from their base at Ras al Khaima (now in modern Oman). Some of the attacked ships were from the East India Company, some were merchant ships of other flags, some were local Arab boats, and many came from Surat in India. One particular capture by the Qasimi was of the merchant ship *Minerva*, taken in 1809. A passenger onboard, one Alimanjee, wrote that about fifty-five Qasimi boats, large and small, with 5,000 Qawasim onboard, attacked the *Minerva*, and over a period of two days succeeded in taking the ship. Alimanjee perhaps exaggerated the number of Qasimi boats and pirates, but in any case, of the seventy-seven strong *Minerva* crew and passengers, forty-five were killed. The rest were taken to the Qasimi capital Ras al-Khaima, where the Qasimi demanded ransom. Most were too poor to pay but the young Armenian wife of Lieutenant Taylor, her infant son, and her servants, were ransomed for $1,400. The handful of Christian males who survived were persuaded to become Muslims, and were forcibly circumcised.[38]

The vessels used by the Qasimi for their piracy were built for operation in narrow waters, and the main boat used was the baghla. This boat had a crew of about 150 to 200 onboard, with a high poop, and a very large sail. An even larger boat was the dow, distinguished from the baghla by having a long gallery projecting from the stern. The dow was capable of carrying 300 to 500 men, and from five to ten guns. The Qasimi mode of attack was as follows:

> They surround a ship, keeping clear of the broadside if she has cannon, and begin the battle with matchlocks, guns and spears … When a favourable opportunity offers, they run their prows over the deck of the vessel they attack … over the heads of the defendants who are completely exposed; and as soon as the dow swings alongside, the men from the fighting stage board, while multitudes of men in fast sailing boats … rush in and overpower the unhappy people they assail.[39]

A typical Qasimi attack was the capture of the *Ahmadi*, sailing from Surat in India in February 1816. This merchant ship possessed a British pass, and hoisted British colours, but this was of little interest to the four baghlas, two dows and two other Qasimi boats lying in wait near Bab el Mandeb, the old ambush location of the Red Sea pirates. Around forty to fifty Qasimi boarded the *Ahmadi* and proceeded to immediately slaughter ten or twelve of those who were on deck. Others of the *Ahmadi* crew escaped to cabins or below decks, or speedily clambered up the masts. One sailor who went up a mast found a Qasimi climbing up after him, and was just about to throw himself into the water when a call went out to stop the slaughter. When this sailor came down from the mast, he saw 'about ten or twelve dead bodies, some of them with their heads severed off … lying about the deck … the remainder had been thrown overboard'. It seems that fifty-six of the people onboard the *Ahmadi* were killed. The *Ahmadi* was one of three Indian ships carrying British colours, and these ships produced about £100,000 in booty to the Qasimi.[40]

The piracy of the Qawasim was widespread, and perhaps employed as many as 25,000 men. Many of the ships taken were from the East India Company, and so the British navy attempted to rein in the piracy with a major attack on Ras al Khaima in November 1809. The navy bombarded the town and then landed troops which sacked the town. This turned out to be a temporary setback to the Qawasim, so in December 1819 the British returned to Ras al Khaima with a battleship, ten other warships, and 3,400 troops, and began a six day siege. In the end, all the boats at Ras al Khamai were destroyed, and the Qasimi fort razed to the ground. This time, the Qawasim recognised the right of the East India Company to sail unhindered, and signed a Treaty or Truce in January 1820, which truce led to the southern shores of the Persian Gulf being known later as the Trucial coast. As it happened, some Qawasim continued to raid, but they were forced to reimburse their victims. Looking at Qawasim piracy overall, it seems that local conditions influenced this piracy to a considerable extent. The Qawasim engaged in piracy partly because they thought it was their right, and partly because it was expected of them by regional politics. Social pressure to maintain the honour of the Qawasim encouraged such piracy, which might be thought of as the kind of traditional raiding normally practiced in the region. Hence, culture, politics, and religion in the shape of Wahhabism, which encouraged maritime plunder, all led to Qawasim piracy. Thus what was tradition in the region of the Gulf became piracy when the East Indian Company and the British became involved.[41]

Piracy in the Eastern seas showed many differences from Western piracy in the size and composition of pirate fleets, in the tactics employed, in the political ambitions of the pirates, and in the complicated rivalry between local rulers as they faced European imperialism and European economic desires. And like Chinese, Indian and South East Asian piracy, pirates in the Arabian Gulf had operated for centuries. Yet Arab Gulf piracy was similar to Chinese, Indian and South East Asian pirates in that during the late eighteenth and early nineteenth centuries, these pirates pursued their activities in the same context of local rivalries and European ambitions. But while Asian piracy continued to flourish well into the twentieth century, there was an earlier nineteenth century outburst of piracy in the Mediterranean and in the traditional areas of the West Indies and the Americas, as the next chapter illustrates.

The Road to Modern Piracy

The first half of the nineteenth century saw a considerable amount of piracy in the Mediterranean, in the Atlantic, off the West Indies, and in the Gulf of Mexico. In the Mediterranean (noted in Chapter 8) the Barbary corsairs did not fully cease operations until 1830, while the disorder created by the Napoleonic wars opened the area to a number of attacks. The end of the Napoleonic wars in 1815 also turned a number of privateers into pirates. But it was the Greek war of independence against the Ottomans, commencing in 1821, which really opened up the Mediterranean to further considerable piracy. This piracy eventually came to an end by 1828 through the actions of the British, French and Russians, who intervened on behalf of the Greeks in 1827. Although both Greeks and Ottoman Turks were involved in piracy throughout this period, it was often Greek sailors who were involved. This was partly because the Greeks had already been outlaws before the war started, partly because they had no other means of survival, and partly because the Greek Provisional Government required Greek ships to stop and search neutrals in order to prevent supplies going to the Ottoman Turks, and these searches often led to outright piracy. Finally, even before the Greek war of independence, there was already some piracy in the Mediterranean, brought about by the conditions created by the Napoleonic wars. These earlier Greek pirates based themselves on the islands of Skiathos and Skopelos, on the islands around Smyrna, at the entrance to the Dardanelles, and on the southern coast of Crete, especially the port of Grabusa.[1]

One such pirate assault, by two Greek ships on a merchant ship in the Mediterranean was recorded by the traveller J.S. Buckingham, in 1812. According to Buckingham, his ship learnt from a Maltese bound convoy that there were a host of pirates infesting the Greek islands, who took their prizes into obscure ports in the Adriatic, where the pirates sold the cargo, destroyed the ship's papers, and then butchered the entire crew. Alert to this very serious problem, Buckingham observed a large lateen rigged pirate, equipped with sweeps, heading toward his ship. Buckingham was especially concerned because his wife and infant daughter were onboard with him, but his ship was unusually well armed, having ten carronades (a large anti-personnel gun), and a number of twelve pounders, although only a relatively small crew of twenty-five men. The pirate ship pulled alongside, intending to board, at which point:

> …we fired a broadside of round [shot], grape, and canister, right into his decks, with a volley of musketry at the same time. His mainmast instantly fell by the board, with a horrible crash, and killed and wounded in its fall perhaps as many as our broadside had done, – the screams and cries of the dying and wounded being most pitiable to hear.

The pirate ship brought out the sweeps and came alongside again, and twice hooked on to the chains, but the ship's carpenter cut away both grapnel hooks, although some pirates got onboard and were cut down. Then a second pirate ship appeared, obviously working in tandem with the first, and fired a twelve pound shot into Buckingham's ship, nearly doing away with his wife and daughter. Next, the first pirate used her sweeps to come under the stern, intending to board at the most vulnerable point of the ship. However, Buckingham's ship was also unusual in possessing two long nine pounder stern chasers, triple loaded with round, grape and chain shot, which, when fired, created very severe destruction in the first pirate ship and immediately sank her. When the second pirate ship saw this, she put out her sweeps and left 'with the utmost speed'.

Buckingham noted that none of his crew was killed, though half were wounded with sabre cuts, musketry, and the most dangerous element of all in naval battles of the time, wooden splinters. He described the scene on his ship afterwards:

> The decks were covered with blood, and the wreck of shattered bulwarks, stranded rigging, split sails, and general dilapidation was so great, that it was a matter of surprise to us how a single gun could have been worked efficiently amidst the darkness and confusion that prevailed.[2]

Buckingham was lucky to escape, and if his ship had been overwhelmed, the end result would have been very unpleasant after the fight his ship put up. Not so lucky were merchant ships in various encounters with Greek pirates in 1827, of which two can be described.

The Maltese merchant ship *Superba* was on a run from Alexandria to Istanbul and Odessa in the spring of 1827, with a French brig doing convoy duty. For some reason the French brig left the fleet, perhaps because of a gale, and the *Superba* then became separated from the fleet, and becalmed as the storm abated. She then noticed a mistico (a coastal vessel with two sails), and a lateen rigged ship with Greek colours approaching. Essentially, the crews of these two ships boarded the *Superba*:

> The men from both [ships] amounted to one hundred and thirty five; they proceeded to bind every person onboard the ship; they struck the captain and threatened him with a drawn sword to extort the money they suspected was onboard to purchase a cargo … They took the steward, beat him, and put him in the hold on the ballast, where several men committed an unnatural crime both upon him and a sailor … They beat the cook and the captain so severely, to make them confess where the money was hid, with sticks and ropes, that they were both much marked.

The pirates then removed everything of value from the *Superba*, and departed for Grabusa on Crete, to sell the cargo, though the captains of the two pirate ships both came from the Greek island of Hydra.[3]

A variation of the previous story comes from the captain of the *Elizabeth*, an English ship, in June 1827. The *Elizabeth* was contracted to sail from Barba Nichola or Tasso (Turkey), with a cargo of vallonia (acorns to be used in tanning, dyeing, and making ink), to Smyrna. On the way to Tasso, the *Elizabeth* was boarded by pirates, who took away all stores, furniture, and the clothes of the crew. Then the pirates 'beat us so unmercifully with ropes, so much so we could scarcely crawl about the deck...' The crew of the *Elizabeth* managed to get their ship into Tasso harbour, where other pirates boarded the *Elizabeth* and forced the captain and crew to abandon her. Then the pirates towed the *Elizabeth* about a mile offshore, where they continued to plunder the *Elizabeth* at their ease. After this, the pirates left the *Elizabeth*, and the captain managed to get the ship towed toward Symi harbour nearby. Once more, pirates in a mistico attacked as the *Elizabeth* approached Symi harbour, but the crew managed to get the ship into the harbour. This was not necessarily the end of the story, as the captain reported to the British consul at Smyrna that the *Elizabeth* was now surrounded by misticos at Symi, and the ship was nearly a wreck. The Royal Navy responded, and HMS *Rifleman* rescued the *Elizabeth*, and re-equipped the ship. Given the numerous Greek pirates around, the *Rifleman* was soon off chasing other pirates.[4]

With the crushing Allied victory of Navarino in 1827 over the Ottoman Turks and Egyptians, and the subsequent Allied demand to the Provisional Greek government that Greek piracy must cease now that there was no Turkish threat, such piracy did come to an end. Following this, the Cretan pirate haunt of Grabusa was destroyed in January 1828 by an Anglo-French fleet, and in 1829 the Ottoman Turks recognised an independent Greece. Thus, peace returned to the Levant, and the short lived Greek piracy crisis was over. However, in another part of the world, at much the same time, piracy was assuming an unusual revival.

Pierre and Jean Laffite

On the coast of Louisiana (which became a state in 1812), and in the Gulf of Mexico, two brothers by the name of Pierre and Jean Laffite operated as slave traders and smugglers in the early nineteenth century. Their head-quarters, just south of New Orleans, was named Barataria, and from here goods were taken in, and then sold in New Orleans. These brothers stayed just on the side of legality between piracy and privateering, using letters of marque or commissions from emerging Latin American states and towns to justify their attacks on Spanish and English ships. Their favourite set of commissions came from Cartagena, Colombia, which was engaged in try-ing to separate itself from Spanish rule, and was happy to print out blank commissions for the Laffites. However, the American government decided to end this slave trading and smuggling ring, and attacked and demolished Barataria in 1814. Just at this juncture, the British, who were involved in a war against the United States between 1812 and 1814, mainly over blockades and the right to search ships, organised an attack on New Orleans. Both the British and the Americans tried to enlist the Baratarians, who decided to support the Americans. Hence, some fifty Baratarians served with the American forces, with the proviso they would later be given a general pardon. It seems that President Jackson especially needed gunflints for his American force of 5,000, and the Laffites possessed thousands of gunflints. Otherwise, the Baratarians had little influence on the Battle of New Orleans in January 1815 except that Pierre Laffite helped with his extensive knowledge of the rivers, swamps, and ground around the general area of the battlefield. Ironically, no one knew that the war had already officially ended on 24 December 1814.[5]

Thus far, the Laffites were technically not pirates, and muddied the waters still further by becoming spies for Spain in the 1815–1816 period. This did not stop them from establishing a new smuggling, slaving and privateer port in Galveston, later Texas, where the Laffites sailed as privateers under the flag of nascent Mexico, using blank commissions. It appears that the Laffites wanted to use Spain to take over Galveston, but then in 1819 decided to support the American adventurer General Long, who led a small army with the idea of reorganising Galveston as a corsair port under his leadership. This did not work out, and in 1820 the Laffites abandoned Galveston, after a wild party involving a great deal of whisky and wine. Galveston was burnt to the ground, and Jean Laffite left with a small squadron of ships. Pierre meanwhile was back in New Orleans, and now Jean Laffite became a true pirate in that he had no commissions from any authority. He captured a Spanish ship in the Gulf of Mexico, with a varied cargo of whisky, oil, quicksilver, indigo, iron and other goods, worth $10,000. He sent the ship to Galveston with the hope that the remnants of the smugglers there could sell the cargo into Louisiana. Meanwhile, the American government was now cracking down on pirates such as Jean Laffite, and so Laffite started to sail in the areas of Cuba and the Bahamas. There he took several ships, including American and British vessels, sometimes ransoming them back to their owners. Around this time, Pierre died of fever, but Jean now received a commission from Colombia, operating out of Cartagena, and once more he became a quasi-legal privateer. This did not help him because in 1823 Jean was killed while fighting two ships in the Gulf of Honduras. This ended the strange saga of the Laffites, who were mostly slavers and smugglers, often privateers, on one occasion American patriots, and only occasionally pirates.[6]

Pirates Operating Out of Cuba

The ending of the Laffites' careers in the early 1820s coincided with the loss of most Latin American commissions, except those from Venezuela and Colombia, so many privateer/pirates were forced to look elsewhere. This move was reinforced by the ending of a number of wars (Napoleonic, Britain versus the U.S. 1812–1814, Latin American), which produced many out of work sailors. So these unemployed sailors and their ships often took the next step to piracy, especially because of increased trade and traffic in the Atlantic and other sea lanes leading to the West Indies and the Americas. Previous pirate bases had been eradicated, hence these pirates started to operate out of Cuba and Puerto Rico, then both still under the control of Spain. A surge of piracy in 1820 saw twenty-seven American ships attacked in the Atlantic and Caribbean that year, and so the United States sent a number of ships into the Caribbean and into the Gulf of Mexico to hunt down the pirates.[7]

A typical pirate at this time was Charles Gibbs. Born in Rhode Island, Gibbs served in the United States navy in the war of 1812. Captured by the British, he was imprisoned in Dartmoor jail, but released through an exchange. Out of work after this, he enlisted in an Argentine privateer, took part in a mutiny, and was voted command of the ship, which he then operated out of Cuba. A brutal pirate, Gibbs' voyages in this ship produced twenty prizes, in which he killed all survivors, except for a Dutch woman, who was abused for some two months before she was poisoned to death. Allegedly he hacked off the arms and legs of one captain, and burnt to death a captured crew. In 1821 an American ship under Lt Commander Kearney surprised Gibbs and his fleet of four schooners as he was plundering three trading ships close to the shore of Cuba. Ever enterprising, Gibbs escaped into the Cuban jungle with most of the loot, and re-enlisted in the Argentine navy as a privateer onboard the *25th of May*. Still later, he served the Dey of Algiers against the French. Following this, Gibbs shipped out on the *Vineyard* from New Orleans, in which he predictably murdered the master and mate and took over the ship. His unpleasant and varied career came to an end in 1831 when he was captured and hung at Rhode Island.[8]

In the years 1822–1823, perhaps as many as 2,000 pirates were attacking ships in the West Indies, mostly operating out of Cuban ports. The United States reacted by organising a special pirate hunting squadron under Commodore David Porter, which captured or killed most of the pirates, including a fierce battle against the Cuban pirate, Diabolito (Little Devil), in his ship the *Catalina*. It seems that Porter employed barges to chase Diabolito onto the Cuban shore, so that the pirates jumped overboard 'like frogs from a bank'. Most of Diabolito's crew was shot in the water, or in the jungle, though Diabolito himself may have escaped to cruise off the Yucatan the next year, 1824. Another violent pirate was Benito de Soto, from Portugal, who originally sailed in a slaver called the *Defensor de Pedro*. Off the African coast, de Soto was part of the crew that took over the slaver, whereupon he shot the mate, and became captain of the ship, which was aptly renamed the *Black Joke*. De Soto sailed for the Caribbean, sold the slaves, and embarked on a vicious campaign of taking merchant ships, plundering them, and then sinking them with the crews locked below decks. In 1828, the *Black Joke* fired on the unarmed British transport ship, the *Morning Star*, homeward bound from Ceylon (Sri Lanka) with invalided soldiers onboard as well as civilians. Summoning the captain of the *Morning Star* aboard his ship, de Soto was enraged that the captain took his time. Shouting 'thus does Benito de Soto reward those who disobey him!' he swung his cutlass and split the unfortunate captain's head in two. Following his normal practice, de Soto looted the ship, the pirate crew raped the women, and then the survivors were locked below deck, holes were bored in the ship, and it was left to sink. The survivors managed to plug the holes and keep the *Morning Star* afloat, and they were luckily rescued the next day. De Soto sold his spoils in Spain, although the *Black Joke* was wrecked off Cadiz. A soldier from the *Morning Star* happened to recognise de Soto in Gibraltar, where he was captured, tried and hung. At his hanging, de Soto coolly rearranged the noose around his neck to achieve a cleaner death.[9]

Perhaps the most infamous of the Cuban-based pirates was the Spaniard Pedro Gibert, who commanded the slave schooner *Panda*. On a voyage from Havana to West Africa in September 1832, the *Panda* overtook the American brig *Mexican*, heading from Salem, Massachusetts, to Rio de Janeiro, with $20,000 in silver onboard in order to purchase goods in Brazil. One of the sailors from the *Mexican*, John Battis, tells the story of what happened. The *Panda* fired a shot and ordered the *Mexican* to heave to, following which five of the pirates came aboard the *Mexican*. One of the five pirates had already asked

Gibert what to do with the crew, to which Gibert reportedly replied, 'Dead cats don't mew – have her thoroughly searched and bring aboard all you can – you know what to do with them.' The pirates searched the *Mexican*:

> …three of the pirates on deck sprang on Larcomb [a sailor on the Mexican] and myself, striking at us with the long knives across our heads. A scotch cap I happened to have on with a large cotton handkerchief inside, saved me from a severe wounding as both were cut through and through. Our mate, Mr. Reed, here interfered and attempted to stop them from assaulting us whereupon they turned on him.

All the sailors of the *Mexican* survived the intial boarding because the pirates needed the crew to pass up the bags of silver to the deck and onto the waiting boat from the *Panda*. The captain of the *Mexican*, Butman, was also beaten up, with the specific object of finding out if any more money was aboard. The pirates followed the normal pattern by saying that if any more undeclared money was found, they would cut the throats of all onboard. Luckily, the $700 Butman had hidden in a false bottom to his chest was not found, and nor was the $50 belonging to the crew of the *Mexican*, which was hidden down in the keel between the inner and outer planking of the ship.[10]

Now came the most dangerous part of the game – the pirates had what they wanted – would they kill the crew? Battis recalls that at this moment all of the *Mexican*'s crew was below, but he decided to take a quick look and see what was going on, 'as I did so, a cocked pistol was pressed to my head and I was ordered to come on deck and went, expecting to be thrown overboard. One took me by the collar and held me out at arm's length to plunge a knife into me. I looked him right in the eye and he dropped the knife…' Then the pirates ordered Battis to get the forecastle doors from below and fix them so as to lock the crew below decks:

> …as I was letting the last one [door] in I caught the gleam of a cutlass being drawn, so taking the top of the door on my stomach, I turned a quick somersault and went head down first into the forecastle. The cutlass came down, but did not find me … Then they hauled the slide over and fastened it, and we were all locked below.

For the next hour, the crew of the *Mexican* heard the pirates destroying the rigging, spars, and sails of the *Mexican*. Lastly, the pirates piled combustibles into the cook's galley, and set fire to the ship. Then the pirates left the *Mexican*, and from the stern windows, Battis could see them rowing over to their own ship. Captain Butman kept calm, and first said a few prayers. After this, Butman found a way onto the deck and ordered the crew to pass him buckets of water, with which he damped down the fire while keeping out of sight of the *Panda*. Butman calculated that he had to stop the fire from spreading, but he should not put it out because he was sure the pirates would return if they saw the fire disappear.[11]

Butman was correct because Pedro Gibert was furious to discover that his pirates had not obeyed orders and killed the crew of the *Mexican*. Gibert actually wanted to return and finish the job, but apparently the smoke convinced him that the *Mexican* was doomed, so the *Panda* sailed away. The crew of the *Mexican* put out the fire after the *Panda* had disappeared, then repaired the ship, and eventually reached Salem in October 1832. As for Gibert and the *Panda*, they were run down on the west coast of Africa by a Royal Navy ship, and most of the crew captured, including Gibert. They were shipped to England in irons, and then to Salem for trial, arriving in 1834. At the trial, death was the sentence for those found guilty, which included Gibert. Before he was hung, Gibert tried to commit suicide with a piece of glass, but this was prevented, and he was duly executed. By the time of this 1834 trial, piracy in Atlantic and American waters, usually originating from Cuba, had essentially come to an end.[12]

Modern Chinese Piracy: Taking Over Steamers

Across the Pacific, piracy in China never really seems to have gone away. In the 1850s, pirate fleets of junks were operating in the South China Sea, while an American pirate named Eli Boggs had joined a fleet of pirate junks in Fuchow Bay, in the Liaotung Peninsula. This Eli Boggs had allegedly once boarded a junk and killed fifteen of its occupants single handedly with pistol and sword. He now served onboard a formidable pirate fleet of pilongs (junks of ninety to 200 tons, which carried six to fourteen guns each, as large as twenty-four pounders, with crews of fifty pirates). In September 1855, Captain Vansittart of HM brig *Bitterne* was searching for Boggs and sighted a pirate fleet of thirty to forty pilongs near Liaotung. *Bitterne* destroyed eight pilongs with gunnery, and then went in search of the others. Along the way *Bitterne* was able to release about 100 trading junks being held by the pirates for ransom off Yingkow. Reportedly, one rich Chinese trader had been cut into four pieces by the pirates and his body sent ashore in buckets to persuade the ransom of others to be paid immediately. The *Bitterne* then sighted another pirate junk anchored very close to shore, so a cutter was sent to take over the junk. But the junk blew up, and Eli Boggs was seen to dive overboard. An American, Captain William Hayes, known as 'Bully' Hayes, was onboard the pursuing cutter, and he dove into the water to catch Eli Boggs. He caught up with Boggs, who was armed with a sword, but Hayes caught Boggs' wrist, and punched him hard on the jaw. Boggs was pulled onboard the cutter, unconscious. Boggs was tried in Hong Kong in 1857, and was acquitted of murder due to lack of witnesses, but found guilty of piracy. He was transported for life. Ironically, 'Bully' Hayes later turned to piracy himself in the South Pacific.[13]

Moving forward in time, Chinese piracy continued, especially in the period before the First World War and in the period before the Second World War. This type of piracy abandoned the usual pirate fleet of junks, and concentrated on taking over passenger steamers in order to seize valuables onboard and demand ransom where appropriate. The method was for Chinese pirates to come onboard the target steamer by booking legitimate tickets for passage, and having weapons delivered onboard to them by stevedores or by accomplices. Sometimes these accomplices were women and children. A typical pirate attack of this type took place in 1913, when the *Tai On* passenger steamer left Hong Kong for the West River, carrying 513 passengers and crew. At about 10p.m. on 27 April 1913, the captain, Weatherell, heard gunshots, and ran out of his cabin with a ten bore shot gun. He immediately saw the chief engineer grappling with a Chinese pirate, and Weatherell shot the pirate, who fell backwards. On the bridge, Weatherell saw another Chinese pirate climbing up, and shot him too. On the other side of the bridge, more pirates were firing through the steel grill that protected the bridge, and Weatherell returned the fire. Other officers supported him, and especially a Portuguese guard who shot five of the pirates. But then the pirates set fire to the forward part of the ship, a tactic that was often employed when the initial attack was foiled. Passengers started to jump overboard, while Weatherell and the chief engineer managed to turn the steamer into the wind, so that the flames shifted to the stern of the ship. But the fire had taken hold, and Weatherell and his officers also jumped overboard. Previously, the chief officer had fired distress flares, and a number of steamers came to the rescue, so that some 160 passengers and crew were pulled from the water, including some of the pirates, who were indistinguishable from the other survivors, having got rid of their weapons. But a number of pirates were identified later, and detained in Victoria Jail, Hong Kong.[14]

Throughout the 1920s, very similar attacks were carried out on a number of steamships, despite the use of steel grills to defend vital areas, and the presence of armed guards. Thus, the steamship *Sunning*, en route from Shanghai to Canton, calling in at Amoy and Hong Kong, with 116 onboard, was pirated just off Amoy on 15 November 1926. At around 4p.m., the second officer suddenly fell flat on his face – he had been tripped up by a pirate. He shouted out 'Pirates!', but it was too late, groups of Chinese pirates onboard had taken over key areas of the ship. There were some fifty pirates involved. The second engineer was hit over the head with a glass bottle, while the chief engineer was hit on the head with the teapot he had just been using. The Chinese pirates herded the ship's officers into an office, while the pirates searched for the comprador, the man responsible for any bullion carried onboard. The comprador carried the only keys to the strong room, so he quickly changed into greasy overalls, and pretended to be part of the engine room. Five of his men very bravely refused to identify him – one was shot dead, and the other four thrown overboard. The *Sunning* was then directed to sail toward the islands at the entrance to Bias Bay, sixty miles east of Hong Kong. The ship's officers decided to fight back before these islands were reached, and at midnight, one officer on the bridge suddenly hit two of the pirates over the head with the deep-sea lead, and the counter attack was under way. Ultimately, the ship's officers gathered on the bridge and beat back pirate attacks with revolver fire, including one attack in which the pirates used a human shield of one officer ahead of them, who unfortunately was shot. True to form, the next move by the pirates was to start a fire aboard, but the captain was able to swing the ship around by letting go the anchor, which drove the fire to the stern. Frustrated, the pirates left by life boat, after which the crew of the *Sunning* was able to put the fire out. Later, some of the pirates were picked up, others had been killed in the fighting, and six were tried and executed in 1927.[15]

Lai Choi San

It was at this time, in late 1926, that the Hong Kong authorities pleaded with the Chinese government in Beijing to put an end to the pirate bases, especially the famous pirate nest at Bias Bay. Little effort was made by the Chinese government, who pleaded inability, but in their place the Hong Kong police waged a long war against the pirates. Similarly, the Royal Navy also patrolled the area, and actually attacked Bias Bay in March 1927, destroying forty pirate junks and burning 140 houses in the village. This action did not bring piracy to an end, as described by the journalist Aleko Lilius, who managed to ship aboard a pirate junk, and visit Bias Bay in 1929. As it happened, the pirate junk he joined was run by a female pirate chief, Lai Choi San. She had inherited pirate junks from her father, added some more herself, and now ran a fleet of twelve armed junks. Her principal method was to collect protection money from the fishing fleets around Macao and Canton, with a guarantee to protect them from other pirate fleets. She also aimed to capture trading junks in order to receive cash for letting them go, and another venture was to hold captured Chinese for ransom. As was normal, refusal to pay the ransom was followed by a finger, ear or nose of the unfortunate captive in order to move the payment along, and then other body parts, if the ransom was still not paid. Final refusal to pay a ransom usually led to death for the captive. In this environment, Lai Choi San prospered, so that her name appropriately meant 'The Mountain of Wealth'. Lai Choi San was married twice, had two sons, and went to sea as undisputed captain of her fleet. When ashore she dressed in a white satin robe with green jade buttons and green silk slippers, but onboard she wore a glossy black jacket and trousers, as worn by many working Chinese women. She did not join in the fighting herself, but directed operations. She had two women amahs with her, who were armed and did fight as required.

Lilius was onboard Lai Choi San's junk when she decided to deal with some competitors. As their junk neared an island close to Bias Bay, where three other junks were anchored, Lilius was ordered below decks by Lai Choi San, and battle commenced:

> …the whole junk shook from a salvo from our guns. The noise was deafening.
> Boom! There went another! And a third, a fourth, a fifth and a sixth! A regular bombardment – but there were no reply shots … The nauseous smell of black powder reached us down below. Then I heard more shouting and many rifle shots…

When Lilius was allowed on deck again, the first thing he saw were two men bound hand and foot, lying on the deck, no doubt destined for ransom.

Some distance away, a junk was sinking with only part of the hull showing. Lai Choi San had dealt with her competitors. Soon after, Lilius left her junk and returned to Macao, and never sailed with Lai Choi San again. Lilius does not relate what happened in the end to this tough Chinese female pirate.[16]

Somalia and the Malacca Straits

Chinese piracy was still happening in the 1960s, and probably still operates today in a minor way. Now, in the modern twenty-first century world, piracy continues in particular areas where there is a lack of maritime control. Two areas consistently turn up in the weekly statistics issued by the International Maritime Bureau: Somalia, and the Malacca Straits between Indonesia and Malaysia.

Piracy off Somalia seems to be conducted by a variety of organisations, some of which are composed of former members of the now defunct Somali navy; some are run by warlords, such as Abdi Mohamed Afweyne, on behalf of the nationalist 'Defenders of Somali Territorial Waters'; some are independent pirates who are too wealthy and strong to be touched by warlords; and some are composed of other nationalist groups such as the National Volunteer Coast Guard, and the Somali Marines, who profess to be protecting Somali waters. The method normally employed by Somali pirates is to capture merchant ships with a view to ransom. Cargo and ships cannot easily be sold in Somalia, so the ship and its crew are held as prisoners until a suitable ransom is paid. Two ships captured in this way in 2005 were the MV *Semlow* and the MV *Torgelow*, which were involved in delivering United Nations aid to Somalia. These ships were held for a month before satisfactory arrangements were made. Owners appear to be paying around $100,000 to $200,000 for each captured ship and crew. Attacks can also be made quite far off the coast of Somalia, using a mother ship to launch smaller boats. A recent assault on the cruise ship *Seaborne Spirit* in November 2005 allowed passengers to see the typical small, fast pirate boat, with a few pirates firing the easily obtained RPG – 7 hand-held anti-tank weapon. The *Spirit* took evasive measures, but such large cruise ships are actually difficult to board or subdue, so the smiling pirates were probably using this occasion as an enjoyable exercise more than anything serious. If they had been serious about taking over the *Spirit*, the pirates would have first disabled the steering mechanism before attempting to board.[17]

Efforts to halt Somali pirate attacks have come primarily from American naval vessels, which caught and destroyed one pirate group. In this context, in January 2006, the USS *Winston Churchill* recaptured the *Al Bisarat*, an Italian freighter being used by Somali pirates. Another entity that did a great deal to stop Somali piracy was the Council of Islamic Courts, whose forces captured Mogadishu in June 2006. Most recently, this Islamic Council has been overthrown by Ethiopian forces, and a war is raging between the two groups. During its short reign, the Council of Islamic Courts saw piracy as illegal, and attacked ports run by pirates, as well as releasing ships under ransom. Thus, in November 2006, Council of Islamic Courts troops recaptured the MV *Veesham*, a United Arab Emirates ship being held off Mogadishu for ransom. The ransom demanded for this ship and its 14 crew, and Ethiopian captain, was $1 million USD. The Council of Islamic Courts threatened the pirates with the sharia punishment of the loss of the left leg and right arm by amputation. Hence, the ship and its crew were readily returned to the United Arab Emirates. In similar fashion, in May 2006, Council of Islamic Courts troops took over the port of Haradhere, a significant pirate haunt, and destroyed a pirate crew onboard a captured oil tanker. But with the recent demise of the Council of Islamic Courts it can be expected that piracy will resume, although the future of Somalia is obviously hard to predict, and it is possible that the Council of Islamic Courts will return in some shape or form.[18]

A second area that is very much a pirate world is the Malacca Straits. This area was always a pirate threat in earlier centuries due to its strategic and maritime importance. With the resignation of General Suharto in 1998, there has been a rise in piracy off Indonesia, partly due to the loss of Suharto's firm but corrupt control of Indonesia, and partly due to an economic recession in the 1990s that turned some individuals and groups to piracy. Much of the piracy in the Malacca Straits involves fishermen and opportunists, who look for easy targets in their spare time. This type of piracy simply seeks to rob ships of articles that can be easily removed. Hence, the head of the Malaysian marine police stated, 'When they rob a ship in the Straits, they steal the safe, watches, cameras, anything they can carry away. The money they get from the safe pays for fuel and another attack.'[19]

Then there are criminal syndicates looking for ships and their cargos. The Malacca Straits are the domain of a criminal syndicate operating out of Singapore, who favour cargos that are easily resold, like refined fuels, oils, rubber, steel, and metals. Once this is done, the syndicate often passes the ship on to other criminals to become a 'ghost ship', carrying either drugs or illegal immigrants. Allegedly, one Chew Ching Kiat, known as David Wong in Singapore, was the local leader of the Singapore crime syndicate, who arranged the hijacking of twenty-two ships in the Malacca Straits and South China Sea. His system was to place an informer on a ship he intended to seize, and then wait for a call on a mobile phone from his informer with details of the ship, crew, cargo, route etc. Then standard pirate procedure called for a fast speed boat to come up on the stern of the ship, board with ropes and grappling hooks, immobilise the crew, and sail to a safe location for further action. For example, this syndicate captured the M/T *Petro Ranger* off Singapore in 1998, which was carrying over 10,000 tons of diesel and jet fuel. The crew were bound with ropes and herded into the officers' mess. The pirates then transformed the ship by painting the blue funnel orange, painting in a new name – *Wilby* – hoisting the Honduran flag, and bringing onboard previously prepared new documents. The ship was taken to Haikou on Hainan Island, where two tankers siphoned off the diesel fuel. Later, the *Wilby* was scheduled to be transformed by the crime syndicate into a ghost ship. However, all this came to light when the *Wilby* was stopped by Chinese authorities and the crime syndicate dismantled.[20]

Sometimes, the pirate hijack becomes deadly, as in the case of the MV *Cheung Son*, a Panama registered bulk carrier heading from Shanghai to Malaysia. This ship was hijacked in November 1998, and the pirate chief apparently required each of his pirate gang to kill a member of the twenty-three strong ship's crew. The ship's sailors were hooded with plastic garbage bags, and were killed in different ways. Then their bodies were tossed overboard, weighed down with machine parts. Six of the dead sailors were later recovered by fishing boats, snagged in nets. Strangely, the ship's cargo of furnace slag was of little value, but it is surmised the ship may have been carrying illegal weapons. The ship was also eventually recaptured by the Chinese authorities.[21]

Another pirate group besides fishermen and criminal syndicates, which may be responsible for some piracy in the Malacca Straits, is the Gerakan Aceh Merdeka, or GAM. This is the Free Aceh movement, based in north Sumatra. Reportedly, the GAM was responsible for the capture of the *Ocean Silver* in August 2001, when the ship and crew were held for ransom. Similarly, the *Pelangi Frontier*, taken in July 2002, was thought to be a GAM operation. The GAM denied these allegations, and it may be that the Indonesian government wished to undermine the GAM with these accusations. However, it is curious that the tragedy of the tsunami of 2004 brought piracy to an end near the Banda Aceh area of Sumatra for six months, and then piracy slowly started again, albeit at a lower level of activity. Thus the GAM might have been responsible for piracy in this area, but other groups are candidates too. Finally, a fourth group allegedly involved in piracy in the Malacca Straits, are rogue elements from the Indonesian armed forces and police. For example, the MT *Selayang* was pirated in the Malacca Straits in 2001. Although the International Maritime Bureau alerted the Indonesian authorities to the location of this ship after it was captured, nothing was done, indeed it is alleged that elements in the Indonesian military informed the pirate syndicate that they were being tracked. Ultimately, the International Maritime Bureau compelled the Indonesian authorities to resolve this situation.[22]

Most recently, piracy is on a modest decline off Somalia and in the Malacca Straits, due partly to political events in Somalia, and partly to greater efforts by the Malaysian and Indonesian governments in the area. On the other hand, attacks on ships at anchor in various ports around the world are on the sharp increase, according to the International Maritime Bureau, mainly because it is obviously easier to attack ships in harbour than try to stop them on the high seas. Ports that are especially vulnerable to this kind of attack at the present time are especially Chittagong, Bangladesh, where forty-seven attacks have been recorded since the end of January 2006, also Lagos, Nigeria; Dar Es Salaam, Tanzania; and some Indonesian ports. The Niger River delta has meanwhile become the centre of a number of attacks and kidnappings due to the ongoing dispute between the self-styled Movement for the Emancipation of the Niger Delta (MEND), and the Nigerian government, over corruption and distribution of profits from the oil industry. This Nigerian form of piracy (or quest for social justice) will likely continue for a considerable period of time.

There is also a slight decline in pirate attacks world wide. The International Maritime Bureau registered 329 attacks in 2004, 276 in 2005, and 168 from the beginning of January 2006 to 30 September 2006. More difficult to assess is the number of pirate attacks on private yachts. The International Maritime Bureau only tracks pirate attacks against commercial vessels, but one or two new internet web sites have recently been created to assist owners of yachts. Often the information is anecdotal, but most stories are credible. John Burnett, the author and reporter, writes of his own ordeal in 1992 off Singapore when his yacht was taken over at night by an older

Indonesian man and his two sons, who roughed him up, stole whatever small items were available, and then left. Burnett was lucky the outcome was not worse, and he probably saved himself by not fighting back, and by being able to speak some of the local language. Part of his account of this incident relates that these Indonesians appeared to be fishermen, but the older son seemed particularly angry:

> As I turned, the surly youth slammed the butt of his rifle against the back of my head. I lurched forward … then slipped to my knees. He yanked me up by my hair and kicked me ahead of him toward the cabin stairs.
>
> The three men stood awkwardly in the narrow cabin below, their assault rifles too large to point. Through tears of pain I watched the old man's eyes scan my seagoing home. The Unicorn had none of the toys found on most blue-water yachts … There wasn't much to steal.
>
> Still dazed, I nodded to them to sit. I reached for the thermos of old coffee that I had made hours earlier and with shaky hands splashed it into some mugs and slid them across the table.[23]

This act of hospitality by Burnett seems to have defused the tension, and the pirates left with only a pair of binoculars and a carton of cigarettes.

Other pirate attacks against private yachts include the incident when the well known New Zealand skipper, Sir Peter Blake, was killed in the mouth of the Amazon River in December 2001. The posthumous lesson from this particularly violent event shows that one should normally not try to fight back. Very recent pirate assaults have been recorded by individuals sending in information to internet web sites, such as the attack on 21 October 2006 off the island of Malaita, in the Solomon Islands. In this case, two adults and two children were on their catamaran when they were boarded at midnight by a small group of men with knives, guns and clubs. Apparently, $10,000 USD was taken. It is difficult to quantify such attacks, but they are happening, and some places which are now mentioned as dangerous by one particular yacht web site include the Red Sea, the Gulf of Aden, Somalia, the coasts of Yemen and Venezuela, and Chaguaramas Bay, Trinidad.[24]

Piracy seems likely to continue and to adapt to changing situations. The world is now a safer place at sea, but piracy can never be totally eliminated because of the vast areas of coast and sea that offer possibilities to impoverished and desperate people, and to criminals of various kinds.

Epilogue

Some important aspects of piracy relate to all centuries and all seas. For example, piracy flourished where control of the seas by declining or growing powers was weak or non-existent. Thus, Muslim pirates operated in the western Mediterranean after the conquest of North Africa in 698, but declined when Byzantine and then Western powers took over. Again, in the sixteenth, seventeenth and early eighteenth centuries, piracy flourished in the Caribbean and the Atlantic until great power rivalries declined, and royal navies established control from the 1720s onward. A similar situation took place with the temporary decline of Chinese piracy after the early nineteenth century outburst.

The next obvious point is that piracy only existed where there were victims to be caught. There was therefore a symbiotic relationship between healthy commerce and piracy – piracy could not exist where there were few ships to capture. In fact, piracy was a sign of economic vitality, so that piracy was actually a by-product of economic progress. A connected point is that pirates also redistributed wealth to eager traders. It is well known that Drake and Hawkins were welcomed by Spanish traders in the Americas, happy to obtain slaves at cheap prices, while at the island of St Mary's,

Madagascar, trade was brisk with pirates, sometimes orchestrated from New York, at other times by local residents, and welcomed by the local inhabitants who valued the pirates 'most as they sell them the best Bargains'.[1] This connection between trade and the redistribution of wealth by pirates is the theme of historian David Starkey's chapter 'Pirates and Markets' in which he emphasises three kinds of demand for pirate goods. These are: firstly, for obvious self sufficiency, secondly, for trading through established trade centres, and thirdly, via state demand.[2] In regard to the last point, the slave trade by the state oriented Barbary corsairs, the Sallee Rovers, and the Knights of Malta (and their licensees), was an example of a high demand state situation.

A further and somewhat obvious point is that the line between piracy and privateering was very often a fine one. In the Ancient and Classical periods, it was usually quite difficult to distinguish between pirates and those who were politically and socially supported. Then, individuals often switched from pirate to privateer according to circumstances. This was the case with Francis Drake, and similarly with privateers in the Caribbean, who switched to piracy when wars were over and their services were no longer needed. In China, pirates became pirate chasers as the great pirate junk fleets disintegrated in the early nineteenth century. The Barbary corsairs and the Knights of Malta can also be seen as privateers rather than pirates.

This leads to the familiar question: who really was a genuine pirate? Even careful definitions do not easily solve this problem. When the Vikings first raided Western Europe in the 780s they can be seen as pirates. But when larger armies of Vikings appeared in succeeding centuries the Vikings really became a political entity rather than pirate raiders. It is also the case that in ancient Rome, the word 'pirate' was often used as an epithet and as a means of discrediting opponents. In the nineteenth century, in South-East Asia and the Pacific, imperial powers like Britain labeled local native leaders and tribes as pirates, with the purpose of suppressing them and gaining economic advantage. Even more problematic, in the Ancient and Classical periods, the question of who was a pirate defies easy analysis. For example, when Antigonus and Demetrius used pirates in their siege of Rhodes in 305–304BC were they still pirates, or had they become something more? Even earlier, was Polycrates a pirate, or was he simply a local tyrant? Was Drake a pirate when he sailed without a written commission, but with the Queen's blessing? And was Henry Morgan a pirate when he sacked the city of Panama in 1671, with a commission from Jamaica, but after peace had been declared between England and Spain? Clearly, in some cases, there is always going to be confusion as to who actually was a pirate.

Another common feature of piracy around the world was the similar targets of pirates. The pirate aim of course was the seizure of wealth, whether through kidnapping and ransom; plunder of valuable commodities, gold, silver, jewelry and coins; sale of captured ship and cargo; or the pillage of vulnerable villages and ports. All this was a constant feature of piracy, although one aspect has tended to change, which is the capture and sale of slaves. This was a major aspect of piracy from the Ancient and Classical periods through the eighteenth century, and only declined with the abolition of slavery and the end of the Barbary corsair/Knights of Malta dominion.

Yet another familiar theme in the history of piracy is that the means used to try and eradicate piracy tended to be the same throughout the centuries. Established states usually either issued pardons or applied maritime power to destroy piracy, or sometimes used both approaches at the same time. Rome's general, Pompey, used both, as did the English monarchy in the seventeenth and eighteenth centuries. Occasionally, however, piracy operated outside the bounds of suppression, by reason of geography or pirate strength, as in the medieval Mediterranean, or perhaps today off Somalia and in the Malacca Straits. And it is worth noting that the frequently mentioned 'golden age' of piracy, from the 1680s to the 1720s in the Caribbean and Atlantic world, is too narrow a vision – in fact, there were always golden ages of piracy around the world which came and went.

A common problem for all pirates was the question of logistics. Whether it was a pirate galley in the Classical period; or Henry Morgan during his several expeditions; or a buccaneer ship facing starvation crossing the Pacific; as in the case of William Cowley; or other buccaneers calling in at the Juan Frenandez Islands for food and water; or a Red Sea pirate waiting weeks for a Muslim ship to sail by, and then calling in at St Mary's for supplies; or William Kidd trying to find provisions on the coast of India; or pirate voyages in the early 1700s sailing between the Caribbean, west Africa and the Americas as Bart Roberts did; pirate captains always had to be thinking of provisions, and water and beer to drink for their crews. In reality, quite a few ships were captured and towns were raided, not in the search for any treasure but because the pirates needed to eat and drink, to say nothing of necessities such as sails, cables and anchors. This was the case with some of Bart Roberts' attacks, because he was the captain of a large number of pirates who simply needed to be kept alive with food and drink before they could operate as pirates. Pirate logistics were normally quite difficult, and could not always be solved through finding turtles to eat.

Finally – why has piracy fascinated writers and readers across the centuries? Part of the answer is the exotic locations, colourful individuals, liberty of action outside social norms, the freedom to roam the seas, and the lure of treasure and instant wealth. But a larger part of the answer is that people seem to be especially interested in those individuals who inhabit the boundaries of society and challenge the social order – criminals like the Mafia, highwaymen, Wild West gunslingers, witches and warlocks, social deviants, religious heretics, mass murderers, social rebels – and pirates. Pirates are among those groups at the ever changing cultural edges of society who are constantly defining what is acceptable and what is not. Perhaps that is why pirates are shape shifters, and thus objects of interest because of their role as social and moral boundary markers. It may even be that the decade of ruthless pirate extermination in the west in the 1720s was a response to the emergence of state formation in the Caribbean and the Americas, which demanded a strong new establishment of social and moral norms.[3]

Whatever the reason for our interest in piracy, society has constantly changed its vision of the pirate over the centuries and will continue to do so, from the enemy of all mankind, to our present image of the historical pirate as a charismatic individual, always ready to drink a bottle of rum and open a dead man's chest.

Abbreviations

Johnson: Charles Johnson, *A General History of the Robberies and Murders of the Most Notorious Pirates*, London, 1724, introduction and commentary by David Cordingly (Lyons Press, Guilford, Connecticut, and Conway Maritime Press, London, 1998, 2002).

ADM: Admiralty files, Public Record Office, Kew Gardens, London.

BL: British Library, London.

CO: Colonial Office files, Public Record Office, Kew Gardens, London.

HCA: High Court of the Admiralty files, Public Record Office, Kew Gardens, London.

PRO: Public Record Office, Kew Gardens, London.

Definitions

Pirate: one who robs or plunders on the high seas, or uses the sea to raid harbours, ports and towns, without social or political authority.

Privateer: an individual or a ship authorised by a letter of marque or a letter of commission, to capture the merchant vessels and cargoes of a hostile nation. Privateers might also carry a letter of reprisal, authorizing reprisal against a foreign subject or ship. Privateers were regulated and had to obey a number of rules concerning codes of conduct.

Corsair: a privateer or pirate who operated in the Mediterranean. These might be from the medieval Mediterranean, or the later Barbary Coast of North Africa, or licensed by the Knights of Malta and the Knights of St Stephen.

Buccaneer: originally used to describe the hunters of cattle and pigs on the island of Hispaniola. Later often used to describe the privateers and pirates who sailed in the Caribbean and in the South Seas.

Filibuster: a term used by French and Dutch writers to describe a pirate in the West Indies, and derived from the Dutch word for Freebooter.

List of Illustrations

1   'A pirate as imagined by a Quaker gentlemen.' Author's collection.

2   'A typical pirate.' Author's collection.

3   'Band of armed pirates.' Author's collection.

4   'A pirate takes aim.' Author's collection.

5   'A pirate shot.' Author's collection.

6   'Pirate Bold and ship.' Author's collection.

7   'Pirate at the wheel.' Author's collection.

8   'A pirate stands over his victim.' Author's collection.

9   'A typical pirate.' Author's collection.

10   'Pirate captain surveys the deck.' Author's collection.

11   'Captain Scarfield.' Author's collection.

12   'Flirting on deck.' Author's collection.

13   'Beach scene.' Author's collection.

14   'Marooned pirate.' Author's collection.

15   'Rescue on its way.' Author's collection.

16   'Stabbed in the back.' Author's collection.

17   'Buried treasure.' Author's collection.

18   'Pirates carrying treasure.' Author's collection.

19   'Discovered treasure.' Author's collection.

20   'Pirates make off with treasure.' Author's collection.

21   'Examining treasure.' Author's collection.

22   'Captain Mayloe shot Captain Brand through the head.' Author's collection.

23   'She would sit quite still, permitting Barnaby to gaze.' Author's collection.

24   'Burning the Ship.' Pirates did often burn the ships they captured, partly in order to prevent their victims from sailing off and revealing where the pirates were, and what they had done. The crews of these captured ships were normally allowed to land or row away. Author's collection.

25   'Pirates used to do that to their Captains now and then.' Author's collection.

26   'So the Pirate Treasure was divided.' Dividing up treasure among a pirate crew was an important process, in

which care was taken to make each share as equal as possible. Some skilled members of a pirate crew, including the captain, surgeon, gunner, and carpenter, would be given more than one share. Author's collection.

27   'Colonel Rhett and the pirate.' Author's collection.

28   'The Pirate's Christmas.' Author's collection.

29   'He lay silent and still, with his face half buried in the sand.' Author's collection.

30   'There Cap'n Goldsack goes, creeping, creeping, creeping, looking for his treasure down below!' Author's collection.

31   'He had found the captain agreeable and companionable.' In the late seventeenth century many colonial governors were sympathetic to pirates, happy to share the spoils. This picture shows the pirate Thomas Tew being entertained by New York Governor Benjamin Fletcher in the 1690s. Author's collection.

32   'How the buccaneers kept Christmas.' Author's collection.

33   'A pirate fighting it out.' Author's collection.

34   'The burning ship.' Fire was always a grave threat, and precautions were taken on all ships to prevent this happening. Pirates usually operated at trade routes fairly close to land because that was where merchant ships were to be found, so crews could normally get ashore if there was a fire. Author's collection.

35   'Pirates fighting.' Author's collection.

36   'Dead men tell no tales.' Some pirate captains did murder their victims. This was especially the case in the nineteenth century, when one pirate captain in 1824 told his men 'dead cats don't mew', obviously instructing his crew to kill their captives. Author's collection.

37   'Daughter of Captain Keitt.' Author's collection.

38   Execution of Stede Bonnet. Stede Bonnet was hung in Charles Town, South Carolina in 1718. Bonnet was an unlikely pirate, being a middle aged plantation owner from Barbados. Bonnet holds a posy of flowers, a common touch with the condemned at hanging, and he is executed using the short rope drop, which took some time to produce death. Author's collection.

39   Cape Corso Castle. A depiction of Cape Coast Castle on the West African coast, where Roberts' large crew were tried, and some of them hung, in 1722. Cape Coast Castle was a Royal African Company factory where African slaves were held before being shipped to their destinations. Author's collection.

40   A wounded Spaniard shot by Capt Low's crew. This scene depicts an event after a Spanish ship was captured off Honduras by Captain Low. One of the Spanish sailors jumped into the water to escape but was recaptured. He begged for mercy but one of the pirates made him kneel down, and placing the muzzle of his gun in the Spaniard's mouth, pulled the trigger. Author's collection.

41   Captain Anstis' mock trial. This mock trial, which took place in 1722, on an island off Cuba, reflected the pirates' attitude toward the justice system of the day. Some pirate humour and some pirate fear both seem to be part of this trial, which was fully reported by Captain Charles Johnson. Author's collection.

42   A symbolic representation of a pirate captain. Note the fashionable clothes, wig and three cornered hat. Also the gentleman's rapier sword and flintlock musket. Courtesy of Joel Baer.

43   Different versions of pirate flags. Two of the flags were designed by the pirate captain Bartholomew Roberts – the lower left flag has Roberts standing on two of his opponent's skulls – A Bahamian's head and a Martinican's head. Courtesy of Joel Baer.

44   Buccaneers attack a Spanish ship in a cannon duel. Normally, buccaneers preferred to take a ship by surprise or by boarding rather than in a fire fight, because Spanish fire discipline was often superior. Courtesy of Joel Baer.

45   Title page of Esquemeling's *The Buccaneers of America*, first published in Amsterdam in 1678. Several other versions followed. Esquemeling is important for his first hand accounts of two of Henry Morgan's expeditions, and for his knowledge of the buccaneers.

46   Esquemeling's vision of a typical French buccaneer on Hispaniola. There were two kinds of buccaneer – those who hunted wild bulls and cattle in a two man operation, and those who hunted wild boars in teams of five or six men. Courtesy of Joel Baer.

47   This is the buccaneer fort constructed on Tortuga by the French adventurer LeVasseur, in the 1640s. He ironically named it his 'Dove Cot'. Interestingly, the fort incorporates the latest 'bastion trace' outline, useful against cannon. Courtesy of Joel Baer.

48   Henry Morgan's raid on El Puerto del Principe, Cuba. The buccaneers took the town, but found only 50,000 pieces of eight, since the Spanish were forewarned. Morgan also forced the inhabitants to produce and slaughter 500 cattle for the buccaneers, who were often short of food. Courtesy of Joel Baer.

49   Portrait of the buccaneer Roche Brasiliano, a Dutchman, but named thus because of his long residence in Brazil. He raided along the coast of Central America, capturing several ships. He hated and tortured Spanish prisoners. But he spent all his plunder on alcohol and women. Courtesy of Joel Baer.

50   Morgan's capture of Panama City in 1671. The buccaneers defeated the Spanish defenders of Panama City in a set battle outside the city, and then plundered Panama and surrounding area for several weeks. Panama was probably set on fire by some of the inhabitants. Courtesy of Joel Baer.

51   William Dampier, painted around 1697. Dampier was a buccaneer but also an acute observer of nature, and published his observations in a number of volumes. The books were readable, satisfied the public's desire for

knowledge about the world, and made Dampier famous. Courtesy of Joel Baer.

52 A map of the Americas from Dampier's book, *A New Voyage Round the World* (1697). It was in this area that the buccaneers operated and raided. Dampier himself joined some of these raids, but also circumnavigated the world. Courtesy of Joel Baer.

53 Dampier's map of the world from his *A New Voyage Round the World* (1697). The map shows that Dampier was vague about North America, but that he knew South America and the Pacific, and in a later voyage he explored parts of Australia. Courtesy of Joel Baer.

54 Hanging a pirate in the eighteenth century at Execution Dock, Wapping, London. At the time, hanging was a slow, unpleasant death due to the 'short drop' which did not break the neck of the condemned. Here, the chaplain, or 'ordinary', tries to elicit a last speech of repentance from the pirate. Courtesy of Joel Baer.

55 A woodcut of the execution of one of Avery's crew in 1696. Bodies of the condemned were placed between the high and low water marks of the River Thames to signify the authority of the High Court of the Admiralty. Courtesy of Joel Baer.

56 A copy of the first page of the 1700 piracy act of William III. This act allowed a seven man jury of officials or naval officers to be assembled anywhere in the world in order to try pirates and execute them if guilty. Courtesy of Joel Baer.

57 A well known pirate, Charles Vane gained fame by refusing to accept Woodes Rogers' offer of a pardon in the Bahamas in 1718. Vane escaped by using a fire ship at night, and then pirated for two years, meeting up once with Blackbeard before being caught and hung in 1720. Courtesy of Joel Baer.

58 Captain Charles Vane. Courtesy of Joel Baer.

59 A report of the trial of the pirate Stede Bonnet and his crew at Charles Town in 1718. Bonnet was unusual in being a gentleman and man of means, who reportedly became a pirate in order to escape his wife. He was no mariner, and was hung along with most of his crew in 1718. Courtesy of Joel Baer.

60 This pirate captain was known as 'Calico' Jack Rackam, due to his penchant for wearing white calico clothes. Rackam was not a very successful pirate, but gained posthumous fame for having two women pirates in his crew, Anne Bonny and Mary Read. He was easily captured, and tried and hung in Jamaica in 1720. Courtesy of Joel Baer.

61 This picture shows the front page of the very lengthy report of the trial of Captain Jack Rackam and his crew, published in Jamaica in 1721. The report also contains the separate trial of the two women pirates in his crew, Anne Bonny and Mary Read. Courtesy of Joel Baer.

62 A portrait of Anne Bonny (or Bonn), who served on Captain Jack Rackam's ship. She abandoned a husband on New Providence in order to run away with Rackam, and became his lover. She was captured and tried along with Rackam, but was spared execution because she was pregnant. She then disappears from history. Courtesy of Joel Baer.

63 A portrait of Mary Read, who served on Captain Jack Rackam's ship. She had allegedly previously served in the army, which helped when she fought a duel with a sailor who threatened her lover. She was captured and tried along with Rackam, but was spared execution because she was pregnant. She died in prison. Courtesy of Joel Baer.

64 Captain Bartholomew Roberts, one of the most successful pirates. In his last battle in 1722, he dressed in a crimson waistcoat and trousers, a hat with a red plume, and wore a gold chain and diamond cross. He was killed in this battle against the Royal Navy, and thrown overboard as he had requested. Courtesy of Joel Baer.

65 Captain Bartholomew Roberts again depicted in fine clothes. He carries a cutlass and a brace of pistols in a sash, as was normal. Roberts was unusual in not drinking alcohol, and in demanding strong discipline in his large crew. Courtesy of Joel Baer.

66 Captain Bartholomew Robert's crew drinking at the slaving port of Old Calabar in 1721. The drink would have been rum or brandy. However, Roberts' pirates fought a battle with the local inhabitants here, and then set fire to the town. Courtesy of Joel Baer.

67 'Extorting tribute from the citizens.' The prelude to torture, when pirates forced individuals to confess where their valuables could be found. This probably relates to Morgan's sack of Panama in 1671. Author's collection.

68 Portrait of Henry Morgan. Technically not a pirate, Morgan launched several raids on Spanish towns, the most famous being the raid on Panama. Esquemeling writes that Morgan's buccaneers cruelly tortured many prisoners in these towns in order to find and seize their valuables. Courtesy of Joel Baer.

69 Morgan fights his way out of Lake Maracaibo, which was blocked by a fort and three large Spanish ships. Morgan used fire ships and boarding to deal with the Spanish ships, and trickery to steal past the fort at night. Courtesy of Joel Baer.

70 'Jack followed the Captain [Blackbeard] and the young lady up the crooked path to the house.' Author's collection.

71 'He led Jack up to a man [Blackbeard] who sat upon a barrel.'. Author's collection.

72 'The combatants cut and slashed with savage fury.' When pirates boarded a ship, the fight was often violent, but also usually short. Blackbeard was killed in 1718 in a ship board struggle, and the fight was bitterly contested with cutlass and pistol. Author's collection.

73 The famous pirate Blackbeard (or Edward Teach) engaged in a fight for his life against Lieutenant Maynard of the Royal Navy. The fight took place in Ocracoke creek, North Carolina, in 1718. Blackbeard sustained many wounds before being cut down by a Royal Navy sailor. Courtesy of Joel Baer.

74   After Blackbeard and his small crew were killed or captured, Lieutenant Maynard had Blackbeard's head cut off, and displayed it from his bowsprit. Allegedly, Maynard threw Blackbeard's body overboard, at which point the body swam around Maynard's ship. Courtesy of Joel Baer.

75   A 1696 broadside or printed sheet of a ballad celebrating the piratical life of Henry Every (Avery). These sheets preserved the memory of Avery and this one presents him as a pirate who made his own future and fortune. Courtesy of Joel Baer.

76   A government authorised version of the trial of six of Every's (Avery's) men. The first trial acquitted these crewmen. But in a second trial, one was spared and turned state's evidence, while the other five were hung as pirates. Courtesy of Joel Baer.

77   Avery is presented here as the king of Madagascar. In fact, although he did put in to Madagascar on his way to the Red Sea, he was far from becoming the king of the island. A more likely king of Madagascar was the trader John or James Plantain. Courtesy of Joel Baer.

78   'Kidd on the deck of the *Adventure Galley*.' William Kidd is here portrayed as an evil pirate, although there is some debate as to whether Kidd was actually a pirate or not. Author's collection.

79   William Kidd is here portrayed turning from good to evil. Historians are divided as to whether Kidd became a pirate, or tried to remain a privateer. The two major ships which Kidd took sailed under French passes, which permitted Kidd to take them legally. However, he was tried and hung in 1701. Courtesy of Joel Baer.

80   Some of the most notorious pirates were hung and then placed in iron chains at a location where all ships' crews entering or leaving the River Thames would see them. Here, it is William Kidd hanging at Tilbury Point in 1701. Courtesy of Joel Baer.

81   'An attack on a Galleon.' Pirates did sometimes attack in small boats, and often from the stern of their target. Surprise was also always a useful weapon. Author's collection.

82   'Capture of the Galleon.' This scene represents the occasion when Pierre Le Grand and his crew captured a Spanish galleon in 1665, and surprised the Spanish officers playing cards below decks. Author's collection.

83   'On the Tortugas.' Henry Pitman, perhaps the model for Robinson Crusoe, was stranded on Salt Tortuga Island with others in 1687. Salt Tortuga lies off the coast of Venezuela. Author's collection.

84   'Marooned.' Many pirates and their victims were marooned, the most famous being Alexander Selkirk, who was marooned on the Juan Fernandez Islands from 1704 to 1709. Author's collection.

85   'Walking the plank.' Very few pirates made their victims walk the plank. After all, wasn't it simpler to just throw the victims overboard? Possibly this myth came from the practice of pirates in the Roman era, who invited their captives to walk home. Author's collection.

86   'Buried treasure.' William Kidd did have John Gardiner bury most of Kidd's treasure on Gardiner's Island, Long Island Sound, in 1699. The treasure was shortly afterwards dug up and sent to Lord Bellomont in Boston after Kidd was arrested. Author's collection.

87   'Who shall be Captain?' Pirate captains were almost always elected by popular vote of the pirate crew, and did not fight to become captain. But pirates did sometimes fight each other.

88   'The bullets were humming and singing, clipping along the top of the water.' Author's collection.

89   'The Buccaneer was a picturesque fellow.' The Buccaneers of the seventeenth century were a very rough looking crew, unlike this individual. Buccaneers were usually based on Hispaniola and Tortuga, and lived by hunting wild cattle and hogs, before turning to piracy. Author's collection.

90   'Then the real fight began.' This picture depicts a mutiny, when some sailors decide to take over a ship. Usually there would be two or three ringleaders, then others would be signed up, and a signal would be agreed to start the mutiny – normally a password, or a cannon ball rolled over the deck. Author's collection.

91   'Captain Keitt.' A romantic and unrealistic image of a pirate captain. Many pirate captains started off as a mate or another senior position on a merchant ship before becoming a pirate. Only a few pirate captains, such as Bart Roberts, lasted more than a year or two.' Author's collection.

92   Capt Edward England. A sketch of the pirate Edward England. He was reported to be kind hearted, and did not abuse his prisoners. He was removed as captain by his crew, and spent his final days in poverty and repentance at St Mary's Island, Madagascar. Author's collection.

93   Anne Bonny and Mary Read. These two women served as part of the crew on 'Calico' Jack Rackam's ship. There were extremely few female pirates in the West, so they gained considerable fame. They were captured along with the rest of Rackam's crew, and condemned to death. But both were pregnant, and so were spared the noose. Author's collection.

94   Capt Bart Roberts. Roberts was one of the most successful pirate captains, taking around 400 ships. He also managed to remain as captain for some four years, before being killed in 1722 on the coast of West Africa. Roberts was unusual in maintaining discipline on his ships, and was reportedly a non drinker. Author's collection.

95   Captain George Lowther. Lowther is shown watching as his ship is careened. This was a difficult task in which the ship was heeled over, and the barnacles and weed scraped and burnt off the hull. Unfortunately for Lowther, his ship was taken in 1723 as it was being careened. Lowther escaped into the jungle where he was found dead with a pistol by his side. Author's collection.

96   Captain Edward Low. An appropriate image of Edward Low, his twisting body reflecting his twisted personality. Low was an unusually cruel pirate captain, often torturing and killing his captives. He seems to have been an unbalanced individual, but he was caught and hung by the French in 1726. Author's collection.

97   'Henry Morgan recruiting for the attack.' Author's collection.

98   'Morgan at Porto Bello.' Author's collection.

99   'The sacking of Panama.' A romantic vision of the ruthless sacking of Panama in 1671 by Henry Morgan and his buccaneers. Author's collection.

100   'Blackbeard buries his treasure.' Blackbeard was rumoured to have buried his treasure on or near Mulberry Island, Chesapeake Bay. If he did, it has not yet been found.' Author's collection.

101   Captain Teach. A portrait of Blackbeard. According to Captain Charles Johnson, Blackbeard did have a long, bushy beard, and he did set fire to lighted matches under his hat, and he did carry three brace of pistols in bandoliers. Author's collection.

102   Captain Avery. A portrait of the pirate Henry Avery or Every. Avery was also called Long Ben, meaning that he was unusually tall. The picture relates to Avery's greatest feat in taking two very valuable ships from India. One of these ships did belong to the Moghul emperor of India, Aurangzeb. Author's collection.

103   'Kidd at Gardiner's Island.' Author's collection.

104   The *Royal Ann*. A typical Royal Navy first rate. Rates were measured by the number of guns they carried – a first rate carried from 80 to 110 guns. The large crew of 780 men was required mainly to work the guns. These ships were not useful for chasing pirates because they were slow sailors, and could not enter rivers or go close to land. Author's collection.

105   The Captain's bridge protected by a grill against Chinese pirates in the 1920s and 30s. Author's collection.

106   Anti-pirate guard ready for action against Chinese pirates in the 1920s and 30s. Author's collection.

107   Lai Choi San. A well known female Chinese pirate in the 1920s, who commanded a fleet of 11 junks. She was to be obeyed, and obeyed she was. Author's collection.

108   Lai Choi San had singled out a large black junk with three yellow sails. Author's collection.

109   Lai Choi San's junk ready for action. Author's collection.

110   Two men bound hand and foot on Lai Choi San's junk afetr action. Author's collection.

111   Some distance to starboard lay the sinking junk – a victim of Lai Choi San. Author's collection.

112   Houses in the pirate lair of Bias Bay, near Hong Kong. Author's collection.

113   The house of torture in Bias Bay, the pirate lair near Hong Kong. Author's collection.

114   The powder magazine onboard Lai Choi San's junk. Author's collection.

115   A typical pirate onboard Lai Choi San's junk. Author's collection.

CHAPTER PAGE ILLUSTRATIONS

p.2   'Band of armed pirates.' Author's collection.

p.5   Skull and cross bones taken from a Howard Pyle illustration (cover design). Author's collection.

p.6   'A pirate takes aim.' Author's collection.

p.7   A woodcut of the execution of one of Avery's crew in 1696. Author's collection.

p.51   Different versions of pirate flags. Author's collection.

p.67   A woodcut of the execution of one of Avery's crew in 1696. Author's collection.

p.83   'On the Tortugas.' Henry Pitman, perhaps the model for Robinson Crusoe, was stranded on Salt Tortuga Island with others in 1687. Author's collection.

p.97   Captain Teach. A portrait of Blackbeard. Author's collection.

p.163   Avery is presented here as the king of Madagascar. Author's collection.

p.181   A portrait of Anne Bonny (or Bonn), who served on Captain Jack Rackam's ship. Courtesy of Joel Baer.

p.205   Captain Bartholomew Roberts, one of the most successful pirates. Courtesy of Joel Baer.

p.235   'A pirate takes aim.' Author's collection.

p.263   Different versions of pirate flags. Author's collection.

p.285   'A pirate takes aim.' Author's collection.

p.286   This pirate captain was known as 'Calico' Jack Rackam, due to his penchant for wearing white calico clothes. Courtesy of Joel Baer.

p.287   'Band of armed pirates.' Author's collection.

p.297   A woodcut of the execution of one of Avery's crew in 1696. Author's collection.

p.309   'Pirates carrying treasure.' Author's collection.

p.314   'The Buccaneer was a picturesque fellow.' Author's collection.

MAPS

All are taken from the author's collection.

Maps

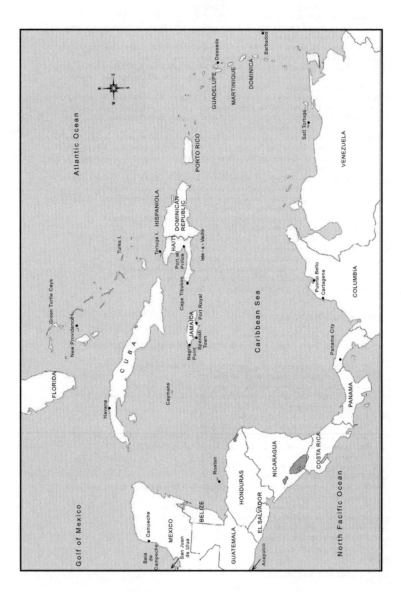

1 The Carribean and the Americas.

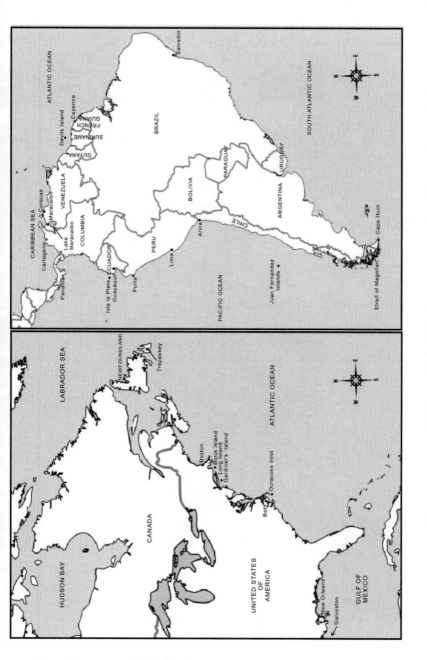

Above: 2a The east coast of North America.
Top: 2b South America.

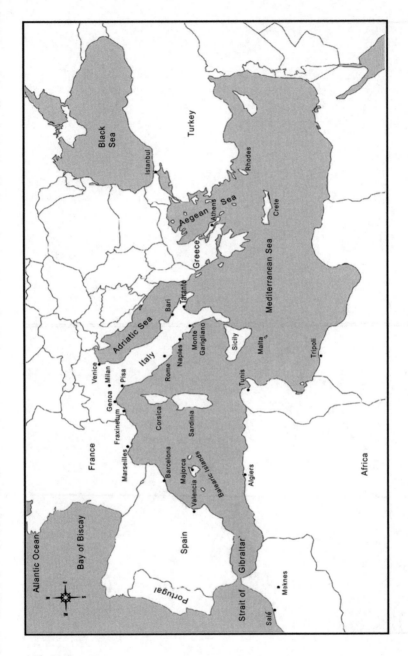

3 The Mediterranean.

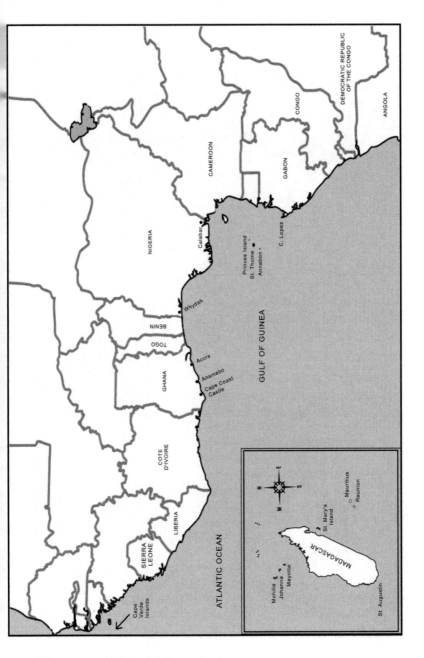

4 The west coast of Africa, and Madagascar (inset).

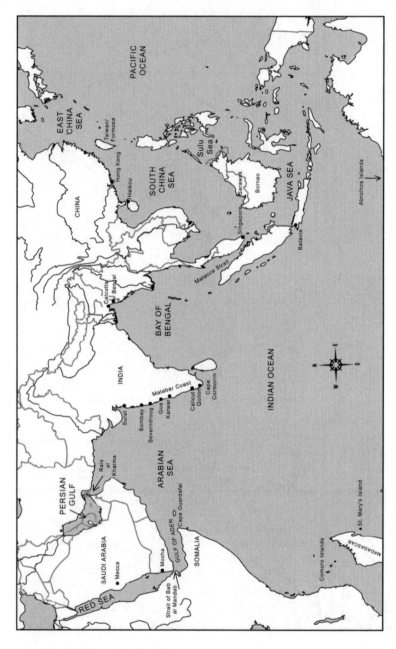

5 Arabia, India, China, and the East Indies.

Notes

CHAPTER 1: THE PIRATE WORLD

1   Captain Charles Johnson, *A General History of the Robberies and Murders of the most Notorious Pirates*, originally published 1724, London, Conway Maritime Press edition, Introduction by David Cordingly, 1998, 2002 [hereafter Johnson], p.265.

    It is significant that Johnson goes out of his way to say that the account of this mock trial was given to him by someone who was actually present, that Johnson describes the precise clothing worn by the judge of the mock trial, and that Johnson reiterates: 'This is the trial just as it was related to me…' p.266.

2   Cordingly, 'Introduction', Johnson, pp.vii – xiv. Defoe seems not to have been Johnson. High Court of Admiralty [hereafter HCA], Admiralty [hereafter ADM], and Colonial Office [hereafter CO], records are held by the Public Record Office [hereafter PRO], Kew Gardens, London, England. First hand accounts, especially of the South Sea men, from the Sloane collection, are found in the British Library [hereafter BL], London, England. There are many excellent books on the pirates, but tribute should be paid to the first good overview, which is Philip Gosse, *The History of Piracy*, first published in 1932. Other fine books are listed in the footnotes and bibliography.

3   Several other authors of pirate stories for children exist, including, for example, Captain Marryat (1792–1848) and more recently, Arthur Ransome (1884–1967).

4   For example, Brad Strickland and Thomas Fuller, *The Guns of Tortuga*, New York, Aladdin Books, 2003, part of the teenage Pirate Hunter Series.

5   Such as *Howard Pyles' Book of Pirates*, New York and London, Harper and Brothers, 1921. Some of the illustrations for the present book come from this work.

6   Among many publications, the following recent titles may be mentioned: Robert Ritchie, *Captain Kidd and the War against the Pirates*, 1986; David Cordingly, *Under the Black Flag: the Romance and the Reality of Life Among the Pirates*, 1996; Aubrey Burl, *Black Barty: Bartholomew Roberts and his Pirate Crew, 1718–1723*, 1997; C.R. Pennell, ed., *Bandits at Sea: A Pirates Reader*, 2001; Richard Zacks, *The Pirate Hunter: the True Story of Captain Kidd*, 2002; Jacques Heers, *The Barbary Corsairs: Warfare in the Mediterranean, 1480–1580*, 2003 (translated from the French, originally published 2001); Peter Earle, *The Pirate Wars*, 2004; Diana and Michael Preston, *A Pirate of Exquisite Mind: Explorer, Naturalist, and Buccaneer: the Life of William Dampier*, 2004; Marcus Rediker, *Villains of all Nations: Atlantic Pirates in the Golden Age*, 2004; Joel Baer, *Pirates of the British Isles*, 2005; and Angus Konstam, *Blackbeard: America's Most Notorious Pirate*, 2006. For modern piracy, there is John Burnett, *Dangerous Waters: Modern Piracy and Terror on the High Seas*, 2002.

7   Richard Burgess, 'Account of the Proceedings of the Essex prize…' 13 August 1699, f. 74; deposition of

Thomas Gulluck, f. 67; CO 323/3, PRO.

8 Johnson, pp.180–181.

9 Ibid, pp.278, 287–288, and 319 for old hands' suspicion of new pirates.

10 Ibid, pp.314–315, 322–323.

11 Ibid, pp.182–183.

12 Charles Johnson, *The History of the Lives and Bloody Exploits of the Most Noted Pirates: Their Trials and Executions*, Guilford, Connecticut, Lyons Press, 2004, pp.128–129. This volume is a reprint of part of the 1726 edition of Johnson's *A General History of the … Pyrates*, with added material.

13 The ideological background to Atlantic piracy is the argument of Marcus Rediker, *Villains of All Nations: Atlantic Pirates in the Golden Age*, Beacon Press, Boston, 2004, passim. For Roberts' ideas, Johnson, p.213.

14 For James, information from Thomas Jones, Captain of the *Ronoke*, 4 August 1699, folio 110, CO 323/3, PRO.

15 Cited in Aubrey Burl, *Black Barty: Bartholomew Roberts And His Pirate Crew, 1718–1723*, Sutton Publishing, Stroud, 2006, p.37. On revenge, Rediker, op cit, pp.86–87.

16 Deposition of Joseph Smollett, 1721, ff. 11–12; deposition of John Stephenson, 9 November 1721, f. 5, HCA 1/55, PRO. On Hamlin, 'Journal of Captain Charles Carlile in His Majesty's ship the *Francis*, 18 August 1683, Gosse /6, Gosse Collection, National Maritime Museum, Greenwich, England.

17 Thomas Lawrence, deposition, 13 February 1723, HCA 1/55; Captain George Martin, HMS *Lizard*, to Admiralty, 1701, M papers, 1698–1701, ADM 1/2090, PRO.

18 Angus Konstam, *Blackbeard: America's Most Notorious Pirate*, Wiley, Hoboken, New Jersey, 2006, pp.257–258, 267–268, 271–272.

19 Examination of Richard Moor, 31 October 1724, HCA 1/55, PRO.

20 Deposition of Thomas Lawrence Jones, 13 February 1723, HCA 1/55, PRO. Johnson, pp.194–195.

21 Deposition of Thomas Lawrence Jones, op cit; Johnson, op cit, pp.262 ff, 194. Johnson mixes up Jones' name on p.262, calling him 'Bones' in the Anstis chapter. It is also on this island that Johnson relates the story of the mock trial, related to Johnson by a participant, op cit, pp.265–266.

22 Johnson, pp.314–315, 317.

23 Ibid, pp.278, 287–288.

24 Ibid, pp.180–181. Johnson noted that the original articles had been thrown overboard when Roberts' crew feared capture, and wondered if these originals had contained something worse. The articles actually mentioned by Johnson had been related to him, presumably by some of Roberts' pirates.

25 Aubrey Burl, *Black Barty*, pp.185–186.

26 Ibid, pp.127 –128.

27 'Journal of our Intended Voyage', Sloane ms 2752, f. 53, BL. Diana and Michael Preston, *A Pirate of Exquisite Mind: Explorer, Naturalist, and Buccaneer: The Life of William Dampier*, Walker and Company, New York, pp.102–103.

28 John Strong, 'Voyage to the Straits of Magellan, 1689–1690', Sloane ms 3295, f. 78, BL.

29 Deposition of Joseph Turner, 12 January 1716, f. 37, HCA 1/54, PRO.

30 Examination of Robert Mason, 27 May 1699, CO 5/1258, PRO.

31 Diana and Michael Preston, *A Pirate of Exquisite Mind*, p.313; Rogozinski, *Dictionary of Pirates*, Wordsworth, Ware, Herts., 1995, Selkirk entry; David Cordingly, *Under the Black Flag: The Romance and Reality of Life Among the Pirates*, (1996) Random House, New York, 2006, pp.139–140.

32 The Pitman story is related by Tim Severin, *Seeking Robinson Crusoe*, MacMillan, London, 2002.

33 John Elting, *Swords Around A Throne: Napoleon's Grande Armee*, Free Press, New York and London, 1988, chapter 30; N.A.M. Rodger, *The Wooden World: An Anatomy of the Georgian Navy*, Naval Institute Press, Annapolis, Maryland, 1986, p.77; Cordingly, *Under the Black Flag*, p.67.

34 David N. Ford, *Royal Berkshire History*, Nash Ford Publishing, Finchampstead, Berkshire, 2005.

35 Cordingly, *Under the Black Flag*, pp.72–74, citing information from Ann Chambers, *Granuaille: the Life and Times of Grace O'Malley, 1530–1603*, Dublin 1979.

36 Cordingly, *Under the Black Flag*, pp.74–75; M.J. Rodriguez-Salgado, *Armada 1588–1988*, Penguin Books, London, 1988, p.266. Bingham, who died in 1599, appears to have been a ruthless and zealous supporter of Elizabeth in Ireland.

37 Johnson, pp.180–181, 315, 278. On the Red Sea pirates' treatment of women, see chapter 6, and Joel Baer, *Pirates of the British Isles*, Tempus Publishing, Stroud, 2005, p.102.

38 See B.R. Burg, *Sodomy and the Perception of Evil: English Sea Rovers in the Seventeenth–century Caribbean*, New York, 1983; Hans Turley, *Rum, Sodomy and the Lash: piracy, sexuality, and masculine identity*, New York, 1999.

39 'A Journal Kept by Bartholomew Sharp…' 7 January 1681, f. 61, ms. 46A, BL.

40 Richard Mandervell or Manderwell, deposition, 1721, ff. 21–22, HCA 1/55, PRO.

41 Padre Dominici, *Trattato delle Miserie*, Rome, 1647, cited in Robert C. Davis, *Christian Slaves, Muslim Masters: White Slavery in the Mediterranean, the Barbary Coast, and Italy, 1500–1800*, Palgrave, MacMillan, Basingstoke and New York, 2004, p.125.

42 Snelgrave cited in Douglas Botting, *The Pirates*, Time Life Books, Alexandria, Virginia, 1978, pp. 17–18; re: Davis, Johnson, p. 134; re: Roberts, Johnson, p. 192; re: Spriggs, Johnson, p. 327.

43 Johnson, pp. 212, 54.

44 Botting, *The Pirates*, pp. 17–18.

45 Johnson, p. 264.

46 Johnson, pp. 335–336.

47 William Cowley, 'Voyage to the Cape Verde Islands' 1683–1686, ff. 7, 16–18, 22–24, 27, ms 54, BL.

48 Johnson, p. 211.

49 Cited in Richard Zacks, *The Pirate Hunter: The True Story of Captain Kidd*, Hyperion, New York, 2002, p. 44.

50 Ibid, p. 44.

51 Ibid, p. 149.

52 Deposition of John Shattock, 18 January 1720, St. Jago de la Vega, Jamaica, Tryalls of John Rackam and others, p. 24, CO 137/14, PRO.

53 Charles Grey, *Pirates of the Eastern Seas*, edited by Sir George MacMunn, Kennikat Press, Port Washington and London, (1933), 1971, p. 35.

54 Witness at the trial of Robert Hudson, 10 March 1720, St. Jago de la Vega, Jamaica, Tryalls of John Rackam and others, p. 36, CO 137/14, PRO.

55 Thomas Grant, 1721, f. 120, HCA 1/54, PRO.

56 Deposition of Clem Downing, 28 October 1724, f. 93; Philip or John Roth, ff. 44–45, 1722, HCA 1/55, PRO.

57 Deposition of Michael Moore, 3 April 1725, HCA 1/55, PRO.

58 Johnson, p. 193.

59 Peter Gosselin, jailor, Guernsey, overhearing John Ashley shouting at John Prie, 1727, f. 20, HCA 1/56, PRO.

60 John Ashley, 1 February 1727, f. 17, and f. 30; John Upton, 1726, f. 27; HCA 1/56, PRO.

61 Deposition of Samuel Perkins, 25 August 1698, f. 390, CO 323/2, PRO.

62 Morgan Miles, deposition, 1721, ff. 9–10; Joseph Stratton, deposition, 14 November 1721, f. 14; HCA 1/55, PRO.

63 Richard Zacks, *The Pirate Hunter*, chapter 15, for the complicated story of the recovery of Kidd's treasure.

64 Alexander Farquharson, deposition, 22 October 1724, f. 90, HCA 1/55, PRO. Barry Clifford tells the story of diving on wrecks at St Mary's in his *Return to Treasure Island and the search for Captain Kidd*, Harper Collins, New York, 2003. It seems that a number of previous treasure hunters have been to St Mary's Island. Barry Clifford and his crew did locate the wreck of Conden's ship, the *Flying Dragon*, and found some gold coins. Kidd's *Adventure Galley* was also located, and a large pewter mug recovered from the wreck.

65 Clement Downing, *A History of the Indian Wars*, 1737, ed. and introduction by William Foster, Oxford University Press, London, 1924, pp. 111–112. Clement Downing, deposition, 28 October 1724, f. 93, HCA 1/55, PRO.

66 Cordingly, *Under the Black Flag*, p. 191. 'Blackbeard Lives', *National Geographic*, July 2006, pp. 146–161.

67 Sloane Collection, ms 50/1070, 1687, BL. This item may or may not have referred to pirates.

68 Johnson, p. 56.

69 'A Narrative abt. the Mocha Frigatt written by William Willocks a Prisoner aboard them 11 Months', f. 729, CO 323/2, PRO.

70 Cited from Pelsaert, *The Unlucky Voyage of the Ship Batavia*, (1647), Amsterdam, 1994. See also Henrietta Drake-Brockman, *Voyage to Disaster: the Life of Francisco Pelsaert*, Angus and Robertson, Sydney, 1963.

71 Ibid. There is a very large historiography of this event, as well as a radio play and an opera.

72 Cited in Cordingly and Falconer, *Pirates: Fact and Fiction*, Collins and Brown, London, 1992, p. 108.

73 Narrative of Phillip Middleton, 4 August 1696, f. 114, CO 323/2, PRO.

74 Johnson, pp. 297–298.

75 Ibid, pp. 298–299.

76 This is the argument of Rediker, *Villains of All Nations*, pp. 170 ff.

77 Johnson, pp. 295, 300, 305–307. The medieval Mongols also cut off ears, but this was simply to count their victims.

78 Ibid, p. 289.

79 Ibid, pp. 327–328.

80 Ibid, pp. 328–330. Rogozinski, *Dictionary of Pirates*, entry for 'blooding'.

81 Nicholas Lawes, Governor of Jamaica, to My Lords Commissioners, 18 May 1722, ff. 152-153, CO 137/14, Part 1, PRO. Peter Earle, *The Pirate Wars*, (2003), Methuen, London, 2004, pp. 199–200.

82 Thomas Grant, deposition, 1721, f. 120; Edward Green, deposition, 29 April 1721, f. 123; HCA 1/54, PRO.

83 Johnson, pp. 177–178.

84 'Piracy', *American Monthly*, February 1824, cited in *The History of the Lives and Bloody Exploits of the Most Noted Pirates*, Lyons Press, Guilford, Connecticut, 2004, pp. 259–265.

85 Johnson, p. 81.

86 V.A.C Gatrell, *The Hanging Tree: Execution and the English People, 1770–1868*, Oxford University Press, Oxford and New York, 1994, on the practice of hanging in England.

87 Rediker, *Villains of All Nations*, p.163. Johnson, pp.256–259, 323–324.

88 Zacks, *The Pirate Hunter*, pp.390–392.

89 Clement Downing, *A History of the Indian Wars*, 1724, p.119.

90 Captain Charles Johnson, ed., Arthur Hayward, *A General History of the Pirates*, Fourth Edition, 1726, Dodd Mead, New York, 1926, pp.590–592.

CHAPTER 2: FROM CLASSICAL PIRACY TO THE MEDIEVAL MEDITERRANEAN

1   Cited in Henry Ormerod, *Piracy in the Ancient World*, (1924), Johns Hopkins, Baltimore, 1997, p.49.

2   Cited in N.K. Sandars, *The Sea Peoples: Warriors of the Ancient Mediterranean*, Thames and Hudson, London, 1985, pp.186–187.

3   Herodotus, *The History: Herodotus*, translated by David Grene, Chicago, University of Chicago Press, 1987, p.229.

4   Philip de Souza, *Piracy in the Graeco-Roman World*, Cambridge University Press, Cambridge, 1999, p.25.

5   Ormerod, *Piracy in the Ancient World*, pp.115–116; Quintus Curtius Rufus, *The History of Alexander*, Harmondsworth, Penguin Books, 1984, p.70.

6   Arrian, *The Campaigns of Alexander*, Penguin edition, Harmondsworth, 1971, p.150.

7   *History of Diodorus of Sicily*, translated by Russell Geer, William Heinemann, London, and Harvard University Press, Cambridge, Massachusetts, 1933, Book XX, vol. 10, pp.355–401.

8   Ormerod, *Piracy in the Ancient World*, pp.139 ff., 222.

9   De Souza, *Piracy in the Graeco-Roman World*, p.140; Philip Gosse, *The History of Piracy*, (1932), Rio Grande Press, Glorieta, New Mexico, 1995, pp.4–8.

10 Ormerod, *Piracy in the Ancient World*, p.227.

11 De Souza, *Piracy in the Graeco-Roman World*, pp.168–175.

12 John Haywood, *Dark Age Naval Power: a re-assessment of Frankish and Anglo-Saxon seafaring activity*, Routledge, London and New York, 1991, passim.

13 Procopius, cited in Archibald R. Lewis and Timothy J. Runyan, *European Naval and Maritime History, 300–1500*, Indiana University Press, Bloomington, 1990 edition, p.11.

14 John H. Pryor, *Geography, technology, and war: Studies in the Maritime History of the Mediterranean, 649–1571*, Cambridge University Press, Cambridge, 1988, p.153 and passim. See also chapters by John H. Pryor and Michel Balard in David Abulafia, ed., *The Mediterranean in History*, Thames and Hudson, London, 2003.

15 Lewis and Runyan, *European Naval and Maritime History*, p.45.

16 Aly Mohamed Fahmy, *Muslim Sea-Power In the Eastern Mediterranean From the Seventh to the Tenth Century* AD, National Publication and Printing House, Cairo, 1966, passim.

17 Ibid, pp.128–132; E. Clutton and A. Kenny, *Crete*, David and Charles, Newton Abbot, 1976, pp.94–95; Pierre Brule, *La Piraterie Cretoise Hellenestique*, Les Belles Lettres, Paris, 1978, p.183. Some historians dispute the label of piracy as applied to the Muslims in Crete.

18 Pryor, *Geography, technology and war*, p.105. Michel Balard, 'A Christian Mediterranean, 1000–1500', in David Abulafia, ed., *The Mediterranean in History*, p.199.

19 Cited in Trevor Rowley, *The Normans*, Tempus Publishing, Stroud, 2004, p.147.

20 Ibid, p.156.

21 Lewis and Runyan, *European Naval and Maritime History*, p.68.

22 Frederic C. Lane, *Venice: A Maritime Republic*, Johns Hopkins, Baltimore and London, 1973, p.29.

23 Rowley, *The Normans*, p.171.

24 Ibid, p.172.

25 Charles Brand, *Byzantium Confronts the West, 1180–1204*, Harvard University Press, Cambridge, Mass:, 1968, pp.208–214.

26 Ibid, p.211.

27 J.K. Fotheringham, 'Genoa and the Fourth Crusade', *English History Review*, vol. 25, pp.26–57; E. Clutton and A. Kenny, *Crete*, David and Charles, Newton Abbot, 1976, pp.99 ff..

28 Steven Epstein, *Genoa and the Genoese: 958–1528*, University of North Carolina Press, Chapel Hill, 1996, pp.180, 120; Lane, *Venice: A Maritime Republic*, p.80.

29 Pryor, *Geography, technology and war*, p.126.

30 Giovanni Boccaccio, *The Decameron*, Laurel edition, Dell Publishing, New York, 1962, p.99.

31 Epstein, *Genoa and the Genoese*, pp.198, 274.

32 Ibid, p.210.

33 Ernle Bradford, *Mediterranean: Portrait of a Sea*, Hodder and Stoughton, London, 1971, p.397.

34 Alberto Tenenti, *Piracy and the Decline of Venice, 1580–1615*, (1961), UCLA Press, Berkeley, 1967, p.82.

35 Susan Rose, *Medieval Naval Warfare, 1000–1500*, Routledge, London and New York, 2002, p.118.

36 Tenenti, *Piracy and the Decline of Venice, 1580–1615*, p.86; Jan Glete, *Warfare at Sea, 1500–1650, Maritime Conflicts and the Transformation of Europe*, Routledge, London, 2000, pp.107–111.

37 Tenenti, *Piracy and the Decline of Venice*, pp.26–27.

38 Ibid, pp.112–147.

39 Cited in Wendy Bracewell, 'Women among the Uskoks of Senj: Literary Images and Reality', in C.R. Pennell, ed., *Bandits at Sea: A Pirates Reader*, New York University Press, New York and London, 2001, pp.324–325.

40 Pryor, *Geography, technology and war*, pp.153–154; see also Glete, *Warfare at Sea 1500–1650*, p.136.

CHAPTER 3: PIRACY IN THE NORTHERN WORLD

1 Anglo-Saxon Chronicle, and Alcuin of York, cited in Else Roesdahl, *The Vikings*, (1987), translated by Margeson and Williams, Penguin, London, 1991, p.193.

2 F. Donald Logan, *The Vikings in History*, Hutchinson, London, 1983, pp.189–190.

3 Ibid, p.191.

4 Roesdahl, *The Vikings*, pp.145–146.

5 Ibn Fadlan, cited in Johannes Brondsted, *The Vikings*, (1960) Penguin, London, 1965, p.265.

6 Ibn Rustah, cited in Ibid, pp.267–269.

7 Benjamin Hudson, *Viking Pirates and Christian Princes: Dynasty, Religion, and Empire in the North Atlantic*, Oxford University Press, Oxford, 2005, p.22.

8 Ibid, p.23. Logan, *The Vikings in History*, p.51.

9 William Ledyard Rogers, *Naval Warfare Under Oars, 4th to 16th Centuries: A Study of Strategy, Tactics and Ship Design*, Naval Institute Press, Annapolis, Maryland, 1940, 1967, pp.78–79.

10 Roesdahl, *The Vikings*, pp.198–199.

11 F. Donald Logan, *The Vikings in History*, p.118.

12 Ibid, pp.130–132.

13 Susan Rose, *Medieval Naval Warfare, 1000–1500*, Routledge, London and New York, 2002, p.29.

14 Ibid, pp.72–73. Phillipe Dollinger, *The German Hansa*, trans and edited D.S. Ault and S.H. Steinberg, Stanford University Press, Stanford, 1970, pp.80–81; Jan Rogozinski, *Dictionary of Pirates*, pp.327–328; Philip Gosse, *The History of Piracy*, Rio Grande Press, Glorieta, New Mexico, 1995 (1932), pp.90–92.

15 Douglas Botting, *The Pirates*, Time Life, Alexandria, Virginia, 1978, p.23.

16 Jan Glete, *Warfare at Sea, 1500–1650: Maritime Conflicts and the Transformation of Europe*, Routledge, London, 2000, p.134.

CHAPTER 4: ELIZABETHAN SEA ROVERS AND THE JACOBEAN PIRATES

1 Nick Hazlewood, *The Queen's Slave Trader: John Hawkyns, Elizabeth I, And The Trafficking in Human Souls*, Harper Collins, New York, 2005, p.34.

2 Ibid, pp.53, 56–57.

3 Harry Kelsey, *Sir John Hawkins: Queen Elizabeth's Slave Trader*, Yale University Press, New Haven and London, 2003, pp.88–89.

4 Ibid, pp.88–106.

5 Harry Kelsey, *Sir Francis Drake: The Queen's Pirate*, Yale University Press, New Haven and London, 1998, pp.64–65. Most of the foregoing information on Drake comes from this book, chapter 3.

6 Ibid, pp.75–86.

7 Ibid, pp.107–109.

8 Ibid, pp.156–157.

9 Ibid, pp.211–218.

10 Ibid, chapter 11.

11 Ibid, p.372.

12 Peter Earle, *The Pirate Wars*, Methuen, London, 2004, pp.60–61.

13 Sir Henry Mainwaring, 'Of the Beginnings, Practices, and Suppression of Pirates', 1618, in G.E. Manwaring and W. G Perrin, eds., *The Life and Work of Sir Henry Mainwaring*, vol. 2, Navy Records Society, LVI, London, (1922), pp.3–49.

14 Rogozinski, *Dictionary of Pirates*, p.243.

15 Earle, *Pirate Wars*, pp.65–66.

16 Information from Johnson on each pirate.

17 Depositions of Michael Moor, aged 17 years, and Daniel McCauley, aged 21 years, 1725, HCA, 1/55, PRO. On the words of the chief mate, Mr. Jelfs, Joseph Wheatley, deposition, 2 September 1725, HCA 1/56, PRO.

18 Ibid, and Johnson, chapter on John Smith/Gow.

CHAPTER 5: BUCCANEERS OF THE CARIBBEAN

1   Information from Rogozinski, *Dictionary of Pirates*, pp.323, 194.

2   Clark Russell, 'Life of Dampier', cited in Gosse, *The History of Piracy*, (1932), Rio Grande Press, Glorieta, New Mexico, 1995, p.143.

3   Cited in Diana and Michael Preston, *A Pirate of Exquisite Mind: Explorer, Naturalist, and Buccaneer: the Life of William Dampier*, Walker and Company, New York, 2004, pp.45–46.

4   Esquemeling, *Buccaneers of America*, (1678–1684), Routledge, London, and E.P. Dutton, New York, 1923, pp.56–57. There is some question as to the reality of the Pierre Le Grand exploit. On the rise of the buccaneers, Kris Lane, *Pillaging the Empire: Piracy in the Americas, 1500–1750*, New York, 1998, chapter IV.

5   Rogozinski, *op cit*, pp.198–199; Lane, *Pillaging the Empire*, chapter 5.

6   Rogozinski, *Dictionary of Pirates*, entry for L'Olonnais; Esquemeling, *Buccaneers of America*, p.103.

7   Esquemeling, *Buccaneers of America*, pp.73–75, Rogozinski, *op cit*, p.42; Gosse, *The History of Piracy*, p.148.

8   Esquemeling, *Buccaneers of America*, p.116.

9   Ibid., pp.173–178.

10 Ibid, pp.185 ff.

11 Ibid, pp.204 ff.

12 Ibid.; Philip Lindsay, *The Great Buccaneer: being the life, death and extraordinary adventures of Sir Henry Morgan*, P. Nevill, London and New York, 1950, pp.143 ff.

13 Lindsay, op cit, 156; Esquemeling, *Buccaneers of America*, pp.215 ff.; Peter Earle, *The Sack of Panama*, Bury St Edmunds Press, Suffolk, 1981, p.223; Dudley Pope, *Harry Morgan's Way*, Secker and Warburg, London, 1977, pp.240 ff. Baer, *Pirates of the British Isles*, Tempus Publishing, Stroud, 2005, p.44.

14 Esquemeling, *Buccaneers of America*, pp.220–223.

15 Ironically, one of Morgan's doctors was Dr. Hans Sloane, who gathered together a large collection of pirate and maritime manuscripts that forms a valuable part of the British Library manuscript collection.

16 Diana and Michael Preston, *A Pirate of Exquisite Mind*, p.34.

17 Esquemeling, *Buccaneers of America*, p.75.

18 Diana and Michael Preston, *A Pirate of Exquisite Mind*, pp.32–51.

19 Bartholomew Sharp, 'Voyage from Jamaica to Porto Bello (1679)', ms. 2752, ff. 29–35, BL.

20 Anonymous, 'Journal of our intended voyage', ms. 2752, f. 37, BL.

21 Ibid, f.38.

22 Ibid, f. 40.

23 Ibid, f. 42.

24 Ibid, f. 42; John Cox, 'John Cox his Travills over the Land into the S/o Seas…' f. 8, 26 April – 13 May 1680, ms 49, BL.

25 Anonymous, 'Journal of our intended voyage…' ff. 43–45; John Cox, 'John Cox his Travills…' f. 8; 'A Journal kept by Bartholomew Sharp…' f. 23, ms. 46 A; BL.

26 John Cox, 'John Cox his Travills', ff. 31–32, ms. 49; Sharp, 'A Journal kept by Bartholomew Sharp', ms. 46 A, f. 65; BL.

27 John Cox, 'John Cox his Travills', ff. 34, 40, 49, ms. 49, BL; Ringrose in Esquemeling, *Buccaneers of America*, p.433.

28 John Cox, 'John Cox his Travills', ff. 42, 64, ms. 49, BL. Joel Baer, *Pirates of the British Isles*, pp.58–59.

29 William Ambrose Cowley, 'Voyage to Cape Verde Islands', ff.1–5, 1684, ms. 54, BL. Diana and Michael Preston, *A Pirate of Exquisite Mind*, chapter VII.

30 Cowley, 'Voyage to Cape Verde Islands', f. 7, ms. 54, BL.

31 Ibid, ff. 10–11. Diana and Michael Preston, *A Pirate of Exquisite Mind*, p.115.

32 Diana and Michael Preston, *A Pirate of Exquisite Mind*, pp.127–128; Baer, *Pirates of the British Isles*, pp.62–63.

33 Rogozinski, *Dictionary of Pirates*, entry for Edward Davis.

34 Diana and Michael Preston, *A Pirate of Exquisite Mind*, pp.132–133, 141–142.

35 Ibid, chapters 11 and 12; Baer, *Pirates of the British Isles*, pp.65–66.

36 Baer, *Pirates of the British Isles*, p.68; Diana and Michael Preston, *A Pirate of Exquisite Mind*, pp.179 ff.

37 Rogozinski, *Dictionary of Pirates*, entry for John Read; Robert Downie, *The Way of the Pirate*, ibooks, New York, 1998, entries for John Read and Josiah Teat; Diana and Michael Preston, *A Pirate of Exquisite Mind*, p.204.

38 Cowley, 'Voyage to Cape Verde Islands', ff. 10–13, ms. 54, BL.

39 Ibid, ff. 16–40.

40 Ibid, ff. 48–49, 53, 65.

41 Cited in Peter Wood, *The Spanish Main*, Time Life Books, Alexandria, Virginia, 1979, pp.144–145.

42 Ibid, pp.150–158.

43 Ibid, pp.159–161.

CHAPTER 6: THE MADAGASCAR MEN

1 Edward Randolph, 'A Discourse about Pyrates', 1695, in GOS/9, Philip Gosse Papers, National Maritime Museum, Greenwich.

2 John Banks, examination, 1699, D74, CO 5/1259, PRO. On privateering commissions, folios D41, D42, 1699, Ibid.

3 File A 14, CO 323/2, PRO.

4 'Abstract of papers relating to Piracy in the East Indies', 20 February 1697, B25, CO 323/2, PRO; Examination of Samuel Perkins, 25 August 1698, CO 323/2, PRO.

5 'Notice from Bombay dated the 15th January 1696/7, and from Calicut dated the 30th November 1696', in CO 323/2, PRO. Richard Zacks, *The Pirate Hunter: the True Story of Captain Kidd*, Hyperion, New York, 2002, pp.197–198, 308, 398.

6 J. South, Dublin, 15 August 1696, A 35, CO 323/2, PRO; Earle, *The Pirate Wars*, Methuen, London, 2004, p.122.

7 'Extract of a Letter to the East India Company from Captain Thomas Warren...' 28 November 1697, CO 323/2, PRO.

8 The Earl of Morton and the Hon. Charles Egerton, 'To the Rt Honoble the Lords Committees of Trade', 1708, CO 323/6, f. 195, PRO. 'The humble Petition of the Pirates and Buckaneers of Madagascar ... and their accomplices by Mary Read [et al]...' 'To the Queen's Most Excett. Majestie', December 1708, CO 323/6, ff. 197–198, PRO. Deposition of Penelope Aubin, 20 January 1709, f. 225, CO 323/6, PRO. Deposition of Elizabeth Woodford, Barbara Ramsey, and Ann Rupert, f. 225, January 1709, CO 323/6, PRO.

9 On George Breholt, Captain George Martin, Royal Navy, to Lords of the Admiralty, 1701, ADM 1/2090, letter 'M', 1689–1701, PRO; on Breholt's plan, John Dovey to Court of St James, 2 June 1709, f. 187, CO 323/6, PRO. It is possible that George Breholt existed separately and was the father or brother or other relation of John Breholt.

10 Lawrence Waldron, deposition, 7 May 1709, f. 222, and Lawrence Waldron and John Clough, deposition, 16 January 1709, f. 223; CO 323/6, PRO.

11 Marquis of Carmarthen to the Queen's Council, 11 June 1709, ff. 188–189; and 'Reasons humbly Offer'd by Peregrine, Marquis of Carmarthen...' June 1709, f. 226; CO 323/6, PRO.

12 Marquis of Carmarthen, 'A Memorial for Suppressing the Pirates of Madagascar...' ff. 220–221, 1709, CO 323/6, PRO.

13 Duke of Leeds, Diary, 19 March 1705, 14 October 1708, 29 March 1712, Carmarthen Papers, Add. Ms. 28041, BL. It seems that Carmarthen separately got into trouble with a certain Mrs. Morton, which resulted in a hearing in the House of Commons, 12 July 1712, Ibid.

14 Ibid., Duke of Leeds, Diary, 13 July 1710.

15 Johnson, pp.25–26.

16 Examination of William Bishop, 15 October 1696, f. 18, HCA 1/53, PRO.

17 Ibid; Narrative of Philip Middleton, 4 August 1696, f. 114, CO 323/2; Examination of Philip Middleton, 21 November 1699, f. 70 ff., HCA 1/53; PRO. Philip Middleton was around 15 years old when examined, so aged about 13 or 14 during the voyage.

18 Narrative of Philip Middleton, 4 August 1696, f. 114, CO 323/2; Examination of John Dann, 3 August 1696, ff. 250–256, CO 323/2; PRO. Other sources for the story include Examination of David Evans, 27 June 1696, f. 28, HCA 1/53; Examination of William Bishop, 15 October 1696, f. 18, HCA 1/53; Examination of John Dann, 8 September 1696; f. 10, HCA 1/53; Examination of Philip Middleton, 21 November 1696, f. 70, HCA 1/53; PRO.

19 Narrative of Philip Middleton, 4 August 1696, f. 114, CO 323/2; Examination of John Dann, 3 August 1696, ff. 250–256, CO 323/2; PRO. Johnson, pp.32–33.

20 Joel Baer, *Pirates of the British Isles*, Tempus Publishing, Stroud, 2005, p.125. Zacks, *The Pirate Hunter*, p.151. For opposite interpretations of Kidd, see Robert Ritchie, *Captain Kidd and the War against the Pirates*, Cambridge, Mass:, 1986, and Zacks, *The Pirate Hunter*. Ritchie sees Kidd as a pirate, Zacks sees Kidd as innocent. On Kidd as a severe captain, Thomas Pattle, chief factor at Karwar, cited in Charles Grey, *Pirates of the Eastern Seas*, ed. Sir George MacMunn, Kennikat Press, Port Washington and New York (1933), 1971, p.199.

21 Zacks, *The Pirate Hunter*, p.361.

22 Colonel Quarry, Philadelphia, 6 March 1699, f. 130; Captain Giles Shelley, f.132; Bartholomew Gracedieu to Lords Commissioners, received 7 May 1700, f. 158; Bartholomew Gracedieu, 9 May 1700, f. 162; CO 323/3, PRO.

23 King in Council, 20 June 1700, f. 205, CO 323/3, PRO.

24 Johnson, chapter on England, and p.88. There is confusion over Taylor's first name – most books list him as John Taylor, but it is clear that his name was actually Richard Taylor, see deposition of Richard Moore, 31 October 1724, HCA 1/55, PRO; and Captain Laws to Duke of Portland, 24 April 1723, f. 314, CO 137/14, Part 2, PRO.

25 Johnson, pp.84–89.

26 Ibid, p.99.

27 Clem Downing, deposition, 28 October 1724; supported by the deposition of Richard Moore, 31 October 1724; HCA 1/55, PRO.

28 Earle, *Pirate Wars*, p.125. Duke of Portland to Lords Commissioners, 25 July 1723, and further discussion in ff. 269 and 272, CO 137/14, Part 2, PRO.

29 Richard Moore, deposition, 31 October 1724, HCA 1/55, PRO. 'Petition of the Pirates', 10 April 1723, f.314; Captain Laws to Duke of Portland, 24 April 1723; Pirates second petition, 26 April 1723, f. 316; Captain Laws to Duke of Portland, 14 May 1723, f. 317; Duke of Portland, 21 May 1723, to Captain Laws, f. 317; Pirates to Captain Laws, 14 May 1723, f. 319, CO 137/14, Part 2, PRO.

30 Duke of Portland to Lords Commissioners, 4 March 1723/4. f. 280; Captain Laws to Portland, 4 June 1723, f. 317; Pirates to Captain Laws, 14 May 1723, f. 317; CO 137/14, Part 2, PRO.

31 Earle, *Pirate Wars*, pp.125–126; Johnson, p.102; Duke of Portland to Lord Cartaret, 24 July 1723, f. 221, and Governor of Panama, J.G. Badillo, to Portland, 5 October 1723, CO 137/14, Part 2, PRO. Charles Grey, *Pirates of the Eastern Seas*, pp.301, 314, argues that Johnson makes some errors in this story.

32 Johnson, p.99–100; Zacks, *The Pirate Hunter*, pp.292–293; Botting, *The Pirates*, Time Life Books, Alexandria, Virginia, 1978, pp.76–77; Clement Downing, *A History of the Indian Wars*, 1737, ed. and Introduction by William Foster, Oxford University Press, 1924, pp.97–104; Charles Collins, deposition, 15 October 1724, f. 75; HCA 1/55, PRO. Conden's name has also been spelt in other ways.

33 J. Andrew, deposition, 1724, f. 94, HCA 1/55, PRO.

34 Gosse, *The History of Piracy*, p.241. Information from various depositions: Charles Collins, 15 October 1724, f. 77; James Holmes, 1724, ff. 81–82; James Duffie, 1724, f. 87; Alex Farquharson, 22 October 1724, f. 90; HCA 1/55, PRO. It seems that the native taken aboard was dropped off at the Cape of Good Hope, along with two native boys, whether by choice or not is unclear.

35 Clement Downing, *A History of the Indian Wars*, pp.105–122. On 1730 as the last of the pirates, see Charles Grey, *Pirates of the Eastern Seas*, p.53. It is curious that Plantain called his location 'Ranter' Bay, since the Ranters were a radical religious and political sect of the Puritan revolution in England in the 1640s – the name may indicate Plantain's political views.

CHAPTER 7: DEATH TO THE PIRATES

1 Marcus Rediker, *Villains of All Nations: Atlantic Pirates in the Golden Age*, Beacon Press, Boston, 2004, p.127; Earle, *The Pirate Wars*, Methuen, London, 2004, pp.162, 207.

2 Johnson, p.60.

3 Ibid, pp.59–60.

4 Ibid, p.61.

5 Ibid, p.46. Is it possible, given Teach/Blackbeard's comparative literacy, and command abilities, that Teach refers to Blackbeard's original profession as teacher? Another name mentioned was 'Titche'.

6 Angus Konstam, *Blackbeard: America's Most Notorious Pirate*, Wiley, Hoboken, New Jersey, 2006, chapter 3.

7 Ibid, pp.157, 91.

8 Ibid, pp.127–130.

9 Ibid, chapters 5 and 7.

10 Johnson, p.55.

11 Konstam, *Blackbeard*, pp.256–257; Johnson, p.57.

12 Konstam, *Blackbeard*, pp.270–274.

13 See Earle, *The Pirate Wars*, p.173 on the functions of the quartermaster.

14 Johnson, pp.107–108; Deposition by Hosea Tisdell, 18 January 1720, St. Jago de la Vega, Jamaica, p.24, CO 137/14, PRO.

15 Konstam, *Blackbeard*, pp.119–120; Johnson, chapters on Read and Bonny.

16 Konstam, *Blackbeard*, pp.120–122; 'The Tryals of John Rackam and other Pirates', 17 and 28 November 1720, St Jago de la Vega, Jamaica, pp.12–19, CO 137/14, PRO.

17 'The Tryals of John Rackam and other Pirates', 28 November 1720, St Jago de la Vega, p.18, CO 137/14, PRO. On cross dressing, see Rediker, *Villains of All Nations: Atlantic Pirates in the Golden Age*, Beacon Press, Boston, 2004, chapter 6.

18 'The Tryals of John Rackam and other Pirates', 28 November 1720, St Jago de la Vega, Jamaica, pp.18–19, CO 137/14, PRO; Johnson, pp.123–124.

19 Johnson, p.131; Aubrey Burl, *Black Barty: Bartholomew Roberts and his Pirate Crew, 1718–1723* (1997), Sutton Publishing, Stroud, 2005, p.149.

20 Johnson, pp.180, 183. Johnson devotes almost a third of his first volume to Roberts' life, and knew a great deal about Roberts. For an over-view of Roberts generally, see Aubrey Burl, *Black Barty*.

21 Burl, *Black Barty*, p.51, claims that Roberts was third mate of the *Princess*, while Johnson has Roberts as second mate, Johnson, p.161, and for Roberts' quoted attitude, Johnson, pp.213–214. Roberts' frequent drinking of toasts suggests that he was not quite a teetotaler. Similar sentiments on the difficulties of promotion come from the sailor Edward Barlow, in his journal, Basil Lubbock, ed. *Barlow's Journal of His Life at Sea*, 2 vols., Hurst and Blackett, London, 1934.

22 Johnson, p.160.

23 Ibid, pp.171 ff.

24 Ibid, p.173; Burl, *Black Barty*, pp.73 ff.

25 Johnson, pp.173 ff.

26 Ibid., pp.186 ff.

27 Ibid., pp.190 ff.

28 Ibid, pp.192–193.

29 Ibid, pp.194–195.

30 Ibid, pp.200–201.

31 Ibid, pp.208–209. Captain Ogle to the Admiralty, 5 April 1722, ADM 1/2242, 1714–1731, Letter O, PRO.

32 Johnson, pp.211–213; Ogle to Admiralty, 5 April 1721, op cit.

33 Johnson, pp.209, 214; Mungo Herdman to Admiralty, 6 August 1723, ADM 1/1880, Letter H, PRO; John Atkins, *A Voyage to Guinea, Brazil and the West Indies*, (1735), Cass, London, 1970, pp.139, 192, 263.

34 Johnson, pp.216–217; Ogle to Admiralty, 5 April 1722, and 8 September 1722, ADM 1/2242, 1714–1731, Letter O, PRO.

35 Atkins, *A Voyage to Guinea, Brazil and the West Indies*, pp.193 ff; Ogle to Admiralty, 14 March 1726, ADM 1/2242, 1714–1731, Letter O, PRO; Burl, *Black Barty*, p.260.

36 Johnson, pp.255–259; Ogle to Admiralty, 26 July 1722, 1714–1731, ADM 1/2242, Letter O, PRO.

37 Archibald Hamilton to Admiralty, 1723, 1720–1724, Letter H; Barrow Harris to Admiralty, 14 October 1723, 1719–1725, Letter H; ADM 1/1880, PRO. The Cork pirate ship was named *The Old Noll*, deposition 6 August 1748, 1736–1749, ff. 108 ff, HCA 1/57, PRO.

38 Robert Harris, affidavit and deposition, 13 August 1722, ADM 1/2096, PRO.

39 Lord Muskerry to the Lords of the Admiralty, 7 December 1722, ADM 1/2096, PRO.

CHAPTER 8: THE BARBARY CORSAIRS OF NORTH AFRICA

1 Jacques Heers, *The Barbary Corsairs: Warfare in the Mediterranean, 1480–1580*, (2001), translated by J. North, Greenhill Books, London, and Stackpole Books, Pennsylvania, 2003, pp.61–66.

2 Ibid, p.86.

3 Ibid, pp.87–89.

4 Ibid, p.90.

5 Robert C. Davis, *Christian Slaves, Muslim Masters: White Slavery in the Mediterranean, the Barbary Coast, and Italy, 1500–1800*, Palgrave, Macmillan, London, 2004 pp.13–25.

6 Curthio Mattei, surgeon of Lenola, Italy, referring to a raid of 4 July 1623, cited in Davis, Ibid, p.39.

7 Davis, Ibid, pp.43–45; Ellen Friedman, *Spanish Captives in North Africa in the Early Modern Age*, University of Wisconsin, Madison, 1983, chapter 2 and Conclusion.

8 Cited in Davis, *Christian Slaves, Muslim Masters*, pp.47–48, 53.

9 Ibid, p.52.

10 Narrative of Richard Hasleton, cited in Daniel J. Vitkus, ed., *Piracy, Slavery and Redemption: Barbary Captive Narratives from Early Modern England*, Columbia University Press, New York, 2001, p.75.

11 Davis, *Christian Slaves, Muslim Masters*, p.51.

12 Ibid, p.53. A more favourable view of corsair behaviour comes from Peter Earle, *Corsairs of Malta and Barbary*, Sidgwick and Jackson, London, 1970, pp.64–65.

13 Narrative of Joseph Pitts, cited in Vitkus, *Piracy, Slavery and Redemption*, pp.228–229.

14 Davis, *Christian Slaves, Muslim Masters*, p.83.

15 Ibid, p.127.

16 Poem, 1624, cited in Vitkus, ed., *Piracy, Slavery, and Redemption*, p.346.

17 Davis, *Christian Slaves, Muslim Masters*, pp.75–82, 129.

18 Heers, *Barbary Corsairs*, pp.212–213.

19 Davis, *Christian Slaves, Muslim Masters*, p.163.

20 Earle, *Corsairs of Malta and Barbary*, p.90.

21 Cited in Davis, *Christian Slaves, Muslim Masters*, p.187

22 Heers, *Barbary Corsairs*, p.204.

23 The story of Pellow's escape is taken from Giles Milton, *White Gold: The Extraordinary Story of Thomas Pellow and North Africa's One Million European Slaves*, Hodder and Stoughton, London, 2004, chapters 10 and 12, and p.255 for Pellow as physician.

24 George Penticost and John Butler, 'A true relation of an Escape made out of Algier the fourth day of July 1640 out of the hands of the cruell Turks...' ms. 3317, BL.

25 W.H. Lewis, *The Splendid Century: Life in the France of Louis XIV*, Waveland, Prospect Heights, Illinois, 1997, p.114.

26 Desmond Seward, *The Monks of War: the Military Religious Orders*, (1972), Penguin edition London, 1995, chapter 15.

27 Earle, *Corsairs of Malta and Barbary*, chapters 6 and 7.

28 Ibid, pp.152–153, and chapter 8.

29 Ibid, p.270; Seward, *Monks of War*, p.310–311.

30 Cited in Milton, *White Gold*, p.275

31 Peter Earle, *Corsairs of Malta and Barbary*, London, 1970, pp.92–3; Linda Colley, *Captives: Britain, Empire and the World*, Pimlico, London, 2003, p.62; Christopher Lloyd, *English Corsairs on the Barbary Coast*, Collins, London, 1981, pp.28, 31; Peter Wilson, *Pirate Utopias: Moorish Corsairs and European Renegades*, Autonomedia, New York, 1995, 2003, p.40.

32 W. Onley, 'The Famous Sea-Fight between Captain Ward and the *Rainbow*', ballad, London, 1680.

33 Cited in Rogozinski, *Dictionary of Pirates*, entry for Ward.

34 Jacques Heers, *The Barbary Corsairs*, pp.226–7, 149; Robert Davis, *Christian Slaves, Muslim Masters*, pp.42–3.

35 Heers, p.162.

36 Milton, *White Gold*, pp.81–2.

37 Joseph Pitts, 'A True and Faithful Account of the Religion and Manners of the Mahommetans ...'(1704), in Vitkus, ed, *Piracy, Slavery, and Redemption*, pp.311–312.

38 Ibid, p.313.

39 C.R. Pennell, ed., *Piracy and Diplomacy in Seventeenth Century North Africa: the Journal of Thomas Baker, English Consul in Tripoli, 1677–1685*, Cranbury, New Jersey, 1989, pp.126, 133–4, 141, 132, 161.

40 Davis, *Christian Slaves, Muslim Masters*, pp.125–127; Wilson, *Pirate Utopias*, pp.184–5.

41 Pennel, ed., *Piracy and Diplomacy*, pp.141–2.

42 On Peter Lyle/Lisle, Seton Dearden, *A Nest of Corsairs: the Fighting Karamanlis of Tripoli*, London, 1976, p.134.

CHAPTER 9: PIRATES OF THE EASTERN SEAS

1 Kwan-wai So, *Japanese Piracy in Ming China during the Sixteenth Century*, Michigan State University Press, East Lansing, 1975, passim; Philip Gosse, *The History of Piracy*, (1932), Rio Grande Press, Glorieta, New Mexico, 1995, p.265; Peter Lorge, 'Water Forces and Naval Operations', in David Graff and Robin Higham, eds., *A Military History of China*, Westview Press, Boulder, Colorado, 2002, pp.92–94.

2 Ray Huang, *1587, A Year of No Significance: the Ming Dynasty in Decline*, Yale University Press, New Haven, Connecticut, 1981, chapter on Ch'i Chi-Kuang. Chi-Kuang, also transliterated as Qi Jianguang (1528–1588), wrote two lengthy military manuals, and went on to defend the northern border of China against the nomads.

3 Peter Lorge, 'Water Forces and Naval Operations', in *A Military History of China*, p.93; A.G. Course, *Pirates of the Eastern Seas*, Muller, London, 1966, pp.130–132

4 Course, *Pirates of the Eastern Seas*, p.134; Peter Lorge, 'Water Forces and Naval Operations', in *A Military History of China*, p.94.

5 Dian Murray, *Pirates of the South China Coast, 1790–1810*, Stanford University Press, Stanford, 1987, chapters 2 and 3.

6 Ibid, p.78, for homosexual quote, and chapters 4 and 5 for information in this paragraph. China has a long tradition of female warriors, and this cultural trait probably led to the prevalence of female pirates and women onboard the pirate junks, Ibid, footnote 76, p.198.

7 Ibid for Chang Pao; Cordingly and Falconer, *Pirates Fact and Fiction*, Collins and Brown, London, p.108, for story by Turner. This episode reminds the reader of L'Olonnais.

8 Murray, *Pirates of the South China Coast*, pp.127, 131.

9 Ibid, pp.63 ff.

10 Ibid, chapter 8.

11 Ibid, p.83 and chapter 5.

12 Ibid, p.64 and chapter 5.

13 Ibid, chapter 6.

14 Report of Commander Dalrymple Hay, *China Mail*, 1 November 1849; Cordingly and Falconer, *Pirates Fact and Fiction*, pp.112–113, 117; Gosse, *The History of Piracy*, pp.281–282; Rogozinski, *Dictionary of Pirates*, entry for Chui Apoo.

15 Basil Lubbock, ed., *Barlow's Journal of His Life at Sea*, 2 vols:, Hurst and Blackett, London, 1934, vol. 2, pp.380–381, 486. Manohar Malgonkar, *Kanhoji Angrey, Maratha Admiral*, Asia Publishing House, London, 1959, p.132, and passim.

16 Malgonkar, *Kanhoji Angrey*, chapter 27.

17 Ibid, chapter 28. For Mr and Mrs Gifford, Clement Downing, *A History of the Indian Wars*, 1737, ed. William Foster, Oxford University Press, London, 1924, pp.41–42. Gosse, *The History of Piracy*, pp.236–237.

18 Malgonkar, *Kanhoji Angrey*, chapter 42; Gosse, *The History of Piracy*, p.246; Downing, *A History of the Indian Wars*, pp.38, 56–57. It seems that the crew of one of Matthews's ships, the *Exeter*, was much given to drunkenness, Peter Earle, *The Pirate Wars*, Methuen, London, 2004, p.125.

19 Malgonkar, *Kanhoji Angrey*, pp.270, 120–124. Malgonkar gets the date of the capture of the *Derby* wrong by attributing this capture to Angrey in 1728, p.292. John Biddulph, *The Pirates of Malabar*, Smith Elder, London, 1907, chapter IX for Matthews, and chapter X for the *Derby*. Clement Downing, on the other hand, says the crew of the *Derby* fought bravely, *A History of the Indian Wars*, p.67.

20 Gosse, *The History of Piracy*, pp.248–249.

21 Ibid, pp.250–252.

22 Nicholas Tarling, *Piracy and Politics in the Malay World: A Study of British Imperialism in Nineteenth-Century South-East Asia*, F.W. Cheshire, Melbourne and Canberra, 1963, Introduction and passim. G.S. Graham, *Great Britain in the Indian Ocean, a study in maritime enterprise 1810–1850*, Clarendon Press, Oxford, 1967, chapters 3 and 6.

23 Harry Miller, *Pirates of the Far East*, Hale and Co., London, 1970, p.26. Possibly these were Balanini pirates.

24 Dampier, cited in Tarling, *Piracy and Politics*, p.10, as absolving the Malays from desiring robbery or piracy in 1689, but for the opposite case, see Diana and Michael Preston, *A Pirate of Exquisite Mind, Explorer, Naturalist, and Buccaneer: the Life of William Dampier*, Walker and Company, New York, 2004, pp.161–162.

25 Abdullah bin Abdul Kadir, Raffles's Malay teacher, cited in Harry Miller, *Pirates of the Far East*, p.36.

26 Harriette McDougall, *Sketches of Our Life at Sarawak*, SPCK, London, and E. and J.B.Young, New York,1882, chapter IV. Although McDougall obviously had a Christian missionary perspective, the details of Malay activities are valuable.

27 Tarling, *Piracy and Politics*, pp.23–26, 65, 111.

28 Cordingly and Falconer, *Pirates: Fact and Fiction*, pp.120–121.

29 Harriette McDougall, *Sketches of Our Life at Sarawak*, chapter XVI: 'Ilanun Pirates'.

30 Ibid, pp.211–212.

31 Ibid, p.214.

32 Ibid, pp.34–35.

33 Henry Keppel, *The Expedition to Borneo of HMS Dido for the Suppression of Piracy*, 1st edition 1846, 3rd edition 1847, new impression of 3rd edition, Frank Cass, 2 vols., London, 1968, vol 2, p.251.

34 Ibid, vol. 2, pp.48–53.

35 Ibid, pp.54–63. Keppel also gives a macabre account of how the Dyaks extracted the brains of the heads they had taken, not unlike the ancient Egyptian practice, pp.63–64.

36 McDougall, *Sketches of Our Life at Sarawak*, pp.37–39.

37 Cordingly and Falconer, *Pirates: Fact and Fiction*, pp.120–121; Tarling, *Piracy and Politics*, pp.135, 144. On Belcher, W. Senior, 'An Early Victorian Windfall', in *Sea Sequel*, Nonesuch and Random House, London and New York, 1935, p.327. It seems that Belcher's ship was only engaged with the pirates for 24 hours.

38 Charles Davies, *The Blood Red Arab Flag: An Investigation into Qasimi Piracy, 1797–1820*, Exeter University Press, Exeter, 1997, p.105.

39 Ibid, pp.228–230.

40 Ibid, pp.112–113.

41 Ibid, pp.268–269.

CHAPTER 10: THE ROAD TO MODERN PIRACY

1 Conditions leading to piracy in the Mediterranean are explained in Lt. Commander C.G. Pitcairn Jones, ed., *Piracy in the Levant, 1827–1828: selected from the papers of Admiral Sir Edward Codrington, KCB*, Navy Records Society, London, 1934, pp.vii–xxxiii.

2 J.S. Buckingham, 'Pirates in the Adriatic', 1812, in *Sea Sequel*, Nonesuch Press and Random House, London and New York, 1935, pp.322–325.

3 Pitcairn Jones, ed., *Piracy in the Levant*, pp.99–100.

4 Ibid, pp.141–146.

5 Information on the Laffites from William C. Davis, *The Pirates Laffite: the Treacherous World of the Corsairs of the Gulf*, Harcourt Brace, Orlando, 2005., passim.

6 Ibid, pp.233 ff., 325 ff., 397 ff., 437, 445 ff.

7 Ibid, p.445 ff.

8 Douglas Botting, *The Pirates*, Time Life Books, Alexandria, Virginia, 1978, pp.178–181; Robert Downie, *The Way of the Pirate*, (1998), ibooks inc., New York, 2005, pp.99–100.

9 Peter Earle, *The Pirate Wars*, Methuen, London, 2004, p.245; Botting, *The Pirates*, p.184; Rogozinski, *Dictionary of Pirates*, entry for de Soto.

10 Narrative of John Battis, from Ralph D. Paine, *Ships and Sailors of Old Salem*, Lauriat and Co., Boston, 1923, cited in Gosse, *The History of Piracy*, pp.217 ff.

11 Ibid, pp.219 ff.

12 Ibid, pp.221–223.

13 A.G. Course, *Pirates of the Eastern Seas*, Muller, London, 1966, pp.173–178.

14 Ibid, pp.200–204.

15 Ibid, pp.219–227.

16 Aleko Lillius, *I Sailed With Chinese Pirates*, Arrowsmith, London, 1930, pp.38–57. See also 'Bok', *Corsairs of the China Seas*, Herbert Jenkins, London, 1936, Foreword.

17 I am indebted for the information in this paragraph to a paper by Robert Forsyth, 'Modern Piracy', University of Victoria, December 2006, citing articles from various newspapers and journals, especially Agence France-Presse.

18 Ibid.

19 John S. Burnett, *Dangerous Waters: Modern Piracy and Terror on the High Seas*, Dutton, New York and London, 2002, p.182.

20 Ibid, pp 226–233.

21 Ibid, pp.224–225.

22 Forsyth, op cit.; Burnett, *Dangerous Waters*, pp.167, 275–280.

23 Burnett, *Dangerous Waters*, p.6.

24 This web site, 'Yacht Piracy', is maintained by Klaus Hympendahl, in Germany. The International Maritime Bureau (IMB) web site reports pirate attacks weekly. As pointed out, the IMB only tracks attacks on commercial vessels, but even here it is likely that some commercial ship owners do not report pirate attacks for various reasons, including insurance premiums.

EPILOGUE

1 Clement Downing, *A History of the Indian Wars*, (1737), edited and introduction by William Foster, Oxford University Press, London, 1924, p.87. The pirate redistribution argument is stressed by Peregrine Horden and Nicholas Purcell, *The Corrupting Sea: A Study of Mediterranean History*, Blackwell, Oxford, 2000, pp.156 ff.

2 David Starkey, 'Pirates and Markets', in C.R. Pennell, ed., *Bandits at Sea: A Pirates Reader*, New York University Press, New York and London, 2001, pp.113–114.

3 This general argument derives from Kai Erickson, *Wayward Puritans: A Study in the Sociology of Deviance*, Wiley, New York, 1969.

Bibliography

PRIMARY SOURCES, MANUSCRIPT

British Library, London
'Account of the capture of an English crew by the natives of Magadoxa … [in] 1700', Ms. 2992.

Anonymous, 'Journal of our Intended Voyage', Ms, 2752.

Carmarthen, 'Duke of Leeds Papers', Add: Ms. 28041.

Cowley, William, 'Journal of the Voyage of W.A. Cowley from Cape Virginia to the Cape de Verd Isles, to China, Java, Cape of Good Hope, and Holland, 1683–1686', Ms. 54 or 1050.

Cox, John, 'John Cox his Travills over the Land into the So. Seas: from thence Round the South parte of America to Berbados and Antegos, 1680–1681', Ms. 49.

Hack, William, 'Sharp's South Sea Waggoner', Ms. 47.

'Journal of a Voyage from Santo Domingo to wreck of Spanish vessel off Porto Plato', 1686–1687, Ms. 50 or 1070.

'Miscellaneous Papers relating to the affairs of Tangier, from May 1671 to May 1674', Ms. 3511.

Penticost, George, and Butler, John, 'A true relation of an Escape made out of Algier the fourth day of July 1640 out of the hands of the cruell Turks…' Ms. 3317.

Sharp, Bartholomew, 'A Journal kept by Bartholomew Sharp of passages in going over land to the South Seas from the island called the Golden Island in April 1680 as followeth', 1680–1682, Ms. 46 A and 46 B.

Sharp, Bartholomew, 'Voyage from Jamaica to Porto Bello', Ms, 2752.

Strong, John, 'Journal of his Voyage to the Straits of Magellan and the South Seas on the *Welfare*', 1689–1690, Ms. 3295.

Whitehead, John, 'His relation of Barbary, 1691', Ms. 90.

National Maritime Museum, Greenwich, London
Philip Gosse Papers.

Public Record Office, London:
Admiralty Files

Colonial Office Files

High Court of Admiralty Files

PRIMARY SOURCES, PRINTED

Arrian, *The Campaigns of Alexander*, translated by Aubrey de Selincourt (Penguin, Harmondsworth, 1971).

Atkins, John, *A Voyage to Guinea, Brazil and the West Indies*, (1735) (Cass, London, 1970).

Barker, Andrew, *Newes from Sea, Of two notorious Pyrates Ward the Englishman and Danseker the Dutchman. With a true relation of the most pinacies by them committed unto the sixt of Aprill* (N. Butter, London, 1609).

Boccaccio, Giovanni, *The Decameron*, (1351–1353) (Dell Publishing, New York, 1962).

Codrington, Admiral Sir Edward, in Lt. Commander C.G. Pitcairn Jones, ed., *Piracy in the Levant 1827–1828: selected from the papers of Admiral Sir Edward Codrington, KCB* (Navy Records Society, London, 1934).

Defoe, Daniel, *The King of Pirates: being an account of the Famous Enterprises of Captain Avery, the Mock King of Madagascar* (London, 1720).

Diodorus, *History of Diodorus of Sicily*, translated by Russell Geer (William Heinemann, London, and Harvard University Press, Cambridge, Mass., 1933).

Downing, Clement, *A History of the Indian Wars*, (1737), edited and introduction by William Foster (Oxford University Press, London, 1924).

Drury, Robert, *Madagascar; or Robert Drury's Journal, during fifteen years' captivity on that island*, (1729) (ed. Captain Oliver, London, 1890).

Esquemeling, *The Buccaneers of America*, (1678–1684), edited by William Stallybrass (Routledge, London, and E.P. Dutton, New York, 1923).

Herodotus, *The History: Herodotus*, translated by David Grene (University of Chicago Press, Chicago, 1987).

Johnson, Captain Charles, *A General History of the Robberies and Murders of the Most Notorious Pirates*, (1724) introduction by David Cordingly (Lyons Press, Guilford, Connecticut, and Conway Maritime Press, London, 1998, 2002).

Johnson, Captain Charles, *The History of the Lives and Bloody Exploits of the Most Noted Pirates*, (1724) (Lyons Press, Guilford, Connecticut, 2004).

Johnson, Captain Charles, *A General History of the Robberies and Murders of the most notorious Pirates: from their first rise and settlement in the island of Providence to the present year*, (1724) edited by Arthur Hayward, fourth edition, 1726 (Dodd, Mead and Company, New York, 1926).

Keppel, Henry, *The Expedition to Borneo of HMS Dido for the Suppression of Piracy*, (1846), 2 vols., new impression of 3rd edition of 1847 (Frank Cass, London, 1968).

Lithgow, William, *The Rare Adventures and Painful Peregrinations of William Lithgow*, (1632), edited by Gilbert Phelps (London, 1974).

Lubbock, Basil, ed., [Edward] *Barlow's Journal of His Life at Sea in King's Ships, East and West Indiamen, and other Merchantmen from 1659–1703*, 2 vols., (Hurst and Blackett, London, 1934).

McDougall, Harriette, *Sketches of Our Life at Sarawak* (SPCK, London, and E. and J.B. Young, New York, 1882).

Mainwaring, Sir Henry, 'Of the Beginnings, Practices, and Suppression of Pirates', (1618), in G.E. Manwaring and W.G. Perrin, eds., *The Life and Works of Sir Henry Mainwaring*, vol. 2 (Navy Records Society, LVI, London, 1922).

Onley, W., 'The Famous Sea-Fight between Captain Ward and the Rainbow' (Ballad, London, 1680).

Pelsaert, Francisco, *The Unlucky Voyage of the Ship Batavia*, (1647) (Amsterdam, 1994).

Pennel, C.R., ed., *Piracy and Diplomacy in Seventeenth Century North Africa: the Journal of Thomas Baker, English Consul in Tripoli, 1677–1685* (Associated University Presses, Cranbury, New Jersey, 1989).

Quintus Curtius Rufus, *The History of Alexander*, translated by John Yardley (Penguin, Harmondsworth, 1984).

Stevenson, Robert Louis, *Treasure Island*, 1883.

Vitkus, Daniel J., *Piracy, Slavery and Redemption: Barbary Captivity Narratives from Early Modern England* (Columbia University Press, New York, 2001).

Woodes Rogers, *A Cruising Voyage Round the World*, (1712) (Dover, New York, 1970).

SECONDARY SOURCES, PRINTED

Abulafia, David, ed., *The Mediterranean in History* (Thames and Hudson, London, 2003).

Antony, Robert J., *Pirates in the Age of Sail* (W.W. Norton, New York and London, 2007).

Baer, Joel, *Pirates of the British Isles* (Tempus Publishing, Stroud, 2005).

Barnby, H.G., *The Prisoners of Algiers: an account of the forgotten American-Algerian War, 1785–1797* (Oxford University Press, London, 1966).

Bawlf, Samuel, *The Secret Voyage of Sir Francis Drake, 1577–1580*, (2003) (Douglas and McIntyre, Vancouver, 2004).

Biddulph, John, *The Pirates of Malabar* (Smith Elder, London, 1907).

Black, Clinton, *Pirates of the West Indies* (Cambridge University Press, Cambridge, 1989).

'Bok', *Corsairs of the China Seas* (Herbert Jenkins, London, 1936).

Botting, Douglas, *The Pirates* (Time Life Books, Alexandria, Virginia, 1978).

Burl, Aubrey, *Black Barty: Bartholomew Roberts and his Pirate Crew, 1718–1723*, (1997) (Sutton Publishing, Stroud, 2006).

Bourne, Joel K., 'Blackbeard Lives', National Geographic, July 2006, pp. 146–161.

Bradford, Ernle, *Mediterranean: Portrait of a Sea* (Hodder and Stoughton, London, 1971).

Brand, Charles, *Byzantium Confronts the West, 1180–1204* (Harvard University Press, Cambridge, Mass., 1968).

Brondsted, Johannes, *The Vikings*, (1960), translated by K. Skov (Penguin, London, 1965).

Browning, Andrew, *Thomas Osborne, Earl of Danby and Duke of Leeds, 1632–1712*, 3 vols. (Jackson, Son and Co, Glasgow, 1951).

Brule, Pierre, *La Piraterie Cretoise Hellenestique*, Les Belles Lettres, Paris, 1978.

Burg, B.R., *Sodomy and the Perception of Evil: English Sea Rovers in the Seventeenth Century Caribbean* (New York University Press, New York, 1983).

Burl, Aubrey, *Black Barty: Bartholomew Roberts and his Pirate Crew, 1718–1723*, (1997) (Sutton Publishing, Stroud, 2005).

Burnett, John S., *Dangerous Waters: Modern Piracy and Terror on the High Seas* (Dutton, New York and London, 2002).

Burns, Robert, 'Piracy as an Islamic-Christian Interface in the Thirteenth Century', Viator, vol. 11, 1980, pp. 165–178.

Cawthorne, Nigel, *A History of Pirates: Blood and Thunder on the High Seas* (Arcturus Publishing, Toronto, 2004).

Clifford, Barry, *The Lost Fleet: The Discovery of a Sunken Armada from the Golden Age of Piracy*, (2002) (HarperCollins, New York, 2003).

Clifford, Barry, *Return to Treasure Island and the Search for Captain Kidd*, (2003) (HarperCollins, New York, 2004).

Clutton, E. and Kenny, A., *Crete* (David and Charles, Newton Abbot, 1976).

Colley, Linda, *Captives: Britain, Empire and the World, 1600–1850*, (2002) (Pimlico, Random House, London, 2003).

Cordingly, David, *Under the Black Flag: The Romance And The Reality of Life Among The Pirates*, (1996) (Random House, New York, 2006).

Cordingly, David, and Falconer, John, *Pirates: Fact and Fiction* (Collins and Brown, London, 1992).

Course, Captain A.G., *Pirates of the Eastern Seas* (Frederick Muller, London, 1966).

Davies, Charles, *The Blood Red Arab Flag: An Investigation into Qasimi Piracy, 1797–1820* (Exeter University Press, Exeter, 1997).

Davis, Robert C., *Christian Slaves, Muslim Masters: White Slavery in the Mediterranean, the Barbary Coast, and Italy, 1500–1800*, (2003) (Palgrave, Macmillan, Basingstoke and New York, 2004).

Davis, William C., *The Pirates Laffite: The Treacherous World of the Corsairs of the Gulf* (Harcourt Brace, Orlando, 2005).

De Souza, Philip, *Piracy in the Graeco-Roman World* (Cambridge University Press, Cambridge, 1999).

Dearden, Seton, *A Nest of Corsairs: the Fighting Karamanlis of Tripoli* (London, 1976).

Dollinger, Phillipe, *The German Hansa*, translated and edited by D.S. Ault and S.H. Steinberg (Stanford University Press, Stanford, 1970).

Downie, *The Way of the Pirate*, (1998) (ibooks, New York, 2005).

Drake-Brockman, Henrietta, *Voyage to Disaster: the Life of Francisco Pelsaert* (Angus and Robertson, Sydney, 1963).

Earle, Peter, *Corsairs of Malta and Barbary* (London, 1970).

Earle, Peter, *The Sack of Panama* (Bury St Edmunds Press, Suffolk, London, 1981).

Earle, Peter, *The Pirate Wars*, (2003) (Methuen, London, 2004).

Elting, John R., *Swords Around A Throne: Napoleon's Grande Armée* (Free Press, New York and London, 1988).

Epstein, Steven, *Genoa and the Genoese, 958–1528* (University of North Carolina Press, Chapel Hill, 1996).

Erickson, Kai, *Wayward Puritans: A Study in the Sociology of Deviance*, Wiley, New York, 1969.

Fahmy, Aly Mohamed, *Muslim Sea-Power in the Eastern Mediterranean from the Seventh to the Tenth Century* AD (National Publication and Printing House, Cairo, 1966).

Ford, David Nash, *Royal Berkshire History* (Nash Ford Publishing, Finchampstead, Berkshire, 2005).

Forsyth, Robert, 'Modern Piracy', University of Victoria, 15 pp., December 2004.

Fotheringham, J.K., 'Genoa and the Fourth Crusade', English Historical Review, vol. 25, pp. 26–57.

Friedman, Ellen, *Spanish Captives in North Africa in the Early Modern Age* (University of Wisconsin Press, Madison, Wisconsin, 1983).

Gatrell, V.A.C., *The Hanging Tree: execution and the English People, 1770–1868* (Oxford University Press, Oxford and New York, 1994).

Glete, Jan, *Warfare At Sea, 1500–1650: Maritime Conflicts and the Transformation of Europe* (Routledge, London, 2000).

Gosse, Philip, *The History of Piracy*, (1932) (Rio Grande Press, Glorieta, New Mexico, 1995).

Graff, David A. and Higham, Robin, eds., *A Military History of China* (Westview Press, Cambridge, Mass., 2002).

Graham, G.S., *Great Britain in the Indian Ocean, a study in maritime enterprise, 1810–1850* (Clarendon Press, Oxford, 1967).

Grey, Charles, *Pirates of the Eastern Seas, 1618–1723*, (1933), edited by Sir George MacMunn (Kennikat Press, Port Washington and London, 1971).

Guilmartin, John Francis, *Gunpowder and Galleys: Changing Technology and Mediterranean Warfare at Sea in the Sixteenth Century* (Cambridge University Press, Cambridge, 1974).

Haywood, John, *Dark Age Naval Power: a re-assessment of Frankish and Anglo-Saxon seafaring activity* (Routledge, London and New York, 1991).

Hazlewood, Nick, *The Queen's Slave Trader: John Hawkyns, Elizabeth I, and the Trafficking in Human Souls*, (2004) (HarperCollins, New York, 2005).

Heers, Jacques, *The Barbary Corsairs: Warfare in the Mediterranean, 1480–1580*, (2001), translated by Jonathan North (Greenhill Books, London, and Stackpole Books, Pennsylvania, 2003).

Horden, Peregrine, and Purcell, Nicholas, *The Corrupting Sea: A Study of Mediterranean History* (Blackwell, Oxford, 2000).

Huang, Ray, *1587, A Year of No Significance: The Ming Dynasty in Decline* (Yale University Press, New Haven, Connecticut, 1981).

Hudson, Benjamin, *Viking Pirates and Christian Princes: Dynasty, Religion, and Empire in the North Atlantic* (Oxford University Press, Oxford, 2005).

Hympendahl, Klaus, Internet web site 'Yacht Piracy'.

Kelsey, Harry, *Sir Francis Drake: the Queen's Pirate* (Yale University Press, New Haven and London, 1998).

Kelsey, Harry, *Sir John Hawkins: Queen Elizabeth's Slave Trader* (Yale University Press, New Haven and London, 2003).

Kemp, Peter K. and Lloyd, Christopher, *The Brethren of the Coast* (William Heinemann, London, 1960).

Kierman, Frank, and Fairbank, John, eds., *Chinese Ways in Warfare* (Harvard University Press, Cambridge, Mass., 1974).

Konstam, Angus, *Blackbeard: America's Most Notorious Pirate* (Wiley, Hoboken, New Jersey, 2006).

Lane, Frederic C., *Venice: A Maritime Republic* (Johns Hopkins, Baltimore and London, 1973).

Lane, Kris, *Pillaging the Empire: Piracy in the Americas, 1500–1750* (New York, 1998).

Lane-Poole, Stanley, *The Barbary Corsairs*, (1890) (Negro University Press, Westport, Connecticut, 1970).

Lewis, Archibald R. and Runyan, Timothy J., *European Naval and Maritime History, 300–1500*, (1985) (Indiana University Press, Bloomington, 1990).

Lewis, W.H., *The Splendid Century: Life in the France of Louis XIV* (Waveland, Prospect Heights, Illinois, 1997).

Lilius, Aleko E., *I Sailed With Chinese Pirates* (Appleton and Company, New York, 1931).

Lindsay, Philip, *The Great Buccaneer: being the life, death, and extraordinary adventures of Sir Henry Morgan, buccaneer and Lieutenant Governor of Jamaica* (P. Nevill, London and New York, 1950).

Llewellyn Smith, Michael, *The Great Island: A Study of Crete*, (1965) (Allen Lane, London, 1973).

Lloyd, Christopher, *English Corsairs on the Barbary Coast* (Collins, London, 1981).

London, Joshua E., *Victory in Tripoli: How America's War with the Barbary Pirates Established the U.S. Navy and Shaped a Nation* (Wiley, Hoboken, New Jersey, 2005).

Logan, F. Donald, *The Vikings in History* (Hutchinson, London, 1983).

Malgonkar, Manohar, *Kanhoji Angrey: Maratha Admiral* (Asia Publishing House, London, 1959).

Miller, Harry, *Pirates of the Far East* (Hale and Co, London, 1970).

Milton, Giles, *White Gold: The Extraordinary Story of Thomas Pellow and North Africa's One Million European Slaves* (Hodder and Stoughton, London, 2004).

Murray, Dian, *Pirates of the South China Coast, 1790–1810* (Stanford University Press, Stanford, 1987).

Ormerod, Henry A., *Piracy in the Ancient World: An Essay in Mediterranean History*, (1924) (Johns Hopkins, Baltimore, 1997).

Pennel, C.R. ed., *Bandits at Sea: A Pirates Reader* (New York University Press, New York, 2001).

Poolman, Kenneth, *The Speedwell Voyage: A Tale of Piracy and Mutiny in the Eighteenth Century*, (1999) (Berkley Publishing, New York, 2000).

Pope, Dudley, *Harry Morgan's Way* (Secker and Warburg, London, 1977).

Preston, Diana and Michael, *A Pirate of Exquisite Mind: Explorer, Naturalist, and Buccaneer: The Life of William Dampier* (Walker and Company, New York, 2004).

Pryor, John H., *Geography, technology and war: Studies in the maritime history of the Mediterranean, 649–1571* (Cambridge University Press, Cambridge, 1988).

Pyle, Howard, *Howard Pyle's Book of Pirates*, compiled by Merle Johnson (Harper and Brothers, New York and London, 1921).

Rediker, Marcus, *Between the Devil and the Deep Blue Sea: Merchant Seamen, Pirates, and the Anglo-American Maritime World, 1700–1750*, (1987) (Cambridge University Press, Cambridge, 1993).

Rediker, Marcus, *Villains of All Nations: Atlantic Pirates in the Golden Age* (Beacon Press, Boston, 2004).

Ritchie, Robert, *Captain Kidd and the War against the Pirates* (Harvard University Press, Cambridge, Mass., 1986).

Rodger, N.A.M., *The Wooden World: An Anatomy of the Georgian Navy* (Naval Institute Press, Maryland, 1986).

Rodriguez-Salgado, M. J., *Armada 1588–1988* (Penguin, London, 1988).

Roesdahl, Else, *The Vikings*, (1987) translated by S. Margeson and K. Williams (Penguin, London, 1992).

Rogers, William Ledyard, *Naval Warfare Under Oars, 4th to 16th Centuries: A Study of Strategy, Tactics and Design*, (1940) (Naval Institute Press, Annapolis, Maryland, 1977).

Rogozinski, Jan, *The Wordsworth Dictionary of Pirates*, (1995) (Wordsworth, Ware, Herts:, 1997).

Rose, Susan, *Medieval Naval Warfare, 1000–1500* (Routledge, London, 2002).

Rowley, Trevor, *The Normans*, (1999) (Tempus Publishing, Stroud, 2004).

Russell, Lord, *The French Corsairs* (Robert Hale, London, 1970).

Sandars, N.K., *The Sea Peoples: Warriors of the Ancient Mediterranean*, (1978), revised edition (Thames and Hudson, London, 1985).

Sawyer, P.H., *Kings and Vikings: Scandinavia and Europe, AD 700–1100* (Methuen, London and New York, 1982).

Sea Sequel To The Week-End Book (Nonsuch Press and Random House, London and New York, 1935).

Senior, C.M., *A Nation of Pirates: English Piracy in its heyday* (Newton Abbot and London, 1976).

Severin, Tim, *Seeking Robinson Crusoe* (Macmillan, London, 2002).

Seward, Desmond, *The Monks of War: The Military Religious Orders*, (1972) (Penguin, London, 1995).

Snelders, Stephen, *The Devil's Anarchy: The Sea Robberies of the Most Famous Pirate Claes G. Compaen, and the Very Remarkable Travels of Jan Erasmus Reyning, Buccaneer* (Autonomedia, New York, 2005).

So, Kwan-wai, *Japanese Piracy in Ming China during the Sixteenth Century* (University of Michigan Press, Michigan, 1975).

Starkey, David, *British Privateering Enterprise in the Eighteenth Century* (Exeter University Press, Exeter, 1990).

Starr, Chester, *The Influence of Sea Power on Ancient History* (Oxford University Press, New York and Oxford, 1989).

Strickland, Brad, and Fuller, Thomas E., *The Guns of Tortuga* (Simon and Schuster, New York, 2003).

Tarling, Nicholas, *Piracy and Politics in the Malay World: A Study of British Imperialism in Nineteenth Century South-East Asia* (F.W. Cheshire, Melbourne and Canberra, 1963).

Tenenti, Alberto, *Piracy and the Decline of Venice, 1580–1615*, (1961) (UCLA Press, Berkeley, 1967).

Turley, Hans, *Rum, Sodomy, and the Lash: Piracy, Sexuality and Masculine Identity* (New York University Press, New York, 1999).

Williams, Gomer, *History of the Liverpool Privateers and Letters of Marque with an account of the Liverpool Slave Trade*, (1897) (Augustus Kelly, New York, 1966).

Wilson, Peter, *Pirate Utopias: Moorish Corsairs and European Renegades*, (1995) (Autonomedia, New York, 2003).

Wood, Peter, *The Spanish Main* (Time Life Books, Alexandria, Virginia, 1979).

Zacks, Richard, *The Pirate Hunter: The True Story of Captain Kidd* (Hyperion, New York, 2002).

Index

Abu Hafs, 58
Alexander the Great, 52–53
Angria/Angrey, Kanhoji, 179, 245, 247–252
Angria/Angrey, Tolaji, 251–252
Anstis, Thomas, 8, 18–19, 29
Antigonus the One-Eyed, 53, 282
Aubin, Penelope, 167
Augur, John, 49
Aurangzeb, Moghul Emperor, 41, 170, 246
Avery, (Every) Henry/Bridgeman, John, 9, 22,
    33, 35, 41, 94, 145, 163–164, 166, 168–171,
    174, 246

Baker, Thomas, 232–234
Baldridge, Adam, 164, 177
Barbarossa, Aroudj, 206–207
Barbarossa, Kheir ed–Din, 206–208, 230
Barlow, Edward, 246
Barrie, J.M., 10
Bellamy, Samuel, 15–16, 36
Bellomont, Lord, Governor of Massachusetts, 34,
    48, 171–172
Blackbeard (Edward Teach), 9–10, 17, 28– 29, 33,
    35–36, 38, 49, 181–188
Boccaccio, Giovanni, 62–63
Boggs, Eli, 271–272
Bonnet, Stede, 184, 186
Bonny, or Bonn, Anne, 9, 24–25, 189–191
Brasiliano, Roche, 137–138, 140
Breholt, John, 166–168

Brihtnoth, 74–75
Brooke, Rajah James of Sarawak, 258–259
Brown, Holy Eleonora, 179
Buckingham, J.S., 264–265
Burnett, John, 278–279

Caesar, Black, 17, 187
Caesar, Julius, 54
Carmarthen, Marquis of, 168
Cervantes, Miguel de, 217, 220–221
Chang Pao, 240–243, 245
Ch'en Tien–Pao, 239
Cheng I, 241–242
Chi–Kuang, Ch'I, 236–237
Ching–Chi–Ling, 237
Ching Shi/Cheng I Sao, 240–243, 245
Chivers, Dirk/Derick, 164–165
Chui Apoo, 245
Clarke, Walter, 165
Clive, Robert, 251
Cockburn, Captain, 175, 178
Conden/Condent/Condon, Edmund, 33, 178
Cook, Captain John, 21, 151, 153
Cooke, Edmund, 26, 147
Cooke, Edward, 84
Cooke, Gerard, 247–248
Cooke, William, 26
Cornelisz, Jeronimus, 39–41
Cowley, William, 30, 145, 151–153, 155, 157–159,
    283

Cox, John, 145, 148–151
Coxon, Captain John, 145–148, 151
Cranston, John, 165
Culliford, Robert, 27, 38, 165, 172

Dampier, William, 21–22, 144–145, 150–151, 153–156, 158–159, 253
Dann, John, 171
Danziker/Danzer, Simon, also Simonson, 93
Davis, Edward, 151, 153–154, 157, 159
Davis, Howel, 16, 18, 28, 44, 45, 94, 192–193
De Pointis, Baron, 160–161
De Soto, Benito, 269
Defoe, Daniel, 9, 21–23
Demetrius, 53, 282
Diodorus, 53
Dick, King, 17, 179
Doughty, Thomas, 89
Downing, Clement, 35–36
Drake, Francis, 84–93, 146, 150–151, 176, 281–282
Du Casse, 159–161

Eaton, John, 21, 152–153, 155, 157–159
Egerton, Honorable Charles, 166–167
Elizabeth I, Queen of England, 25, 84, 86, 88, 91, 92
England, Edward, 49, 94, 173–174, 177
Esquemeling, Alexandre, 99, 137–138, 140–141, 143–145

Fletcher, Benjamin, 165

George of Antioch, 60
Gibbs, Charles, 268
Gibert, Pedro, 269, 271
Glasby, Harry, 32, 196
Green, John, 165
Guiscard, Roger, 60
Guiscard, Robert, 59–60
Guzman, de, Governor of Panama City, 141–142

Hands, Israel, 9, 182–183, 186, 188
Harris, Peter, 146–147
Harris, Robert, 201–204
Harvey/Chown/Gifford, Mrs., 248–249
Hawkins, John, 28, 43, 84–86, 281
Hayes, William "Bully", 272
Henszlein, Klein, 81
Hornigold, Benjamin, 184
Houblon, Sir James, 168

Ibn Fadlan, 70
Ibn Rustah, 70–71
Ismail, Moulay, 221

Jacobsz, Ariaen, 39–40
James, Commodore, 251, 258
James, John, 11, 16
James I, King of England, 92, 229
Janssen, Jan/Murat Rais, 206

Johnson, Captain Charles, 8–9, 14–16, 18–20, 26, 32, 38, 42–43, 48, 50, 171–174, 177, 182–185, 187–189, 191–194, 200–201
Jones, Cadwallader, 165
Jones, Thomas Lawrence, 18–19

Kennedy, Walter, 31, 44–45, 194–195
Keppel, Admiral Sir Henry, 255, 257–259
Kidd, William, 9–11, 31, 34–35, 48–49, 154, 171–173, 246, 283
Koxinga/Zheng Chenggong, 237–238, 241
Kuo P'o Tai, 242

La Buze/La Bouche, Olivier, 28, 175
Laffite, Jean, 11, 266–268
Laffite, Pierre, 266–268
Lai Choi San, 273–275
Laws, Captain, 176
Le Grand, Pierre, 99–100
Le Testu, 88
Le Vasseur, 100
Leeds, Duke of, 168
Lithgow, William, 229
Lorrain, Paul, 47
Low, Edward, 42–44
Lowther, George, 12–14, 19–20, 26, 39, 94
Luke, Matthew, 44

Macarty, Dennis, 49–50
Macrae, James, 174
Mainwaring, Henry, 92–93
Martin, Captain George, 167
Martin, Captain William, 25
Matthews, Captain Thomas, 175, 178–179, 248–250
Maynard, Lieutenant, 186–188
McDougall, Harriette, 255–257, 259
Modyford, Thomas, 139–140, 144
Moore, William, 31, 171, 173
Morgan, Henry, 44, 139–144, 146, 151, 282–283
Morton, Earl of, 166–167
Murat Rais (Janssen, Jan), 206
Murat Rais (Lyle/Lisle, Peter), 234
Murat Rais (Albanian), 233
Muskerry, Lord, 201–204

Nau, Jean/L'Olonnais, 43, 100, 137–139
Nutt, John, 93

Ochiali/Euldj'Ali/Uluc Ali, 208, 225, 230–231, 234
Ogle, Captain, 197–201
O'Malley, Grace, 25–26

Pellow, Thomas, 221–223, 231–233
Pelsaert, Francisco, 39–41
Phillips, Frederick, 164
Phillips, John, 12, 14, 19–20, 26, 39, 48
Pitman, Henry, 22–23
Pitts, Joseph, 212, 232

Plantain, John or James, 35, 177–179
Polycrates, 52, 282
Pompey, Roman General, 55, 283
Portland, Duke of, 175–177
Pyle, Howard, 9–10

Rackam, Calico Jack, 9, 16, 24, 166, 188–192
Raffles, Stamford, 253–254
Ragnall, 72
Read, John, 155, 157
Read, Mary, 9, 24, 166, 189, 191
Ringrose, Basil, 145, 150, 154–155
Roberts, Bartholomew, 9, 12–14, 16–20, 26, 28, 29–32, 39, 44, 47–48, 94, 182, 192–201, 283
Rogers, Woodes, 22, 49–50, 189

Sawkins, Richard, 146–148
Selkirk, Alexander, 21–22
Shap–'ng-tsai, 245
Sharp, Bartholomew, 26, 145–146, 148–152
Smith/Gow, John, 32, 94–95
Snelgrave, William, 16, 27–29, 31
Spriggs, Francis, 28, 43–44
Sores, Jacques, 97–98
Stevenson, Robert Louis, 9
Stortebeker, Klaus, 80
Stradling, Thomas, 21

Swan, Charles, 153–155
Swann, John, 27

Taylor, Richard, 17, 31, 173–178
Teach, Edward (see Blackbeard)
Teat, Josiah, 155, 157
Temenggon, Ibrahim, 253–254
Tew, Thomas, 33, 163–165, 169
Timocles, 53
Trott, Nicholas, 33, 165, 170
Tryggvason, Olaf, 73

Usamah, 62

Vane, Charles, 31, 188–189

Wafer, Lionel, 150–151, 159
Walden, John, 197
Waldron, Lawrence, 167
Wang Zhi, 236
Ward, John, 93, 229–230, 233
Watling, John, 20, 149
Watson, Rear Admiral, 251
Welch, Edward, 177
William the Striker, 20–21, 149, 152
Woodford, Elizabeth, 167